The state and ethnic p
Southeast Asia

Given the increasing number of ethnic disputes around the world, David Brown has written a timely work on the nature of ethnicity and the ways in which it is affected by the composition, structure and policies of the state.

The book provides discussions of ethnic politics in Burma, Singapore, Indonesia, Thailand and Malaysia, and offers a coherent interpretation of the variations in the nature of ethnic consciousness and the causes of ethnic tensions in these countries.

This ethnic consciousness is defined in terms of a psychological and political ideology that is crucially influenced by the character of the state. The argument is developed through an examination of differing conceptualizations of the state relating to neo-patrimonialism, corporatism, ethnocracy, internal colonialism and class, so as to show how these different perspectives each generate distinct explanations of ethnic politics.

The State and Ethnic Politics in Southeast Asia is aimed primarily at Southeast Asia specialists, but will also be of interest to students of comparative politics.

David Brown is Senior Lecturer in the Department of Political Science at Murdoch University, Australia.

Politics in Asia Series
Edited by Michael Leifer
London School of Economics

The state and ethnic politics in Southeast Asia

David Brown

London and New York

First published 1994
by Routledge
11 New Fetter Lane, London EC4P 4EE

Simultaneously published in the USA and Canada
by Routledge
29 West 35th Street, New York, NY 10001

Reprinted 1994, 1995

First published in paperback 1996

© 1994 David Brown

Typeset by Florencetype Ltd, Stoodleigh, Devon
Printed in Great Britain by
TJ Press (Padstow) Ltd, Padstow, Cornwall

British Library Cataloguing in Publication Data
A catalogue record for this book is available from the British Library

Library of Congress Cataloguing in Publication Data
A catalogue record for this book is available from the Library of Congress

ISBN 0-415-04993-8 (hbk)
ISBN 0-415-12792-0 (pbk)

Contents

Tables

Preface

Ethnicity is one of those subjects where explanation tends to become intertwined with moral evaluation. Enquiry tends to be permeated and inhibited by the preconception that it involves either a primitive and backward instinctual trait (tribalism), a moral sickness (racism, chauvinism), or a progressive virtue (the communitarian spirit, the 'people', for some, the nation). Faced with one or other of these assumptions or feelings, any attempt at extended explanation is likely to be criticized in so far as it fails to accord with, or provide ammunition for, the given evaluation. The best that one can hope for, and the purpose of this book, is that in outlining one partial perspective as regards some of the terrain, the discussion provokes critical reflection and offers occasional enlightenment.

My initial interest in ethnic politics developed out of research on local-level politics amongst the Ewe community of West Africa. From this research grew the perception that fluctuating political alignments within an allegedly 'tribal' community, and in relation to other such communities, could be explained only by rejecting any primordialist assumptions and examining the shifting situations engendered by successive state régimes. This in turn generated an interest in the comparative politics of ethnicity, from which developed a concern to make sense of the variations in its manifestation. My move to Southeast Asia in 1982 then implied the need to re-examine and re-evaluate my understanding as to how political science might contribute to illuminating the ethnic politics of this particular region.

The book developed out of an initial suggestion by Professor Chan Heng Chee for a set of edited readings on ethnic politics. The task of searching for coherence in the writings of others evolved gradually into the attempt to elaborate my own framework. Thus when Peter Sowden of what was then Croom Helm visited Singapore in 1988, I optimistically announced that the book had been conceived, was indeed already fully formed in miniature, and could be delivered within two years. But pregnancy has its drawbacks. Teaching and research are certainly compatible in that it is in the process of convincing the naive students of the validity of one's argument that one first glimpses its obvious fallaciousness. But they are also in tension with each other; quite simply, teaching takes away the vital time and energy needed for research – at least for those of us without sabbaticals. I suppose it was a natural birth, and the occasional relaxation exercise did help ease the pain, though the labour was certainly much more prolonged than had been anticipated. It is, by the way, crucial to have one's wife present at the birth, and I thank Diana sincerely for her support, and her help with the breathing. Finally, there is the brutal question which all parents ask themselves sooner or later. Was the resultant baby worth all the effort? That, however, is for others to judge, and this parent for one will irresponsibly abandon the child for others to play with or worry over as they wish; pausing only to acknowledge the paternity, and to plead guilty to any genetic deformities which become apparent.

My thanks go to Chan Heng Chee for facilitating my teaching and research in this area, and to Michael Leifer and Donna Pankhurst for their encouragement at various stages. My thanks also to the following colleagues for their helpful advice on specific chapters: David Martin Jones, Hussin Mutalib, Bilveer Singh, A. Mani, Leo Suryadinata, Ho Khai Leong and James Jesudason. I am also grateful to the following ex-students who helped me with bibliographical work and translations: Peggy Lim, Jean Ng, Noorlinah Mohamed and Siti Mariam.

David Brown
National University of Singapore
December 1992

Introduction

This book seeks to describe some aspects of ethnic politics in Southeast Asia. More importantly, however, it seeks to organize this material so as both to explain the events and to develop a distinctive explanation as to the general nature of ethnicity and the causes of ethnic politics.

The very proliferation of ethnic tensions in the contemporary world militates against systematic examination as to the causes. It sometimes seems as if ethnic loyalties and rivalries are universal and fundamentally unexplainable expressions of human nature. On the other hand, it also seems as if each ethnic conflict arises out of a unique interplay of specific historical, cultural, socio-economic and political circumstances, so that the best we can hope for by way of explanation is the careful documentation of the chain of events and the listing of all contributory factors.

The purpose here is to reject claims as to both the universality and the uniqueness of ethnic tensions, and to offer an explanation of the uniformities and the variations in ethnic politics in one region. Ethnic tensions are common to all the countries of Southeast Asia, but they take diverse forms, ranging from the sustained violence of Burma's ethnic rebellions to the polite expressions of ethnic concern in Singapore's press. Instead of trying to explain such variations in terms of differences in the cultural composition of each country, the focus will be on examining how the development and political manifestations of ethnic consciousness are related to differences in the character of each of these states. Such a focus on the character of the state offers a basis for exploring the underlying nature of ethnic consciousness in relation to the power structure in society, and also a focal point through which to explain variations in the impact of ethnic behaviour upon political stability and unity.

Ethnicity constitutes one of several forms of association through which individuals pursue their interests relating to economic and political advantage. But there is more to ethnicity than this, since it appears to offer intrinsic satisfaction as well as instrumental utility. Individuals seem to need to distinguish between 'us' and 'them' communities, and ethnic consciousness arises when such psychological constructs are attached to observable differences of language, religion, lifestyle or physiognomy. But ethnicity is not reducible to such objective distinctions. It involves the translation of sometimes minor linguistic gradations or physical variations into cultural boundary markers which are believed to be intrinsically significant and clearly demarcated, and which designate a particular cultural group as a distinctive 'people' with a unique history, homeland and way of life. On the basis of these perceived cultural affinities, the group claims a common destiny and thence the political rights necessary for the attainment of that destiny.

Such an initial formulation of ethnicity indicates that the term should be used to refer to a distinctive form of politics relating to culturally-based entitlement claims, irrespective of whether those claims are based on a perceived similarity of race, or of language, or of religion. If this is so, then the tightness of the concept of ethnicity must be sought not by limiting the range of cultural attributes to which it attaches, but rather by explaining precisely the type of political consciousness and behaviour to which it refers. The attempts to find such precision have produced a continuing debate as to the relationship between ethnicity and the state, and the primary axis of this debate has stretched between the polar positions of primordialism and situationalism, so that a brief examination of these two approaches constitutes a necessary preliminary to the present discussion of state–ethnic relations.

Those approximating the primordialist position have taken as their point of departure the apparently common-sense view of ethnicity as a culturally embedded group loyalty.[1] Ethnic consciousness is thus seen as an ascriptive, communal allegiance which inheres in the particular linguistic, racial or religious attributes defining the parameters of the group. This view of ethnicity connects with the widespread assumptions that language carries with it cultural connotations, that religious values carry over into the values underlying wider social and political behaviour, and that the sharing of common genes engenders feelings of common identity.

The particular way in which the cultural attributes generate a sense of ethnic identity is variously formulated. The simplest position is to portray ethnicity as an instinctual bond which is 'ineffable', 'unaccountable', and thereby inaccessible to reason or explanation.[2] Its power and origins are thus regarded as essentially 'shadowy and illusive',[3] as indicated by the term 'primordial', which refers, in Jungian terms, to an 'archetype of the collective unconscious'.[4] In sociobiology, attempts have been made to give more precision to the primordialist argument by positing the existence of an evolutionary mechanism directing behaviour towards the survival of the individuals' genes and those of their 'genetic relatives'.[5] Alternatively, ethnic identity is sometimes portrayed as arising out of the primary and pervasive socialization into the linguistic, religious or 'way of life' community into which the individual is born, so that the defence of one's unit of culture comes to be perceived as fundamental to the survival of the core moral values and identity of oneself and one's children.[6] But central to all versions of the primordialist approach is the proposition that the ethnic affiliation must be seen not only as 'fixed' in the sense that it is ascriptive, but also as 'fixed' in that it constitutes the conceptual given from which political analysis must begin. If the concept of ethnicity is to be linked to the concept of the state, then the primordialist perspective indicates that attention must necessarily focus on the ways in which the immutable ethnic identities impinge on the character and activities of the state.

The primordialist perspective asserts that people are naturally ethnocentric, exhibiting trust and preference for those of their own cultural group while feeling more distant from, and distrustful of, those of other cultural groups. It would follow that societies made up of markedly different cultural communities would have problems in managing their inter-group relations; and since most contemporary societies are multicultural, ethnic conflict of one sort or another is indicated as the norm.

The dominant image of politics generated by the primordial perspective has therefore been the 'plural society' argument, developed by J.S. Furnivall, and subsequently modified by M.G.

Smith, Rubushka and Shepsle, and others.[7] The argument is essentially that if a society consists of discrete ethnic segments, each with dissimilar and antithetical cultural values and political goals, then attempts at responsive, democratic, or alliance-based government will tend to degenerate into political instability and disintegration. This approach recognizes that the composition and viability of a government will be affected by the cultural configuration of the social structure (multiple minorities, majority/minority, bipolar, etc.). Nevertheless, the prospects for governmental and social stability are enhanced to the extent that the state can so far distance itself from societal influences as to be unrepresentative of, and unresponsive to, the divergent values and interests of the disaggregated society. The political implication of the primordial perspective, as formulated in the plural society argument, is thus clear: the greater the tendency to cultural pluralism, the more likely it is that political instability can be avoided only by some form of authoritarian state.

This suggestion that the stability of the state might correlate with its unresponsiveness to societal ethnic influences serves to complement the primordialist stress on the unresponsiveness of ethnic identities to the influence of the state. While it is indeed recognized by the primordialist position that assertions of ethnic identity might remain latent until stimulated by the incursions of an interventionist state, it is nonetheless argued that the political situations engendered by the state merely provoke the articulation of the pre-existing identities already defined by the cultural givens; they do not serve to determine the boundaries, content and character of ethnicity. We are thus brought by the primordialist and plural society approaches to the conclusion that, just as the policies and preferences of the authoritarian state are largely independent of ethnic societal influences, so is the character of ethnicity largely independent of the state. While this perspective stresses that ethnicity is the dominant fact of the social structure, it implies that it is necessarily only marginal to the functioning of the unresponsive state.

This theoretical implication of the primordialist/plural society position has posed a problem for students of Southeast Asia. It has been evident that ethnicity is of particular political salience in each of the states of the region, and this has been reflected in the numerous country studies that have been done. But the incorporation of this into the theoretical work on state–society relationships has been inhibited by the dominant influence of the primordial and plural society approaches, arising in part from the fact that both Furnivall and Geertz did their seminal work in this region. The result has been twofold. Firstly, it has been noticeable that much of the work done on domestic politics in this region, including the ethnic dimension, has concentrated on asserting the uniqueness of each country's history, social structure, culture and politics, and has rejected, or only paid lip service to, the contributions of analytical and comparative political science. In the words of Richard Robison:

> There is a fairly general suspicion of theory by many scholars of Southeast Asian politics based upon the proposition that theory is too rigid and deterministic to take account of the diversity and uniqueness of specific situations.[8]

The second implication has been that those studies which have adopted a specifically theoretical approach to the characterization of state–society relations in Southeast Asia have either employed characterizations of the state which do not relate it to the phenomenon of ethnicity, or have failed to explore any ethnic implications.[9] There has therefore been a failure to systematically explore the relationship between ethnicity and the state in Southeast Asia; a failure which this book seeks to repair.

It would be misleading to give the impression, however, that those writers on ethnicity who approach it from a primordialist perspective have taken the political salience of ethnic loyalties entirely for granted and completely ignored the role of the state. Some primordialists, including Clifford Geertz, argued that the process of modernization would involve shifts from irrationality to rationality, from ascription to achievement, and from particularism to universalism, such that ethnic loyalties would be eroded by the process of national integration. The state could play a role in increasing social interactions between cultural communities so as to promote the progressive replacement of ethnic consciousness by state-national loyalty.[10] Other primordialists have argued, however, that the modernization process might actually promote ethnic conflict.[11] They have stressed that such increasing social interactions might lead 'objective' cultural groups, whose ethnic consciousness had hitherto remained latent, to develop increased subjective ethnic consciousness as external rivalries and threats developed. Walker Connor in particular has focused attention on the expansion of the state as the dominant factor provoking the translation of 'latent' ethnic consciousness into manifest ethnic-nationalist assertions.[12] For such primordialists, the alternative to ethnic political conflict lies in the prescription of forms of political autonomy to each community possessing 'ethno-national' consciousness.[13]

In either case, whether the role of the state in political development is seen as implying the erosion or the strengthening of ethnic consciousness, the specific connection between the subjective and objective aspects of ethnicity still remains rather unclear; and since primordialism is defined precisely by its assertion of such a connection, it begins to lose its explanatory coherence. Why does a sense of community develop in some cases at the level of variations in dialect or sect, while in other cases it adheres to the encapsulating linguistic or religious collectivity? Why have some multicultural groups managed to come together in a 'melting pot' community while others indulge in mutual hostility? The primordialist approach seems to assume, rather than explain, the strength and political salience of ethnic consciousness, and seems unable to explain changes in the cultural attributes and cultural boundaries to which it refers. It is here that the opposite perspective, that of situationalism, makes its contribution.

The situationalist approach begins with the observation that individuals might be members of social and cultural groups without necessarily recognizing them as 'conscious aggregations' having ideological and political significance.[14] In sociology and anthropology, ethnic attachment has frequently been explained as a response to situational threats from dominating others, so that individuals react by forming appropriate defensive groups. The perception of the 'them' is mirrored by the development of the sense of 'us'. The particular cultural grouping which comes to be the focus for ethnic attachment will thus vary depending upon the source of the perceived situational threat. While it is recognized that ethnic attachments thus form as responses to situations of perceived insecurity, the focus of attention is not the nature and origin of any emotional need for security, but rather the depiction of ethnicity as an appropriate resource, rationally chosen in pursuit of individual and group interests, so that it is the instrumental and fluid aspects of ethnicity which are stressed.[15]

In social psychology, situationalism has implied a focus on the mechanisms whereby individuals adapt to social expectations and conform to social group norms. Thus, feelings of ethnic loyalty and attachment to particular cultural communities are explained as the result of an individual's continuing suscepti- bility to socialization and conditioning, and thence as the devel- opment of a rationalistic concern for the defence of the relevant groups.[16] While ethnic attachment is thus explained in terms of responsiveness to environmental realities, any apparently irra- tional behaviour, such as ethnic prejudice, is attributed to faulty perception or faulty judgement.

The situationalist perspective on ethnicity has been explored by several writers on ethnic politics in Southeast Asia, such as Judith Nagata on Malaysia, William Liddle on Indonesia, Robert Taylor on Burma, and Charles Keyes on Burma and Thailand; and their works have helped to shift attention away from the cultural attributes of society and towards the situational factors which influence ethnic consciousness.[17] The causes of ethnic conflict are located, for example, in the mobilization activities of manipulative élites or in the economic disparities between regions and communities. Ethnicity is thus seen as a conse- quence of change in the social, economic and political arenas.

The situationalist approach depicts ethnicity as one resource among many which individuals may employ in their efforts to respond, pragmatically and rationally, to the environment. The picture of ethnicity which emerges is one which stresses its derivative nature. The relative strength of the racial, linguistic or religious attachments, and the level of inclusiveness at which their boundaries are demarcated, will be determined by, and vary with, the situation. Ethnicity acts as a political resource, promoting group cohesion and thereby facilitating the political articulation of both group and individual interests. The result- ant politics may either be those of competitive pluralistic bar- gaining, or of inter-group conflict; but there is no presumption, in the situationalist perspective, that ethnic politics need be any more problematical than any other type of politics.

A focus on the situational context as the crucial factor in determining ethnic consciousness is clearly useful in explaining variations in the boundaries and political salience of ethnic communities, but that very insight seems to make it vulnerable to the criticism of crudely overestimating the flexibility of ethnicity. Perhaps more importantly, it seems unable to explain the particularly powerful emotional appeal of ethnicity. Cultural affinities are certainly only one of several bases for political affiliation from which people may choose, but people rarely seem to perceive themselves as choosing their ethnic group; and compared for example to class, ethnicity often appears to offer a more all-embracing and emotionally satisfying way of defining an individual's identity. If individuals do indeed often rally around cultural attributes as a set of symbols which will generate and sustain their sense of identity, then what exactly is the appeal and power of such symbols?

The primordialist and situationalist approaches can thus both be seen to offer valuable insights as to the nature of ethnicity and its role in politics, but the adoption of either approach on its own seems to be misleading. Ethnicity appears to exhibit both primordialist and situationalist attributes. It surely functions both as an interest resource and as an emotional loyalty. It is in part generated by the political and socio-economic structure of society, but is also in part a 'given' which plays a causal role; it is neither fully determined by the cultural structure of society, nor is it a totally elastic response to situational variations. It would thus be tempting to adopt a position in the middle of the axis, but that would simply combine antithetical perspectives so as to generate ambiguity. If a way of synthesizing the insights of both perspectives is to be sought, then it cannot be one which depicts ethnicity as somehow both a loyalty and a resource.[18] It must offer a distinctive perspective. The proposal here is to seek such an analytically coherent perspective in the depiction of ethnicity as a form of ideological consciousness.

Several recent writers on ethnic politics have characterized ethnic groups as 'kinship communities', because it is the claim to common kinship which appears to get to the essence of how ethnic attachments are actually perceived by those involved.[19] Nevertheless, the way in which this 'family resemblance' has been interpreted has varied greatly. For those of a primordialist tendency the ethnic group has been depicted as a real extension of the genealogical hierarchy, while for the situationalist-inclined the belief in common kinship has been viewed simply as a perceptive description, rather than an explanation of what constitutes ethnic consciousness. But the major significance of the view of ethnicity as a kinship community is as an analogy, which provides the key to understanding how the situationally fluid ethnic consciousness can nevertheless constitute an emotionally powerful and politically influential allegiance.

The view of ethnicity presented in the subsequent chapters recognizes, therefore, that ethnic consciousness may attach to groups claiming affinities of language, race, religion or territorial homeland; and that such groups may be designated as tribes, sects, nations, or just 'communal groups'. It is suggested that such situationally fluid ethnic consciousness derives emotional power from its characteristic as a specific psychological and political ideology which promises certainty to individuals experiencing insecurity, by 'mimicking' the family. In order to examine the circumstances influencing which particular cultural aggregation becomes the focus for the ethnic bond, attention is focused upon the role of the state in determining the structure of insecurities in a society. It is then argued that the way in which we perceive and portray ethnicity, and its relationship to the unity and stability of the nation-state, is dependent upon the way in which we portray the character of the state. The exploration of alternative conceptualizations of the state thus serves to generate differing portrayals as to the character and political salience of ethnicity. The differences in ethnic politics between neighbouring countries are thus explained, not in terms of their unique histories nor the variations in their cultural pluralism, but rather by means of a comparison as to the composition, capacity, ideology and strategy of the state.

In order to employ this approach to the study of ethnic politics in Southeast Asia, five countries have been selected – Burma, Singapore, Indonesia, Malaysia and Thailand – so as to explore five different conceptualizations of the state. Since there is clearly no one objectively correct characterization of the state which would apply to all such countries, or indeed to any one; the choice of which perspective to employ for the examination of each country is in part based on the subjective criterion of assessing which perspective appears to offer the most interesting and illuminating approach to understanding that country's ethnic politics. In practice, however, the choice of approach is made easier by the recognition that, although the politics of each country has been discussed by different writers from numerous perspectives, there has in each case developed a dominant or at least a popular approach which provides a literature whose coherence and implications can be examined. Thus, for example, while class analysis of the state has been employed for each of the countries, its influence on studies of the state and of ethnicity has probably been greatest in the case of Malaysia. Similarly, while the state élites of Thailand and Indonesia have both been portrayed in bureaucratic, technocratic or corporatist terms, it is the Singaporean state which has most consistently been examined from this perspective, and where its implications for ethnicity are clearest. In Chapters 2 to 6 therefore, the ethnic politics of each country is examined in turn, each from the perspective of the one characterization of the state which appears, from a review of the literature, to offer the most useful insights as to the causes and political impact of ethnicity.

The purpose of examining the relationships between the characterization of the state and the nature of ethnic politics is thus a dual one: to offer explanations for the variations in ethnic politics in each of the countries examined, and to explore the implications for ethnicity of each of the models of the state.

These discussions of the nature of the ethnic ideology and of ethnic–state relationships offer a basis for some conclusions as to the causes of ethnic tensions. While it is clear that there are potential problems as to the relationship between the assertion of ethnic claims and the claims of the nation-state, it is equally clear that there are several ways in which these problems might be managed, with each of the characterizations of the state examined here suggesting one possible strategy for ethnic management. The frequent incidence of ethnic conflict seems to indicate, however, that there are factors inhibiting successful management, and the concluding chapter examines two of these factors, relating to the ways in which the ideologies of state nationalism and of democracy are employed in ethnic politics.

Studies of politics which focus on a particular region frequently do so because they consider that common cultural, historical or geopolitical circumstances have produced a distinctive character which is shared by each of the states in the region. The present study is based on no such assumption that Southeast Asia is unique as regards the causes and character of its ethnic politics, or that all the countries of the region share any significant political features. Indeed, the intention is to explore the differences in their ethnic politics and to suggest that the characterizations of ethnicity and of the state which are explored here might, with equal validity, be employed as the starting point for examining ethnic politics elsewhere.

Chapter 1

Ethnicity and the state

One of the most widespread features of the Third World since the Second World War has been the expansion of the state in both its spatial and policy realms. Régimes which hitherto had displayed only spasmodic and limited capacity outside their core regions and their capital cities, have sought increasingly systematic control over peripheral regions through the expansion of their administrative bureaucracies, their armies and their educational systems. At the same time, the range of governmental interference has expanded beyond a concern with raising revenue and maintaining order, as the need to direct, train and motivate labour has increased. The effectiveness of such state interventions has varied greatly, however. The expansion of the state has not implied its strengthening; and the various agents of the state have only rarely managed to bring about the intended structural or cultural changes. Nevertheless, they have frequently had sufficient impact to impinge on social groups, sometimes disruptively and unintentionally, so as to modify societal consciousness and behaviour. There has thus developed a close relationship between ethnic consciousness and relationships on the one hand, and the activities of the state on the other. The purpose here is to examine that relationship by explaining how ethnicity functions as an ideology whose cultural focus and political implications are crucially influenced by the character of the state.

Ethnicity is interpreted here as an ideology which individuals employ to resolve the insecurities arising from the power structure within which they are located. Accordingly, the explanation of ethnic politics must begin with the examination of the state's influence upon that power structure.[1] It is clear that the state plays a major role in influencing the distribution of power, status and wealth in society, and hence in the type of situational insecurities and threats with which individuals and groups are faced. This role involves not only the state's influence on socio-economic disparities, but also its influence upon the advantages which accrue to those possessing a particular language, religio-culture or racial identity. The state also provides legitimation for the power structure in the form of a more or less explicit nationalist ideology, and this state-promulgated national ident-ity defines the ideological parameters within which ethnic consciousness develops and operates.[2] Since both cultural state nationalism and ethnic ideology employ the same type of cultural markers (race, language, religion and territory) in depicting the respective communities, then ethnic ideology must necessarily define itself as a reaction to, or a constituent of, the state-national ideology.

The concept of the state refers to the governmental and administrative institutions of a society, and to the ideological claim as to the sovereignty of those institutions. A 'statist' analy-sis of politics is thus one which assumes coherent organizing principles connecting the disparate administrative agencies in any particular state system, and assumes also that the state functions as an independent actor in politics, rather than simply as an arena for societal contention. The danger of such a state-centred approach is that it ceases to be simply a heuristic device, and leads to an overestimation of the co-ordination between discrete governmental agencies and their boundedness from society – and an overestimation of the capacity of those agencies for controlling social change.[3]

It is clear, however, from the extent of state-ethnic conflict in the contemporary world, that no states are able to fully control the ethnic consciousness and behaviour of those they purport to govern. In developing a 'statist' explanation of ethnicity – one which focuses on the impact of the state upon ethnic poli-tics – it is necessary, therefore, to recognize the limitations upon the state's ability to control ethnicity; also to indicate the varying degrees of its resilience to ethnic pressures. The limi-tations on the state's ability to control ethnicity relate in part to the intrinsic character of ethnic consciousness, which makes it inherently resilient to attempts by state élites to transform or control it, and in part to the relative weakness of the state, in terms of the varying degrees of its resilience to societal pressures.

States diverge greatly in terms of their legitimacy, autonomy, capacity, and organizing principles. The autonomous state would be one where the policies and preferences of state élites were determined by their professional interests as state officials, rather than by the demands of any societal segments. In terms of ethnicity then, the autonomous state would either be ethnically impartial, proclaiming ethnically colour-blind national values and depoliticizing ethnicity, or it would employ ethnicity as a resource for the promotion of a state-initiated formula for state development and national integration.[4] This would contrast with the non-autonomous state, where the state élites act in response to societal ethnic pressures. Politics in such a state would revolve around assertions of, and questions of access to, the benefits of membership of the various ethnic communities.

Such variations in state autonomy in relation to ethnic interests are not necessarily connected with the capacity of the state to dominate and control society.[5] Variations in state capacity may be indicated by the broad distinction between reactive, responsive and manipulative patterns of state impact upon ethnicity. The more radical the social restructuring attempted by the state, and the less effective its administrative capabilities, the more likely it becomes that its interventions in society fail to produce the intended effects, with the state having sufficient capacity to influence and perhaps to disrupt the social structure, but insufficient capacity to control the impact of its interventions. In such a case, attempts to modify ethnic consciousness would have the effect merely of disrupting the cohesion of target communities, thence promoting the possibility of a defensive assertion of ethnic solidarity directed specifically against state interventions. The classic example of such a reactive impact would be the incidence of ethnic separatist rebellion amongst ethnic minorities faced with assimilationist state policies.

In some cases, however, the state may indeed be in a position to achieve a responsive impact, so as to implement its policies on ethnicity effectively and to promote the type of changes in consciousness and behaviour intended. The intermediate situation is that where state interventions on ethnicity generate a manipulative politics. Target communities cannot escape the interventions of the state, but they might be able to treat such interventions as resources to be employed for their own advantage, so that the outcome differs significantly from that intended by the state. In the case of the Indonesian Chinese for example, it appears likely that assimilationist state policies have been utilized in such a way as to generate a modified *peranakan* Chinese ethnic consciousness, rather than to achieve an assimilationist outcome.[6]

These distinctions concerning state autonomy and capacity are important for two reasons. Firstly, they mean that an explanation of ethnicity in terms of the character of the state does not imply that it is the state which *determines* ethnicity. The state may impact in a variety of ways upon ethnicity, not necessarily or solely in ways intended by the state élites. Secondly, the state may function as a causal agent in politics irrespective of whether it is autonomous of societal groupings. Thus a state which is the agency of one particular ethnic segment in the society, or of a class, is one which lacks autonomy; but it may at the same time be a strong state with a high capacity to influence the consciousness and behaviour of its citizens.

The tendency towards the weakness of the state has been particularly well documented in the case of developing countries.[7] Some Southeast Asian states have indeed displayed the symptoms of the 'weak state', but, with the exception of Burma, it is noticeable that they have not been overwhelmed by the forces of ethnic disintegration, as has been the case in several African, and more recently Eastern European, countries. While they have not managed to exert full control over ethnic consciousness and ethnic politics in their countries, neither have they failed completely in their efforts to influence, manipulate, and contain ethnicity. Ethnic politics has indeed been problematic, but the Southeast Asian states have displayed a resilience in the face of ethnic disintegration tendencies.

We need therefore to explain the extent of the Southeast Asian states' successes in managing ethnicity, while also showing the limitations of such management efforts. The discussion must therefore be in two sections. The first task is to examine the relative resilience of ethnicity in the face of state control. This is explained here as arising from its character as a psychological and political ideology. Secondly, the relative resilience of the state in Southeast Asia is examined. This is explained here as arising in part out of the 'soft authoritarian' features of several of the states, and in part also out of the type of ethnic strategies which have been adopted. Thereafter, the extent and limitations of each state's ethnic management strategies will be examined by exploring several distinct characterizations of the state.

THE RELATIVE RESILIENCE OF ETHNICITY

Ethnicity is not simply a response to external stimuli such that it is fully determined and shaped by situational factors. Individuals are indeed influenced, in terms of their communal affiliations and relationships, by the external societal and political agencies which exert power over them, but they do not adopt a new ethnic consciousness in response to every new 'them' which they encounter. Such situational influences serve rather to modify the boundaries or strength or political salience of a prior communal consciousness, rather than creating it anew.

The simplest way of asserting this resilience of ethnicity would be to explain it as a primordial given, providing the individual with a primary and permanent sense of identity. But such a position would overstate the immutability of ethnicity and understate the influence of situational factors such as the state. The alternative position adopted here, therefore, is one which seeks to explain both the situational malleability of ethnicity and also its resilience. Such a perspective is offered by the depiction of ethnicity as an ideology.

The general argument which will be developed is that the resilience of the ethnic attachment derives from its ability to provide, for the individual, a simple psychological formula which resolves the ambiguities and uncertainties as to the relationship with society and with the state.[8] The psychological formula employed is that of the kinship myth: the endowment of the 'imagined' cultural community with the attributes of the real family. This myth may attach to any cultural community available to the individual, depending upon situational factors, but thereafter it functions both as a psychological ideology and as a political ideology in the form of the ethnic nationalist claim. The power and resilience of this kinship myth is explained here in psychoanalytic terms.

The notion of ethnicity as ideology is not completely absent from either the situationalist or the primordialist perspectives.

For the primordialist, the ethnic community employs ideology in the form of the rights claim which the nationalist argument embodies. In the situationalist position the ethnic community is depicted as a particular type of interest group which employs ideology as a resource whereby élites can mobilize the communal group solidarity necessary for political action. But while both the justification of entitlement claims and the mobilization of group cohesion are important functions of ideology, they do not form the core of the concept.

The term 'ideology' is contested in the sense that there is disagreement as to its relationship to objective truth; whether it refers to a rational distillation of reality, a distorted, irrational view of the world, or a hermeneutic interpretation. But common to each of these approaches is the view of ideology as a mental construct offering an apparently coherent formula which makes sense of that of which the individual is least certain. Ideology provides certainty in that it defines the location of the individual in the wider society and in that it provides a diagnosis of contemporary ills and a prescription for their remedy. Ideology then, refers both to a psychological belief system, and also to the articulation of that belief system in the form of a programme for political action. Thus, the ethnic ideology will be depicted here as offering certainty to the individual by locating him or her within a defined ethnic community and then further locating that community within the nation-state system. Political problems are then diagnosed in terms of a dislocated relationship between the 'kinship' community and the nation-state.

The ethnic ideology is made concrete for the individual in the form of the specific myths and symbols which are attached to a particular cultural group. The myth of kinship thus grants the individual his own specific name, history and destiny. It is:

> a device men adopt in order to come to grips with reality. . . .
> A political myth is always the myth of a particular group. . . .
> It renders their experience more coherent; it helps them understand the world in which they live. And it does so by enabling them to see their present condition as an episode in an ongoing drama. A political myth may explain how the group came into existence and what its objectives are; it may explain what constitutes membership of the group and why the group finds itself in its present predicament; and, as often

as not, it identifies the enemy of the group and promises eventual victory.[9]

The kinship myth, then, is a foundation myth of common ancestry, origin, migration or history, which gives specific and dramatic meaning to the ethnic ideology.

Ideological consciousness is frequently contrasted with 'pragmatism', so as to distinguish between the adaptability and responsiveness of the latter way of thinking as compared to the relative inflexibility of the former. The argument is that once an individual employs an ideological formula as a means of comprehending the world, there develops a concern to retain the integrity of that formula such that new information is filtered, perhaps distorted, so as to accord with the formula, rather than being responded to 'realistically'. Thus, once a particular cultural aggregate has come to be perceived as a 'kinship myth' community, the resultant ethnic consciousness will continue for some time after the situation which generated it has ceased to exist. Even when new situations generate a new pattern of ethnic identity, it will probably be internalized as an ethnic consciousness which modifies rather than replaces the earlier ethnic identities; employing the same historical myths but for amended purposes. For example, while the boundaries of the Hmong of Northern Thailand have shifted over time, and the term Hmong clearly does not refer to one 'consistent genetic-linguistic grouping', it is nevertheless the case that the Hmong kinship myth, originally generated to distinguish the Hmong from the Chinese, is retained and employed in markedly different situations, to distinguish them both from the Lao and the Thai.[10] Hmong consciousness displays situational fluidity, but also historical resilience; it has developed as a response to external pressures, but also as an independent political factor to which the Thai state has had to respond.

Ethnicity as a psychological ideology

Although the history of psychoanalysis lies in the study of repression and alienation in the bourgeois capitalist societies of the West, it claims also to offer insights as to the psychic mechanisms by which individuals relate to other social conditions: to the strains of the decolonized Third World experiencing early capitalism and westernization in its various forms, just as much as to those of the bourgeois environment of the developed states.[11] Nevertheless, any explanation which rests on psychoanalysis must contend with the doubts as to its scientific status, and the inconsistencies in its formulation. There is certainly no consensus within the various strands of psychoanalysis as to the basis for ethnic affiliation, but there is a significant convergence of the contending formulations in that they each illuminate how the relationship between the adult individual and the group affiliation is explainable in terms of, and derived from, the relationship between the infant and the family. The theme is that 'the individual and the group perform functions for each other that replicate the early life functions of child and parents'.[12]

The appeal of the psychoanalytic explanation of ethnicity is that it allows us to go beyond the oft-stated but unspecified assertion that ethnicity satisfies the 'natural' individual needs for identity or security. Psychoanalysis has been directly concerned with explaining how the unconscious mind develops out of the interweaving of the instincts with the social environment, so that: 'what appears to be natural and inescapable is in fact socially constructed'.[13]

The central propositions may be initially summarized. The conscious, rational individual (the ego) is depicted as inherently fragile and in danger of being overwhelmed by the demands of the complex external world on the one hand, and by the demands of the unconscious instinctual drives (the id) and the conscience (approximating the super-ego) on the other. The fragile ego seeks support and reinforcement, therefore, in the attempt to gain a strong sense of individual identity, emotional security, and moral authority. Communal affiliation provides one possible avenue for reinforcement, and this occurs at three 'levels'. First, at the ego level: the sense of individual identity is strengthened when we seek a sense of our individual uniqueness by the belief that we belong to a unique and real sub-category of humanity. Second, at the level of the id: our sense of emotional security is strengthened by the belief that we belong to a community offering us unconditional protective love, similar to that offered by the mother and the womb. Third, at the level of the super-ego: the individual's fragile sense of moral certainty is strengthened by erecting a mythical ethnic stereotype embodying the norms and values to which the individual can submit. In these various ways then, the individual affiliates to the cultural community by perceiving it as a mythical family. This explanation as to the psychological power of the ethnic attachment provides the basis for explaining the widespread appeal of the political ideology of ethnic nationalism, which translates each of the psychological mechanisms of the kinship myth into legitimatory symbols.

The ego: the individual's need for a sense of unique identity

Several psychoanalysts have focused attention on the ways in which the individual develops a sense of ego; a sense of individual identity as a unique and rational actor distinct from others. It is ironic that probably the most interesting explanations of the individual's search for an integrated ego come from divergent ends of the psychoanalytical spectrum – from the ego psychology of Erik Erikson; the object-relations psychoanalysis associated with Melanie Klein, which stresses the fragility of the ego; and the Lacanians, to whom the ego is a fiction.

Melanie Klein argued that the infant experiences an overwhelming anxiety in the face of the innate destructive impulses and the ambiguities inherent in personal relationships. She depicted the main defensive response of the fragile ego as that of 'splitting'. Instead of experiencing the external world directly, we experience it through the filter screen of internal phantasies, and we create a phantasy duality, between the idealism projected onto the good objects and destructiveness projected onto the bad objects. In this way, we perceive our relationships with others in schizoid terms, as split into the good and the bad. Through this splitting, ambiguities are denied, in that the negative attributes of the good object can be projected onto the bad object, and the admired qualities of the bad object can be distorted so that admiration manifests itself in its destructive form as envy.

Although the ego of healthy adults gradually becomes more integrated, so that splitting declines and they can recognize and deal with ambiguities in the environment, 'splitting . . . remains an important defence which is always available'.[14] The implication for ethnicity is clear: that individuals who feel threatened by the complexity and contradictions of their environment might retreat into this schizoid mechanism of splitting the social world up into the 'good us' and the 'bad them'. The 'bad them' then becomes the repository upon which feelings of aggression can be projected, so that even qualities in the 'them' which might otherwise be admired now become perceived in negative terms. For Melanie Klein, therefore, ethnocentrism and racism represent widespread but fundamentally regressive strategies for promoting a sense of ego identity.[15]

Some recent object relations theorists have denied this regressive implication of the ethnic attachment, and have tended to stress rather that ethnic affiliation constitutes a normal aspect of development. In a recent work which reviews this literature, the American 'Group for the Advancement of Psychiatry' has argued that the mental process of splitting has its origins in the neurological developments of early life, and that the sense of self-esteem provided by ethnicity is both central to ego development and functional to individual and group survival:

> At the moment of birth man is thrust from intrauterine union into a world of dichotomy, self and other . . . . Parents then naturally divide and redirect their children's ambivalence, finding good within the family and bad outside. This precedent sets the stage for society to do the same not only with its individuals, but also on the group level. The faculty of individuals to reunite and fuse with the group appears to be deeply embedded behavior that assures the survival of the individual, the group, and therefore the species.[16]

A contrasting depiction of the ego, and how it might be strengthened by the ethnic attachment, is that offered by Jacques Lacan. He depicts the ego not as the emergence of a realistic and rational sense of autonomy, but as the erection of a fragile linguistic fiction. For Lacan, the self does not exist apart from or prior to society, so that the ego is simply the inherently fragile fiction of a coherent self which is determined by the pre-given structures of the culture, and specifically of language, into which the individual is inserted.[17] Faced with the disintegrative chaos of desires and of the external world, the individual seeks fictions of certainty.[18] The first crucial stage in the creation of the imaginary selfhood is the so-called 'mirror phase', where interactions with others lead to the false perception of a unified self. The imaginary self is constituted by reference to the imaginary other; and it is the structures of language which define the relationship of the ego to 'The Other'. The main linguistic categories by which the sense of self is defined and located are those of kinship and gender, and this distinction between the self and The Other has been employed, for example by Franz Fanon, in explaining racism.[19]

As Stephen Frosh has noted, Lacan's formulation signifies that the racist is one who maintains his own fiction of wholeness and coherence by perceiving the cultural attributes of The Other, in this case the physiognomy, as embodying the threat of fragmentation and disorder.

> It is the visual image of The Other that makes it possible for it to become a container for the racist's internal otherness, for the fragmentation that is central to the experience of infancy and, indeed, to the experience of modernity itself. The immense terror around which the psychology of the racist centres derives . . . from the threat to the precarious sense of ego-integrity that proceeds from an encounter with the black other: the *visibility* of difference undermines the abstract sense of homogeneity which so shakily supports the ego . . . Racism becomes a fortress for the fragments of the self.[20]

The third psychoanalyst who offers an explanation of how ethnicity serves to strengthen the ego, is Erik Erikson. He argues, in contrast to Lacan, that the ego is potentially strong and effective.[21] Ego development is seen as dominated by the search for a sense of uniqueness as a person, and crucial to this is the need for a clearly defined role and place in society. As individuals who are born alone and helpless, we have a need 'to know where we come from, and where we stand, where we are going, and who is going with us'.[22] The search for identity thus necessarily involves the search for a category of society to which the individual can affiliate. Such a collective identity involves the stereotyping of self and the stereotyping of others.

> The positive identity must ever fortify itself by drawing the line against undesirables . . . . Man always seeks somebody who is below him, who will be kept in place, and on whom can be projected all that is felt to be weak, low and dangerous in oneself.[23]

The sense of individual identity thus involves the location of oneself at the centre and the drawing of boundary lines between such a centre and the periphery. This psychic development of the ego has directly political implications, since it emerges in the individual's capacity to imagine communities of affiliation and of exclusion.[24] The psychological development of the individual ego thus involves the formation of an ideological vision which defines these 'mythological' communal entities. This process of ideologizing the individuals' sense of their positive identity, by imagining an 'us and them' distinction, is referred to by Erikson as 'pseudospeciation'. For Erikson, the developing child finds the first 'pseudospecies' in the family, but further development leads to the perception that the family is itself located within a larger community of the race or the nation.

> The human being has a built-in tendency to think of the 'subspecies' to which he or she belongs – family, class, tribe, nation – as *'the* human species'. . . . A sense of irreversible difference between one's own and other 'kinds' can attach itself not only to evolved major differences among human populations, but to small differences that have come to loom large. . . . In the form of ingroup loyalties, pseudospeciation can contribute to human being's highest achievements; in the form of outgroup enmities, it can express itself in clannish-ness, fearful avoidance, and even mortal hatred.[25]

The explanation of ethnic categorization as one aspect of our search for a sense of our own unique ego identity thus refers partly to a cognitive process – a search for a way of comprehending a complex world by erecting simplifying myths – but it also reflects the search for significance and importance; an awareness of oneself as a coherent and purposeful actor in the world. Ethnic affiliation and categorization promote such a sense by linking the individual ego to the perceived authenticity of one demarcated community.

This brief outline of competing formulations as to the relationship between the search for ego identity and the ethnic affiliation is sufficient to indicate how they concur in showing that the potentiality for ethnic affiliation arises, not from instinct, but rather from the influence of the environment upon the development of the unconscious, and thence upon the ego. They therefore offer a first step towards explaining the psychological resilience of ethnicity.

The id: the individual's need for emotional security

The simplest explanation for the emotional power of ethnicity is that version of sociobiology which suggests that there exists an instinct leading us to give prior affection to those who appear to be genetically similar to us. Psychoanalysis does recognize that individuals have instinctual needs for emotional oneness with others, but one of its major messages is that while the healthy individual might channel these needs into equal, loving relationships with other individuals, it is the less mature or more neurotic individual who might retreat from the responsibility and freedom of equal affiliations and seek instead to satisfy his or her instinctual needs by relations of emotional dependency on 'similar' others. In such unequal dependency relationships emotional security is attained by infantile, submissive love; and ethnic affiliation is frequently depicted, in psychoanalysis, as a neurotic distortion of the child's love for the family.

Erich Fromm is the psychoanalyst who most directly discusses the relationship between the individual's need for love and the communal affiliation. Fromm was concerned primarily with the need of the individual to confront and find resolutions to the 'existential dichotomies' which arise from the fact that he is both a part of nature, and alone, apart from nature. Faced with these dichotomies, the individual exhibits an anxiety about his aloneness which emerges in a 'fear of freedom'.[26] He tries to escape from intolerable feelings of helplessness and aloneness by seeking for a return to 'natural roots', and the 'most elementary of the natural ties is the tie of the child to the mother'. The individual exhibits 'a deep longing for the security and rootedness which the relationship to [the] mother once gave him', and he locates such security in the idea of the communal group. 'The family and the clan, and later on the state, nation or church, assume the same function which the individual mother had originally for the child.'[27]

The fixation on the mother is thus manifested as a desire for the protection and security which comes with the abandonment of individuality and submersion in the group. Various psychic mechanisms are involved in this escape from freedom through group affiliation. They include elements of moral masochism, in which the individual exhibits a neurotic need for affection; and also elements of what Fromm calls 'automaton conformity', i.e.

the attempt to wipe out the separateness of individual existence by extreme submissive conformity, so that the group-self is substituted for the real self. Narcissism, instead of being directed to the self as self-love, becomes focused upon the group, so that the group is seen as more important than the self.

For Fromm, the attachment to the ethnic group is one of several neurotic responses which individuals have had to the sense of aloneness engendered by modernization and capitalism:

> Man – freed from traditional bonds of the medieval community, afraid of the new freedom which transformed him into an isolated atom – escaped into a new idolatry of blood and soil, of which nationalism and racism are the two most evident expressions . . . . Those who are not 'familiar' by bonds of blood and soil (expressed by common language, customs, food, songs, etc.) are looked upon with suspicion, and paranoid delusions about them can spring up at the slightest provocation. This incestuous fixation not only poisons the relationship of the individual to the stranger, but to the members of his own clan and to himself. The person who has not freed himself from the ties to blood and soil is not yet fully born as a human being; his capacity for love and reason are crippled; he does not experience himself nor his fellow man in their – and his own – human reality. Nationalism is our form of incest, is our idolatry, is our insanity.[28]

Fromm is not denying that individuals need to develop bonds of love for others. Indeed, his concern is precisely to stress that individuals have fundamental human needs for what he terms 'relatedness', 'rootedness', a 'sense of identity' and a 'frame of orientation and devotion'. But for Fromm, the healthy individual is one who satisfies these needs by a love of all humanity, by a love and respect for oneself, and by equal loving relationships with other individuals. The tie to the ethnic group constitutes for Fromm a retreat from humanity, in that it is based instead on neurotic ties of narcissism, incest and herd conformity.

Fromm's view of ethnicity is thus much more negative than is Erikson's. Whereas for Erikson the individual gains his sense of unique identity by ethnic affiliation, for Fromm, the appeal of ethnicity is precisely that the individual can lose himself in the 'herd'. He gains a sense of security precisely by losing his sense of individual identity. The incompatibility between these two formulations raises the possibility of a distinction between two types of ethnic affiliation – the 'healthy' attachment which offers identity with security, and the 'neurotic' attachment in which security is attained at the cost of identity.

The super-ego: the individual's need of authority

It is already clear that the classification of people into one or other ethnic category involves their moral grading, so that the us group is characteristically defined as morally superior to the them group. But the identification of the us group with moral virtue goes even deeper than this. When the individual affiliates to an ethnic community he suspends his own moral judgement in favour of the moral authority provided by the group stereo-type. The ethnic community is perceived as embodying a set of authoritative moral norms, inherent in the group's language, culture and religion, which define 'correct' behaviour. It is this function of communal affiliation, as an 'expression . . . of man's irrational longing for the return of authority'[29] which Sigmund Freud himself stressed. For Freud, the submission of the child to the authority of the father becomes the model for the adult individual's subsequent submission to social authority. This sub-mission to authority is internalized (introjected) to form the unconscious moral super-ego within the individual, in which the aggressive impulses towards authority are turned inwards to generate guilt feelings directed against the self. The super-ego impels obedience to internal moral ideals in the same way that the infant was compelled to obey external authority. Subsequently, when adults submit themselves to the communal group, they enter into a relationship of dependence in which they each identify with the leader or the authority principle of the group. This ideal authority principle is then internalized into the super-ego, thus repeating the submissive response of the child to the parents. In the extreme case of the 'authoritarian personality' it was argued that the emotional need for uncondi-tional submission to authority predisposed the individual both to ethnocentrism and to fascism.[30]

This portrayal of the relationship between leader and follower in the group, in which submissive love and identification with moral authority intertwine, has essential similarities with the Weberian notion of charisma. Freud saw authority as always being personified in the individual leader, but he did this, as Rieff notes, because he 'profoundly overestimated the community of groups' by thinking of politics as if it were 'a permanent mass meeting.'[31] However, it is clear that in large non-face-to-face groups authority is not always personified. In an 'imagined community' like the ethnic group, it is the myth of the stereotype group character which replaces and performs the role of the individual, charismatic father-leader in embodying moral authority. This stereotype group character is in fact the totality of the imagined community. Instead of consisting of real individuals with whom one has actual, affective ties, the imagined community consists of strangers on whom are projected the idealized stereotype. Thus, identification with the group is identical to submission to the authority of the moral ideal embodied in the group stereotype. The individual perceives the ethnic community with which he identifies as embodying the moral authority for which he yearns.

Ethnic prejudice

The explanations of identification with an 'in-group' have immediate implications for our understanding of attitudes and evaluations towards 'out-groups'.[32] The phenomenon of ethnic prejudice becomes understandable, therefore, in terms of three processes corresponding to the three bases for ethnic affiliation. First, if the individual seeks ego identity through affiliation with an 'us' community which is defined as that which is both central and significant; then the 'them' communities necessarily come to be perceived as peripheral, marginal and of inferior status. Second, if the individual finds id satisfaction within the communal group in the form of submissive, affective bonding; then the aggression and hostility which is repressed is then projected onto the 'out-group' (who are thence depicted as aggressive); or, if the aggression is not repressed, it is displaced away from expression within the in-group and takes the form of hatred redirected towards the scapegoated out-group.[33] The third process, which arises from the stereotyping of the in-group as a moral authority ideal, involves the projection onto the out-group of negative values, and the displacement onto them of guilt feelings. The moral virtue of the in-group is thus counter-posed by the moral degeneracy of the out-group; the fiction of the one being maintained by the fiction of the other.

Thus, while the identity of the in-group may be defined in a variety of cultural terms depending upon the situational insecurities engendered, prejudice against cultural out-groups of one type or another is seen to be endemic. It involves much more than simply faulty evaluations which arise from cognitive ignorance of other cultures. Rather it is the corollary of in-group attachment, and involves both a hostility towards the other and also the erection of a moral justification for that hostility.

The kinship myth

If it is sensible to argue that ethnic affiliation is powerful because it offers one means of channelling fundamental psychological drives, there nevertheless remains a crucial question as to why the individual should seek in-group satisfaction within specifically *cultural* groups, perceived in terms of language, religion or race; rather than within any other form of communal grouping.

The perception of a cultural group as an ethnic community involves the belief on the part of the individual that his affiliation to that group is ascriptive, that the group possesses historical permanence in that it claims a common history and constitutes a common descent group, and that the distinctive cultural attributes of the group are such as to define clear boundaries from other such groups. These perceptions do not, however, derive from the accurate observation of social realities, which would show rather the malleability and porousness of linguistic, religious or racial variations. They derive, as we have noted, from the needs of the fragmented psyche for myths of certainty and coherence. The primary image of certainty for the individual is that offered to the infant by the family; embodying the promised source, if not the actuality, of individual identity, security and authority. The adult, in contrast, is exposed to the complexity and uncertainty of the modern world, and the search for certainty through the formation of attachments to the ethnic community is, in essence, an attempt by the adult to return to and replicate the security of the family. If such an attempt is, as psychoanalysis sometimes implies, a neurotic one, then it is a particularly widespread neurosis. If this insight of psychoanalysis is valid – that the adult in politics seeks an image of security which accords to the image of the family – then it becomes clear why it is the cultural group which so often becomes the focus for such an attachment. It is the ease with which the cultural group can mimic the family, can portray itself as a 'family writ large', which explains its appeal.

The family consists of individuals who look similar and who share similar values because they have a common genetic ancestry and shared experiences. When cultural groups claim common attributes, common history and common ancestry they are claiming to *be* the family. To be sure, communal groups of other types also make claims to mimic the family, and thus to offer the promise of certainty and security to the individual. For example, the class community claims to be a brotherhood and the feminist community to be a sisterhood. Most importantly, however, the state frequently claims not to be just a political community based on the volition of its citizens irrespective of cultural attributes, but also a cultural community defined by the same type of attributes to which ethnicity refers. In this way, the state, in claiming to be a cultural nation, seeks to arrogate to itself the power of the ethnic kinship myth.[34] Thus communities based on cultural similarities have decided advantages in their abilities to mimic the family. Similarities of lifestyle, clothing, worship, dialect and physiognomy can all be adduced as 'proof' of the claim to common ancestry; and once this claim is made, the cultural group appears not only as *similar* to the family – though manifested in the larger public sphere rather than in the smaller private realm – but also as a *version* of the family; an extension of a mythical hierarchical chain which is extended outwards from the nuclear family, through the clan and the tribe, towards the nation and the race. The kinship myth, therefore, is the belief by the adult individual that the sense of identity, security and authority which the infant experiences within the family can be found within a cultural group, a group which mimics the family in its claim to constitute an ascriptive and common ancestry group. The individual comes to believe that the cultural aggregate with which he identifies does in reality constitute an ascriptive kinship unit. The corollary is that other such cultural aggregates come to be perceived as potential threats to the identity, security and authority which the individual finds in the ethnic bond.

This explanation of ethnicity as the kinship myth has the implication that individuals will tend to seek certainty in the linguistic, racial or religious grouping only in so far as they *fail* to find that security within the real, face-to-face kinship communities of the family and the locality. Such an argument would be in line with the fact that the ethnic revival in the developed West began to be noticed from the late 1960s onwards, at the same time as did the impact of late capitalist society in weakening the integrity of the nuclear family.[35] In the case of the 'Third World', the implication would be that it has been the weakening of the extended family and village community (and also perhaps of their traditional patronage structures) by the combined impact upon rural societies of education, urbanization, and capitalism, which has promoted the increased salience of the kinship myth of ethnicity as a potential alternative basis for a sense of certainty.

Ethnicity as a political ideology

The explanation of ethnic consciousness in terms of the psychology of the kinship myth does not, of itself, provide an adequate answer to the question of why the ethnic bond is so powerful. There remains a significant distinction between the feelings of dependent attachment to the cultural group which have so far been discussed, and the conscious belief by an individual that the group to which he feels attachment constitutes a distinctive people, a nation or a potential nation which has rights of political priority or autonomy for which that individual would be willing to die, and perhaps also to kill. We need to explain, in other words, why the ethnic attachment can apparently so easily be translated by political élites into commitment to the ethnic nation, so that individuals are mobilized into ethnic nationalist political movements.

The shift from the psychological ethnic ideology to the political ethnic nationalist ideology involves more than just an increased level of consciousness as to the ethnic bond. It involves also the translation of the unconscious psychological motives of the individual to the status of publicly legitimate claims. Moreover, while the significance of the psychological ethnic ideology is that it offers a sense of certainty and authenticity to the individual; the significance of the political ethnic nationalist ideology is that it functions also at the level of the community; it provides a sense of authenticity for the group as a whole by asserting the distinctiveness and status of the community *vis à vis* other communities, through the depiction of it as a nation.

Although the literature on nationalism is particularly diverse in its depiction of the relationship between group consciousness – the subjective sense of nationhood – and objective group attributes – the possession of the cultural attributes of a distinctive people – there is general agreement that the community with the strongest claim to nationhood is that which possesses both.[36] Thus, the starting point for the nationalist ideology is the assertion that the nation is the community which possesses both cultural distinctiveness and group consciousness; in other words, that there exists an ethnic community. The incipient sense of ethnic-national consciousness can be promoted by the ideologues through the fostering of various symbols of cultural distinctiveness, such as the promotion of the language and literature of the group or the lauding of its distinctive dress and lifestyle.

The second stage in the ideological argument is the assertion that the community possesses its own distinct history, and therefore its own destiny. The generation and articulation of the community history involves, characteristically, the myth of common ancestry or migration, the existence of a mythical previous golden age, the depiction of an evolutionary development towards the present, and the possibility of the resolution of contemporary problems through a future regeneration.

The promotion of historical myths is frequently intertwined with the third theme of the nationalist argument, that of the territorial claim. The nationalist vision is one in which all individuals are born into one or other distinct national community, each with its own territory. The nationalist ideology therefore depicts either the territory of origin or the territory of current residence as more than just the land which is worked. It is depicted rather as the concrete symbol of nationhood, the Homeland.

The final stage of the nationalist argument is the assertion that the community which possesses ethnic consciousness, a unique history, and a specific homeland, is deserving, therefore, of political autonomy. This argument claims to derive, if tortuously, from liberal ideas of popular sovereignty. If individuals

have inalienable natural rights to their own liberty and autonomy, then it might follow by analogy that groups of individuals
also have such rights, or that political authority derives from the
'will of the people'. The argument culminated in the doctrine of
national self-determination; that if governmental legitimacy
came only from the will of the people, then each people should
constitute a civil society with its own unit of government.[37]
The nationalist ideology is clearly a particularly powerful
force in contemporary politics. But it is not powerful merely
because it is simple and readily understandable, nor just because
it often offers a ready-made legitimation for the pursuit of
power by self-interested élites. It is argued here, rather, that its
fundamental power derives from the particular way in which the
distinct themes of the nationalist ideological argument correspond to, and buttress, the psychological mechanisms which
underlie the ethnic bond. It is the specific connection between
the psychological structures of the ethnic bond and the ideological structures of nationalism which allows the first to be so easily
translated into the second.
The links between the nationalist ideology and the psychological bases of ethnicity can be clarified if we return briefly to the
three aspects of the ethnic bond: the search by the individual for
a sense of ego identity, for id security and for super-ego
authority.
The individual gets a sense of ego identity not only by locating
himself in relation to others, but also by relating himself to his
own past. A sense of permanence, and of continuity with one's
own past, is crucial to the development of personality. Erikson,
for example, sees the attainment of a 'historical perspective' as a
crucial stage in individual development, a stage in which the
individual gains 'a sense of the irreversibility of significant
events' so as to attain a 'unity of personality which is acceptable
. . . as an irreversible historical fact'.[38] If the individual seeks his
sense of ego identity through attachment to the cultural group,
therefore, he will also seek a sense of his own permanence and
distinctiveness through identification with the development of
that community. Identification with a community which apparently has historical permanence and distinctiveness serves to
strengthen the ability of the ethnic attachment to provide a sense
of identity for the individual. It also provides a specific link
between individual and group identity: the individual is able to

assert his own sense of distinct and permanent identity by appealing to the unique history and the destiny of the community with which he identifies. The individual, indeed, comes to believe that the history of his own cultural community constitutes the *only* valid history. As Claude Levi-Strauss notes,

> It seems . . . as if something is happening only in his own culture, as if only his culture is privileged to have a history that keeps adding events to one another. For him, only this history offers meaning and purpose . . . . In all other societies, so he believes, history does not exist: at best, it marks time.[39]

Thus, the sense of the developing identity of the individual is articulated in the form of the assertion of the historical development of the identity of the community. The private psychological is thereby linked to the public political.

> The nation, with its stress on a beginning and flow in time, and a delimitation in space, raises barriers to the flood of meaninglessness and absurdity that might otherwise engulf human beings. It tells them that they belong to ancient associations of 'their kind' with definite boundaries in time and space, and this gives their otherwise ambiguous and precarious lives a degree of certainty and purpose. By linking oneself to a 'community of history and destiny', the individual hopes to achieve a measure of immortality which will preserve his or her person and achievements from oblivion. . . . In this sense, ethnic nationalism becomes a 'surrogate' religion which aims to overcome the sense of futility . . . by linking individuals to persisting communities, whose generations form indissoluble links in a chain of memories and identities.[40]

This formulation by A.D. Smith of the power of historical myths is similar to Kenneth Minogue's view as to the essential appeal of the nationalist ideology: its ability to provide 'an escape from triviality . . . which dignifies a man's suffering'.[41] By providing myths and symbols of the history of the ethnic community, the nationalist ideology thus directs the individual's search for identity towards a commitment to fulfilling the historical destiny of the ethnic nation.

The second basis for ethnic affiliation involves the 'retreat from freedom' on the part of the isolated individual, and his attempt to attain, through herd conformity with the group, the kind of emotional security and protection which was given by the mother. The group is thus perceived as a kinship community arising out of 'ties of blood which give man a sense of rootedness and belonging'.[42]

In Fromm's formulation, this tendency to 'herd conformity' in the group is traceable to the yearning for the security of the mother, for the womb and, fundamentally, for a return to 'natural roots'. He identifies 'a deep craving in man not to sever the natural ties, to fight against being torn away from nature, from mother, blood and soil'.[43]

It is this connection between the notion of the family and the notion of a natural home which explains the powerful appeal of the nationalist ideology's claim of the Homeland. The Homeland claim reinforces the claim of the ethnic community to constitute a 'family', and it offers the image of a physical home which can provide both security and protection. The argument is that,

> nations and territories belong together and . . . every nation has its rightful place on earth, which belongs to it and to it alone, and . . . only in its recognized 'home' will exile and self-estrangement wither away, allowing its members, at last, to realize their real selves in the collective soul or 'essence'.[44]

As Walker Connor notes, this homeland myth is powerful because it evokes images of the family:

> As manifested in emotion-laden terms such as *home*land, *native* land, or land of my fathers, territory becomes mixed in popular perceptions with notions of ancestry and family, that is to say, blood . . . . This emotional bond to homeland flows from a perception of the latter as the geographical cradle of the ethnonational group.[45]

What is happening then, is that the individual's search for emotional security through a 'retreat from freedom' into submissive dependency within the 'womb' of the group, is being translated into the argument that the group itself can attain security if it claims its own home. Thus, territory which hitherto had been taken for granted now becomes significant as the symbol of primordial natural roots.

The third aspect of the psychology of ethnicity relates to the search for moral authority. The individual seeks an external moral authority to which he can submit, and ethnic affiliation provides such an image of authority in the form of the ethnic stereotype, which takes the form of the idealized moral norms associated with the ethnic community. This ideal then provides the standard by which the individual, as well as others, can be morally judged.

The nationalist ideology is able to employ this psychological basis for ethnic affiliation in generating the argument that ethnic nations possess inherent political rights. The moral right becomes translated into the political right. That is, the belief that the ethnic community embodies a moral ideal becomes restated as the argument that the ethical character of the ethnic community gives it the moral right to determine its own political destiny. This translation from moral rightness to political rights is one which arises out of the depiction of the ethnic community in terms of the Rousseauean General Will. The argument is simply that if the ethnic community is indeed depicted as embodying moral values, then it follows both that the individuals have a supreme duty to submit to the authority of the moral community, and also that the legitimacy of government derives solely from the same authority. In Rousseau's terms, sovereignty belongs solely to the community, both in that the individual must submit himself to the general will, and also in that government is simply the agent of the community, to formulate and implement the general will.[46] Thus, the argument that the ethnic nation has the right to self-determination is derived directly from the assertion that the ethnic nation embodies moral authority; and the individual's need for submission to authority can become the basis for his ideological commitment to national autonomy.

The relationship between the ethnic affiliation and the nationalist ideology may thus be summarized. The kinship myth of the ethnic community provides the starting point for the nationalist ideology; and the ideology is powerful because it provides an assertion of legitimate group rights which expresses and develops the psychological processes underpinning the individual's ethnic attachment. In this way the personal search for identity is translated into the group's claim to historical authenticity; the individual's search for security is translated into the group's claim to the homeland; and the individual's search for authority is translated into the claim of the group to political autonomy.

The explanation of the power of the ethnic bond over the

individual is thus not that it constitutes an instinct, nor that it constitutes a political resource for the rational pursuit of interests; it is rather that it constitutes a powerful myth of certainty, the kinship myth, which functions both as a psychological ideology and also, potentially, as a political ideology.

Ethnicity has a resilience of its own. It is indeed influenced by the state, but it is never determined by the state. This means that the politics which result from the state's attempt to influence ethnicity, are always a problematical politics. It is therefore possible that the resilience of ethnicity will overwhelm the fragile state. But there is no inevitability about the collapse of the state in the face of ethnicity. Indeed, some states have shown themselves sufficiently strong to influence and manipulate ethnicity in ways conducive to the pursuit of state goals. It is to the resilience of the state that we now turn.

THE RELATIVE RESILIENCE OF THE SOUTHEAST ASIAN STATES

It has frequently been argued that Southeast Asia has a better record than Africa for example, as regards political stability and unity, economic development, and ethnic harmony. Of course, such a comparative statement is selective – ignoring the chaos of Burma, the decay of the Philippines, and the underdevelopment of Indo-China. Nevertheless, it offers a comparison which needs explaining. Indonesia, Thailand, Malaysia and Singapore have each managed in their different ways to escape from the 'dependency trap' characterized by the weak state and the underdeveloped economy. Explanations have come from three main quarters. 'Cultural' explanations have focused on the political implications of Asia's deferential and communitarian traditional values, so as to show how they have legitimated the paternalistic strategies which most states have pursued. The Southeast Asian variants of Confucianism, Buddhism and Islam have thus each contributed to political stability, it is argued, in that they have facilitated the process of depoliticization, and thence the autonomy of the state. Political economy explanations, for their part, have stressed the implications for political stability of Southeast Asia's location in the world economy. Attention has focused, therefore, on how the economic strategies of export-oriented economic diversification have produced sufficient economic growth to give substance to the states' claims to 'technocratic' legitimacy. The third approach has been the 'statist' one. This approach has stressed the way in which the post-colonial Southeast Asian state-élites have been able to transform themselves, by primarily bureaucratic-authoritarian strategies, from being weak states with fragile legitimacy, low autonomy from social pressures and low capacities for social control; into strong states which have been able to combine the use of authoritarian controls and democratic legitimation.

The ability of these states to make this latter transformation derives in part from the advantages to the state of historical continuity. In contrast to the largely artificial African states created by colonization, the Southeast Asian states have had significant pre-colonial antecedents, with traditional kingdoms and core cultural communities providing a basis from which modern nation states might emerge and legitimate themselves. The dominant factor, however, has been the adoption by post-colonial state-élites of strategies which have been termed 'oligarchic democracy' or 'soft authoritarian'.

These terms direct attention to two tendencies. The decolonization period involved a high level of mass politicization in nationalist movements, but it also involved, even in the Indonesian case, a negotiated transfer of power from one élite group to another. The inheriting élites, which had used the politicized masses in order to attain power, increasingly sought to retain that power by employing state institutions in authoritarian ways, so as to exclude political opposition and to exert bureaucratic control over their societies. These authoritarian tendencies have been balanced, however, by the employment of democratic electoral procedures. These democratic procedures were introduced either to legitimate the decolonization process (Malaysia and Singapore) or to legitimate the accession to power of new nationalist élites (Thailand and Indonesia). These procedures were retained (or at least periodically revived), and have provided channels whereby the state élites can engineer mass support and thereby periodically demonstrate their democratic legitimacy. These procedures have been, however, only semi-competitive. They have contained sufficient restrictions on political debate and organization so as to have successfully avoided the dangers of disunity which more fully competitive forms of democracy might invite.

The balance between the authoritarian tendencies and the democratic characteristics has varied between the different states, but there has also been a general shift over time. In broad terms, the period from the 1960s to the 1980s was dominated by the 'authoritarian' tendency towards increasing state autonomy and capacity; while since the mid-1980s there has been some shift in the 'democratic' direction, towards increasing state responsiveness.[47] But the combination of authoritarian and democratic features has remained the most significant characteristic of these states, and provides the major explanation for their comparative resilience. They have been relatively strong states in that they have succeeded, to varying degrees, in adopting strategies which have avoided both the illegitimate coerciveness of overt ('hard') authoritarianism and the dangerous dissensus of ('soft') liberal pluralism.

In terms of their stance towards ethnicity, there is, however, a more specific factor which has contributed to the ability of some Southeast Asian states to contain tendencies towards political instability. This relates to the types of ethnic management strategy they have adopted. Elsewhere, states faced with the potentially destabilizing impact of politicized cultural pluralism have sometimes opted for radical strategies which have involved the fundamental restructuring of cultural consciousness, cultural attributes and behavioural patterns. Such strategies would include attempts at enforcing the assimilation of minority cultural segments so as to adopt the attributes and the consciousness of the cultural majority; excluding specific cultural minorities from the political arena, forcible population movement between regions or between states so as to achieve what one can now term 'ethnic cleansing', and the suppression of ethnic affiliation from the language and practice of politics so as to achieve – by authoritarian means – the de-ethnicization of politics.

Such strategies could, theoretically, be successful where the state possesses sufficiently high capacity in its coercive, control or indoctrination capabilities. But the limited capacity of most states, including those of Southeast Asia, combined with the inherent resilience of ethnicity, would seem to ensure the failure of such policies and the probable destabilizing impact of their attempted implementation.

With the clear exception of Burma, the Southeast Asian states examined here have opted for less radical ethnic strategies which have been much more in line with the limitations of the states' implementation capacities. Instead of trying to eradicate or restructure ethnic affiliations, they have attempted in very different ways to accommodate, manage or manipulate them so as to try to turn ethnicity from a potential problem into a potential resource. While none of these strategies has been unproblematical, it is nevertheless significant that each of the strategies we shall examine (again excepting Burma) has been partially successful. While ethnic–state confrontations have not always been avoided, they have in each case been sufficiently contained so as not to threaten the overall stability and survival of the state.

Thus, the relative resilience of the Southeast Asian states examined here arises, in general terms, from their combination of democratic legitimation with bureaucratic-authoritarian political control. More particularly, their capacity to contain the problematical politics of ethnicity arises out of their adoption of appropriate ethnic management strategies which have reflected the character and capacities of the state. The relationships between the state and ethnicity can, therefore, most appropriately be explored by examining, in the case of each country, the relationship between the character of the state, its ethnic strategies, and the resultant ethnic politics.

In the chapters that follow, five distinct ways of portraying the state are explored; they refer to the variations in state character, autonomy and capacity, and make explicit their implications for ethnic politics. These five models of the state may be briefly indicated. First, the ethnocratic state model explains the causes and the consequences of the domination of the state by one ethnic community within a multicultural society, and will be illustrated through a discussion of anti-colonial nationalism and ethnic rebellion in Burma. Second, the corporatist model of the state is employed in order to discuss the impact of state management upon ethnic politics in Singapore. Third, the role of ethnic communalism in Indonesian politics is explored through a discussion of the neo-patrimonial characterization of the state. Fourth, Thailand is discussed so as to illustrate the internal colonial model which depicts the state as promoting regional economic disparities in pursuit of the development of the core region, so as to stimulate a reactive rebellion on the part of peripheral communal groups. Finally, the class perspective on the state is discussed in relation to the ethnic politics of West Malaysia.

The choice of these conceptualizations of the state, and the choice of illustrative cases, arises from a variety of considerations which relate partly to a view of political science as an interpretive discipline, and partly also to a view of polities in Southeast Asia which stresses diversity.

Political science has generated numerous typologies of 'forms of government' or 'political systems', but because of the extent to which these typologies have sought to cluster the polities of the world into discrete, definitional categories (most famously, democratic, authoritarian or totalitarian), they have been vulnerable to the charge of trying to pattern the unpatterned – trying to force the complex multidimensional world of politics into simplistic, two-dimensional conceptual boxes. One response to such an accusation has been to seek, not descriptive categories, but 'ideal-type' conceptualizations. This involves recognizing that science cannot hope to encompass and comprehend all of reality, but must content itself instead with approaching reality from one partial perspective at a time, determined by the particular interests and values of the observer. The 'ideal-type' conceptualization involves, in Weber's words:

> the one-sided accentuation of one or more points of view and . . . the synthesis of a great many diffuse, discrete, more or less present and occasionally absent concrete individual phenomena, which are arranged according to those one-sidedly emphasized viewpoints into a unified analytical construct.[48]

The ideal-type conceptualization is thus a heuristic device which is employed only in so far as it is illuminating. Rather than being an attempt to pin down the true essence or core of a complex situation, it seeks to illuminate one particular aspect by employing one partial perspective. Alternative, competing perspectives cannot be combined into one overarching, unified understanding, though there exists the possibility of employing, in turn, several different conceptualizations in order to see how each can contribute to our understanding by illuminating different aspects of a situation.

It is from this interpretive perspective on political science then, that the different ways of characterizing the state are approached. Each of the Southeast Asian states to be discussed has been characterized in a variety of ways by different observers who disagree not so much about the facts, but rather about the most appropriate way to explain and interpret those facts. It is noticeable, moreover, that there is considerable overlap as to the range of approaches employed to examine the politics of each country, and that these approaches derive, in the most part, from the various schools of thought which have emerged in the social science literature on development. While the five models selected for detailed examination here are not the only ones to have been employed in the analysis of Southeast Asian politics, they are nevertheless the most widely used, and arguably the most interesting.[49]

Although the writers employing these various approaches sometimes treat them as descriptive models, they are revisited here rather as ideal-type conceptualizations focusing on one particular facet or dimension of politics. It is thus the specific character of recent or contemporary ethnic politics in each country that determines the choice of which conceptual approach to employ in the characterization of the state. In making explicit the ethnic implications of a particular way of characterizing the state, light will be shed not only on the nature and role of ethnicity in politics, but also upon the utility and coherence of the conceptualization of the state.

The character and issues of ethnic politics of each of the five countries differ markedly. In the case of Malaysia, the dominant tension is that between the Malays and the Chinese, and this tension appears repeatedly to focus upon the issue of their relative economic positions and the impact upon this of the government's economic policies. This issue of ethnic economic rivalry has generated a flourishing literature on class, ethnicity and the state, so that a clarification of the relationship between the class character of the state and the structure of ethnic politics appears to offer a potentially illuminating approach.

In the case of Burma, one of the dominant issues of contemporary politics is clearly that of the ethnic rebellions against the central state, and the domination of that state by ethnic Burmans. This suggests the potential utility of an examination of the relationship between these two phenomena: the ethnocratic character of the state and the ethno-regional rebellions. In

Thailand, the ethnic unrest amongst the northern hill tribes, the northeastern Isan, and the Pattani Malays of the South, has frequently been related to the impoverishment of these peripheral regions and the increasing prosperity of Bangkok and the Central Plains. The internal colonial characterization of the state, which seeks precisely to explain the origin and impact of such regional economic disparities, thus appears to offer a potentially fruitful approach.

In the case of Indonesia, one of the most pervasive issues of contemporary ethnic politics relates to the attempt by the state to deal politically and economically with the grievances of Muslims and outer islands communities who perceive themselves as losing out in the distribution of state patronage. While the examination of the ethnic implications of a patrimonial characterization of the state is clearly not the only way of elucidating this issue, it is, nevertheless, a particularly useful one if it can explain the variations in the impact of ethnic communalism upon Indonesia's national integration.

Finally, in Singapore, the dominant issue of contemporary ethnic politics concerns the impact of what appears to be a shift in the strategy of the state towards ethnicity. Whereas the state used to stress the depoliticization of ethnicity, it has recently taken various initiatives designed to strengthen and politicize ethnic affiliations, initiatives which appeared to some to throw into doubt its claim to ethnic neutrality. The politics of such state 'engineering' of ethnicity seems most amenable to an approach which focuses, as does the corporatist characterization, on the state's interventionist management of society.

CONCLUSION

This chapter has sought to connect the ideas of ethnicity and of the state so as to establish the argument that an understanding of the former can usefully be attained through an examination of the latter. The view of ethnicity as a form of ideology indicates that it constitutes a situationally generated form of political consciousness in that it is a response to environmental factors which may potentially attach to any cultural aggregate, but that it also has sufficient psychological power to act as an important causal factor in politics. Both in its consequential and its causal roles, ethnicity refers directly to the power structure of a society, and specifically to the focal point in that power structure, the state. The character of the state influences the nature and political salience of ethnic consciousness because the state and the state-nation ideology have a crucial impact upon the types of disparity and tension that characterize the social structure; but the resultant ethnic consciousness also constitutes an ideological assertion to which the state has to respond. The way in which we choose to characterize the state will thus influence our understanding as to both the causes and the consequences of ethnicity.

While the following chapters may be read independently, they each constitute stages in this overarching argument relating ethnicity to the state. Each of the depictions of ethnicity is distinct in that it derives from a specific state situation, but the various depictions do not thereby constitute fundamentally inconsistent views of ethnicity. Whereas a Marxian position might assert the universal priority of economic relationships in generating ethnic consciousness, or an 'ethnic entrepreneurial' position might insist on the causal priority of élite rivalries; the 'statist' position adopted here shows how potentially any aspects of the situational environment – economic, social or political – may provide the stimulus for the development of ethnic communal attachments. It is the character of the state which crucially influences the pattern of situational insecurities in a society, and thence the pattern of ethnic consciousness and relationships. The alternative depictions of ethnicity refer, therefore, to contingent differences, and derive from the competing characterizations of different states.

Chapter 2

The ethnocratic state and ethnic separatism in Burma

There are several cases of ethnic-separatist rebellion in Southeast Asia.[1] Each has its own distinct origins, grievances and goals, but the aim here is to examine one theme which recurs in most discussions of ethnic rebellion: the argument that the cause of such movements is the domination of the state by the ethnic majority community.[2]

Burma offers a useful case for the study of ethnic rebellions. The cultural and linguistic structure of Burmese society is complex, but the majority-minority dimension is clear. The majority linguistic group are the Burmans,[3] who comprise about two-thirds of the total population and who have traditionally inhabited the central Irrawaddy plain. The largest minority groups are the Shan, Kachin, Chin and Karen.[4] The earliest of the rebellions involved communist and separatist unrest amongst the Arakanese, in the western Irrawady plain. The conflict between Karen and Burman armed forces began in 1949 and stimulated similar outbreaks amongst Karenni, Mon and Pao groups. By the late 1950s, the further expansion of state intervention had precipitated separatist rebellions amongst the Kachin and the Shan. Since then, virtually all of the minority linguistic groups in Burma has been involved, at one time or another, in insurgency against the state. While some of this dissidence has taken a communist direction, ethnic disaffection has remained a central factor.[5] Some of the movements have demanded outright secession, though most would apparently now settle for some form of autonomy within a federal Burma, but repeated attempts at negotiation have failed.

The confrontational and protracted nature of the disputes can be traced in part to military stalemate, but there is also a more fundamental reason. They have come to be perceived by all parties, not as negotiable political issues, but rather as clashes between absolutist and irreconcilable ideologies: the imperative of state nationalism confronting the imperative of ethnic nationalism. Explanation of the rebellions must be sought, therefore, in examination of the processes have which generated such antithetical perceptions of state and ethnic nationalisms.

The argument which emerges is in three stages. First, the 'capture' of the state by the majority Burman ethnic group will be explained as arising out of the impact of the introduction of the modern state system upon the authority structure of Burman society so as to impel displaced élites and dislocated masses to rebuild authority on a new ethnic nationalist basis. Second, the domination of the state by this one ethnic group will be related to the 'ethnocratic tendency', in which the state acts as the agency for that community in promoting its ethnic values as the core component of the nationalist ideology. Third, it will be argued that the ethnic separatist rebellions are explainable as reactions to the disruptive penetration of peripheral communities by the weak ethnocratic state. This penetration provoked the collapse of their authority structures and the dislocation of their societal cohesion so as to generate the invention, by displaced or emergent élites, of new levels and forms of ethnic consciousness. The focus, therefore, is on the disruption and restructuring of communal authority structures as the basis for explaining both the origin and the impact of the ethnocratic state.

Several writers have noted that in pre-colonial Burma, political alignments were not primarily based upon stable linguistic cleavages, but were instead characterized by fluctuating patron-client linkages and were related to distinctions between lowland wet rice communities and upland swidden agricultural communities, between those who adopted Buddhist culture and those who did not, and between those within the monarchical states and those outside.[6] Politics, indeed, frequently focused on tensions between majorities and minorities, but these terms referred not to ethnic categories, but to disparities of power, amongst the competing power centres of the various Buddhist kingdoms (Burman, Mon, Shan and others), and between these power centres and those lacking power – primarily non-Buddhists in the uplands and in the lower Irrawaddy delta.

This fluidity in political alignments corresponded with a fluidity in communal affiliations. Amongst both valley peoples like
the Mon and Burman, as well as amongst hill peoples like the
Shan, Kachin and the upland Karen, loyalties were to kin, clan,
patron, locality and region.[7] Moreover:

> While valley peoples may have thought of hill peoples as 'wild
> heathen', such a categorization did not exclude their eventual
> incorporation into 'civilization' by acculturation. The hill
> peoples seemed to have shared this view. It was not ethnic
> diversity, but cultural practice which divided people socially,
> not necessarily politically. For the Buddhist Shans, the dis-
> tinction between them and the lowland Burmans and Mons
> amounted to cultural variations rather than significant cul-
> tural differences.[8]

This does not imply that the numerous linguistic groups in
pre-colonial Burma lacked any communal consciousness which
might be termed ethnic; it is rather that ethnicity did not denote
either fixed social or political boundaries:

> Historically these relationships were never stable with a single
> established pattern or response . . . . A Kachin under certain
> circumstances might act as a Shan, or a Mon as a Burman.
> Wars that were commonly regarded as ethnic may have had
> their origins in such economic causes as control over areas of
> surplus rice production and their populations, or over highly
> strategic trade routes . . . . Colonial rule changed this
> situation.[9]

The fluidity in political alignments and communal identities
changed from the early nineteenth century onwards: it gave way
to a politics which was based, increasingly, on stable ethnic
alignments and on ethno-national consciousness. The explanation for this change in communal political consciousness lies in
the impact upon Burmese society of the modern state structure.
This refers to the early colonial state, which was imposed on the
peoples of the Irrawaddy valley, and also to the post-Second
World War Burmese state, which has encroached upon the hill
peoples. Whereas Burman–minority relationships had previously been characterized by fluidity and accommodation, as
well as by shifting power rivalries, the colonial system imposed
an institutional separation between the Burman dominated

'Burma Proper' and the hill areas inhabited by the minorities. This administrative rigidity was reinforced by a conceptual rigidity:

> It became normal to speak of the Burmans, Chins, Shans, Kachins, Kayahs, Mons, Arakanese, Tavoyans, and Karens as if they were unified national groups with ancient historical antecedents. This ascriptive conceptual mode for intellectually mapping the structure of Burma has been so widely accepted by Burma's political élite that they, like the Europeans who created it, have tended to accept the broad ethnic categories as embodying living social formations with political imperatives . . . . It is now impossible to avoid the use of broad ethnic labels even while attempting to demystify them.[10]

Ethnicity has become, therefore, the main structural basis for political alignments and for communal consciousness in independent Burma. Ethnicity has indeed become so institutionalized and ideologized that it constitutes, in the form of Burman ethnic nationalism, the core component of Burmese state identity. It is this phenomenon, the identification of the state with the dominant ethnic community, which must first be examined.

THE ETHNOCRATIC STATE

It is noticeable that, as Myron Weiner recently noted:

> In country after country, a single ethnic group has taken control over the state and used its powers to exercise control over others. . . . In retrospect there has been far less 'nation-building' than many analysts had expected or hoped, for the process of state building has rendered many ethnic groups devoid of power or influence.[11]

The term 'ethnocratic state' is employed here to signify the situation where the state acts as the agency of the dominant ethnic community in terms of its ideologies, its policies and its resource distribution. This involves three propositions. First, the ethnocratic state is one in which recruitment to the state élite positions, in the civil service, armed forces and government, is disproportionately and overwhelmingly from the majority ethnic group. Where recruitment of those from other ethnic origins does occur, it is conditional upon their assimilation into the dominant ethnic culture. Moreover, the state élites use these positions to promote their ethnic interests, rather than acting as either an 'autonomous' state bureaucracy or as representatives of the socio-economic class strata from which they originate.

Second, the ethnocratic state is one which employs the cultural attributes and values of the dominant ethnic segment as the core elements for the elaboration of the national ideology, so that the state's depiction of the nation's history, the state's stance on language, religion and moral values, and the state's choice of national symbols all derive primarily from the culture of the ethnic majority. Thus, the national identity which is employed to define the multi-ethnic society is neither ethnically neutral nor multi-ethnic, but rather it is mono-ethnic. It must be recognized, however, that precisely because of the ethnocentric assumptions underlying this, the ethnic particularism will not usually be made explicit, but will emerge clothed in the language of universalism. As Lucien Pye noted in his study of Burma:

> In reflecting the communal base of politics [political parties] tend to represent total ways of life. . . . Nationalist movements in particular have tended to represent total ways of life . . . because such parties are inclined to feel they have a mission to change all aspects of life within their society, even conceiving of themselves as a prototype of what their entire country will become in time. Members of such movements frequently believe that their attitudes and views on all subjects will become the commonly shared attitudes and views of the entire population.[12]

The third attribute of the ethnocratic state is that the state's institutions – its constitution, its laws and its political structures – serve to maintain and reinforce the monopolization of power by the ethnic segment. Thus the channels which the state provides for participation are such as to either restrict all avenues for politics or to secure the disproportionate representation of the ethnic segment.

It should be noted at the outset that ethnocracy constitutes a tendency which is manifested to varying degrees in a large number of states, rather than being a descriptive category to which any actual state fully conforms. Nevertheless, there is a

criterion for distinguishing those states with significant ethnocratic tendencies from non-ethnocratic states. The ethnocratic
tendency implies that politics primarily takes the form of ethnic
alignments, and that the penetration of the state into the peripheries of society takes on a distinctly centralizing and assimilationist character. The ethnocratic character of the state means
that state expansion takes the form of attempts to introduce the
values and institutions of the dominant ethnic groups into the
peripheral communities so that, in Cynthia Enloe's words:

> supposedly 'integrative' policies in, say, language or adminis-
> tration are likely to be perceived by those not members of the
> ruling group as not so much ethnically neutral as simply
> favouring the regime's own constituents over members of
> other communal groups.[13]

State penetration thus implies the assertion that the values of
the subordinate communities are in some way inferior, so that
only by adopting the more advanced culture of the dominant
ethnic groups can members of peripheral communities gain full
entry into the nation. Ethnocratic states might indeed vary as to
whether, and to what extent, they grant the members of the
subordinate ethnic segments access to the culture of the dominant ethnic segment and thereby grant access, through assimilation, to the opportunity of upward socio-economic and
political mobility. Even where effective assimilation is not feasible in practice, state penetration is seen by peripheral communities to be assimilationist in intent. State penetration implies the
marginalization of the ethnic minority groups both in their
exclusion from positions of power in the state machinery, and in
the subordination of their languages, religions and cultures
in the portrayal of the nation.

If the ethnocratic character of the state implied only that
access to national élite status and resources could be gained
solely by assimilation into the dominant ethnic culture, then the
most appropriate and widespread response of those of other
cultures might be to seek such assimilation where available. But
the communal consciousness of an ethnic group is not just a
situational response to external 'others'; it is also the outcome of
a discourse within the ethnic community itself as to how to
respond to the disruptive impact of those 'others' upon the
society. It is this process – the dialogue between various élite and

mass groups within the ethnic community, each seeking to resolve the particular dilemmas which the 'others' have posed for them – which provides the focus for explaining both the causes and the consequences of the ethnocratic state.

Burma is not an 'ideal-type' ethnocratic state. Each of its constitutions have enshrined the right of ethnic minorities to practise their cultures; the five stars clustered around the larger star in the Burmese flag symbolize 'unity in diversity' rather than assimilation; and Buddhism has never been explicitly and consistently employed as a state ideology to promote Burman culture. Some studies of Burma have indeed managed to ignore the Burman dominance of the state.[14] Nevertheless:

> all the systems in Burma that allow growth, development and mobility are those dominated by the Burman cultural tradition. . . . Minority languages are relegated to one's home and cannot be used for other than local purposes. Education is in Burm[an]; the symbols of the state and the deployment of power are Burman. . . . The 'Burmese Way to Socialism' might more accurately be termed the 'Burman Way to Socialism' because it reflects Burman cultural, political and nationalistic norms.[15]

This ethnocratic tendency is clearly related to the fact of Burma's cultural and linguistic diversity, and to the large Burman majority; so that it might be tempting to argue simply that it is the latter which caused the former: that it is the fact of a Burman-speaking majority in society which inevitably generated the Burman character of this state. A framework for such an argument is indeed offered by M. G. Smith's version of the plural society model. Whereas Furnivall had argued that the plural society could be held together by the unresponsive authoritarian state, Smith suggests that in the post-colonial situation this would inevitably translate into the capture of the state by one ethnic segment:

> Given the fundamental differences of belief, value and organization that connote pluralism, the monopoly of power by one cultural section is the essential precondition for the maintenance of the total society in its current form.[16]

But Smith recognized the potential instability of such a state. Just as it was 'natural' for one ethnic segment to capture the state, so was it 'natural' for the subordinated ethnic minorities to oppose such domination. As Smith continues:

> The dominant social section of these culturally split societies is simply the section that controls the apparatus of power and force, and this is the basis of the status hierarchies that characterize pluralism . . . . In such situations the subordinate social sections often seek to regulate their own internal affairs independently of their superiors . . . . In desperation, the subordinate cultural section may either practice escapist religious rituals or create a charismatic leadership as the organ of sectional solidarity and protest.[17]

But such a simple and 'common-sense' argument has several problems. There is a danger of inconsistency; treating the communal cohesion of the dominant segment as an analytical 'given' (and by implication as a primordial affiliation), while explaining the communalism of the subordinate segments as generated situationally, in reaction to their position of subordination. What is needed is an argument able to explain in compatible terms the development of both Burman ethno-nationalism and that of the minority communities. Just as a plural society argument tends to skim over the explanation of how and why ethnic consciousness developed, so does a situational reaction argument tend to skim over the explanations of why reactive opposition rather than deferential responsiveness might occur, and what internal mechanisms exist within communal groups to produce either reflex. There is surely no inevitability of a linguistic group developing the political consciousness, cohesion, and organization necessary to 'capture' a state, either by electoral or by insurrectionist means; nor is there any inevitability about the 'sectional solidarity' of a 'subordinate cultural section'. It is, therefore, neither the fact of societal pluralism itself, nor the inherent tendency of political domination to induce an autonomy reaction, which generates the ethnocratic state tendency and the minority ethno-nationalist rebellions. Their origins are located rather in the responses of both élites and masses to the disruption of communal authority structures brought about by the development of the state system.

The disruption of the Burman authority structure

The cause of the ethnocratic state tendency in Burma was the colonial disruption of the Burman authority structure, which produced a power vacuum from which new and displaced élites sought release by creating new positions of authority in their society, and from which dislocated village communities sought release by finding a new basis for communal order and authority. Both levels of society resolved their dilemmas in a new Burman ethnic nationalism directed against colonial rule.

The imposition of colonial rule upon the Burman speakers of the fertile Irrawaddy valley served to fundamentally disrupt the authority structure of the Burman monarchical empire which had developed since the eleventh century. This authority structure was based on Buddhism, both in terms of the role of the Buddhist *sangha* (monkhood) from which the political and administrative élite were recruited, and in terms of the value system which sustained the empire. Nevertheless, although many of the peripheral groups subject to Burman suzerainty were also Buddhist, the Buddhist *sangha* and the Buddhist religion did not act as a force for integration of the Burman empire into a united nation, partly because of the localized structure of the village monastery system.[18]

The colonial military conquest of the Burman monarchical state began in 1824, and was completed by 1886. The British imposed direct rather than indirect administration upon the Irrawaddy plains designated as 'Burma Proper', and replaced the Buddhist *sangha* authority system with their own bureaucratic administration. While 'Burma Proper' was effectively controlled in this way so as to facilitate the export of its rice to India, the less immediately economically productive upland regions were administered only lightly and intermittently through systems of indirect rule, and were designated as the peripheral 'Frontier Areas'.

The colonial state system thus removed the Burman ruling élites from positions of power and influence. Since the élite class had been directly dependent on royal patronage, the removal of the king meant the end of the traditional ruling class.[19]

> The British conquest . . . destroyed more than a traditional regime. It eliminated not only the seat of secular authority,

the monarchy, but obliterated the religio-mystical functions of the head of state and all the institutions and customs that were predicated on his role . . . . In the absence of a professional bureaucracy, as in the Sinocentric societies, his removal caused the collapse of the court-focused state. Dacoity and rebellions spread after his ouster. They were not only directed against a foreign invader but were in response to a political vacuum that succeeded the demise of traditional administration.[20]

The disruption of the Burman authority structure involved also the dislocation of leadership at the local community level.[21] Local-level authority in rural Burma lay primarily with the *myothugyi*, the hereditary leader of a village group. This leader had acted as the link between local community and central government, but the British introduced a new administrative system which ignored the *myothugyi*, and was based instead upon a smaller unit, the village. In the process, the *myothugyi* was bypassed and the village headman, the *thugyi*, was enrolled as a government functionary.[22] The indigenous authority system had functioned to protect the interests of village communities in their dealings with the Burman monarchical officials, but this was dislocated by the new system:

> The role of headman atrophied. Although he continued to settle disputes informally, so as to avoid government inter-ference with village life, he lost both his ability so serve as an efficient mechanism for autonomous local administration and growth and his role as the nexus of village life.[23]

The dislocation of village life caused by the effects of colonialism on the authority system was exacerbated by hardships brought about by the depression and its impact on rice incomes, and from the disruption of land and of populations caused by the fighting in the War. The resultant discontent could no longer be articulated through the channel of the headman, but the authority vacuum was filled by the village monks, who sought to carve out a new role for themselves. 'Monks, the alternative leaders of the old society, now arose to take a political role in their communities, abetted by the British inability to maintain the authority of the central monastic institutions.'[24]

By the 1920s, the village-level monks were active in promoting political agitation, and had organized a general council of the monkhood to direct such activities:

> Attacking foreign rule, village headmen, the police and courts, tax collectors, and Indians . . . . Theirs was a defensive position that rested upon the values of traditional society, but their organization, tactics and issues were new. Significantly . . . the political monks remained in close contact with the peasantry in the *wunthanu athin* [own race societies].[25]

The most radical outburst of such peasant unrest was the Saya San rebellion of 1938, led by a former monk and an activist of the village *wunthanu athin* organizations.

Thus, the decline of the authority of the central monastic institutions which followed on from the British destruction of the monarchical system had left the village-level monks free to search for a new role in society as the leaders of anti-colonial agitation in rural Burman communities during the 1920s and 1930s.

To replace the traditional administration, the colonial system sought administrative coherence through the recruitment of Burmans as lower echelon clerks and functionaries in the civil service and in private economic enterprises. This involved the development of a western-oriented education system and the emergence of a new aspiring élite of young men, initially recruited primarily from the towns of Lower Burma.[26] This new urban élite sought to reconcile their Buddhist background with their western education and attempted thereby to establish themselves as moral and political leaders in their society in order to fill the vacuum left by the collapse of the traditional Buddhist authority structure. In 1906 they formed the Young Men's Buddhist Association (YMBA), a coalition of Buddhist modernist groups, as a vehicle for the articulation of a modern Buddhist cultural identity.

Buddhism became increasingly the 'most important element of Burman identity'[27] and the cultural basis for an emergent Burman ethno-nationalism. Moreover, Buddhism offered a 'safe' channel through which Burman discontent and emergent nationalism could be developed.[28] After 1917, the younger and more radical elements in the YMBA formed the General Council of Burmese Associations (GCBA) to campaign for greater Burmese representation in the legislative council. At the same time, the GCBA supported student demonstrations at the new University of Rangoon demanding an expansion of educational opportunities, and supported efforts to create a school system which would unify the society around the teaching of the Burman language, culture and history.

Initially there was a tension between the interests of the GCBA urban élite and the interests of the village-level authority activists.[29] However, the tension began to ease during the 1930s, partly because of the failure of the Saya San rebellion, which indicated that peasant rebellion was not feasible, and partly because of their coincidence of interests in curtailing the immigration of Indians, who by 1931 constituted 53 per cent of Rangoon's population, and who threatened the employment prospects of non-educated and educated alike.

But it was primarily the rise of a new generation of students, the *Thakin* (masters) which fostered the growth of a more united nationalist movement. The *Thakin* were a radical student movement, initially focused at Rangoon University, which grew out of the *Dobama Asiayone* (We Burmese Association) founded in 1932. They sought a role as co-ordinators of peasant and labour unrest, and they employed various strands of socialist thought to link the discontent of aspiring élites with that of dislocated masses so as to organize the anti-colonial movement. 'The most important contribution of Marxism and the Left to Burma's nationalist efforts . . . was not in ideology or in garnering international recognition; rather, it was in the concept of mobilizing indigenous mass support'.[30]

The *Thakin* provided the leadership for the Burmese nationalist movement, the Anti-Fascist People's Freedom League (AFPFL), founded in 1944. This began as an umbrella organization to co-ordinate the resistance movement to the Japanese, and initially it included communists and non-communists, as well as Burman, Karen, Shan, Kachin, Chin and Arakenese groups. However, the organization's unifying impact was inhibited, from the outset, by mutual distrust engendered by the Japanese preference for recruiting Burmans and the British preference for recruiting hill peoples.[31] Moreover, in the negotiations with the British the AFPFL claimed to speak for all Burmese, but made no attempt to promote a sense of Burmese identity, rather it 'appealed for support of the indigenous peoples as members of separate ethnic, religious and political groups and not as Burmese.'[32] This united front soon split, but the AFPFL continued for some time to include affiliated groups representing the ethnic minorities. Accordingly, it adopted a federated structure with branches in most minority areas. Nevertheless, in terms of its decision-making structure, the AFPFL remained a highly centralized body dominated by Burmans, and by 1948 it had lost most of its non-Burman support.[33]

Thereafter it developed as an essentially Burman ethnic-nationalist movement which articulated the goal of Burmese independence in the name of a defence of Burman ethnic language and culture, and of the Buddhist religion, portraying the independent Burmese state as rightful successor to the Burman dynasties of the past.[34] Thus the AFPFL mission which went to London under Aung San's leadership in 1946 to demand independence consisted entirely of Burmans,[35] and in the early 1950s all of its chief officers, under the Presidency of U Nu, were Burmans.[36] The provisions of the 1947 Constitution in fact exacerbated this tendency towards Burman dominance since, although the British had taken various measures to protect the minority peoples from Burman domination, including the granting of a secession right to the Shan and Kayah states, the states were in fact given extremely little independent power. Thus, the overwhelming victory of the AFPFL in the constituent assembly elections of 1947 and in the national elections of 1951 and 1956, meant that the non-Burman ethnic groups came under the governmental control of a predominantly Burman political élite. It is certainly the case that there were several non-Burmans in the AFPFL-dominated governments, but as Hugh Tinker noted in 1956:

> It is noticeable that, when a choice is possible U Nu and his Burm[an] colleagues choose frontier leaders for office who identify themselves most closely with their Burm[an] cousins. A high favourite is the Sima Duwa . . . . He is one of the few Kachin Buddhists (he was educated in a monastery), he is married to a Burm[an] lady, and he has adopted a Burm[an] name (Kyaw U) . . . . The avowed aim of the AFPFL government is the integration of all the peoples of Burma into a unified whole . . . . But it is not pleasant to see Burm[an] public men behaving towards their frontier colleagues like

a 'master race', insisting that the only true Burm[ese] is a Burm[an] Buddhist.[37]

The image of 'unity in diversity' was illusory, though it probably reflected Aung San's personal liberal stance towards diversity and autonomy.[38] It was the views of his successor U Nu however, which had more impact on the actual character of the Burmese state. U Nu was 'ethically colour-blind', but was committed to the idea of Burma as a unitary, cohesive and assimilated society in which there was no place for ideas of minority rights. He envisaged the 'submersion of local identities and mutual mistrust in favor of creating a new identity equally shared by all and based on new community values and ideals'.[39]

However, the cement of these new national values was, for U Nu, the combination of Buddhism and socialism which the Burman-dominated AFPFL had espoused; so that despite his own commitment to democracy and equality, the call for assimilation into a new Burmese culture became in effect a call for assimilation into Burman culture. This tendency was further enhanced by the entry of the military into the political arena as the caretaker government from 1958 to 1960, and by the imposition of military rule under General Ne Win from 1962 onwards. In 1940 the Burma army had been only 12.3 per cent Burman, and 27.8 per cent Karen, but after the Karen rebellion the army was reorganized under Burman officers.[40] The officers training college was linked to the University of Rangoon, and officers were trained in a specifically Burman-oriented curriculum. The military thus became closely identified with the Burman majority, especially in the senior ranks.[41]

It has been argued so far that the emergence of Burman ethnic nationalism, in the form of the Burmese AFPFL nationalist movement and thereafter of the Burman domination of the Burmese state, did not reflect either a traditional Burman ethnic consciousness or an inevitable outcome of Burma's demographic structure: rather it constituted a response to the colonial disruption of the traditional Burman authority structure. Burman nationalism provided a vehicle whereby aspiring student élites and displaced Buddhist élites could both gain positions of power and authority in their society. They were able to employ this ideology to mobilize mass support because the social disruption generated by the collapse of the traditional authority structure had produced village communities desperate for a myth of communal certainty. This myth depicted the emergence of a new communal unity and cohesion which was legitimated in terms of nostalgia for a unity and cohesion of the past. Thus, ethnic nationalism served to provide the disrupted society with a new basis for cohesion, with Burman ethnicity providing the basis for Burmese state nationalism.

But the development of a state structure dominated by ethnic Burman personnel and values did not of itself precipitate the ethnic rebellions. It was only when the state began to try to expand its control beyond the core areas of the colonial 'Burma Proper' that those in the hill areas began to feel that 'Burmanization' constituted a threat. Among some of the non-Burman valley peoples, including the Mon and the valley Karen, colonial rule had, as with the Burmans, involved the displacement of traditional élites and the emergence of new aspiring élites, but it was only the combination of this change with the onset of pressures towards Burman assimilation and political centralization which generated ethnic unrest.

The assimilationist and centralizing character of state penetration

All developing states have experienced political tensions between attempts by central governments to expand their influence and attempts by peripheral communities to defend their autonomy. In this respect Burma is, to use Barry Buzan's term, a 'weak state' in that 'its ideas and its institutions are internally contested to the point of violence. They do not offer clear referents as objects of national security because they are not properly national in scope'.[42]

If the state is depicted as a centralized state which has penetrated the peripheral communities, then it has clearly not done so in ways which have produced the outcomes and responses contemplated by the state élite. Not only has it failed to generate a national consensus, it has in fact generated precisely the opposite outcome to that intended. Its penetrations have succeeded in provoking rebellion. But this cannot be explained simply as an outcome of the tension between centralization and autonomy; rather it is the ethnocratic character of the state, the consequent assimilationist character of its penetration into

peripheral communities, and the effect of this upon their authority structures, which have determined the character of the
ensuing politics.[43]

The periodic expansion of previous Burman kingdoms had
provoked numerous incidents of rebellion, from the 11th century onwards, on the part of the peripheral minorities. These
rebellions provide historical legitimation for, but do not of
themselves explain, the contemporary minority nationalist
movements. Although both the Karen and Shan rebellions
began as responses to disruptive military interventions in their
communities, in 1948 and 1952 respectively, they took on the
form of nationalist movements because of the assimilationist
character of Burmese government policies. It soon became clear
that the state machinery in independent Burma was, in Geertz's
words 'to a very large extent the obvious agency of a single
central primordial group'.[44]

The Burmanization of the Burmese state and nation occurred
simply because the Burmans who led the nationalist movement
and manned the state machinery considered themselves to be
the most advanced, the most modern, and the most 'nationalist'
community:

> It seemed natural to those in power who came largely from
> this community that Burm[an] should be the lingua franca of
> the nation; and while they did not say it, implicit in the idea of
> the language of the majority as the national language was the
> concomitant idea that Burman dress, manners and religion
> should also take precedence over all others.[45]

This ethnocentric basis for government policies was reinforced by the values of uniformity and centralization implicit in
the socialist and democratic ideologies of successive Burmese
governments. Ne Win, despite policy modifications, continued
to see the aim of his government's national unity policy as being
'to make those lagging behind us come up on level with us'.[46]
There thus began a slow process of Burmanization so that
'insofar as members of the minorities have a role in the power
structure, they have performed that function in a Burman context, subject to Burman approval'.[47]

The assimilationist character of state expansion was evident in
official language and education policies. The Burman language
was made obligatory for all government business from 1952

onwards and was in widespread use by government clerks in the Shan states by 1956. In the schools, Burmese history was taught from the standpoint of Burman nationalism, and from standard four onwards the sole language of education was Burman. This meant that upward social mobility implied assimilation:

> It was necessary to become fluent in Burm[an] in order to progress up the educational ladder; further [a student] had to leave his local home area to advance his education because secondary schools were located in the cities and larger towns and the universities were situated in Burma proper . . . . By moving to Rangoon or Mandalay for his higher education, a student became part of Burman culture, and in order not to stand out or to be treated as a rustic, he tended to modify his dress, speech, and living pattern so that he fit in.[48]

Burmanization was also implemented through the establishment of the Ministry of Culture and the Mass Education Movement which sought to promote the values of the indigenous culture of the Burmese people, and in practice to give primacy to Burman history and culture. The National Solidarity Association established by the military caretaker government was similarly distrusted by the minorities, who saw it as 'a new means for Burman domination'.[49]

Assimilation was promoted further by the spread of Buddhism through missions to the various hill peoples, especially the Karens. These missions were organized under the auspices of the Ministry of Religious Affairs and the *Buddha Sasana* Organization. This was done when Buddhism was not a state religion as such, having only a 'special position' under the 1947 constitution. In 1961, for a brief period, Buddhism was established as the state religion, though this was amended and retracted by the military government in the face of protests from non-Buddhists and outbreaks of religious conflict. The military government did indeed abandon attempts at systematically using Buddhism as a resource for nation-building, partly because of the independence of the Buddhist monkhood.[50]

Assimilation was accompanied by increasing administrative centralization. During the 1950s traditional rulers in the ethnic minority areas were effectively bypassed as educated non-traditional élites, political bosses allied to the AFPFL, and military personnel were recruited to administrative positions.

Administrative centralization culminated in the formation of the Burma Socialist Programme Party (BSPP) and the Military Revolutionary Council in 1962. From that time onwards Burma was administered through a centralized hierarchy of administrative councils manned by the military, the BSPP (from 1972), and the civil service, which was an appendage of the BSPP. This meant, in effect, the administration of the non-Burman states by predominantly Burman officials. In Silverstein's words:

> With no ethnic leaders who opposed the military in positions of authority, the hierarchy of councils was able to extend the policies emanating from Rangoon more effectively than any previous government had been able to do. While the military leaders, like their civilian predecessors, spoke in ways that seemed to lend support to the ideal of unity in diversity, they pursued a variety of policies that led to the assimilation of peoples into a common culture and a common loyalty. Thus they emphasized the nationalization of the society and the Burmanization of its culture.[51]

The introduction of the 1974 Constitution, the coup of 1988, the replacement of the BSPP by the National Unity Party, and the 1990 elections have not reduced either the centralization or the Burman domination. Indeed, it is not the formal provisions of the constitutions and the enacted laws which ensure that state penetration has involved a progressive centralization and Burmanization, but rather the dominance of Burmans in the state élites, and their assumption of Burman cultural superiority.

It is the perception of the assimilationist implications of state penetration that has provided the focus, at the level of consciousness, for the minority ethnic rebellions. What remains is to explain how such consciousness developed, and how it emerged in ethno-national form. As Silverstein notes:

> What moved them were their common fears of Burmanization, loss of cultural identity, interference in their affairs by the national government and a belief that the Burmans were creating an internal colonial system in which they would not share the wealth of the country, the growth of the economy and the right of self-determination.[52]

The development of minority consciousness

The process of incorporation into and penetration by the modern state is clearly a major situational change for the peripheral communities; and it has produced correspondingly major changes in their communal identities.

Each of the peripheral communities has come to see the expanding state as the dominant influence upon them, and to identify themselves in relation to this dominant other. They were labelled as subordinate groups having the marginal status of 'second-class citizens', were designated as a minority in someone else's homeland rather than inhabitants of their own, and were subject to policies which led to the deprivation of their region and community. They began, therefore, to correspondingly modify their sense of identity, and to develop an awareness of their relative deprivation within the state. This became the basis for an incipient sense of ethnic solidarity. The process was furthered where the impact of military intervention and of administrative and economic restructuring was a divisive and destabilizing one, disrupting the coherence of political, kinship and locality communities. The experience of contemporary disruption came to be contrasted with a potential (or a mythical past) image of communal unity and stability.

The state policies of centralization and assimilation, and the consequent disruption of communal authority structures, thus engendered a sense of minority consciousness in which the recognition of disunity itself provided a basis for ethnic unity. However, the specific impact of minority consciousness upon ethnic consciousness can vary. At a minimum, it may provide a sense of group identity as an inferior and subordinate community; and if this were to be articulated and ideologized by the state, then it could be used to legitimate state domination. Alternatively, it might come to be employed by the oppressed community itself and adapted 'to serve its own purpose in any eventual liberation struggle'.[53] Whether minority consciousness leads towards political acquiescence or rebellion will depend on whether, and how, it can be ideologized by political élites.

The perception of oppression, and thus of minority-consciousness, has been promoted partly by the threat state penetration has posed to the peripheral communities' links with co-ethnics across the state borders. The Burmans are the only

major ethnic group not divided by the Burmese state boundaries, and the effect of state penetration in disrupting interactions with ethnic cohorts outside Burma has given rise to
concrete grievances amongst the Shan, Karen, Arakanese and
others, and has helped to stimulate myths of communal
unity.[54] Probably a more significant factor, however, has been
the impact of state policies in provoking amongst the peripheral communities an awareness of their economic deprivation.
The virtual exclusion of minority communities from representation in the ethnocratic state means that they tend to be
denied access to the resources and benefits at the disposal of
the state.[55]

In Burma, ethnic separatism amongst the upland minorities,
including those in Karen state, can be correlated with the dearth
of investment in these regions. Industry and development have
been located to a very large extent in the lowland areas and
especially around Rangoon. In the case of the Shan, the region is
in fact rich in such resources as teak, oil, gems and silver, but the
Shan people have lacked the expertise, infrastructure and
investment funds to exploit these resources, and no government
aid has been forthcoming. The rice-based economy was destroyed by the devastation accompanying the Kuomintang
(KMT) incursion, and the benefits of the opium trade have gone
primarily to the various armies in the area rather than to the
Shan farmers.[56] It is clear that such visible economic disparities
play a major part in promoting a sense of deprivation at the
hands of the state; and when the state is seen as an assimilationist
one, treating the peripheral communities as second-class citizens, then the development of minority-consciousness amongst
such communities is facilitated.

This minority-consciousness has promoted the emergence of
new ethnic identities. Groups where communal consciousness
had hitherto been focused at locality and kinship group levels
were now impelled, by the common threat of the expanding
state, towards a new sense of pan-ethnic solidarity. Dialect and
cultural distinctions previously denoting differences between
such groups could now be reinterpreted as minor variations
within a broader community.

In the pre-colonial period, the political alignments and communal identities amongst the Shan were not based on any Shan
ethnic nationalism:

Whenever the Shans came into close proximity with the Burmans, they tended to merge with them through assimilation of customs, traditions and social values. Those Shans who remained separate were organized in numerous sub-groupings each under the absolute authority of a hereditary chief or *sawbwa*. Because of the hostility, mistrust and jealous rivalry between these chiefs, the Shans were unable to unify into a single nation as the Burmans had done.[57]

Under the colonial system, the Shan states were administered separately from the other hill peoples, through two federations of Shan states and the Federal Council of Shan Chiefs; and the 1947 constitution provided for one united Shan state.[58] Nevertheless, it was only in the 1950s that a sense of Shan unity began to develop, when their system of *muong* village groups under *sawbwa* leadership failed to protect their autonomy. This was when KMT and Burmese government troops began disrupting the area. The atrocities and lawlessness of the Burman military provoked both resentment and ethnic consciousness:

Ordinary Shans, for the first time since pre-colonial days in the nineteenth century, came in close contact with the Burm[ans], and the ethnic differences became more apparent. In the eyes of the Shan farmers, who had little or no knowledge of the Burm[an] language, the government troops were just as alien as the KMT. In the countryside, an unarticulated discontent started to grow.[59]

This emergent Shan pan-ethnic consciousness was paralleled amongst other hill tribes in Burma at this time,[60] but it was only amongst the Karen that the shift from locality to pan-ethnic consciousness had fully developed. The various dialect and village communities amongst the Karen had been too divided to resist the initial stages of Burman oppression up to the early 19th century.[61] By the late 1940s, however, when the Karens faced both 'betrayal' in the constitutional negotiations and marauding communist, PVO[62] and army mutineer bands, they had become sufficiently conscious of themselves as a betrayed and disregarded minority to respond and rebel on the basis of Karen pan-ethnic consciousness.[63]

But the case of the Karen merely illustrates the dilemmas facing the other peripheral communities. Karen ethnic consciousness had been formed, not on the basis of growing minority consciousness alone, but by the activities of new Karen élites, who had been generated by the long contact with Christianity and colonialism, and who could articulate and develop this minority consciousness.

In the absence of any such mobilizing élite within the community, the inchoate minority consciousness at mass level would not be ideologized, and would thus fail to develop into politically salient ethnic nationalism. Indeed, without such a linkage between mass and élite, the more likely scenario seems the opposite one. 'Minority consciousness' refers to what in other contexts has been termed the 'colonial mentality'; the feeling of inferiority in relation to the dominant other, and a consequent response of deference, admiration and awe. Such a response implies a state of psychological dependence which seems particularly conducive to successful political domination by the state. Assimilation, rather than separatist rebellion, would thus seem to be indicated.[64]

If we are to explain why minority consciousness did promote separatist rebellions in the case of the particular communities referred to here, we will need to explain how minority consciousness at mass level became linked to, and mobilized by, the ethnic minority political élites. This necessitates a shift of attention towards the impact of state penetration upon the indigenous political élites of these communities so as to explain why it was they, rather than the state, who became the relevant political mobilizers.

The search for élite legitimacy

Separatist ethnic nationalism arose in these peripheral communities because the development of minority-consciousness was accompanied by the erosion of the power, status and authority of their traditional indigenous élites, and the emergence of new élites; these changes being caused by the assimilationist character of state penetration.

In those cases where the development of minority consciousness was not accompanied by a dilemma of élite legitimacy, separatist ethnic nationalism did not develop. This has been argued, for example, by Taylor as regards the Chin minority in Burma.[65] Separatism would similarly have been inhibited had the state been willing to channel sufficient amenity resources to these communities, and to funnel them through indigenous élites who could then have retained dominance as communal patrons and brokers. But since the scope for this was limited by the economic policies of the state, traditional or emergent élites had to look elsewhere for means to retain or attain their political influence. The most feasible means to revive their authority and support has been for them to make use of the emergent sense of minority-consciousness amongst their communities.

By articulating the sense of communal vulnerability and dislocation in the form of an assertion of ethnic unity, and by giving voice to a sense of resentment against the dominating state in the form of a demand for increased autonomy, the élites have been able to assert their right to act as the spokespeople and leaders of their communities, and have thereby managed to revive or establish their authority. Moreover, by expressing these ideas in the context of an ethnic nationalist ideology – i.e. the assertion that the cultural integrity of the community makes self-government not just a desirable goal, but an inalienable right – the ethnic élites ensured the escalation of political tension with the expanding state into a direct confrontation between state nationalism and ethnic nationalism.

The problems of élite legitimacy amongst minority communities took various forms. The main processes may, however, be briefly stated. First, the extension of education to peripheral communities led to the emergence of a new educated generation who were disadvantaged in relation to the better educated ethnic majorities if they opted for a career in the state structure. Moreover, they often lacked the traditional cultural credentials for gaining high status within their own communities. The educated youth varied in both size and significance, but in each case they constituted a rising counter-élite in search of legitimacy.[66]

Second, in some cases state education threatened the legitimacy of traditional élites in the peripheral communities, sometimes by its secular nature, and sometimes because of its assimilationist character. The teaching of an alien language and culture was especially disruptive of traditional authority in those societies with what David Apter used to call 'consummatory belief-systems', i.e. tightly integrated cultures resistant to adaptation, like that of the Shans.

Third, since in agrarian societies the authority of traditional élites is always associated with their control over land, state interventions in land-holding were similarly disruptive of traditional authority. Where the traditional élites were perceived as owners of the land, as with the Shan, their position was directly threatened by the state policies of land nationalization and redistribution.

Fourth, the authority of indigenous élites was also directly eroded by the administrative policies of the state. Where the state attempted to recruit indigenous élites into the state machinery it placed them in a classic role-conflict position – inhibiting them from articulating communal discontent against the state, and laying them open to charges of pursuing self-interest at the cost of their communities. On the other hand, where the state removed indigenous élites from positions of political and administrative power and replaced them by members of the dominant ethnic majorities as administrators over these regions, the indigenous élites were even more clearly isolated from their communities and thus deprived of their support bases.

It is these threats to indigenous élite legitimacy, therefore, produced by state expansion, which combined to create a situation where educated and traditional élites each sought ways to regain contact with and support in their communities, and were thus in a position to take advantage of the incipient communal consciousness by articulating and ideologizing it. The process can be briefly examined as it has occurred, in rather different ways, amongst the Shan and the Karen.

The Shan   In 1947 the Shan traditional élites, the *sawbwas*, allied with the Burman dominated AFPFL in order to safeguard their own positions as well as the autonomy of the Shan. They succeeded in securing both the creation of a Shan state and their own positions in the governments at both Shan state and federal levels. The Shan *sawbwas* elected twenty five seats in the Union Chamber of Nationalities and formed the Shan State Council. They exercised limited judicial powers, acted as the administrative authority over their traditional domains, and had the right to levy taxes and other revenues.[67]

But the AFPFL government soon showed that it had no intention of preserving such a status quo and, of all the Burmese states, it was the Shan state which suffered most from the disruptive effects of central state interventions. As early as 1950 the *sawbwas* had to agree to forego their judicial powers. Then, in 1952, most of the southern Shan states were put under military administration, with the *sawbwas* being sidestepped. This was interpreted as an unwarranted interference in Shan internal affairs and 'evidently another move to undermine the power of the Saohpas'.[68] From then on, most of the *sawbwas* were reduced to trying to negotiate favourable conditions for the renunciation of their powers. In 1959 they agreed under pressure to the ending of their administrative powers in return for financial compensation and the retention of their titles and personal estates.[69]

It was not however the case that the *sawbwas* could forego their official positions while still retaining their traditional status, because by 1959 their traditional authority had already been undermined. This was partly because, so long as they had held administrative positions in the state machinery, they had been thereby constrained from showing support for the popular discontent amongst the Shans arising from the Burmese government's disruptive activities in the area.[70]

> The peasants who had suffered the most became increasingly desperate, vulnerable to any and all types of agitators and hotheads, and more and more disillusioned with their own leaders, their parliamentary representatives, and the existing political and administrative institutions.[71]

The *sawbwas'* traditional authority was further eroded both by their inability to retain traditional consultation and coalition-building practices in their state administrative roles, and also by the government's attempts to implement land nationalization measures in the Shan region, which directly threatened the main basis of *sawbwa* dominance. The cumulative effect of these pressures on the *sawbwa* was, as noted by Wiant, 'like a cancer slowly eating away at the structural fabric of the sub-nuclear societies.'[72]

The erosion of traditional authority did give rise to some 'anti-feudalist' sentiment, particularly in the southern Shan states. Most of the *sawbwas* responded, however, by seeking and finding a new platform upon which to base their claim to leadership. It was, as Taylor noted, claims 'that they were speaking on behalf of Shan nationalism [which] continued to provide the Sawbwas with a platform from which to maintain their local authority and make claims against the central state'.[73]

In 1957 some of the *sawbwa* had formed a Shan State Unity Party to try to lead them out of the federation constitutionally, 'rather than surrender their powers'.[74] When this failed, the more radical *sawbwa*, together with 'young aristocrats with close *sawbwa* connections'[75] formed the *Noom Sukhan* (Shan State Independence Army) in 1958 as a secession movement; and in March 1959, when the Shan State Council voted to end 'feudal' rule, the first clashes with the Burmese army occurred.

In an effort to resolve the issue, the senior Shan *sawbwa*, Sau Shwe Thaike, submitted a proposal to U Nu for a looser federation which would give real autonomy to the Shan state; and this led to the conference with U Nu's government in February 1962. But with the coup in April 1962 Sau Shwe Thaike and the other participants in the meetings were arrested, and the secessionist rebellion further escalated. The 1962 Coup provoked more of the Shan *sawbwas* to open insurrection; a development which was epitomized in the appointment of Sau Shwe Thaike's widow, Hearn Kham, as the first leader of the new Shan State Army in 1964.

The role of the Shan *sawbwas* in articulating a separatist Shan nationalism was directly related, therefore, to their concern to find new sources of authority after the loss of their state administrative positions and the decline of their traditional communal authority. But the traditional élites have been challenged in the leadership of the Shan rebellion by educated youths who have remained overtly socialist and 'anti-feudalist' in their leanings. In the 1940s the first defenders of Shan autonomy against the Japanese were educated Shan young men who allied with the AFPFL and formed the Shan State Peoples Freedom League to oppose *sawbwa* domination.[76] When the *sawbwas* began allying with the AFPFL so as to gain guarantees for the retention of their authority in the Shan states, the 'anti-feudal' youths and students – including those at the universities of Rangoon and Mandalay, moved away from the AFPFL, and began responding to the developing sense of Shan minority status by promoting Shan cultural nationalism through student associations and literary societies.[77] This cultural nationalism became politicized and radicalized when the government began military activities in the

Shan states, and segments of the educated youth went into the jungle as guerrilla fighters for Shan autonomy – in units such as the *Noon Seek Harn* (Young and Brave Warriors).[78]

Subsequently, various political movements and armies were formed, and although some of the educated youth were themselves members of the traditional aristocracy, the dominant trend was for the students to assert their leadership of the Shan national movement by forming bodies, like the Shan State Independence Army and the Shan State Progress Party (formed in 1971) which articulated 'anti-feudalist' programmes. Increasingly, a younger generation of 'barefoot teachers' was emerging to assert their own leadership of the Shan rebellion, and relations between the educated youth and the *sawbwas* have remained a major source of factional disunity within the nationalist movement.[79]

Thus, both the development and the disunity of Shan nationalism are illuminated if we recognize that the two groups – the educated youth and the *sawbwas*, were each seeking positions of legitimate dominance in the Shan community, and were each attempting this by translating the incipient sense of Shan minority status into calls for Shan national autonomy from the expansionist state.

The Karens The development of Karen ethnic nationalism is explainable as the outcome of two factors: the disruption of Karen social cohesion, mainly from Burman interventions; and the emergence of new élites in search of communal authority. But Karen nationalism developed in stages. The first stage, in which a pan-Karen consciousness developed, arose out of the combination of Burman interventions against Karens, for example in 1852 and 1886,[80] and the emergence of a Christian educated group who aspired to be a pan-Karen élite.

The second stage, that of Karen national rebellion, began in the 1940s both as a response to the disruption of Karen society at the hands of the armed incursions, and as a reaction to the dislocation and division of the Karen élite by their 'betrayal' in the decolonization negotiations. Until this time the Christian educated Karens could both act as leaders and spokesmen of Karen ethnic nationalism, and also pursue their careers and status within the colonial administrative structure and the governmental advisory bodies representing Karen interests.[81]

From the 1940s onwards, however, they were faced with a dilemma in that they were increasingly forced to choose between their career interests in the administration of an ethnocratic Burman state – which implied assimilation into Burman culture – or the retention of their position of communal authority within the Karen nation. Karen nationalism was thus articulated in the first phase by an emergent élite seeking legitimacy as spokespeople of communal unity; and it was characterized in the second phase by the displacement of that élite from their positions in the state administration, and their consequent articulation of an anti-state ethnic nationalism.

The first stage of Karen ethnic nationalism, the shift from village- and dialect-level political organization towards a pan-ethnic consciousness, was not simply an extension of the idea of Karen village identity, nor was it simply an outgrowth of pan-Karen cultural similarities. It should be understood, rather as a political myth created and propagated by the new educated élite who emerged during the colonial period. From about the 1850s the American Baptist missions began producing a new Christian educated generation, who were literate in the Sqaw Karen dialect, for which the missionaries developed a script. They articulated a Karen nationalism which was embodied in Karen myths of origin and migration and which legitimated the claim that the Karen constitute a distinct people with a right to their own homeland, 'Kawthoolei'. But this cultural nationalism was a new phenomenon:

> Karen identity is . . . an *invention*, rather different from the way that Karen in village communities identify themselves, and . . . the Karen 'nation-state' is, to use Anderson's term, an 'imagined political community' . . . . Karen nationalism undoubtedly has cultural roots [but] a national consciousness must be seen as a product of literacy . . . . The use – or perhaps one should say the *possession* – of a Karen 'national language' (Sgaw Karen) and a script . . . in these schools, as well as in administration and other forms of communication, is also symbolic and serves to establish, simultaneously, Karen identity and differences between Burmese and Karen.[82]

These educated Karens had an interest in promoting Karen unity so as to establish themselves as the first pan-Karen élite. In 1881 they formed the Karen National Association:

The association was a political organization designed to utilize the pervading clannish spirit of the Karens in order to bridge the gap between Christian and non-Christian Karens as well as between the various Karen language groups. Its announced objectives were to facilitate understanding and co-operation with the British rulers, to promote through education and self-help the social and economic advancement of the emerging nation, and to protect all Karen groups against any future threat of the restoration of Burman domination.[83]

The KNA benefited the educated élites themselves as well as the wider Karen society, since the emergence of Karen nationalism legitimated their recruitment within the colonial administration as the representatives of Karen interests. Until 1940 Karens formed the majority of the indigenous military forces, and many Karens were also recruited into the lower echelons of the civil service. At the élite level, the first Karen was appointed to the Legislative Council in 1916, but the KNA succeeded in getting five Karen communal seats on the Council in 1922, and in raising this to 12 in the House of Representatives and two in the Senate in 1935. By the 1930s educated Karens comprised a significant and influential segment of the governmental élite. Increasingly, they sought to promote Karen interests by ensuring the formation of a strong and autonomous Karen state. But by the 1940s it was becoming increasingly difficult to both effectively represent Karen interests, and to pursue their own interests in the Burmese state administration.[84]

In 1942 Burman members of the Burma Independence Army massacred Karens in the Salween District, whom they regarded as British collaborators. This heightened Karen distrust of Burman domination so that, in the decolonization negotiations after the war, the Karen élites became preoccupied with the problem of how to form a Karen state which could be autonomous of Burman domination. By 1947 many of them were demanding the formation of a British Karen colony which would remain separate from 'Burma Proper'. When the British failed to back this demand, the Karens felt betrayed; and when the Communist and PVO rebels threatened Karens, the Karen National Defence Organization (KNDO) began to act directly to protect the Karen communities.

This posed a dilemma for the Karen élites. Their careers in the governmental and administrative hierarchy led them to varying degrees of accommodation and assimilation with the dominant Burmans. Some, like Mahd Win Maung and Aung Pa (General Secretary of the Karen Youth Organization), were Burman speaking Karens who came to renounce Christianity for Buddhism.[85] Moreover, there were younger educated Karens who felt disgruntled at their exclusion from the authority positions in their own community, and from the élite positions in the administrative hierarchy; and such groups accordingly advocated pro-AFPFL positions in the 1947 negotiations as a way to 'satisfy their personal desires'.[86] As Cady notes:

> The apparent Burmese policy of dispensing economic and political favors to break the unity of the Karen National Union was measurably effective, but it was not calculated to dispel Karen distrust which was itself the basis of the obdurate and, from the Burman point of view, unreasonable Karen demands for independence.[87]

Faced with the growing incompatibility between their two roles – as spokespeople for Karen nationalism and as figures in an increasingly Burman ethnocratic state hierarchy – some of the educated Karens gave way to assimilationist pressures, but others sought to retain and strengthen their élite positions within the Karen community by calling for the defence of Karen nationalism against the threats posed by the state.[88] As Taylor notes:

> Since they were not traditional leaders . . . their claim to a political role had to be based on arguments of the existence of a separate Karen nation. Unwilling to undermine their own positions, the KNDO leaders rejected the compromises of the 1947 constitution . . . . Because of the early and firm acceptance by Christian and western educated Karen leaders of the notion of the unique historical place of the Karens, the depth of their conviction has made accommodation with the central state impossible.[89]

The increasingly Burman ethnocratic character of the state has eroded the opportunity for educated Karens to function within the state as '*loyal* Karens', this displacement from the state administration led them, rather, towards rebellion as 'loyal *Karens*'.[90]

SEPARATIST ETHNIC NATIONALISM

The import of this discussion of élite responses has been that the minority élites were led to establish themselves as spokesmen and leaders of movements for ethnic autonomy through their concern to resolve threats posed by the state to their career and authority positions. This connects with the impact of the state upon the peripheral communities at the mass level. The argument has been that the penetration of the state produced instability and disunity in the peripheral communities at the local level, and that the weakening of the authority structure in these communities engendered feelings of insecurity out of which a new basis for communal identity, based on minority consciousness, was beginning to develop. The élites' search for legitimacy in their communities thus coincided with the search at the mass level for communal unity and identity. Minority consciousness, which hitherto had implied dependence upon the state, became translated by the mobilization activities of the ethnic élites into a stance of ethnic autonomy against the state.

What is significant about this formulation is that both the élite and the mass-level behaviour can be understood in the same terms, as attempts to resolve problems of insecurity. Donald Horowitz has shown that security tends to be perceived in terms of group worth relative to other groups, and that the insecurity of 'backward' groups can develop into an anxiety in which 'every issue can . . . become a survival issue'.[91] The assimilationist expansion of the ethnocratic state constituted such a threat to both élites and masses when it led to the disruption of communal authority structures at the periphery. For the élites, the dilemma was that they had come to rely increasingly upon the state for their career and authority positions, but the state seemed now to undermine and threaten these positions. It was essentially the feeling that they had been betrayed by the state which led them to find a new basis for attaining security – by opposing the state. For the masses, insecurity appeared in the form of the disruption of their communities, and the solution was to find new myths of communal unity, again by opposing the state.

We do not, therefore, need to distinguish between élite behaviour as being 'rational' or 'manipulative' and mass behaviour as being 'irrational' or 'primordial'. Both élites and masses were equally threatened by the weakening of the communal authority structures, and ethnic-nationalist rebellion provided for both a response which offered a symbolic solution, – the assertion of group worth, status and rights – and also, potentially, a practical solution – authority positions for the élites and communal stability for the masses.

Numerous approaches to the study of ethnic separatism have been developed and refined in the context of the global upsurge of ethnic unrest since the late 1960s. Studies have focused on the fact of cultural pluralism and the weak state, on regional economic disparities, on state expansion, or on manipulative élites, these approaches being each depicted as if they offered alternative and incompatible explanations, so that to combine them would generate only ambiguity. However, once attention is focused upon the character of the state as the key causal agency of ethnic rebellion, then many of the apparent tensions between the different approaches begin to disappear. In the sub-category of ethnic rebellion examined here, the cultural pluralism of the social structure, the limited capacity of the state, the economic exploitation of the periphery, the defence of autonomy by peripheral communities, and the self-interest of minority élites can all be accommodated into a theory of the origins, character and impact of the state. The recognition that several factors interact does not imply any abandonment of 'mono-causal' theory if the interaction of the factors can be shown to constitute a coherent causal chain which links the origins, character and impact of the state. It was the colonial impact upon the authority structure of the majority community which generated the ethnocratic state tendency, and it was the ethnocratic character of the weak state which caused state penetration to take on an assimilationist form which provoked the disruption of communal authority structures amongst the peripheral communities. The outcome was the emergence of minority consciousness and the translation of this by displaced élites into ethnic nationalist rebellion against the state.

This depiction of ethnicity as arising out of the disrupted traditional authority structures is therefore dependent upon, and derives from, the portrayal of Burma as a weak ethnocratic state; and another way of characterizing the state would correspondingly generate an alternative depiction of ethnicity. If there were an 'opposite' to the weak ethnocratic state which generates a reactive form of ethnic consciousness, it would be the State which is depicted as ethnically neutral, and which has sufficient legitimacy, capacity and autonomy to generate a responsive pattern of ethnic consciousness and ethnic behaviour in society. In order to examine such a contrasting model of state–ethnic relationships, the case of Singapore will be explored in the next chapter.

Chapter 3

Ethnicity and corporatism in Singapore

Singapore is a multi-ethnic society of largely immigrant stock. In ethno-linguistic terms it comprises mainly Hokkien, Teochew and Cantonese Chinese – making up 78 per cent of the population – Malays, including Javanese and Boyanese who comprise 14 per cent; Indians, mainly Tamils, Malayalees and Punjabis, constituting 7 per cent; and 'others', including Eurasians.[1] Overlapping with this ethno-linguistic pluralism are the distinctions between Buddhist, Islamic, Christian, Hindu, Sikh and other religious groups. As is the case with Burma, discussions of Singaporean politics usually take this ethnic pluralism as their starting point. In line with the plural society model, the tendency has been to show that the Singaporean state has succeeded in combating the destabilizing and divisive tendencies of ethnic pluralism only by modifying western-style responsive democracy towards more authoritarian, bureaucratic, administrative or paternalistic patterns. But the character of the Singaporean state is not just a reaction to its ethnically plural society, since the state itself has clearly had sufficient strength to significantly modify the development of ethnic consciousness and the manifestations of ethnic politics – not simply by a strategy of coercive suppression, but rather by adopting a strategy of increasingly interventionist management.

A focus on this politics of ethnic management suggests a characterization of the state as being autonomous in relation to societal pressures and ethnically neutral in its national ideology. Such a view of the state is offered by the corporatist perspective. The purpose here, therefore, is to use a corporatist characterization of the Singaporean state to explain the development and implications of its ethnic management politics.

The first task of any discussion of ethnic politics in Singapore is clearly to explain how and why political stability and ethnic harmony have been sustained from Independence to the present day; and as most of the literature on Singapore has noted, the key to this lies in the avowedly ethnically-neutral character of the state.[2]

There is, however, a second feature of contemporary Singaporean politics that demands attention. During the 1980s there was clearly a shift in governmental attitudes concerning ethnicity, involving statements and policies on ethnic issues previously considered too sensitive for public discussion. Although it is difficult to quantify the impact of these initiatives, a perusal of the public debates, and also discussions with university students and others since 1982, indicates that there has developed a degree of confusion and anxiety. This is focused on the possibility that relations between Chinese and non-Chinese are less harmonious than hitherto.[3] This anxiety frequently takes the form of a question: Why would a government which proclaims its commitment to ethnic neutrality issue statements and policies which have seemed sometimes to favour the Malays, but which at other times, and increasingly, seem to reflect a new pro-Chinese stance?[4]

In order to explain both the long-term political stability of ethnic relations in Singapore and also the contemporary confusions, we must proceed by examining the development of the Singaporean state. It will be argued that both facets of ethnic politics in Singapore can be illuminated if we understand the state as developing in a corporatist direction.

THE CORPORATIST STATE MODEL

As with all key concepts in political science, the term 'corporatism' is contentious and ambiguous.[5] It is so precisely because it directs attention towards a central issue of contemporary politics. Corporatism refers to attempts by an avowedly autonomous state élite to organize the diverse interest associations in society so that their interests can be accommodated within the interdependent and organic national community. It points to:

The ideal of a harmonious, well-regulated, nonconflictive society, based on moral principles and well-defined norms which are issued and maintained by the public authority, the state . . . . There should be some intragroup autonomy and self-regulation, but the very existence of groups and their relationships with each other are granted and regulated by the state . . . . It is the state that legitimates and enfranchises group and individual participation in public affairs . . . . This is exactly the opposite of the . . . Western European tradition, in which society and its groups legitimate the power of the state.[6]

The term 'corporatism' has its origins in the medieval tradition rooted in the philosophy of absolutism and divine authority, and in the organic view of society whereby different status ranks and feudal estates were seen as coexisting in interdependent harmony. As feudalism began to give way to capitalism and industrialization, corporatism survived in the Catholic nostalgia for the feudal order and in the argument that the state should act as the moral guardian, organizing social cohesion for the greater glory of God. God and corporatism were not against capitalism as such, only against the rising tide of liberalism which accompanied it in the West. More recently, the place of God has been replaced by the idea of the nation, and the corporatist idea has been developed and applied to the state-dominated nationalism of twentieth century fascism, to the bureaucratic-authoritarian regimes of Latin America, and to the collectivist tendency recently evident in some Western European democracies.

In so far as the concept has been applied to developing countries, it has been related to two main strands of thought. One strand grew out of the observation that the post-colonial states were 'overdeveloped' in that the bureaucratic state structures tended to be particularly large and powerful, and to appropriate to themselves a disproportionate share of state revenues. This state machinery did not function solely as the agency of any one particular class, but displayed relative autonomy in relation to all class groups so as to maintain control over the whole society.[7] The second strand developed from the study of military régimes (particularly in Latin America) in which the state machinery was highly institutionalized, centralized and monopolistic, and in which the masses were deprived of opportunities for autonomous political participation.[8] In some cases, limited political participation was restored by these bureaucratic-authoritarian states, but the form and content of such participation was restricted to ensure that it posed no threat to the stability, unity and economic development of the system.

Corporatism constitutes a strategy which has been employed in states facing crises of both early and late industrialization, but its emergence in Third World states has tended to be sparked off particularly by the need to curtail populist participation when new economic policies demand sacrifices from the emergent working class. The restriction of mass participation initially enables the technocratic élite to concentrate on the administration of economic development. But if they are to get the active co-operation of the masses in economic restructuring, then the élite must move towards reliance, not on coercive or authoritarian domination, but rather on rebuilding a co-operative partnership between state and society, initially by employing strategies of economic tripartism which institutionalize state-supervised co-operation between state, management and workers' unions. In promoting such institutions for corporatist participation, the state élite seeks to attain both legitimacy and control.

For the concept to be useful as an empirical model, it is necessary to specify the extent of state domination, and since this clearly varies greatly in practice, the proponents of the concept have suggested employing the distinction between several sub-types of corporatism, with 'state corporatism' and 'exclusionary corporatism' at the authoritarian-state end of the scale, and 'societal corporatism' and 'inclusionary corporatism' at the end where the organic community is built on a more genuinely consensual partnership between state and society.[9] It is, however, precisely this stretching of the term to refer to very different empirical situations which evokes criticisms of ambiguity from its critics. It sometimes appears to be used as, in Williamson's words, 'a handy label which can stick to any surface'.[10]

Nevertheless, as Williamson continues, it is indeed possible to discern a 'reasonably substantial core'.[11] The essence of corporatism is the attempt to reconcile two apparently antithetical ideas:

the image of society and state as comprising a natural, organic, *gemeinschaft* community; and the image of society as an unintegrated aggregation of disparate groups. The two ideas are reconciled in the view of politics as state management. The corporatist characterization of the state thus implies, in the contemporary context, the state that is dominated by bureaucrats and technocrats who are depicted as acting according to the imperatives of statehood and as comprising a professional state élite trained as legal, managerial and economic experts; rather than as comprising a state bourgeoisie promoting their own class interests. The state is perceived as autonomous of society, and as the neutral agency seeking the stability, unity and development of the society through efficient management. Thus the corporatist state 'is not subject to effective challenge from popular or particularistic demands. In this respect . . . the corporatist state is a dominant state.'[12]

But the unity and development of the national society is problematical in that it is seen as no longer possessing a natural communal cohesion and evolution, and so must be held together and developed 'artificially' by the strong, autonomous state, which must co-opt the various groups in society whose co-operation is necessary for the state goals. This state control and management is then legitimated by a nationalist ideological myth which portrays the nation as if it were a consensual, organic community. The nation is depicted as a 'multicellular organism' in which the tension between pluralism and monism disappears.

This notion of the national community as a multicellular organism displaying both organic unity and also pluralistic heterogeneity, involves the postulation of a threefold distinction which, it is suggested here, is central to the corporatist definition of politics and will thereby be central to our discussion of the corporatist politics of ethnicity. This is the distinction between *political authority*, *cultural identity*, and *interest association*.

Political authority is portrayed in monistic terms as absolutist loyalty to the nation-state, such that any other sub-national or cross-national political loyalties are deemed antithetical and illegitimate. The state demands of its citizens that they give full political commitment to the organic national community and to the consensual goal of national economic development. Since the national community and the national goal constitute moral imperatives, it follows that the state élites who define them should be seen as the moral guardians as well as the expert-managers of the community. Thus:

> The state [is] . . . endowed with a moral authority to serve the greater glory of 'God' or the nation's interest, and ha[s] the right to intervene in economic and social affairs whenever they conflicted with God's will or the national interest.[13]

This absolutist national political loyalty is distinguished from the depiction of the national *cultural identity*. The nation does indeed possess a distinctive and morally superior cultural ident-ity, but this is seen as a layered or tiered structure, rather than as a monolith. It is comprised of component cultural values, such that the various distinct groups within the complex society are recognized as having values which differ from each other but which are compatible, so that they constitute a nested hierarchy of values forming the building-blocks for the 'umbrella' national cultural values and identity.

The third dimension of the corporatist nation refers to the *interest structure* of the society. In order to engineer national unity and development, the managerial state élite create mono-polistic institutional and ideological channels through which the interests of those socio-economic groups which are recognized as legitimate may be articulated. These state-sponsored channels for mobilized participation function also as means of political control, by co-opting the interest associations and defining the ideological parameters of interest articulation. In Schmitter's formulation:

> The constituent units are organized into a limited number of singular, compulsory, non-competitive, hierarchically ordered and functionally differentiated categories, recog-nized or licensed (if not created) by the state and granted a deliberate representational monopoly within their respec-tive categories in exchange for observing certain controls on their selection of leaders and articulation of demands and supports.[14]

It will be argued here that Singaporean politics is becoming increasingly corporatist. But since various commentators have argued that Singapore is moving in precisely the opposite direction – towards liberalism – it is necessary to briefly examine the dynamics of corporatism.

Corporatism may well be adopted as a deliberate strategy of state management, but it refers fundamentally to a particular tendency or pattern of state development, which has its own dynamics, so that political change becomes partially independent of the conscious strategic goals of political élites. Thus, once policies of interventionist economic management are initiated, they may have an inbuilt dynamic such that exclusionary corporatism (where institutionalized co-operation is restricted to a small élite) gives way to inclusionary corporatism, in which the network of corporatist institutions for controlled, mobilized participation is broadened to incorporate wider segments of society, to the point where it begins to provide the dominant basis for politics.

It would seem that the main 'engines' for a tendency towards inclusionary corporatism are first, the 'managerial egotism' of the state élites, which persuades them that their interventions as 'experts' are necessary and fruitful, and that the non-expert masses are not to be trusted with autonomous political participation; second, the recognition by state élites that moves towards inclusionary corporatism, involving the broadening of institutionalized consultation procedures, facilitate claims to democratic legitimation; and third, the perception by those outside the corporatist network that there are benefits to be had from being 'licensed' and co-opted by the state.

The question of whether corporatism develops in such an inclusionary direction or gives way to a liberal-democratic tendency, seems to relate directly to the question of the relationship between the state and an emergent 'middle class'.[15] In various countries there has been a relationship between the growth of an educated, affluent socio-economic stratum, loosely referred to as the middle class or bourgeoisie, and the emergence of political liberalism. This has generated the widespread view that industrialization generates a middle class which necessarily constitutes a liberalizing force in politics, exerting political pressure to reduce the extensiveness and intensity of state control. Such a shift from corporatism towards liberalism would involve a change from controlled, mobilized participation towards autonomous participation; from pragmatic interventionist government towards limited government; and from moral and political absolutism towards moral and political pluralism. Clearly, the term 'liberalism' should not be employed simply to denote the shift, within corporatism, from an authoritarian style towards a more caring paternalism.

Some observers have indeed characterized recent changes in Singaporean politics as involving 'an experiment with some degree of liberalization'.[16] But since it is acknowledged that the 're-politicization' in Singapore is 'filtered through changes in the goals of the political élite', who 'put a premium on strong leadership and a tightly disciplined society, but less emphasis on functioning pluralism', then such 'liberalization' begins to look rather similar to inclusionary state corporatism.

The Singaporean 'middle class' does not conform to the 'liberal' model of professionals who, because of their wealth, skills and predominantly private-sector occupations, are economically independent of the state, and therefore also politically independent. Thus the percentage of the educated élite employed by the state remains remarkably high, averaging about 40 per cent,[17] and the combination of a stress on deference (promoted as an 'Asian value') and of material prosperity, has produced a 'depoliticized culture' which is not conducive to the spread of ideas of individual or group liberty rights against the state.[18] Thus Ho Wing Meng has argued that:

> Prosperity and material well-being . . . have given rise to . . . the growing cult of materialism, and with it, the related phenomena of cupidity, philistinism, political apathy, alienation and, for many people, a sense of spiritual deprivation. For most Singaporeans, this cult of materialism takes the form of an obsessive preoccupation with the pursuit and acquisition of pecuniary and material gains and the honorific display of wealth.[19]

It seems possible, moreover, that the wealthy, English-educated socio-economic élite is even more imbued with the culture of *kiasu* (competitive selfish anxiety) which sustains corporatism, than are other segments of society. They are the products of an education system which seems to promote, rather than reduce, this culture, since:

> The aim of the government's policy on education is strictly practical and pragmatic, namely, that of job training through

the inculcation of knowledge and expertise relevant to the kinds of professional skills required by the public and private sectors of the economy . . . it goes down well with most Singaporeans, despite occasional grumblings about the tendency of the system to encourage rote learning, cramming, lack of creativity, and the breeding of obedient bureaucrats and technocrats.[20]

While there is thus no evidence that the growth in the size and proportion of wealthy and educated 'white collar' Singaporeans has led to any liberalizing pressure on the government, the increase in specialist professionals, with their own interests and expertise, has increased the complexity of occupational and interest-groups within Singaporean society. If corporatism is to cope with such a change, then it must expand its network of institutionalized channels for controlled participation. Such an expansion of corporatist consultation is not to be confused with, and does not necessarily imply, any move towards political liberalism. Indeed, it suggests a political change in precisely the opposite direction – towards an expansion, rather than an erosion, of corporatism.

Although several writers, such as Deyo, Rodan and Anantaraman, have referred to Singapore in corporatist terms, it should be noted that there have been some objections to applying the model to Singapore.[21] It has been argued that there is such a high centralization of power in the state that the strategies of state control have been direct and authoritarian, rather than corporatist in nature. Approached from the other side, this takes the form of the argument that the labour force and other social groups have been so acquiescent and deferential that corporatist measures of state control have not been needed. Also connected with these arguments is the suggestion that state controls in Singapore are often informal, rather than being institutionalized in ways which can be labelled as corporatist.[22]

There is indeed some truth in each of these observations, although the extent of state domination and of political acquiescence evident in the 1970s should be recognized as being the outcome of PAP strategies which had significant elements of 'exclusionary corporatism'. Nevertheless, it is only the widening of the political arena during the 1980s and early 1990s that demands the corporatist label. Moreover, it is indeed significant that state control of political participation in Singapore sometimes occurs informally, as with Stephen Milne's example of the relationship between the state and the Chambers of Commerce.[23] This feature does, however, correspond to one of the distinctive attributes of corporatism noted by Guillermo O'Donnell when he comments that 'the state exercises control over the dominant sectors by less direct and much less coercive means than those applied to the popular sector', since such organized interests can be represented within the institutional areas of the state itself.[24] This probably applies especially to a small state such as Singapore, where the relationships between the state élite and the commercial and other élites are particularly close and multiplex. Corporatist institutionalization is thus often more evident in the relationships between the state and 'the masses', than at the intra-élite level.

The application of the corporatist label to Singapore signifies only that corporatist characteristics have become an increasingly dominant aspect of government. It does not imply that Singapore is, or is likely to become, fully and explicitly corporatist. This is partly because of problems inherent in attempts by the state to engineer consensus. But corporatism is also inhibited by the impact which the anti-corporatist values of western liberal-democracies have had on Singaporean society, which ensure that government leaders, even while pursuing policies with corporatist implications, continue to legitimate them in part by acknowledging liberal and pluralist ideals; hence the cryptic and illusory quality of much of the language and practice of Singaporean politics.

Corporatism and ethnicity

The connection between corporatism and ethnicity is a contingent one, since it is quite feasible that a technocratic-bureaucratic state élite might restrict a corporatist strategy to the realm of economic tripartitism. Even if corporatism is extended to the political and social realms, the 'cells' employed for the building of the national organic community might relate either to occupational categories, to administrative units, or to ideological groupings, rather than to ethnic communities. Indeed, virtually all the writers on corporatism define the concept in terms of the state's relationship to the private enterprise production process, and most of them similarly restrict their focus to the examination of the economic realm. The present discussion seeks to extend the concept to the examination of state-ethnic relations on the basis of two key propositions.[25]

First, it is suggested that the development of corporatist tendencies in the culturally plural society leads inexorably to the state becoming involved in attempts to engineer ethnic consciousness. The state demands a monopolistic and absolutist national political loyalty, and must therefore condemn other competing sub-national loyalties, including ethnic loyalties, as subversive. On the other hand, unless the state were to adopt an assimilationist stance, it must recognize that the corporatist national identity has to be built on a multicellular rather than a unicellular basis. It must therefore seek to modify ethnic affiliations so that they can become compatible with, and component elements of, the organic national identity. Thus, at the same time as the state is seeking to erode ethnic political loyalties, it must promote and develop the approved ethnic cultural values.

The second proposition is that, just as the state might employ economic organizations as corporatist intermediaries, so might it seek to promote social and economic order by extending this strategy of control and consultation to other social groupings. Specifically, the state may seek to organize ethnic communities as 'singular, compulsory, non-competitive and hierarchically ordered' categories on 'Schmitterian' lines. The articulation of ethnic interests could thus be promoted as a legitimate political activity, with the state more effectively supervising ethnic demands by licensing and controlling the type of issues and the organizational channels recognized as legitimate.[26]

The extension of the corporatist strategy to ethnicity thus involves the state in an attempt to structure politics around a distinction between three different facets of ethnicity: as a subversive political loyalty which undermines national loyalty, as a cultural component for the national ideology, and as a legitimate interest association. If the corporatist state is to sustain and enforce such inherently subtle distinctions, then it must exert a correspondingly high degree of influence over the political socialization processes, in particular over those relating to the formation of ethnic consciousness. The danger is clearly that there are inherent problems in dividing ethnic consciousness up into 'loyalty', 'value' and 'interest' compartments, and that such an exercise is likely to be misunderstood by the populace. If this is so, then the employment of corporatist strategies to promote national unity and political stability may begin to have the unintended consequence of actually promoting new sources of political disquiet and uncertainty. In this respect, the attempt to extend corporatism may expose inherent tensions which lead eventually towards dissensus rather than consensus.

In the case of Singapore, the corporatist tendency has extended to incorporate the ethnic dimension to such an extent that the state élites have developed a marked predisposition to depict and to organize Singaporean society along primarily ethnic lines, even for the discussion of economic, political and social issues which do not relate directly to the ethnic realm of linguistic, religious or racial matters. There would appear to be three main reasons for this. The heritage of the Singaporean state élites made them particularly prone to see politics in ethnic terms; first, because of the geopolitical factor whereby the political consciousness of the Chinese majority in Singapore is dominated by their self-perception as a minority within a predominantly Malay region; second, because of the impact of the racial division of labour and racial stereotyping which accompanied British colonial rule in Singapore; and third, because of the perceived link, during the 1950s, between Chinese 'chauvinism' and pro-communist agitation, which predisposed the PAP moderates towards a view of the disruptive potential of ethnic loyalties.

In relating the model of the corporatist state to the discussion of ethnic politics in Singapore, three periods or phases will be distinguished. From the time of self-government up to the separation from Malaysia in 1965, the state lacked any major corporatist features and retained both the authoritarian and the incipient liberal-democratic features which had been inherent in colonial rule. Nevertheless, it was during this period that the governing PAP élite began to develop the network of political and legal institutions, and some of the ideological perceptions, which were to provide the basis for subsequent corporatist developments.[27] In the second phase, from the mid-1960s until the end of the 1970s, the state was still not fully corporatist, but did increasingly possess certain prerequisites of corporatism. It had a high level of autonomy from the dominant socio-economic groups,[28] and it was dominated by a technocratic élite who sought to control the process of economic development by a strategy of 'depoliticizing' society. During this phase the Singaporean state was frequently characterized as an 'administrative state' or as a 'bureaucratic' or 'bureaucratic-authoritarian' system.[29] It also clearly exhibited some other corporatist characteristics, especially as regards its relations to labour and the trade unions. It is only in the most recent phase, however, from the early 1980s onwards, that Singapore may be described in corporatist terms, and as moving progressively towards an inclusionary form of corporatism.

ETHNIC MOSAIC POLITICS 1959–65

The governing PAP élite frequently reminds its citizens of the major problems facing them with the onset of self-government. How was it to rapidly build a sense of national identity amongst its largely immigrant and culturally plural society; and how was it to do so, given its predominantly Chinese population within a Malaysian federal state where the Malays were politically dominant? Singaporean society was portrayed from the outset, explicitly and almost exclusively, as structured on a racial basis; as an ethnically plural society whose unity was both fragile and problematical.

It was clear that the geopolitical circumstances inhibited any development of a Chinese state, a 'third China', and it was similarly evident that the government at the time lacked the capacity to implement any policy of assimilating the different racial, religious and language groups either into a Singaporean nation based on Chinese culture, or into one integrated around western and Anglophone values. The realistic formula which was adopted was that of portraying the Singapore nation as a unique 'ethnic mosaic', and the key terms used to designate this formula were those of 'multiracialism' and 'unity in diversity'. It was symbolized in the adoption of four official languages, Malay, Mandarin, Tamil and English.

This form of national identity was employed, not just at the level of symbolic national ideology, but also at the level of political resource allocation. The PAP was careful to allocate cabinet, parliamentary and senior civil service posts in terms of 'ethnic arithmetic'.[30] Similarly, education policies were 'ethnically balanced' by the use of a policy of bilingualism, and by the preservation of different ethnic 'streams' of schooling.[31]

The stress on the 'ethnic mosaic' character of Singapore served to promote national unity and political stability in two ways. It provided a way for the English-educated PAP and governmental élite to associate themselves with, and to proclaim their admiration for, the unique richness and diversity of the Singaporean society. It thus bridged the gap between the westernized élite and the non-westernized masses. Moreover, it was translated into government policies and education programmes which stressed the civic virtues of mutual tolerance and admiration between ethnic communities; so that the government could hope to convince the various migrant communities that their ethnic attachments would not be threatened by the development of new attachments to Singapore.

It is important to note that such policies of ethnic accommodation, which had in fact been initiated by the previous colonial governments,[32] did not imply that each ethnic group would receive equal attention, only that allocations would be based on some criterion of 'fairness'. In practice, this meant a stress, both in national ideology and in resource allocation, on the constitutionally guaranteed 'special position' of the Malays.[33] The Malay language was promoted as the national language and the 'lingua franca'; and Malays, unlike the other racial communities, received free education. Given the numerical and socioeconomic predominance of the Chinese, it was inevitable that the stress should be on the danger of unfairness to the minorities, and in particular to the Malays, who were believed to be the least economically and educationally advanced racial group.[34] Moreover, the government was impelled to downplay its concern to protect Chinese interests while displaying its concern for the Malays because of its desire to attain independence within the Malaysian Federation.[35]

The 'ethnic mosaic' approach to Singaporean national identity and political allocations was significant so long as the PAP government remained concerned to develop its support base amongst each component ethnic group, and so long as Singapore's merger with Malaysia continued. By the mid-1960s, however, both these circumstances had changed, and the 'ethnic mosaic' depiction of Singapore began to give way to a rather different portrayal, that of 'meritocracy'.

THE POLITICS OF ETHNICALLY NEUTRAL MERITOCRACY IN THE 1970s

The term 'multiracialism' has continued to be pervasive in the political discourse of Singapore, but with a marked shift in its significance. Whereas up to the mid-1960s it referred to the character of the state, implying accommodationist politics and an 'ethnic mosaic' national ideology; it began to be used in the 1970s to describe the racial composition of the society, and to celebrate the virtue of inter-ethnic tolerance in an achievement-oriented society committed to economic development.[36] The character of the state, the political arena, and the national ideology, began to be portrayed in terms of ethnic neutrality instead of in ethnic balance terms as previously.

This shift reflected the facts that the PAP élite had by then attained effective and unchallenged governmental authority, and that Singapore had separated from Malaysia. The government was thus in a position to concentrate on the central task of industrialization, and it sought to inculcate into its citizens a new set of national values conducive to such development. These values, promulgated in the schools, the media and the governing élite's political speeches, focused around the ideals of discipline and rugged self-reliance, pragmatism, egalitarian competition, and the pursuit of excellence. National identity was not to be based then, on any specifically Singaporean culture, but rather on 'a philosophy of national development'.[37] These values were epitomized in the portrayal of Singaporean national identity in terms of 'meritocracy'. The image was of a society in which political, economic and social status positions were to be allocated on the grounds of ability and desert – as measured by the state – rather than on grounds of ethnic arithmetic. But if ethnicity were to be depoliticized, this would have to be achieved through the deliberate state management of ethnic consciousness.

The concern to promote a Singaporean national identity which was meritocratic and ethnically neutral was reflected in various shifts of governmental policy. The PAP continued to recruit and promote non-Chinese into political and governmental positions, but it was now claimed that they were there solely on merit, and that they should not be considered as representatives of any ethnic constituency.[38] In economic terms, the government now laid stress on the fact that the Malays could not expect positive discrimination and should increasingly move towards 'self help' by taking advantage of the equal opportunities open to all Singaporeans in education, politics, and career advancement. In the social realm, education and housing policies began to reflect an increased concern with promoting racial integration.[39] By 1966 the government had ceased its annual campaigns to promote the Malay language and began to concentrate instead on promoting English as the common language of meritocratic economic development.[40] By 1979, 91 per cent of Primary 1 school enrolments were in English-stream schools, which consequently performed a major integrative role.[41]

This shift from 'ethnic mosaic' to 'meritocracy' had important implications for the nature and role of ethnicity in Singaporean politics. The aim was to change ethnicity from being a problem in the way of national integration, towards making it a resource conducive to both unity and development. This took two main forms. First, ethnic attachments were depoliticized through state policies aimed at revising their content so as to 'sanitize' them of political connotations. Ethnicity was then promoted as a 'high culture' located outside the political arena. Second, the state promoted national unity by fostering a 'garrison mentality' in which the potentially destabilizing and subversive implications of ethnic loyalties were stressed. The articulation of this distinction between ethnicity as a legitimate source of values and identity at the level of high culture, and ethnicity as a subversive political loyalty, was to provide an important basis for the subsequent development of corporatism.

The depoliticizing of ethnicity

The portrayal of Singapore as a meritocracy implied the adoption of an ethnically neutral portrayal of the Singaporean national identity, but it had the additional function of legitimating the government's strategy of discouraging political participation. The meritocratic argument asserted that there was equality of opportunity in the hierarchically organized and highly competitive society, and that the resultant socio-economic inequalities were the just and fair outcome of universalistic procedures. In terms of politics and power, the implication was that those who attained political élite positions did so because they had most merit and were best fitted for government by their expertise. It followed that the job of government should be left to these experts, while the ordinary people pursued the non-political occupations for which their own levels or forms of merit best suited them.

The government encouraged, therefore, the process of 'de-politicization', in which politics became translated into the idea of rational administration. Depoliticization in turn implied the encouragement of political acquiescence. Organized political opposition was neutralized, for example by the 'Operation Cold Store' detention of the opposition activists in 1963, and by the outmanoeuvreing of the Barisan Socialis over the merger issues in 1965.[42] Labour unrest was tackled by means of the PAP's promotion of the pro-government National Trade Union Congress (NTUC), the deregistration of the pro-communist Singapore Trade Union Congress (STUC), and the 'harassment' of its successor, the Singapore Association of Trade Unions (SATU).[43] Various pieces of legislation were introduced which strengthened employers' controls over labour and restricted opportunities for labour strikes.[44] In addition, the PAP government sought to inculcate what has been termed a 'spectator' political culture[45] into the populace.

The aim was:

> to create a nonideological [national] identity, or if this seems to be a contradiction in terms, an identity through an 'ideo-logy of pragmatism'. Discussion of basic questions of political philosophy and ideology, even political discussion in general, was severely curbed until it flowed at a low ebb out of public purview.[46]

The depoliticization of ethnicity was just one facet of this wider process of modifying the cultural attitudes of Singaporeans towards politics.

During the 1960s several outbursts of ethnic rioting occurred,[47] and these events were perceived by the government as evidence of the primacy of ethnic attachments over Singaporean national loyalty. Moreover, they appeared to arise out of political attachments outside Singapore; the feelings of loyalty felt by Singaporean Malays to their co-ethnics in West Malaysia, and the communist and pro-Beijing affiliations of many Chinese. Such ethnic attachments were clearly antithetical to political stability, to national unity, and to the prospects for meritocratic economic development. The Singaporean government thus embarked on the task of modifying the ethnic ties so as to rob them of such destabilizing characteristics.

Singaporean society is complex in its ethnic diversity (with, for example, at least forty-two dialect/language groups) but the government sought, with increasing intensity during the 1970s, to promote the image of an 'official four race model' of society.[48] The diverse cultures of each racial group were 're-created' into four cultural compartments, portrayed as internally homogeneous and mutually distinctive.[49] Thus, for example, Malay and English-speaking Baba Chinese were educated in their 'mother-tongue' which, according to government ideology, is Mandarin.[50] The content of each official 'racial culture' was promoted through the schools and portrayed on television dramas, in 'cultural shows', and as an 'instant Asia' display for tourists.

The implication was that all Singaporeans were impelled to strengthen their cultural attachments to one or other of the racial communities. As Geoffrey Benjamin noted:

> If a corporate, organismic view of the state is espoused, then it will follow that each constituent 'race' will have ascribed to it a stereotypic list of defining behavioural characteristics. In so far as full Singaporean identity at the personal level will depend largely on the extent to which the individual is able to claim membership of one of the four 'races', then we should expect that actual behaviour would show a tendency to conform to the expectations that derive from those 'racial' stereotypes. In other words, Singapore's Multiracialism puts Chinese people under pressure to become more Chinese, Indians more Indian, and Malays more Malay, in their behaviour.[51]

This promoted political stability in two ways. It removed ethnicity from the political arena and defined its location in the non-political social realm, and it also provided individuals with the 'cultural ballast' which is, according to the government model, necessary in order to prevent the alienation (cultural and also potentially political) of the 'rootless' individual.

The promotion of the four 'official' ethnically-defined cultures was thus not incompatible with the government policy of promoting ethnically-neutral meritocratic politics. Indeed, as Chew Sock Foon has argued, the expression of ethnic identity as 'cultural ethnicity' was directly conducive to the development of national identity as a political loyalty.[52] The depoliticization of ethnicity served to promote the de-ethnicization of the economic and political arenas. In economics and politics, acquiescent individualism could thus more easily be promoted, though this is not to say that there was not a burden on Singaporean citizens enjoined not only to learn two languages, but also to inhabit two worlds, the non-political ethnic and the non-ethnic political.

The depoliticization of ethnicity and the 'sanitization' of the ethnic cultures during the late 1960s and the 1970s led to various problems. The attempt to generate a sense of national identity based upon the values of economic pragmatism and meritocracy faced the intrinsic difficulty that such values appeared too loose and unspecific to provide a strong sense of distinctive Singaporeanness. They were also too closely associated with western and Anglophone cultures to bridge the gap between the English-speaking élite and the 'vernacular'-speaking masses. As Chan and Evers noted:

> The attempt of the Singapore PAP leadership is suspected by members of individual ethnic communities as being in fact nothing but the expression of values prevalent among the English educated élite, and by those with socialist leanings as being an ideology of a capitalist economic system with totalitarian political features.[53]

Moreover, given the need to develop political attachments to the ethnically neutral and meritocratic state at the same time as promoting cultural attachments to the ethnically plural society, the Singapore government had to continually find ways of reinforcing its definition of the dividing line between politics and culture. The government thus looked for short-term ways of dramatizing its argument that loyalty to nation constituted a morally absolute commitment.

The main response of the government to these problems has been to promote repeatedly the 'garrison mentality'; to publicize the various dangers and threats facing Singapore which make the defensive unity of the whole community imperative to the country's very existence. It is this siege view of politics which lies behind the idea, promoted by the government after 1965, that Singapore's national ideology was the 'ideology of survival'.[54]

The government found various ways to convince Singaporeans of the fragility of Singapore and the imperative of national unity. There has indeed been no shortage of evidence supporting such an argument. The government was able to point to Singapore's minute size, compared especially to that of Indonesia and Malaysia, its vulnerability as a predominantly Chinese country in a Malay-dominant region, and the fragility of the economy given its dependence, especially on the USA. In addition, there have been a series of specific external threats: the Communist uprising of the 1950s in Malaya, Singapore's experience of *Konfrontaci* with Indonesia between 1963 and 1965, the 1965 expulsion from Malaysia, and the threat to security and the economy posed by the 1968 announcement of the impending withdrawal of the British military base.

National unity has also been promoted by the state's articulation of another more general external threat, that of 'westernization'. During the 1970s, the Singapore government sought to promote the universalistic and pragmatic values associated with the adoption of western technology, but at the same time sought to prevent Singaporean society from becoming 'de-ethnicized' by being assimilated into what Lee Kuan Yew has disparagingly termed a 'pseudo-western' cultural community. In particular, it was convenient to see social problems such as youth alienation and drug abuse as arising not because of tensions inherent in Singapore's social development, but as being imported by 'infections' from the West. The need to protect and guard Singapore against such 'contamination' from the West thus became a legitimatory rallying cry which was employed by the state throughout the 1970s. Increasingly, the West came to be depicted as the source of social degeneracy and political instability.

In addition to these external threats, there have been a series of internal threats which have been proclaimed as dangers to unity and stability. The government has pointed at various stages of the country's development to the threats from internal communism. Detentions of those alleged to be involved in communist activities occurred periodically from the mid-1960s to the mid-1970s,[55] and reappeared with the discovery of the 'Marxist conspiracy' of 1987. However, perhaps the internal factor most consistently depicted as a threat to Singapore's unity and stability has been that of ethnicity. Ethnic strife has been depicted both as a danger in itself, and also as the Trojan horse which threatens Singapore's ability to defend itself against external threats.

Singaporeans have thus been repeatedly reminded of the ethnic tensions of the 1960s in order to maintain a garrison mentality, and the PAP leaders have frequently employed the spectre of ethnic unrest to combine calls for national unity with the mobilization of support for the PAP. They have depicted opposition politicians as 'playing up communal issues which could tear the Republic apart',[56] and have then equated support for the PAP with the safeguarding of Singapore's future:

> Unleashing communal passions . . . can do more damage than even the atom bomb. It will rip society apart, not just bridges and buildings. The explosion once it starts is of indefinite duration. It can go on not just for a few months and few years, but for generations.[57]

Singaporeans who listened to the 'drumbeats of primitive tribalism' played by opponents of the PAP, were 'endangering themselves and generations yet unborn'.[58] Such warnings were directed especially at the younger generation who, as Lee Kuan Yew repeatedly noted, had no experience of any instability or insecurity in Singapore, and who thus might not otherwise appreciate the rationale behind the imperative of national unity.

This portrayal of politicized ethnicity as an illegitimate and subversive threat to national unity thus served to dramatize and promote the moral absolutism of national loyalty, and also served to sustain the state's stance of depoliticization.

The dynamics of meritocracy in the ethnically plural society

Although the stress on meritocracy was intended to promote both the authority of the governing PAP élite and also the process of state-directed economic development, there was evidence by the early 1980s that it had not been entirely successful. It appeared, both in the 1981 by-election and in the 1984 general election, that there was a significant reduction in popular support for the PAP.[59] Moreover, by the late 1970s economic strains were becoming evident, and the government decided on an economic restructuring policy which implied the need for a further increase in state intervention. Both trends seemed to imply the need for new measures to promote the ideological legitimacy of the PAP-dominated state.[60] The meritocracy of the 1970s also seems to have promoted certain other problems and tensions relating to ethnicity, which provided impetus for further progress towards corporatism.

The tendency towards meritocracy had not served to reduce the socio-economic disparity which existed, especially between the Malays and the Chinese. Indeed, as Tania Li has argued, the position of the Malays relative to the Chinese declined from 1959 to 1980, with that decline being most marked during the late 1970s. Between 1975 and 1980, the percentage of Chinese in the low income group (earning less than S$400 per month) fell from 67.15 per cent to 41.8 per cent, but during that same period, the percentage of low-income Malays rose from 62.55 per cent to 64.1 per cent. A similar trend was evident in terms of educational attainment. While the percentage of Chinese proceeding to upper secondary and tertiary education was high and increasing during the 1970s, the percentage of Malays was low and declining.[61] Of itself, the increasing disparity might not have been politically significant, but the Malays still had expectations of upward mobility, partly because of the promise of special consideration for Malays which had characterized the earlier 'ethnic mosaic' period, and partly because of the actively pro-Malay policies of the Malaysian government across the causeway, which became increasingly evident after 1969.

Meritocracy appeared to be promoting racial inequality rather than equality, and there were signs that this was beginning to engender a degree of political alienation and ethnic discontent amongst the Malay community. By 1983/4, Tania Li found:

> The widespread and deeply held belief among Malays in Singapore is that their problems and disadvantages have been imposed on them on a racial basis by the Chinese majority. Discrimination by Chinese against Malays is based on the Chinese opinion that Malays are culturally inferior and incapable of hard work.[62]

The Malay community had been encouraged to lower their sights and to accept, for example, that the Malay language would have to take second place to English. But some Malay

activists opposed this trend in ways which provoked their detention by government,[63] and the apparent widespread acquiescence perhaps arose more from an absence of Malay political
leadership, from the Malay community's recognition of their
own weak numerical position, and from awareness of the PAPs
intolerance of 'communalistic' politics, than from an absence of
grievances. Nevertheless, some dissatisfaction at various PAP
policies continued to be voiced within the Malay community,
and it emerged in reduced Malay support for the PAP.[64] Given
the government's general planning perspective, this problem of
Malay alienation and inter-communal suspicion had to be
'nipped in the bud'.

Within the Chinese community, the decline of the Chinese-
medium schools in the face of the promotion of English as the
language of economic mobility provoked some discontent which
was articulated most clearly in 1970 by the Chinese newspaper,
Nanyang Siang Pau,[65] and which was met by the detention of
several of its staff in 1971.

The other problem generated by meritocratic politics related
to the weakness of the symbols and values available as bases for
Singapore's national identity. The attempt to employ strategies
of siege nationalism in order to buttress and supplement the
level of national consciousness provided by the rather unspecific
values associated with 'meritocracy' was, by its very nature, a
short-term and inadequate one. Specifically, the younger generation – those most deeply imbued with the universalistic values
of meritocracy – were likely to perceive the spectre of collapse as
far-fetched and unconvincing. A further impetus for a renewed
attempt to promote a stronger and more specific sense of
national identity was the impending change of political leadership in Singapore. While the older generation of political
leaders, especially Lee Kuan Yew himself, had attained strong
legitimacy as the 'fathers of the nation'; the second generation
leaders, who began to be groomed by the 'old guard' in the mid-
1970s, had no such strong base. They could attain strong legitimacy only if they could cement the idea that the PAP was itself a
'national movement', and if they could thereby associate themselves with a strengthened sense of national loyalty on the part
of Singaporeans.

The weakness of meritocracy as a basis for national identity
was initially articulated in the form of repeated warnings that

Singapore was in danger of becoming too westernized, and that the depoliticization of ethnicity might have led to an erosion of the vitality of the traditional ethnic cultures. During the 1980s, such warnings were buttressed by the argument that westernization was leading to a religious revivalism, especially in the form of the conversion of young, educated Chinese to Christianity, which threatened both to generate the spread of a communist inspired 'liberation theology'[66] and, through the spread of proselytism, to promote intolerance and suspicion between the various religious communities.[67] If the governing élite were to resolve the perceived problems of emergent ethnic discontent and of a weak sense of national identity amongst all sections of society, then it appeared that a way must be found to bring ethnicity back into the political arena in a form which could strengthen national consciousness.

TOWARDS INCLUSIONARY CORPORATISM

In general, Singaporean politics moved in a corporatist direction in the 1980s and early 1990s. If Singapore were to achieve a 'second industrial revolution', this would necessitate, as Rodan has noted, the shift to a 'qualitatively new phase' in state intervention.[68] The employment and trade union legislation of the 1960s and 1970s had embodied some clearly corporatist elements, but these were now extended. PAP leaders and members were appointed to key NTUC posts, and the larger and more powerful unions were dismembered and replaced by smaller industry-based and house (company-based) unions, so as to facilitate the 'overriding authority of the political leadership'.[69] Moreover, the 1982 Trade Union Act extended government controls over unions and redefined their roles in line with Lee Kuan Yew's call that they 'support management and government in a joint effort to realize our full potential'.[70] This stress on tripartite co-operation under government supervision was further promoted by the establishment in 1981 of the Committee on Productivity, and by the launching of campaigns to promote a Japanese-style management ethos of 'teamwork', through such institutions as Quality Control Circles (QCCs) and Work Improvement Teams (WITs).[71]

The new stress on 'teamwork' contrasted sharply with the earlier focus on 'rugged individualism', and it was extended well beyond the workplace into a campaign aimed at modifying wider cultural values and inculcating nationalist commitment. The government launched a campaign of TV and cinema advertisements to urge the civic virtue of the co-operative community. Singapore was deluged with songs and slogans such as 'Count on me, Singapore' and 'This is my Home'.

In the overtly political realm, the corporatist tendencies emerged both in the 1982 reconstitution of the PAP to strengthen its élitist organizational structures and to define it explicitly as a 'national movement',[72] and also in the moves to incorporate political opposition by ensuring that it was articulated through institutionalized governmental channels. Lee Kuan Yew announced that 'constructive' opposition would henceforth be fostered so as to provide the PAP parliamentarians with 'sparring partners',[73] and this was implemented by the 1984 offering of 'non-constituency MP' places to the defeated opposition candidates who gained the most votes, and also by the appointment after the 1988 election of 'Nominated MPs'. The trend towards a corporatist national identity was also signalled in various initiatives designed to promote an image of government as based on community-wide consultation and consensus-building. Such channels for 'controlled participation' as the Government Feedback Unit (1985), the PAP Youth Wing (1986), the PAP Women's Wing (1989), and the 'meet the people/walkabout' sessions by MPs and government leaders, were intended to boost the PAP's electoral support by promoting it as the key central element in the tightly knit national society.[74] The new parliamentary and advisory committees, inviting views and comments from the public, but acting also as platforms for the legitimation of government decisions, could similarly be seen as having corporatist implications.[75] The identity of the nation and of the PAP continued to be portrayed in morally absolutist terms. Goh Chok Tong, then Deputy Prime Minister, stated this explicitly in April 1989, when he asserted that politics is 'a perpetual struggle between good and bad forces . . . . The good can continue to win decisively if Singaporeans continue to elect their Government and MPs responsibly.'[76] The 'forces of good' were presumed to be embodied in the PAP.

Thus, during the 1980s, there was a general shift away from 'departicipation' and towards the governmental provision of channels for participation through institutions which were created or licensed by the state, and which were within the ideological parameters of corporatist nationalism promoted by the state. In the words of Goh Chok Tong, the government was moving to 'involve Singaporeans in discussion of major policies, and create avenues for them to air their views and will see these views channeled in a constructive manner'.[77] It is within this context that the changing role of ethnicity in Singapore politics should be understood.

Political loyalty

The garrison ideology which had been stressed during the 1970s has continued to be employed.[78] Singaporeans are still repeatedly reminded that ethnic political loyalties ('ethnic ties to countries inside and outside the region'[79]) constitute primordial and irrational bonds which are easy to ignite and which constantly threaten to explode. But this argument has been increasingly supplemented by a more positive and future-oriented assertion of the imperative of national loyalty. The Singaporean nation has increasingly been depicted in terms of its future greatness. The symbolism of the vision varies – the image is of the 'tropical paradise', the regional 'hub city', 'number one', 'the top league', the 'dynamic, culturally vibrant society', and so on. The argument is that the achievement of this destiny depends on the full commitment of Singapore's 'only natural resource', its people. The goal cannot be attained unless all individuals commit themselves to 'total defence' and to putting 'nation before self'.

It seems likely that the state élites have had some success in inculcating the necessary strong sense of national loyalty. This is difficult to substantiate, but is indicated by various surveys, which have found, for example, four-fifths of Singaporeans willing to die (at least hypothetically) for Singapore. This high level of national political loyalty – patriotism – is, moreover, to a large extent independent of ethnic attachments.[80] This would seem to imply that the large majority of Singaporeans do not regard their high level of patriotism as being in tension with their ethnic attachments, and therefore that those ethnic attachments no longer encompass political loyalties to race or to overseas homeland which would be antithetical to national loyalty.

Such a distinction, between the moral imperative of national political loyalty, and the moral subversion of ethnic political loyalty, would be a central component in the effective corporatist management of ethnicity.

Ethnic cultural values and national identity

Instead of depicting the nation of Singapore as an ethnic mosaic (stressing the differences between the component cultures), or depicting it as meritocratic and ethnically neutral, the state élites have, since the early 1980s, increasingly sought to inculcate a new sense of Singaporeanness which stresses the emergence of a consensual culture at the level of the national community; a consensus based on 'Asian values'. The core proposition is that the ethnic cultures of Singaporeans have now been largely 'sanitized' by the state so as to remove their politically destabilizing connotations. The society is depicted, for almost all purposes of political, economic and social analysis, in terms of comparison between the official racial categories; and while the ethnic values which they embody are clearly distinct, these are no longer regarded as either incompatible with each other or antithetical to the encapsulating national community. Therefore the ethnic cultures can be employed as the distinct but compatible building blocks for the articulation of the new 'umbrella' national culture of Asian values. Thus, to counteract the divisive and disruptive effects of western individualism, Singapore can now be portrayed as moving towards the kind of organic, communitarian and corporatist culture which, allegedly, promoted economic development and political stability in Japan and the other Asian NICs.[81]

Singaporeans are portrayed as each belonging to a set of 'nested' identity groups, i.e. family, ethnic community, and nation; which have similar and complementary cultural values. The government has promoted this image of Asian values through a variety of policy initiatives. Throughout the 1970s government leaders had warned of the dangers of western infection, but from the late 1970s onwards there was a shift of argument. With his National Day Rally speech of 1978, Lee Kuan Yew began to argue that Singapore had already been infected, and that the antidote was now necessary. There needed to be a strong assertion of the Asian values common to all Singapore's ethnic groups, stressing the virtues of individual subordination to the community so as to counteract the disruptive individualism of western liberalism.[82]

The concern to prevent the spread of western individualism was directed particularly at the Chinese, who were seen to be most at risk. This was pursued by the sustained campaigns to promote Confucian values, and to promote the Mandarin language; campaigns which began, respectively, in 1978 and 1982. Both campaigns were implemented through changes in the school curriculum and through media advertising. 'Chineseness' was portrayed as a traditional culture, encapsulated in Confucianism and Mandarin, and embodying the values of discipline, respect for authority and commitment to the community. Confucianism was not associated with a backward China, but rather with the dynamic societies of Taiwan and Japan; and it was portrayed as being compatible with and conducive to economic development, political stability, national unity and, potentially, democracy. Defined in such ways, 'Chineseness' could be depicted as a central building block out of which the consensual national identity was being created. Given the numerical and socio-economic predominance of the Chinese in Singaporean society, this image of Chinese culture inevitably provided the major component.[83] Moreover, it was argued also that Confucianism should not be seen as associated specifically with the Chinese; it was adhered to also by the Japanese and Koreans, and could thus claim to be the core component of a truly 'Asian' culture.

With regard to the Malays, the government has sought to assert the compatibility of Malay identity with a Singaporean national identity based on Asian values through two main strategies. First, the government has promoted the acceptance amongst the Malays of the 'Malay cultural-weakness orthodoxy', whereby the Malays are persuaded to see their own internal cultural attributes as responsible for their socio-economic problems, instead of blaming the Chinese or the government.[84] It is the lack of achievement motivation, or the rural orientation of Malays, which is, in this view, the cause of their 'predicament'. Such a view has been promoted, not just through repeated government speeches, but also through the formation in 1982 of Mendaki, (the Council for the Education of Muslim Children), which was established to 'reform Malay attitudes and values',[85] particularly concerning education.

The second aspect of government policy towards the Malays has been its concern to influence the development of Islam in Singapore. During the 1970s there was a global resurgence of Islam, which in many countries – including Malaysia – took a radical and highly politicized form. The government has consequently tried to exclude this type of Islam from Singapore by refusing admission to 'inflammatory' foreign preachers and by warning Malays of the imperatives of loyalty to Singapore and of keeping religion out of politics. On the other hand, the government has tried to promote another vision of Islam as a set of values which can promote family and community cohesion, whereby alienated Malay youths could be instilled with discipline and social commitment.[86] If the Islamic revival could be channelled into a non-proselytizing and non-political direction which was tolerant of other religious communities and which promoted the resilience of Malay families, the neighbourhood mosque communities, and the wider Singaporean Malay-Muslim community, then it would offer a valuable contribution to Singapore's national cohesion.

The promotion by the state of such distinct but compatible ethnic values, for the non-Chinese communities as well as for the Chinese, provided the basis for the articulation of an overarching Singaporean national culture. The intention to erect such a national culture was indicated in the proposal made by Goh Chok Tong in October 1988, that these Asian values common to each of the ethnic cultures, be specified in a National Ideology. He argued that 'such a National Ideology, setting out society's guiding principles, will help Singaporeans keep their Asian bearings as they approach the 21st century'.[87]

This national ideology would specify the 'core values' necessary to define the national identity of Singaporeans and to delineate the morally absolute values within which consensual politics could be conducted. The government initially suggested that four core values might be identified: the value of ethnic and religious tolerance embodied in the idea of multiracialism, the commitment to making decisions by consensus rather than by contention, the putting of the needs of society over the needs of individuals, and the upholding of the family as the core unit of society.[88]

It is important to note that these 'core values' were perceived by the governing élite as being antithetical to pluralism, and perhaps even as inherently corporatist. This is implied not only by the focus on consensus, but also by the argument that Asians, and particularly Chinese, think politically in terms of absolute loyalty to a strong government, rather than in western 'give and take' terms.[89]

There were immediate expressions of suspicion that such a national ideology could be used either to promote Chinese Confucianist values at the expense of the non-Chinese, or to serve as an ideological prop for PAP political dominance; and probably in response to these criticisms the government proposal was subsequently modified to focus on the inculcation of such core values through the schools, rather than on the promulgation of an official state ideology. If consensus were to be maintained, then the values of the national ideology would have to be imbued 'from the bottom up', in the schools, rather than imposed 'from the top down'.

The government had begun the promotion of Asian values in the schools in 1982, when the Ministry of Education proposed the teaching of religious knowledge (later renamed moral education) as a compulsory subject, with students of each racial category studying their respective religion.[90] Within a few years, however, it began to be argued that this had been a mistake. The teaching of religion might have contributed to the religious revivalism in Singapore, affecting Christianity, Buddhism and Islam in particular, which threatened ethnic harmony because, it was argued, 'It is impossible to fulfill both the Christian vision of a perfect order and the Muslim ideal of an Islamic state in Singapore.'[91] The state might thus have been inadvertently encouraging religious intolerance, and discriminating against the minority religions. This was tackled by the change of policy in 1989 in which the teaching of religious knowledge was abandoned in favour of 'civics' – the teaching of 'aspects of nation-building, awareness of shared values and an appreciation of Singapore's major religions and races'.[92] The focus thus shifted from one which stressed the distinctiveness of each religious group to one which stressed the mutual compatibility of all religious values. This proposal was accompanied in 1990 by the Maintenance of Religious Harmony Act, which attempted to distinguish more clearly the promotion of religion as a unifying 'cultural anchor' from the 'subversive' promotion of divisive religious values in politics.[93]

By the end of the 1980s then, the state élites had moved a long way in asserting a corporatist Singaporean national identity. In the schools and in the media, Singaporeans were faced with assertions of the primacy of the national community over the individual, and of the associated Asian values over those of westernization. This was done primarily through the reassertion of ethnicity as embodying the core values which provided 'cultural roots' for the individual and communal cohesion for the nation. Since 1991, explicit promulgations of Singapore's 'shared values' have waned, but their core moral imperative, that of 'community before self', remains pervasive in characterizations of Singapore's 'Asian' national identity. The transition towards this 'Asian communitarianism' was accompanied by the state's fostering of another new role for ethnicity, that of legitimate interest association.

Interest associations

Throughout the 'meritocracy' period, Singaporeans had been warned that issues relating to religion, language and race were too sensitive to be openly discussed. This changed during the latter half of the 1980s, when the government began not only to raise ethnic issues explicitly, but also to encourage public debate on these issues. By 1991 it was becoming clear that Singapore was moving towards the 'balanced institutionalization' of ethnic interests, whereby each ethnic community would have its own state-licensed organizations through which ethnic interests could be articulated and through which state policies could be promoted. This change was interpreted in several different ways: as a shift away from ethnic neutrality on the part of the state, as part of a process of liberalization, and as part of an escalation of state intervention into new areas. The argument here is that it reflected the shift towards a more inclusionary corporatist strategy.

The general argument is that it was the government's initiatives in remoulding the ethnic cultural values to form the base for an 'Asian values' national identity which necessitated, in turn, the creation of state-licensed channels for the articulation of ethnic interests. Any attempt to impose, in an authoritarian manner, changes in the language, religion or cultural values of the ethnic communities would be both ineffective and disruptive, unless it were accompanied by the provision of channels through which the communities could air their doubts or grievances concerning these cultural policies, and air also their views and interests as to how these changes affected their socioeconomic position in the society. By providing such channels, the government promotes the expression of ethnic interests, which can then be defused or responded to by the government, but they also gain new forums through which government policies can be legitimated, and which can be employed to delineate the boundaries between acceptable ethnic interests and subversive communalist views. Therefore, in adopting such a stance towards ethnic groups, the government has sought to exert 'various controls on their selection of leaders and articulation of demands and supports'.[94]

Chinese ethnicity as 'legitimate interest association'

The shift of government policy towards the remoulding of Chinese culture through the promotion of Confucianism and Mandarin has sometimes been interpreted as marking a move away from ethnic neutrality and towards a pro-Chinese stance on the part of the state. It should be noted, however, that in promoting Chinese values, the government was not responding to Chinese demands, but was imposing what many of the Chinese initially perceived as new and unwelcome pressures: to learn Mandarin, to adopt Confucianism, to reject western values, to have more children, to welcome Hong Kong immigration, and so on. The government was apparently trying to modify and strengthen the Chinese identity against the initial wishes of at least some of the Chinese populace, in order to promote Chinese cultural values as a building block for the ethnically impartial Asian communitarian national identity.

The government's concern, therefore, has been to offer the Chinese populace avenues through which they could express such worries, but to do so in ways which would promote the mobilization of support for its policies rather than undermining them. Initially, the government favoured the strategy of launching a series of debates based upon initial 'position statements' made by a government leader, in most cases by Lee Kuan Yew.

The subsequent public discussions were conducted within boundaries indicated by the government and they served, with some success, as exercises to mobilize support and legitimacy for government policies affecting the Chinese. This strategy was not immediately supplemented by the formation of a specifically Chinese ethnic interest organization, because the Chinese, as the majority community, were able to employ the existing state-controlled or state-approved channels for articulating their interests, including parliament and the mass media; and it appeared that government leaders, and Lee Kuan Yew in particular, wished to retain direct control over the ways in which Chinese ethnic issues were articulated and handled.

The decision to change strategies, and to establish a Chinese interest association through which government could promote and administer its policies towards the Chinese, and through which responsible community leaders could represent their views, arose from the dynamics of inclusionary corporatism. Ethnic neutrality, which had initially referred to the depoliticization of ethnicity, was now perceived by the government increasingly in terms of an idea of an impartial ethnic management which implied a 'balanced' approach reminiscent of the ethnic arithmetic of the earlier 'ethnic mosaic' period of politics. Since the government had begun tackling the grievances of the lower socio-economic groups in society by creating ethnic interest associations for the Malays and for the Indians, then to be balanced, it must offer the Chinese their own ethnic interest association.[95] Accordingly, in July 1991 Prime Minister Goh Chok Tong announced that he favoured the formation of a 'Chinese Mendaki', and by late 1991 several groups of Chinese-educated professionals had responded to this state initiative with plans for a Chinese Development Assistance Council to promote Chinese education and to channel educational assistance to poorer Chinese. The CDAC was accordingly launched in April 1992, and the Prime Minister, as its patron, appointed the Foreign Minister, Wong Kan Seng, to be Chairman of its Board of Directors.[96] Henceforth, the Chinese community would have a specific licensed interest organization, as well as the 'licensed debates', through which their interests could be mediated.

During the late 1980s the government launched a series of licensed debates related to Chinese values and interests, in which the public airing of grievances and criticisms provided the basis for 'exercises in persuasion' aimed at convincing the Chinese populace to become 'more Asian' and 'more Chinese'. During 1989 the government sought to mobilize Chinese support for various measures aimed at reversing the decline in the Chinese proportion of the population. The public discussion on this issue, instigated by Lee Kuan Yew's speech in August, sought to reassure the populace that measures to increase the Chinese birth rate, reduce Chinese emigration, and encourage Chinese (Hong Kong) immigration, would benefit all races; since the large Chinese majority had proved conducive to economic development because of the commercial abilities of the Chinese, and had also promoted racial harmony.[97]

The issue of the teaching of Mandarin became another focus for public debate. The government facilitated the articulation of discontent amongst non-Mandarin speaking Chinese parents concerning the pressures upon their children to learn a 'mother tongue' not used in the home.[98] This debate provided a platform for the government's defence of its stepped-up campaign to promote Mandarin, reassuring the parents as to its practical benefits as a source of both morality and status.

The role of Confucianism in society similarly became a focus for debate. Many Chinese still regarded Confucianism as incompatible both with modernization and with democracy, and the public discussions on this facilitated the government's assertion of the opposite view. The government's argument that a Confucianist route towards development was suitable for Singapore was promoted by the formation of the Institute of East Asian Philosophies, which hosted prestigious international conferences on 'Confucianist Modernization'.[99]

The 'licensed debate' took a slightly different form in the case of the discussion on the significance of the 1991 election result. The result was, of itself, an inconclusive one, in which Prime Minister Goh received almost the same electoral support as he had previously, as Deputy Prime Minister in 1988,[100] but the government decided to interpret it as an expression of discontent by the poorer and older sections of the Chinese community at the ways in which their culture (including the Chinese dialects) had been neglected in favour of the English-speaking Chinese. The prescription which followed this diagnosis was the suggestion that Chinese clan associations should take over the running of selected schools so as to improve the quality of Chinese-medium education.

The government has thus provided channels through which the ethnic interests of the Chinese, relating to their cultural values, language, education, demographic and socio-economic position, can be articulated. Such mobilized participation has enabled the airing of ethnic grievances and has facilitated government responsiveness to these grievances. But these 'democratic' aspects of ethnic interest articulation have gone hand in hand with the corporatist control aspects, whereby governmental supervision of the interest articulation process has enabled it to use the debates to promote its policy goals and to establish the demarcation lines of legitimate Chinese interests.

Malay ethnicity as legitimate interest association

With regard to the Malays, the government's primary concern has been to allay discontent at the erosion of their socio-economic position during the 1970s, and to find ways to counteract this tendency during the 1980s. This concern was motivated partly by the need to preserve national unity, and partly to try and counteract the perceived decline in PAP support amongst the Malays.

The government has sought to develop official channels through which Malay concerns could be articulated and through which government policies could be more effectively implemented and communicated to the Malays. Some such channels already existed, such as the Presidential Council for Minority Rights, the Minister in charge of Muslim Affairs, the PAP Malay Affairs Bureau, and the Islamic Religious Council (MUIS). Two major new institutions were added in the 1980s: the Council for Malay Education (Mendaki), formed in 1981, and the specially designated Malay MPs in the Group Representation Constituencies (GRCs) introduced in the 1988 elections.

The membership of MUIS and Mendaki is partly appointed directly by the government, and partly selected by the government from nominees submitted by Malay organizations. Mendaki is headed by the Minister in charge of Muslim Affairs, and has the Prime Minister as the Chairman of its Board of Advisors. The Malay Affairs Bureau is composed of the Malay PAP MPs. Currently, Mendaki's chief executive officer is also the

President of MUIS.[101] These various bodies thus have overlapping membership and contain a small group of educated,
pro-government Malays, dominated by the PAP Malay MPs,
who act as the legitimate intermediaries between the government and the Malay community.

The Council for Malay Education was formed as a
government-appointed committee to promote the upward socio-
economic mobility of the Malays by encouraging their education. In 1989 it was strengthened and given wider responsibilities in the administration of educational funds. In line with this,
it was renamed as the Council for the Development of the
Singaporean Muslim Community, and was redesignated as
'Mendaki II'. While its overt function was thus as a channel
through which government could promote Malay special interests, it also provided a platform from which the pro-government
Malay élites, under the chairmanship of the Minister in charge
of Muslim Affairs, could mobilize support amongst the Malay
community for government policies, through seminars, conferences and speeches. In 1990 the corporatist organization of
Malay interest articulation was apparently threatened by the
emergence of the Association of Malay Professionals amongst
young educated Malays who were critical of the extent to which
the Malay PAP MPs had protected Malay interests. Initially
suspicious of the AMP, the government quickly sought to
accommodate it by offering to recognize it as a 'Mendaki
Swastra' (private sector Mendaki). The government then sought
the co-operation of the AMP by allowing it to administer a
proportion of the funds allocated to the Malay community, on
condition that it worked alongside Mendaki and promoted
Malay unity. Prime Minister Goh stated: 'I have no objection to
this, so long as our objectives are the same – to uplift the level of
the Malays in Singapore – and so long as you do not divide the
Malay community.'[102]

By recognizing the AMP and accepting it as a legitimate
channel for the articulation of Malay interests at the same time
as employing it as a channel through which government funds
can be channelled to the Malays, the government hoped to
regain the political support of those Malays who apparently have
been moving away from the PAP, and ensure the co-operation
of Malay élites who might otherwise become oppositionist.[103] It
should be noted that the government's efforts to improve the

socio-economic position of the Malays, through these ethnic interest associations, have apparently had some noticeable success during the 1980s, with the proportion of Malays in lower income groups (below S$1,500 per month) falling from 85 per cent to 36 per cent.[104]

The government's second initiative was a response to the under-representation of Malays (and Indians) in parliament and the government. By introducing Group Representation Constituencies for the 1988 election, the government ensured that a minimum number of minority race MPs, nominated by the PAP or any other party, would enter parliament. It was specified that the group candidacies in three-fifths of the GRCs had to include one Malay, and it was clear that the Malay and Indian GRC MPs were expected to act as ethnic spokesmen and as channels for the communication of government policies to the minority communities.[105]

These institutions have been used as channels for a series of 'licensed debates' directed towards the Malays, on a similar basis to those directed towards the Chinese. Much of the public discussion has been instigated by government reminders of the distinction between illegitimate political loyalties and legitimate social and cultural interests, and Malays have been repeatedly warned about their alleged lack of loyalty to the nation and the government. The major thrust of such debates concerned the government accusations of Malay disloyalty when they protested at the visit of the Israeli President, Chaim Herzog, in November 1986, the Prime Minister's National Day speech in 1987 (in which he asserted that Malays were 'not yet in the mainstream' of Singapore society, and expressed doubts as to their degree of loyalty),[106] the February 1987 speech by Brigadier-General Lee Hsien Loong justifying restrictions on Malay recruitment into the Singapore Armed Forces, and the allegation by Goh Chok Tong that the Malays had failed to support the PAP in the 1988 election.[107]

The introduction of the GRCs provoked a debate on the issue of whether, and to what extent, Malays should receive 'positive discrimination' in Singapore. Some Malay leaders expressed doubts concerning this scheme, arguing that it might result in the Malay GRC MPs being regarded as second-class MPs, and that it might have an ethnically divisive effect by encouraging voting on ethnic lines.[108] Probably the most lively debate arose over the 1989 proposal by Goh Chok Tong concerning the strengthening of Mendaki, which focused on the government's suggestion that the Malays should no longer regard the educational subsidy as a constitutional right, but rather as a temporary support for poorer Malays only.[109] This discussion of Malay 'special privileges' was in fact aimed at both the Chinese and the Malays, and was concerned on the one hand to reassure the Chinese that such privileges are minimal and temporary and do not compromise essential meritocratic principles, while at the same time mobilizing the Malays to unite behind their 'responsible' leaders to support government policies. The suggestion to end the automatic education subsidy for Malays initially aroused vocal opposition from Malay groups, and especially from the Malay students. The Malay intermediaries, and the government spokespeople, repeatedly justified the proposal, and the Mendaki Board duly decided to support it.[110]

With regard to the articulation of Malay interests then, as with the Chinese case, the government has been able to show that it allows and even encourages the voicing of discontent and criticism on ethnic issues. In doing so, however, it has been able to specify the channels and the range of views regarded as legitimate, and it has shown its ability to manage the resultant public debates so that they serve the purpose of legitimating the government's policies and contribute to the moulding of ethnic consciousness.

The discussion has so far been restricted to the issue of Chinese and Malay ethnic identities in Singapore, since it is with regard to these communities that state intervention has been most active. There have, however, been signs of increasing political activism amongst the Indian communities, and an increasing concern by government to 'manage' Indian ethnicity in a way which balances its concern with Malay and Chinese ethnicity.[111]

The Sikh community comprise about 8 per cent of the Indians in Singapore, and they have been an energetic and upwardly mobile minority group, who have accordingly developed strong attachments to the PAP and to the Singapore nation. In its efforts to promote Sikh cultural identity as a component part of a corporatist national identity, the government began, during the late 1980s, to promote the teaching of the Sikh religion and the Punjabi language in schools.[112] This was aimed also at helping the Sikh community to combat erosion through the loss of young people marrying out of the community, losing competence in the language, or converting to Christianity.[113] Such action to promote Sikh cultural identity was accompanied by repeated government warnings against Sikh political affiliations to the activities of Punjabi nationalists in India. The government has also been active in fostering and 'licensing' Sikh intermediaries. The main body recognized as the channel for transmitting Sikh interests to the government, and for mobilizing Sikh support for government policies, is the Sikh Advisory Board, appointed by the government.[114] Also, in 1988, the PAP selected a Sikh as a 'minority' member of one of the GRC constituencies.

Despite the generally positive attitudes of Sikhs towards their position in Singapore society, there was increasing concern during the 1980s that, while the government was active in promoting Chinese values, and in responding to Malay grievances primarily through the strengthening of Mendaki, it had failed to treat the Sikhs with the consideration commensurate to their contributions to society. They perceived the government as claiming a 'balanced' stance towards the ethnic groups in society, and therefore began to demand 'fair' recognition. This emerged most clearly in the calls for the creation of a Mendaki-type body for the Sikh community; and in the creation of a Sikh Research Panel, which was approved by the government as a first step in this direction.[115] The next step was the inclusion of the Sikh Advisory Board within the Singapore Indian Development Association (SINDA), established in 1991 as the Mendaki for the Indian community as a whole.

The government has sought to inculcate into the Sikh community then, a distinction between ethnicity as the illegitimate political loyalties towards the Punjab, ethnicity as the identification with Sikh values which provide a cultural anchor and a basis for Singaporean identity, and ethnicity as the legitimate socio-economic interests of the Sikh community. As with the other ethnic groups, it seems possible that some Sikhs might find such a distinction difficult to comprehend.[116]

The case of the Tamils has been rather different, since they had by and large been excluded from the government's 'corporatist net' until the establishment of SINDA. They had been treated by the government, rather, with 'benign neglect'. During the 1980s there was no government-sponsored institution or leadership group which acted as intermediary between the Tamils and the government. There were indeed some Tamil MPs, including two government ministers, but they tended not to present themselves, or be seen by the Tamils, as representatives of the Tamil community, partly because they were English-speaking, mostly with limited command of Tamil. But the emergence of a Tamil leadership group had also been inhibited by, on the one hand, the government's commitment to treating 'Indian' rather than Tamil as the legitimate interest group; and partly also by the decentralized structure of the Hindu and Tamil communities.

The government was, however, active in its portrayal of Tamil political affiliations as politically dangerous and subversive, as in its frequent references to the dangers posed by Sri Lankan ethnic conflict; though these warning were not always seen as pertinent by Singaporean Tamils, the large majority of whom are of Indian stock, with no affinity to the Sri Lankans. Moreover, amongst Singapore Tamils the Hindu–Muslim and Hindu–Sikh tensions of Indian politics are of little relevance.

Regarding the promotion of Tamil values as a 'cultural anchor', the government has indeed promoted the Tamil language in the schools, and has protected the rights of Hindus to worship freely. It is certainly the case that the cultural identity and cohesion of the Tamil community is relatively healthy.

Despite the general low profile of the Tamil ethnic community, they developed an awareness of socio-economic grievances which were increasingly directed at the government.[117] It was recognized that very few Tamils were reaching top positions in Singapore; and while this was partly seen as arising from cultural and social problems intrinsic to the community, it was also connected with the perception that government resources were going into pro-Malay and pro-Chinese directions, rather than to the Indians.[118] There was also apparently some unease amongst the Indian communities over the treatment of ex-President Devan Nair and his replacement by a Chinese President; and also over the then Prime Minister Lee's assertion that he preferred Goh Chok Tong as his successor to Mr. Dhanabalan, then Minister for National Development, on the grounds that 'Singapore is not yet ready for an Indian Prime Minister'.[119] Such perceptions of political neglect, together with the awareness that the predominantly Tamil Indian communities were falling behind in educational and economic terms, combined to produce the call for an Indian Mendaki.[120] SINDA is in part, therefore, a symbol of government's concern to promote Indian cultures and interests. It provides a government-approved channel through which 'responsible' community leaders can articulate Indian interests, and through which government policies towards the Indian community can be implemented.

IMPLICATIONS

The general argument has been that ethnic consciousness in Singapore should be understood primarily as a response to the particular character of the Singaporean state and to the way in which the state has developed. The extent of public discussion of ethnic issues has increased enormously since the 1970s, but this has not primarily taken the form of the autonomous airing of ethnic demands from the various communal groups in society. Rather it has taken a corporatist form; the instigation by the government of specific 'licensed debates' on ethnic issues, and the development of specific government-licensed ethnic interest organizations. The government has employed these means to facilitate its policies aimed at eradicating ethnic political loyalties, moulding ethnic affiliation into a cultural building block from which an Asian communitarian form of national identity can be created, and promoting the controlled articulation of legitimate ethnic interests.

The state has thus sought to change ethnic consciousness from an all-embracing racial affiliation into a compartmentalized distinction between ethnicity as a politically disruptive loyalty, ethnicity as a component cultural basis for national identity, and ethnicity as a legitimate interest association.

The development of corporatism is not a tension-free process. In the case of Singapore, the government leaders have repeatedly argued that their intention is to achieve a more consultative form of government, and to accommodate political opposition and critical comments. At the same time, however, they have stressed that there must remain limits to such participation. Political comments should not be made by organizations not registered as political parties; participation will only be allowed if the government believes it to be 'constructive' and conducive to the building of consensus, and the views which are aired should not be partial, articulating sectional 'vested' interests, but must be motivated by concern for the common good.[121] The tension between the two themes is clear, and one result is simply that there exists a degree of confusion about the direction of Singapore's politics.

This confusion extends to the area of ethnic relations in Singapore, and although it has not become politically destabilizing, the potentiality is there. To a significant extent, the present problems arise out of the difficulties in making the three-fold distinction of ethnicity comprehensible to the society.

There are several areas of confusion. First, there is confusion about the distinction between cultural values and political loyalties. This is evident, for example, in the government's promotion of Chinese values as a cultural basis for an ethnically-neutral national identity, which seems to have been misinterpreted by some non-Chinese as involving the assertion of Chinese political loyalties and as the promotion of a pro-Chinese national identity. Thus the campaigns to encourage the use of Mandarin and the adoption of Confucianist values, appear to some as manifestations of a new (and puzzling) pro-Chinese ethnic bias, contravening the previous and contemporary claims to ethnic neutrality. There is an irony here, in that the very measures which non-Chinese might perceive as evidence of a shift towards a 'pro-Chinese' state, are measures which themselves are also seen as suspect by some of the Chinese. Dialect-speaking Chinese grandparents, English-speaking Chinese parents, and educated Chinese youth influenced by western liberalism, might each have 'vested interests' in tension with the government's attempt to inculcate 'Chinese' values.

The problems of distinguishing the cultural anchor aspect of ethnicity from the political loyalty aspect are exacerbated by the fact that the government sometimes seems to 'draw the line' as it goes along. Thus, for example, the Sikh temple communities which held prayers for the assassins of Mrs. Gandhi, and which in various other ways showed solidarity with Punjabi nationalists, no doubt believed that they were expressing the legitimate cultural value of Sikh unity, until informed by the police that their action constituted an illegitimate expression of involvement in Indian politics.[122]

The second basis for confusion relates to the distinction

between ethnic political loyalties and ethnic interests. This confusion was one element in the controversies concerning the 'Herzog affair' and the SAF affair.[123] In the SAF case, Malays had previously expressed discontent that the government's principles of meritocracy were not practised in the area of SAF recruitment and promotion, and that an apparent anti-Malay bias existed in practice. But the discrimination was never publicly acknowledged until its apparent endorsement by Brigadier General Lee. His statement seemed to some to grant anti-Malay discrimination a new legitimacy and respectability. While he appeared to argue that Malay commitment to Islam constituted a potentially politically subversive loyalty which justified their exclusion from key posts in the nation's defence forces, Malays for their part argued that they were being deprived of legitimate career opportunities in a prestigious arm of the public services. They could, moreover, claim that their commitment to Islam was a 'cultural anchor' which was compatible with, and indeed contributed to, their loyalty to the Singaporean state.

In the case of the Herzog affair, Malay expressions of opposition to the official visit of the Israeli President were regarded by the government as evidence of the politically illegitimate affiliation (or subordination) of Singaporean Malays to their more vocally anti-Zionist co-ethnics in Malaysia; whereas for many Singaporean Malays the articulation of criticism to the visit seemed to constitute a politically legitimate defence of Islamic interests which implied no lack of commitment to the state.

The confusion between ethnic interests and ethnic loyalty was again manifested in perplexity as to where government drew the line. In the GRC scheme, voting on ethnic lines, which had previously been condemned by government as 'dangerous communalism', appeared to be suddenly promoted by government as the legitimate articulation of ethnic interests. As regards the Maintenance of Religious Harmony Bill, spokespeople for the Catholic Church, for example, were worried that the concern for social issues, which they had hitherto regarded as reflecting the legitimate Church interest in social justice, was now being defined by government as a political commitment antithetical to state loyalty.[124]

Finally, we may note one general source of confusion. The government is seeking to promote strong, distinct, ethnic identities which will function as a base upon which the overarching national identity, focused on Asian values, can be erected. Thus, while the 'top layer' of national identity involves a synthesis of aspects of the ethnic values, these ethnic values remain distinct at the subordinate level. Some Singaporeans, however, find this too confusing, and continue to see the question of identity in zero-sum terms, such that to be more Singaporean is to be, necessarily, less Chinese, or Indian, or Malay.

These problems all relate to the issue of what meaning to give to the term 'ethnic neutrality' when the government adopts, not a 'hands off' authoritarian or liberal approach to ethnicity, but rather an increasingly interventionist stance. Whereas in the meritocratic 1970s ethnic neutrality referred to the impartiality both of the content of government policies and also of its national development goal; in the inclusionary corporatist 1990s the avowed ethnic neutrality of the national goal is pursued by a series of specific policies which appear to favour first one ethnic group and then another. The government is seeking to create a 'level playing field' where each ethnic group receives equitable treatment, in order to rectify perceived imbalances in their political, cultural or socio-economic interest situations. Corporatist management thus begins to give way to a 'balancing act' in which government legitimates itself by appearing to give simultaneous 'priority' to all ethnic segments of the community.[125] What began as pragmatic interventionism comes to be perceived, by government as well as by society, as an ideological commitment to the political arithmetic of ethnic equality:

> In Singapore, whatever community you belong to, whatever the size of your community, we give you equal treatment. . . . It is not a one race, one culture Singapore . . . . It is a Singapore based on many races, many cultures, but one Singapore.[126]

But each intervention in favour of one ethnic community threatens to provoke the perception amongst those of other ethnic groups that government is ceasing to be ethnically neutral, and that this may be corrected only by a further intervention to rectify the new imbalance. The expectation develops that each ethnic group deserves its own Mendaki,[127] its own 'cultural month', its own language and values promoted through the schools, and its own representative élites within the

PAP and the government. In the context of Singapore, where ethnic balance must inevitably refer to the demographic predominance of the Chinese, the translation of ethnic neutrality into the language of ethnic equality could eventually generate a politically dangerous tension in which the Chinese populace interprets ethnically-neutral Asian communitarianism as granting legitimate dominance to their culture and interests; while the non-Chinese interpret ethnic neutrality as granting them some form of parity with the Chinese. It was precisely to avoid such ethnic tensions that the Singaporean state élite initially took the path of ethnically-neutral management. To promote ethnic consciousness as a resource for nation-building and political development, while at the same time guarding against the emergence of competitive ethnocentrism in society, is indeed to undertake a problematical balancing act.

Singapore is not yet at the stage where ethnic neutrality begins to change into an explicitly consociational politics which would politicize the distinction between equality and proportionality; but the dynamics of an inclusionary corporatist approach to ethnic management do lead in that direction. As of now, Singapore's ethnic management must be judged a success, but the strategy which has been adopted puts increasingly heavy demands upon both the ethnic managers themselves and on their subjects.

During the 1950s, the PAP leadership attained governmental power by 'riding the tiger' of communism. Today's tiger is perceived to be that of ethnicity, and the strategy has been to tame and house-train the beast through corporatist management. Given the strength of the Singaporean state, the strategy has been implemented with a high degree of effectiveness, and the system is probably resilient enough to cope with the resultant tensions. These ethnic tensions do not relate primarily to the danger that the ethnic beast might break loose and run wild, but rather to the possibility that state-managed ethnicity becomes a performing animal, enfeebled and confused by overtraining, and consequently unable to offer protection and security to its handlers. If ethnic consciousness refers, essentially, to a kinship myth in which the ethnic community provides the sense of security to the individual which the family offers to the infant, then it would seem likely that the attempt to unravel such a myth, by dividing it into loyalty, identity and interest compartments, runs the risk of robbing ethnicity of its intrinsic power and appeal, so that it becomes eventually a new source of anxiety and confusion rather than a source of security.

Chapter 4

Neo-patrimonialism and national integration in Indonesia

The corporatist perspective on the state seeks to comprehend both those states like Singapore which accommodate and manage societal interests, and also those which seek to exclude and suppress them. Indonesia has sometimes been depicted in such exclusionary state corporatist terms so as to focus on the unresponsiveness of the state to societal interests, but this has not been the dominant model. The most pervasive characterization of the Indonesian state has rather been that which stresses élite factionalism and the personalistic use of governmental power; and this approach has similarly been employed primarily to stress the insulation of the state from the wider society.[1] The intention here, however, is to explore the alternative perspective, which shows how the personalist characterization of the Indonesian state illuminates the interconnections between state and society. The suggestion is that the inherent fragilities of the neo-patrimonial state generate the development and politicization of ethnic communalism, either in the form of integrative communal patronage networks, or as the mobilization of ethnicity for purposes of electoral opposition, or as ethno-regional rebellion.

These links between the neo-patrimonial characterization of the state and the political impact of ethnic communalism are examined, in the Indonesian context, in order to gain an understanding of the ethno-regional politics of the province of Aceh. The most widespread explanation of Aceh's unique political history is that which sees its primordial cultural, linguistic and religious distinctiveness as the cause of its history of political autonomy, oppositionism and insurrection. By contrast, the nature of Aceh's ethnic politics, and the impact on national political unity and stability, are explained here in terms of the shifting neo-patrimonial relationships between competing central élites and competing provincial élites.

The focus is therefore on the 'ethnic entrepreneurial' behaviour of political élites who seek access to state power, and who manipulate ethnicity to that end by employing it as an ideological weapon or by acting as communal patrons. There is no assumption that these communal patrons are 'selfish' in giving priority to their own personal interests over the goals of the communal group they claim to represent. Indeed, what is distinctive about such politics is the extent to which the interests and values of the clientele and of their patrons become inextricably intertwined. It is the ability of the leader to define and articulate the myths and symbols of a community, and thus to interpret its identity in relation to the wider society, that generates his influence and power in the community.[2]

It should be noted, however, that such a focus on élite behaviour is frequently objected to on the grounds that the presence of élites articulating political opposition or disunity does not of itself indicate whether the élite behaviour constitutes a cause of such politics, or is merely the symptom of more fundamental socio-economic or cultural realities. Only in a situation where politics changes rapidly or frequently, between opposition and support, between unity and disunity, would we be able to discern the extent to which élites play a causal role. The intention here, therefore, is to argue the utility of explaining politics in terms of élite behaviour by examining just such a situation as it relates to fluctuations in the national integration of Indonesia.[3]

The specific argument, illustrated through the discussion of the political mobilization of Acehnese communalism, is that ethnic oppositionism may be explained in terms of a lack of congruence between the cohesion and strategies of élites at the level of the central state and those at regional level. While central élites seek to co-opt regionalist élites so as to extend central political control, and regionalist élites seek central allies in order to gain access to state resources, their mutual alliance strategies may fail to mesh when élite cohesion at one level coincides with factional dissensus at the other level. Thus, when regional élites seek alliance with a divided centre, they may find themselves as allies of a marginalized élite faction lacking access to state resources. When a cohesive centre seeks a regional alliance in a situation of regional élite factionalism, its alliance with one faction will exacerbate regional disunity and conflict, rather than promoting the desired central control and political cohesion. In both of these circumstances, political oppositionism at regional level arises more as the unintended outcome of unanticipated events than as the manifestation of a consistent tradition of ethno-regional autonomy. In this type of state, therefore, national political integration is not a 'process' arising from cultural, social, or economic integration, but is rather an inherently fragile and contingent situation dependent upon changes in élite cohesion at central and regional levels, and upon the outcome of their politics of mutual manipulation.

The view of politics which focuses upon the competition for power amongst competing influential individuals is made explicit in the concept of the patrimonial state. In the model of a traditional patrimonial system, both élite cohesion and leader-follower relations are stabilized by institutional and cultural constraints as to how the rivalry for power could be conducted. But in the contemporary world, such constraints are weakened, and patrimonialism appears in a modified form characterized by various tensions which reduce its stability. The term 'neo-patrimonial' is thus not employed here loosely to refer just to a Third World state in which some remnants of traditional personalist rule persist. Rather, it indicates the specific political tensions that characterize personalist politics within the institutional and ideological framework of the modern state.

PATRIMONIALISM AND NEO-PATRIMONIALISM

For Max Weber, a traditional patrimonial system was one in which:

> The object of obedience is the personal authority of the individual which he enjoys by virtue of his traditional status. The organised group exercising authority is, in the simplest case, primarily based on relations of personal loyalty, cultivated through a common process of education. The person exercising authority is not a 'superior', but a personal 'chief'. His administrative staff does not consist primarily of officials, but of personal retainers . . . . What determines the relations

of the administrative staff to the chief is not the impersonal obligations of office, but personal loyalty to the chief.[4]

What holds such a system of government together then, is the personal bond between the individual governmental leader (chief, king, sultan, etc.) and the influentials whom he appoints to positions of power within the state machinery. These influentials, in turn, each have their own retinue of followers bound to them by similar bonds of personal loyalty; and this network of patron–client ties may extend all the way 'from the village to the palace'. The patrimonial state is thus the governmental apex of a society characterized by traditional patron–client relationships. In such a social structure the inequalities of wealth and power are such that the mass of ordinary subjects have no access to the benefits of statehood other than through their dependence upon an influential patron who can offer protection in return for loyalty. This patrimonial system is sustained and legitimated by traditional conceptions of personalized power, and by political cultures of deference embodied in religious and cultural values. In such cultures, power generates its own authority in that those who attain positions of dominance are assumed to have deserved it because of their skill and moral virtue.[5] The potential stability of such a system arises both from these legitimating values, and also from its institutionalization in a hereditary monarchical system, in a legal framework of feudal obligations, and in some cases in imperial systems of territorial administration.

Although the system of patron–client linkages which sustains such a patrimonial system is by its very nature one of personal ties, the linkages are not thereby restricted to one-to-one relationships. Whole communities might be dependent upon the good will and protection of one or more individual patrons; and the awareness of their mutual dependence upon such patrons might itself serve to promote a sense of communal solidarity amongst the followers. By co-opting such communal patrons into his retinue, the patrimonial ruler thereby extends his political control both over these patrons and over their communal clienteles.

Some of these patrimonial features are no doubt to be found in every society and every state, but the influence of the modernization paradigm led to the widespread assumption that patrimonial forms of politics would erode. When political scientists began to notice that in some Third World states the modern democratic or constitutional forms of government were something of a facade, and that politics was characterized by personalized alliances and factional rivalries, they sought to revive and revise the concept of patrimonialism.[6] On the one hand, patrimonial alliances seemed to offer a functional basis for government in societies where the imported western forms of government lacked legitimacy, and where alternative institutional or ideological bases for political cohesion were absent. On the other hand, it seemed that once patrimonial politics was removed from its traditional context, it implied the politics of corruption and nepotism, which undermined political cohesion.

The central distinction between traditional patrimonialism and contemporary neo-patrimonialism lies in the changed equation relating leaders to followers. In the traditional system, the patrimonial élite constituted a privileged class who were able to rely upon rigid status hierarchies in the society to monopolize the resources of the state and exclude the masses from power and wealth. The exchange which occurred between patron and client was largely the non-material one in which the client's duty of deferential loyalty to the patron ensured, in return, his protection and security. In contemporary neo-patrimonialism, however, the decline of traditional deference, the increased mobility of society, and the spread of expectations of development and democracy, make it increasingly difficult for the patrimonial élite to maintain the exclusion of the masses. The patron–client exchange begins to change. The leader's provision of security and protection must be supplemented by the provision of material resources; and the follower's provision of passive loyalty is liable to be supplemented by the mobilization of active political support. Thus the traditional exchange of protection for loyalty gives way, at least in part, to a more pragmatic exchange of material resources for political support.

As the traditional ideologies and institutions which sustained patrimonialism are eroded, the effectiveness and stability of the system depend increasingly upon the particular manipulative skill of the leader, who must retain monopoly control of resource distribution, and employ it to reward support and to buy-off opponents, à la Machiavelli, so as to inhibit factional rivalries amongst the patrimonial élites, and to maintain the support of the clientele-followers.

THE CONTEXT OF INDONESIAN NEO-PATRIMONIALISM

When the concept of patrimonialism was 'rediscovered' from the late 1960s onwards, Indonesia was one of the states most frequently cited. Both Gunther Roth and S.N. Eisenstadt illustrated their arguments by reference to Indonesia,[7] and amongst subsequent students of Indonesian politics the focus on patrimonial politics has remained 'the conventional wisdom or "mainstream" approach'.[8] Patrimonial tendencies in Indonesian politics have most usually been explained as responses to three interrelated elements in the society: the continued salience of a traditional conceptualization of power as manifested in precolonial Javanese monarchies, the continued importance of patron–client linkages as a basis for social relationships, and the continued prevalence in this predominantly rural society of a 'culture of deference'.

Benedict Anderson sought to delineate the way in which power was perceived in precolonial Java, and has offered a portrayal of contemporary politics in terms of the continuing influence of such perceptions.[9] Power, he argues, has traditionally been understood as something concrete, residing in an individual ruler able to 'concentrate within himself apparently antagonistic opposites'.[10] This centralization of power implies the development of a class of retainers or bureaucrats sharply distinguished from the masses who remain excluded from power and its perquisites; but the Javanese conception of power, as something which diminishes with distance from the individual at the centre, serves to obscure the development of sharp class cleavages. Political relationships are instead perceived as non-conflictual hierarchies of clientage.[11]

Such a conceptualization of power is manifested in the social structure. Pervasive patron–client relationships, extending in a vertical chain through all levels of Indonesian society, are sustained by the cultural values of *bapakism*, i.e. the relationship between father (*bapak*) and children (*anak buah*).[12] Thus gross disparities of wealth and power, instead of inspiring discontent, will inspire deference and loyalty so long as the *bapaks* fulfil the responsibilities of their role; though such a social structure remains vulnerable to factional segmentation.[13]

In addition to the prevalence of clientelist social relationships, Indonesia also exhibits another feature frequently seen as promoting patrimonialism: its cultural heterogeneity and weak infrastructural development. Gunther Roth, for example, cited Indonesia to argue that those societies which lacked effective institutional links between centre and periphery, and lacked cultural consensus, could only attain political unity and stability through the development of government based on personal linkages and alliances between the various regional- and communal-based élites. The expectation was that 'personal rulerships can be more responsive to cultural and social diversity than intensely ideological leaders are willing to be', and that the bargaining politics of such 'personal patrimonialism' might provide a route to unity more akin to 'empire building' than to any process of cultural or institutional integration.[14]

Indonesian society is indeed remarkably diverse, and colonialism did little to strengthen and institutionalize the linkages between its various islands and communities. The communal cleavages are complex in that they involve several distinct but overlapping dimensions.[15] First, Indonesian society is divided along religious and cultural lines into different *aliran* (streams).[16] Perhaps 90 per cent of Indonesians are Muslims, but they divide between the devout Muslims, the *santri*, and the more nominal Muslims, the *abangan*. Most of the Javanese, (perhaps 60 per cent) probably fall into the *abangan* category, while many of the coastal peoples of the Outer Islands espouse stricter forms of Islam. Herbert Feith related this variation to the history of Islam as the culture of the coastal trade, and distinguished between the 'Islamic entrepreneurial' culture of the maritime sultanates, and the eclectic 'Javanese aristocratic' culture of the Javanese traditional élite,[17] a culture which overlaps with Geertz's *priyayi* culture. Most of the contemporary bureaucratic élite is of Javanese *priyayi* background.

The second dimension of communalism relates to ethnolinguistic and racial distinctions. Indonesia is usually depicted as having about 25 different language groups and over 250 different dialect groups. The Javanese (of central and eastern Java) constitute perhaps 45 per cent of the population, while the Sundanese, of West Java, comprise 15 per cent. The remaining groups on the outer islands are much smaller and include the Minangkabau (4 per cent), Bataks (2 per cent) and Acehnese (1.4 per cent). The most obvious politically salient feature is thus that of Javanese dominance in numerical (as well as in socio-economic) terms. The other major distinction is that between the indigenous communities and the 'alien minority', the ethnic Chinese (3 per cent).

The final distinction is that regarding the regional and locality bases of communalism. Indonesia has a population of about 180 million spread throughout 6,000 inhabited islands, over an area of three and a half thousand miles east to west. There is a clear core–periphery relationship between Java and the Outer Islands. The development of locality and regional communal identities is reinforced by Indonesia's administrative structure, despite its unitary constitution. For purposes of civil and military adminis-tration, resource allocation, and electoral representation, Indonesia is divided into twenty-seven provinces, and thereafter into districts, sub-districts, municipalities and villages; with each unit, including the villages, having a government-appointed head. The political significance of the administrative units arises not just because of their role in resource allocation, but also because they overlap significantly with the ethno-linguistic groupings. With the exception of the Chinese community, the various ethno-linguistic groups all either occupy or identify with particular homeland localities and regions within Indonesia.[18]

Indonesians thus function within overlapping communities relating to various levels of *aliran*, linguistic, and locality affili-ation. Each of these may become the focus for politically salient ethnic consciousness, and the relationship of such ethnic com-munal consciousness to an overarching Indonesian identity has been, from the outset, a contingent one. Indonesia's unity has clearly been fragile. The years of revolution against the Dutch no doubt forged a sense of national unity, but the departure of the common enemy meant that this unity was immediately threatened by intense rivalries for the fruits of decolonization. If an ideology of Indonesian nationalism was not, on its own, sufficient to hold the society together, then the élite alliances of neo-patrimonialism would have to supplement it.

The relationship between communalism and clientelism is variable. Patron–client and patrimonial networks sometimes cut across and weaken communal affiliations, especially where patron–client relationships arise out of the competition for individual goods such as licences, contracts or jobs. Where, however, the focus of politics is the pursuit of community resources such as public amenities and development projects, then the politicization of regional and ethnic communalism is promoted.[19] The politicization of ethnicity becomes even more likely where patrimonial élites seek to mobilize popular support so as to promote their own individual political positions, since appeals to communal solidarity have the advantage of cutting across and inhibiting class alignments.

In the urban areas of Indonesia, many patron–client relationships are probably not communally based. But the large majority (about 85 per cent) of Indonesians live in rural village communities, and the patrons with major social and political influence are those community leaders who have access to material resources or elements of traditional authority. In a study of voting in the 1977 election, Tjan Silalahi found that rural voters were influenced by three types of communal patrons. The most influential were the formal government-appointed heads of the administrative units, the provinces, districts, and villages. Their main influence derived from the fact that they had access to government patronage for their communities, but in many cases they were men who also had high traditional status. The second category, with considerable influence only in a limited number of communities, were from the families of the traditional aristocracy in the various ethno-linguistic communities. The third type of patron was the religious leader, both Islamic teacher and Christian minister, having an influence over the community which extended well beyond the spiritual sphere.[20] Silalahi found that, 'The majority of voters in the rural areas tend to vote on the basis of what they perceive to be their patron's preference.'[21] The communal basis for political affiliation remained strong, and by the time of the 1987 elections, considerations of traditional deference and loyalty were beginning to give way to more material considerations.

Communal patrons act, in politics, as brokers. They enter into patron–client relationships and provide channels through which the members of their communal group can hope to gain access to the governmental patrimonial élites and their resources. At the same time, they act as the channels through which these governing élites can hope to mobilize, when necessary, the support of the communal group. The functioning of the patrimonial system is thus closely intertwined with the communal structure of the society.

THE TENSIONS INHERENT IN NEO-PATRIMONIALISM

The neo-patrimonial state does promise to provide a patronage umbrella under which communalism can be mobilized by cohesive élites in the service of national integration. But the promise is a fragile and tentative one. The tensions within neo-patrimonialism threaten to generate political instability and disunity should the patrimonial ruler run out of the necessary skill and resources with which to contain them. Since the ruler must perforce sleep, blunder and die, the tensions are unlikely to be contained indefinitely.

Three neo-patrimonial tensions will be explored in order to elucidate the role of ethnic communalism in Indonesian politics. The first is that between the cohesiveness of the patrimonial élite, and the counter-tendency towards élite factional disunity. The second tension is between the claim to universalistic administration and the practice of political favouritism. Third, there arises the tension between the concern of the patrimonial élites to exclude mass political participation and their countervailing interest in mobilizing mass political support without, at the same time, creating channels for oppositionist participation.

The tension between élite cohesion and élite factionalism

The tendency towards élite factionalism constitutes one basis for the politicization of communalism in that ethnicity may be employed as a resource in élite factional rivalries – either by disgruntled élites attempting to put pressure on the leader, or by dominant élites seeking to discredit their rivals. Such factional tendencies are to some extent countered by the awareness of neo-patrimonial élites that they constitute a privileged class within the society with a common interest in maintaining this position. Indeed, the patrimonial bureaucracy is rather similar to the neo-Marxist description of a bureaucratic bourgeois class which derives its economic wealth and power from its access to the state apparatus.[22] However, since each member of the neo-patrimonial élite is in rivalry for resources and for the favour of the patrimonial leader, there is a strong counter-tendency towards élite factional disunity. The bureaucratic class is characterized, in Karl Jackson's terminology, by competing 'circles' of patrimonial factions.[23] The tendency to élite disunity is further exacerbated in that the neo-patrimonial leader cannot count on strong traditional loyalty, and so must repeatedly redistribute resources to inhibit incipient disaffection amongst rival élites. These élite rivalries are intensified by the manoeuvring for succession, since neo-patrimonialism lacks the legitimate succession mechanism previously provided by hereditary monarchy.

Once dominant factions seek to deny subordinate factions access to the patrimonial network of state resources, the excluded élites may respond by putting pressure on the state to accommodate them. In such circumstances:

> Nation-building becomes, instead, faction-building . . . . As élite cohesion declines or disintegrates altogether, the élites are forced to seek new sources of support and new means of retaining their followings. In this situation, appeals to primordial sentiment are almost inevitable. Communalism, like opposition, is often inseparable from intra-élite conflict and factionalism.[24]

The tension between the factional and cohesive tendencies was evident in Indonesia's 'democratic' politics from 1949 to 1957, when the parliamentary system allowed competing élite-patrons to share power and resources at the centre, while mobilizing their communal clienteles through the four national political parties, the Indonesian Nationalist Party (PNI), the Communist Party (PKI), the reformist Islamic party, *Masjumi*, and the more traditional Muslim party, *Nahdatul Ulama*. The intensity of élite rivalries was increasingly evident in the successive coalition cabinets between 1949 and 1957, and within each of the political parties themselves. These rivalries involved struggles for high office between ambitious individuals, but they also evinced various cultural patterns as factional alliances developed amongst leaders of similar backgrounds.

Between 1945 and 1953, the struggle for power at the centre focused increasingly around two cleavages: first, that between the bureaucrat administrators and the communal patrons (in

Feith's words, the 'solidarity makers') who had led the revolution;[25] second, between *santri* Muslim élites calling for an Indonesian state which could accommodate some recognition of Islamic law, and those *abangans* and non-Muslims concerned to promote a more secular state. In 1945 Sukarno and Hatta had sought to build a bridge between the latter *santri* and *abangan* factions by articulating the *Panca Sila* principle of belief in one deity, as a nationalist 'umbrella'.[26] But the mutual suspicions between rival élite groups inhibited this, and between 1945 and 1953 this issue was employed increasingly as a resource which rival élites, competing for governmental positions, could manipulate.[27]

Elite rivalries, primarily but not solely between PNI and *Masjumi* leaders, were intensified by the prospect of Indonesia's first elections scheduled for early 1954.[28] The PNI élites sought to delay the elections because they feared a major swing towards the Islamic parties, particularly *Masjumi*, and they sought to validate this fear that they would lose governmental power by depicting *Masjumi* as a threat to national unity, arguing that elections might herald a replacement of the *Panca Sila* state by some form of 'Islamic state'.[29] This ideologizing of élite factional rivalries engendered a polarization which was further intensified by Sukarno's Amuntai speech in January 1953 in which he contrasted a 'national state' with a 'state based on Islam', and argued that:

> If we establish a state based on Islam, many areas whose population is not Islamic, such as the Moluccas, Bali, Flores, Timor, the Kai Islands and Sulawesi, will secede. And West Irian, which has not yet become part of the territory of Indonesia will not want to be part of the Republic.[30]

Once the struggle for élite power at the centre had been articulated and ideologized as a struggle between nationalism and Islam, the success of PNI élites in ousting *Masjumi* élites at the level of cabinet politics was bound to translate into a sharp decline in the receptiveness of central government to Islamic interests. Moreover, this pattern of factional rivalries was repeated within *Masjumi* itself, as the party came increasingly to be dominated by administrators who sought to defend their leadership of the party against the communal patrons with regional power bases.[31]

The impact of this cementing of élite factional rivalries in reducing governmental receptivity to Islamic religious demands was reinforced by the collapse of the federal formula for Indonesian independence, and by the concern on the part of the central government to combat centrifugal tendencies through policies of administrative centralization.[32] A federal arrangement, combined with a multi-party system, had appeared to offer the best prospects for mediating the cleavages between nationalist leaders and accommodating the aspirations of the diverse office-seekers within an élite coalition. But Hatta and Sukarno quickly came to realize that they had no option but to abandon federalism in favour of a unitary system, both because the administrative incoherence of the federal arrangement clashed with the need for efficient central control in the immediate post-colonial period, and also because the federal arrangement was fatally compromised by association with Dutch rule. But the ability to dispense rewards was crucial to the stability and legitimacy of the neo-patrimonial system, and the move to a unitary state after 1950, and towards increasing administrative centralization, made it particularly difficult for the government to contain the intense struggle for power by rewarding and accommodating all the communal patrons who had contributed to the nationalist revolution as 'regional army leaders, guerrilla leaders, political propagandists, and religious leaders'.[33]

Such élite factional rivalries led not only to increasingly weak coalition cabinets, but also to regional insurrections, as some of the communal patrons perceived that they were losing out in the competition for state power and sought to exert pressure by threatening to mobilize regional rebellion.[34] As Ruth McVey has argued, the major regional rebellions of the 1950s should be understood as:

> The settlement of a quarrel among aspiring élites – for the most part regional in origin but not regionalistic in outlook – who were agreed on the basic idea and outlines of an Indonesian nation-state but not on how power should be distributed among those who had claims to form its ruling élite . . .
>
> Eventually, the effort of the Outer Island élites to gain concessions from Jakarta led them to refuse its authority and finally to threaten revolt; but these were desperate

manoeuvres rather than real steps towards a new state formation. Indeed, the leaders who provided the military backing
and much of their political impetus were territorial army
commanders, sometimes but not always native to the region,
who had engaged in a contest for overall command of the
army and who, having lost in the round of manoeuvring in
the capital, were making a last-ditch effort to overturn the
decision by pressure from the provinces.[35]

The South Moluccas rebellion of 1950, for example, arose out
of the attempt by members of the regional government created
by the Dutch, and especially the former regional Justice Minister
Soumokil, to avoid their displacement by the new nationalist
central government. Soumokil was able to generate strong communal support based on Ambonese nationalism before the
revolt was quelled. In the case of the 1958 rebellions in Sumatra
and Sulawesi, it was the regional military commanders who
staged first a coup attempt, and then regional rebellions, as a
response to the threat to their positions from moves towards
military centralization.

This collapse of élite cohesion led Sukarno to move away from
parliamentary democracy towards a 'guided democracy' which
was, in effect, an alliance between civilian administrative élites
and military leaders. When this new élite alliance itself collapsed
because of rivalries between Sukarno and his army commanders, the army leaders under Suharto took over and established a 'New Order', in which the factionalism of neo-
patrimonial politics was avowedly to be replaced by 'depoliticized' efficient management, with military officers identifying
themselves as an administrative élite and a technocratic expert-
class, rather than as agents of authoritarian coercion. The immediate problems of national integration were to be solved by
restricting the options for political participation.

But this New Order 'corporatism' camouflaged, rather than
replaced, the reality of neo-patrimonial politics. Central government has continued to be characterized by neo-patrimonial tendencies towards élite factional rivalries; and while the options
available for marginalized élites to politically mobilize communalism have been restricted, they have not been eliminated. In the
New Order régime, therefore, élite factionalism has ensured

the perpetuation, indeed the escalation, of nepotistic practices which undermine the claims to meritocratic technocracy.

The tension between universalism and nepotism

This second tension within neo-patrimonialism arises from the clash between the universalistic·claims that all sections of the community be treated equally or fairly in the distribution of state offices and resources, and the imperatives of neo-patrimonial politics which dictate the discriminatory dispensing of patronage. One facet of such neo-patrimonial favouritism is the practice of ethnic bias, in which the leader gives preferential treatment to those of his own regional, cultural, religious or language group in the belief, which may or may not be valid, that such individuals will exhibit greater loyalty. The practice is self-fulfilling in the sense that it generates a sense of alienation and grievance amongst the leaders of those ethnic communities discriminated against. The favouring of *abangans* and *priyayis* over *santri* Muslims in Indonesia's élite politics, has already been noted. What has made this even more politically salient has been its interweaving with the preferential treatment of Javanese over non-Javanese.

In traditional patrimonial systems, the private interests of the ruler were perceived as compatible with, and indeed the articulation of, public societal interests. In contemporary states, however, including neo-patrimonial states, public interests are portrayed in terms of the universalistic norms which are implicit in the ideology of national liberation from colonialism, and which are also attached to modern bureaucratic and democratic claims.[36] There thus develops a direct clash between the politics of personal power, and the public norms and universalistic ideologies available to legitimate that power. It is this gap which is referred to when neo-patrimonial states are depicted as characteristically corrupt.[37]

From the outset, the leaders of the Indonesian nationalist revolution sought to unite the various linguistic, religious and regional communities by proclaiming an Indonesian nationalism based on 'unity in diversity' embodied in the eclectic slogans first of *Panca Sila*, and then also of NASAKOM (the concern to give fair consideration to the claims of nationalism, religion and communism as a basis for national identity). In these formulations of the Indonesian nation, all indigenous communities would retain their integrity and identity and would receive equal or fair treatment in the allocation of resources. The major nationalist symbol of this commitment was the decision to adopt Malay, rather than Javanese, as the national language. As Leo Suryadinata has noted, in Indonesian nationalism:

> the indigenous minority groups are not expected to be absorbed into Javanese society. The Indonesian national culture is seen as a new culture based on various indigenous ethnic cultures, of which Bahasa Indonesia is the major vehicle. Islam is part of the culture, but not the dominant one . . . the minority groups are tolerated/encouraged to retain their ethnic cultures provided that they accept the authority of the national government and national education.[38]

This image of ethnic accommodation, rather than of assimilation into Javanese culture, lies at the cornerstone of the sense of Indonesian national identity. But the claims to equitable accommodation are undermined by the neo-patrimonial politics of favouritism. Neo-patrimonial rulers seek stability by surrounding themselves with (and giving favourable treatment to) retainers chosen on grounds of personal affiliation rather than on merit. The ruler favours those individuals tied to him by personal bonds of kinship, culture, training, or common career background.

In the competition for administrative positions and state resources, the exercise of patronage leads to imbalances in which particular branches or levels of the state machinery, in extreme cases, may come to be regarded as the preserve of a particular section of the community. This may occur to the extent that the state comes to be seen as 'owned' by a particular patrimonial leader and his clientele, in which case a 'zero-sum' view of politics is generated. Politics comes to be seen as a conflict for monopoly access to the state rather than, as proclaimed in the national ideology, a process of equal or fair access for all groups. Rather than legitimating patrimonial rule, the national ideology of universalism and fairness becomes a resource available to excluded entrepreneurs seeking to mobilize disadvantaged and disaffected communities. The incumbent élites can be portrayed as self-interested, nepotistic or 'tribalistic', in that their behaviour falls short of their own proclamations of ethnic neutrality or ethnic balance.

Many observers of the Suharto government have focused attention on the incidence of 'familism'; the favouring by Suharto of his immediate family members.[39] But nepotism in Indonesia also involves an ethnic dimension in that recruitment, promotion and resource distribution have been based, to a significant extent, upon an ethnic favouritism which favours members of the Javanese *abangan* and *priyayi* groups. A Javanese predominance at élite levels, which initially reflected only the population, economic, educational and training advantages arising from residence in Java, has been progressively exaggerated as Javanese leaders have become increasingly suspicious of factional threats from non-Javanese, and have developed ties of trust and affinity with those with whom they have had closest interactions – mostly their co-ethnics.

In most states of the world the majority cultural group is over-represented in the governing élites, but the distinctive feature of the Indonesian case is that such over-representation has been steadily increasing over time. In the first cabinets of the independent Indonesian Republic there was no over-representation of Javanese, and the leaders of the main political parties were drawn from various ethnic groups, with Outer Island élites being well represented.[40]

Nevertheless, there were some complaints of Javanese dominance, partly because Sukarno was Javanese (and part Balinese), and partly because the Javanese were over-represented within the state bureaucracy, probably initially for educational reasons. The shift away from parliamentary democracy to bureaucratic control in the late 1950s served both to reduce the concern of the régime to appear ethnically representative, and also to make this Javanese domination of the civil and military bureaucracies more politically salient. Anne Gregory found that the extent of Javanese domination amongst the decision-making élite went from 50 per cent in the revolution period, to 55 per cent under parliamentary democracy, 57 per cent in the transition towards guided democracy, 66 per cent under guided democracy, and then to 64 per cent in the early New Order régime.[41] The extent of ethnic bias in Indonesian patrimonialism has been most clear amongst the military élite, and has been most dramatic during the New Order régime of Suharto. At the beginning of this régime, the Javanese constituted about 66 per cent of the military élite. By 1977 the figure had risen to 74 per cent, and by 1978 it was roughly 80 per cent. By that time also, fourteen out of the fifteen Regional and Territorial Commanders of the Outer Islands were Javanese.[42] In her study of the military élites Gregory found that:

> In general, recruitment into the political élite in Indonesia has been increasingly dominated by those from the Javanese ethnic group, particularly from Central Java and from social groupings hostile to orthodox and modernist Islam. The military segment of the political élite is even less representative of the society than are the civilian segments. Those from the Outer Islands found it necessary to resocialise themselves as Javans in order to make it in civilian and military politics . . . . For the military as an institution is deeply influenced by Javanese values and ways of thinking.[43]

In the late 1950s the Military Academy (AMN) was established overtly to counteract the previous military training advantages of the Javanese, but even after its graduates had risen to senior posts in the 1980s, the percentage of Javanese in the officer corps still remains 'well over 70 per cent'. 'Thus the ascendancy of AMN Javanese probably occurred in the 1970s by a selective promotion process – whether for political reasons or not remains uncertain.'[44]

In repeated factional rivalries, non-Javanese officers have been defeated by Javanese factions, and have, in the process, been either retired, diverted into powerless, symbolic governmental positions or simply passed over for promotion,[45] and the main explanation for the resultant disparities is, according to Gregory, that:

> for military factions divisional identification and ethnic background are, in general, congruent, and . . . are the most important fctors in terms of military factions. However, when divisional and ethnic lines are not congruent, army leaders often choose a faction composed of people from their ethnic background, not their army division.[46]

Such an ethnically selective promotion process in the armed forces implies that the composition of the military élite, and to a somewhat lesser degree of the governing élite as a whole, is now

dominated by Javanese to such an extent that factional cleavages
no longer reflect ethnic divisions. While this is sometimes quoted
as evidence of the political unimportance of ethnicity, it should,
more accurately, be seen as the direct result of the ethnic bias of
Indonesian neo-patrimonialism.

The fact of Javanese domination, and the perception of this as
arising from neo-patrimonial favouritism, have been repeatedly
referred to by non-Javanese critics of central government in
order to legitimate political opposition. But the extent of overt
opposition has been inhibited by the efforts of Indonesia's
leaders to reduce and control the extent of political discussion
and activity.

The tension between the political exclusion of the masses and their political mobilization

The neo-patrimonial élites, like their traditional counterparts,
prefer to maintain élite privileges by insulating themselves from
the wider society, monopolizing power and resources while
relying primarily on the culture of deference to maintain political stability, but also where necessary on authoritarian means.
They are, however, subjected to various counter-pressures.
They perceive that the traditional culture of deference may be
declining and that mass expectations of developmental
resources are increasing. They also wish to claim democratic
legitimation, and this implies the need to mobilize mass participatory support. Such mass participation carries with it the
danger, however, of articulating populist discontent against the
patrimonial régime. The dilemma is captured in Ruth McVey's
discussion of Indonesia's 1955 elections:

> [The national élite] were anxious on the one hand to put
> down deeper roots into the society, to establish a real relation-
> ship with the mass clienteles they claimed to represent, and to
> link to themselves those lower-level leaders who might other-
> wise compete for the loyalties of the mass; at the same time,
> they were unsure of the extent of their public support, uncer-
> tain of how to go about securing it, and uncomfortable with
> the idea of sharing power with leaders who did not come
> from their own cultural milieu.[47]

The response of the neo-patrimonial state is to seek to limit and control the options for participation. But they may lack the capacity to exercise such controls effectively, as excluded élites seek to utilize the participation options offered by the state so as to mobilize communal opposition.

Each strategy (departicipation or participation) is attractive, but each has its dangers. If the deference culture is indeed being eroded, then the departicipation strategy might generate mass alienation unrest. If the mobilized participation strategy is attempted, then it must be tied to the skilful distribution of developmental resources and the skillful deployment of coercion, co-optation and 'divide and rule' tactics, otherwise the participatory options will be employed by disgruntled élites and disgruntled communal clienteles for oppositionist purposes. Thus, whereas traditional patrimonialism is stable in that it can employ deference and loyalty so as to exclude mass participation, neo-patrimonialism is fragile. The pressures for it to move towards the mobilization of mass participation imply the possibility of unleashing the resentment of patrons and clienteles who feel that they have done badly in patronage politics.

Although Indonesia's period of parliamentary democracy was characterized by unstable coalitions at the centre and insurrection in the peripheral regions, the mass mobilization activities of the various national political parties illustrated the way in which ethnic communalism might be mobilized in the service of national integration. The experience of participation in a national political party, espousing national issues, served to promote the idea that local and national issues were interconnected. Individuals came to make sense of both their own individual identity, and the identity of the nation, through the 'lens' of their communal affiliation. These connections between communal identities and national identities were then made concrete by the network of patron–client linkages which connected the rural village to the central government.

Each of the four major political parties had as its core a particular communal group. Thus the PNI had its base amongst the Javanese *priyayi* bureaucracy; the PKI (Communist Party) had its core among the poorer elements of Javanese *abangan* society; the *Nahdatul Ulama* relied on the support of the rural *santri*; while the *Masjumi* (the reformist Islamic party) relied primarily on the Muslim commercial and urban groups. Nevertheless, as Liddle has shown in his studies of the Sumatran

Bataks, each party was constrained to mobilize support beyond
its core group:

> Whatever the nature of the conflicts which divide the parties
> at the national level [the parties tend at the local level] to take
> on the coloration of local primordial cleavages . . . . Each
> party sought popular support by devising policies and pro-
> grams according to the patterns of interests, loyalties and
> hostilities in each locality.[48]

Political mobilization occurred, then, as the political parties
employed 'patron-client pyramids' linking village communities,
ethno-linguistic and regional communities, with *aliran* communities.[49] When religious, linguistic and local communities
participated in national politics specifically to defend or promote
their own communal interests by seeking access to state resources, such participation served to strengthen and politicize
their communal affiliations:

> Competition for scarce values and material goods, – land,
> certain kinds of employment, education, status, – led indi-
> viduals to begin to perceive themselves as members of distinct
> ethnic groups, based on common language, culture, clan
> membership and to some extent religious affiliation, whose
> interests they defended against incursions from other groups
> . . .
> Modernization . . . may produce a new kind of leadership,
> rooted in primordialism, but oriented toward the national
> community, and eager to play a 'broker' role on behalf of its
> constituency through participation in a national system.[50]

The electoral politics of the 1950s thus had the effect of
promoting national integration by mobilizing support on a communal basis, and bringing the various communal groups
together in an umbrella coalition of political parties at the
centre; each party comprising chains of vertical links between
patrons and their communal clienteles. The umbrella failed,
however, to work effectively. The 'new kind of leadership', i.e.
the communal brokers in search of resources, became restless
when the system failed to produce the promised resources, or
seemed to channel them primarily into Javanese and *abangan*
hands. At the centre, élite cohesion was maintained only at the

cost of immobilism and corruption, and when élite factional rivalries proliferated, they provided the justification for Sukarno to end electoral political participation. Thereafter the political parties began to atrophy.

After the overthrow of Sukarno, the New Order régime pursued a policy of depoliticization, and ruled primarily through authoritarian and bureaucratic means. With its reliance on the centralized military and administrative institutions, the New Order régime could, initially at least, pursue the traditional patrimonial strategy of excluding the masses both from political participation and from many of the resource benefits associated with governmental power.[51] Mass political participation was thus perceived as a threat to patrimonial control; and after having defeated the Communists, the main political concern of the New Order élite was to defuse the perceived threat of political Islam. To this end, the New Order élites sought to either co-opt or coerce Islamic leaders, or alternatively to undermine their position as communal patrons by making alliance with, and distributing resources through, their rivals. In no case though, could the Islamic leaders be allowed to mobilize mass support for the goal of an Islamic state implementing Islamic law in pursuit of an Islamic society. The New Order élites were impelled, however, to restore limited political participation through their concern to contain the mounting frustrations arising from escalating economic inequalities and from the régime's increasing reliance on repression. The new generation of army officers, groomed in the military academy rather than in the nationalist revolution, were increasingly alienated from such behaviour, and sought administrative rather than coercive means of maintaining the régime. This implied the provision of new options for the articulation of interests, but options which the state would be able to control and contain.

Since the early 1970s, therefore, the Indonesian state élites have tried to develop an institutional and ideological framework within which mass political participation may be mobilized on a communal clientele basis in support of the state-élite patrons. They have successfully established *Golkar* as a political machine for the downward distribution of resources in return for mobilized supportive participation. State control over political participation was ensured by the formation of *Golkar* as the party of the government and administration, and the amalgamation of all other parties into two approved groupings, the PPP, containing the Muslim parties, and the PDI, containing all others.

In each of the elections which have been held since 1971, *Golkar* has achieved majorities of over 60 per cent; and these are attributable mainly to the fact that it is widely perceived as a monopolistic state patronage machine. *Golkar* has mobilized support primarily through employing patron–client networks, gaining the support of communal patrons by appealing both to traditional ties of deference, and also to the concern for material resources:

> Golkar provides various interests with the benefits and material incentives in the form of contracts, or the favourable allocation of development projects, in return for support . . . Golkar as a machine stresses parochial loyalties to the virtual exclusion of ideology and class policy, and with regard to its base it is neutral, allied to those elements which can organize and deliver the votes upon which it depends for victory. However, since the majority of Golkar's support is derived from the traditional sector where deference to authority and symbolic goals are of major importance, Golkar does not always stress machine-style incentives to build support.[52]

For its part, the Islamic PPP, which has emerged as *Golkar's* major rival, continues to rely primarily on the communal influence of religious leaders; and this ensures that the *santri–abangan* cleavage in Indonesia remains a politically salient and potentially destabilizing one. For each party, political mobilization involves communal patrons persuading their clientele communities to give their support either on the basis of traditional deference or on the basis of actual or promised resource distribution.

Indonesian governments have thus shifted between strategies of exclusion and of participation; and in seeking to avoid the problems of both, the New Order government has developed a strategy of controlled participation. Despite the attempt to provide one umbrella institution, *Golkar*, within which the various clientage networks can be contained, the present system has failed to resolve the tensions associated with communal mobilization. *Golkar* has still failed to entice many of the *santri* Muslim voters, who remain wedded to the PPP; and it remains predominantly an alliance of communal groups – locality, ethno-linguistic and religious – in which perceptions of iniquitous resource allocation continually threaten to provoke communal rivalries.

The three neo-patrimonial tensions which have been identified, relating to élite factionalism, ethnic favouritism, and the mobilization of oppositionist communal participation, do not function independently of each other. They intertwine when élite groups who are defeated in élite factional rivalries and then excluded from the patrimonial resource network perceive their exclusion as arising from ethnic bias, and seek to improve their bargaining position in élite politics by mobilizing oppositionist communalism. In order to illustrate this intertwining, and its implications for the relationship between ethnic communalism and national integration, the discussion will shift focus, to the impact of the neo-patrimonial state upon politics at the ethno-regional level.

THE CASE OF ACEH[53]

The neo-patrimonial characterization of the state is useful in combating the argument that some states are doomed to disintegration by the facts of their ethno-regional composition, whilst others can rely on their cultural integration for national political integration. It suggests rather that the question of whether and how ethno-regionalism becomes politicized, depends on how élite rivalries at the centre influence the prospects either for communal 'umbrella' alliances, or for oppositionist communal mobilization by marginalized élites.

In the Aceh case, the provincial élites have not themselves been involved in politics at the centre; but they have sought alliances with central élites in order to promote their influence as communal patrons, and they have threatened to mobilize communalism against the centre when they felt neglected or aggrieved. An explanation of communal politics must focus, therefore, on the alliance decisions and strategies of the individuals who have sought influence as communal patrons. As Morris notes with reference to Aceh:

> People, not regions, act politically. Thus we need to ask who
>   formulates identity symbols, who provides the 'definition of
>   the situation', and who mobilizes a group on the basis of this
>   identity . . . . In examining the emergence, maintenance and

transformation of ethnic and regional identity symbols, attention must be focused on leadership groups who define the
symbols.[54]

Aceh's political oppositionism, both electoral and insurrectionist, has sometimes been interpreted as reflecting its
unique position amongst Indonesia's regions in terms of its
strong ethnic cohesiveness, its history of political independence,
the intensity of its commitment to Islam, its relative social isolation from the political centre, and its 'internal colonial' economic relations with central government. However, although
Aceh is not typical of Indonesian provinces in its history of
political oppositionism and in its regional characteristics, the
nature of the linkages between Aceh's objective attributes and its
political orientations can nevertheless be understood in similar
terms to those operating elsewhere in Indonesia; in the interactions between regional élites seeking central alliances, and
central élites seeking regional control.[55]

Neo-patrimonialism in Old Order Indonesia, and its impact on Acehnese communalism

During the colonial period, Aceh's traditional élite, the *uleebalang*, acted as the administrative agents of Dutch rule, and thus
provided an effective linkage between the central government
and the region. This link was severed, however, by Aceh's
'social revolution' of 1946 in which the *uleebalang* were ousted by
the reformist Islamic leaders, the *ulama*, who sought an alliance
with the parliamentary governments at the centre. It was the
impact of élite factionalism at the centre in undermining these
alliance attempts which provoked the marginalized Acehnese
ulama to mobilize communal opposition in the form of
the Acehnese rebellion. The lack of congruence between the
alliance strategies of the neo-patrimonial centre and those of the
Acehnese élites resulted in the failure of the former to co-opt
the latter, and the failure of the latter to gain access to the state
resources of the former. The rebellion was a result of this
breakdown of negotiations, but it also served to put pressure on
the central government to reopen them. It was, however, only
when élite cohesion was subsequently restored at the centre in
the early guided democracy period, that the centre was able to

build a fragile alliance linkage with the Acehnese *ulama* by promising them state resources, thus ending the rebellion. The impact of these events was, however, the revival of élite factional disunity within Aceh.

The Acehnese rebellion is thus typical of the widespread regionalist unrest in Indonesia in the 1950s, in that it was instigated by regional leaders who mobilized ethnic consciousness in opposition to the state so as to exert pressure in their struggle for access to the resources and power of the centre. Aceh appears to be typical also in that support for the rebellion was based on a traditional communal clientelism, in which village communities followed their village leaders, in this case the reformist *ulamas*. It should be noted in this context that while in pre-colonial Aceh the *ulamas* had comprised a 'type of free-floating intelligentsia',[56] they subsequently developed as village-based leaders. They were thus able to combine two levels of communalism – the village community and the Acehnese community, for purposes of political mobilization.[57] It is thus the extent of village *ulama* influence, and their personal political orientations which, above all, explains the extent of support for the 1953 rebellion in the different parts of Aceh.[58]

Factional disunity in Aceh: ulama *versus* uleebalang

The *uleebalang* were the hereditary territorial chiefs of the Acehnese Sultanate.[59] They were retained by the Dutch as their administrative officials after the destruction of the Sultanate in 1903; and they articulated a version of Acehnese communalism which stressed the traditional *adat* continuity of Aceh's regional development and its territorial administration.[60] Their claim to Acehnese leadership was challenged, from the 1920s onwards, by the spread of the *madrasah* movement in Aceh, led by the reformist *ulama*, who organized themselves in 1939 into the 'All-Aceh Ulama Association' (PUSA), under the leadership of Teungku M. Daud Beureueh.[61] PUSA articulated an alternative image of an Acehnese community, revitalized and unified by the administration of Islamic law.[62] This rivalry, between the reformist *ulama* articulating religious Acehnese communal values, and the *uleebalang* articulating a regionalist Acehnese communalism, has been identified as the major basis for élite factional rivalry within Aceh and thence as the major key to understanding its relations with the centre.[63] It has not been, however, the only level of factional rivalry within Aceh. The rise of the reformist *ulama* constituted a challenge to the authority not only of the *uleebalang*, but also to that of the more conservative or orthodox *ulama*. Moreover, within the reformist Islamic camp itself, there developed a tension between the PUSA *ulama* and those reformist Muslims occupying secular occupations, the *zuama*, whose occupational interests led them to stress regional autonomy as the key to the achievement of an Islamic Aceh.[64]

The harshness of Dutch administration and the spread of reformist Islamic ideas combined to erode the *uleebalang*'s position of dominance, and in 1946 the PUSA *ulama* were able to use their more militant youth wing (*Pemuda* PUSA), trained in the Japanese *Giyugun* military units, to organize for the defence of Aceh against a Dutch return; and also to lead a popular 'social revolution' against the attempt by *uleebalangs* to restore their authority.[65] The PUSA leaders then set about establishing their new position as the dominant Acehnese communal élite. In August 1946 they established a network of religious courts, *Makamah Sjariah*, throughout Aceh, to be manned by themselves.[66] This served both to implement the goal of an Islamic Aceh on which their communal influence depended, and also 'to provide jobs for the large number of *ulamas*'.[67] It strengthened their position as the Acehnese élite by providing 'a kind of insurance for Atjenese *ulamas* against the resuscitation of *uleebalang adat* authority'.[68] PUSA leaders also took over administrative positions in the Aceh Residency from the ousted *uleebalang*, and exercised effective control of trade and of the military forces. During 1946 also, the PUSA leaders who took over the Residency administration decreed, without central approval, that the *madrasah* schools be recognized as state schools, with their teachers to receive government salaries. In order to consolidate their position and implement their religio-communal goal, however, it was necessary that they get official recognition from central government as Aceh's administrative, military and judicial élite.

Elite cohesion in Aceh: the ulama's alliance strategy with the centre

The situation was that Indonesia's Republican leaders had given tentative recognition to PUSA's de facto control of Aceh after the 'social revolution',[69] and in January 1947 the Republican Governor of Sumatra appeared to recognize the Islamic courts which had been established in Aceh.[70] Then in July 1947 the Republican leaders appointed Daud Beureueh as Military Governor.[71] In June 1948, Sukarno met Daud Beureueh in Aceh and promised 'to do his best at least to make Aceh an Islamic nation'.[72] Most crucially, in December 1949 the temporary 'Emergency Government' based in Sumatra, led by the *Masjumi* leader, Sjafruddin, acceded to PUSA calls for Aceh to be recognized as a separate province; though this remained unratified by the Ministry of Home Affairs.[73] On the basis of this provincial status, Daud Beureueh was proclaimed Governor, and a provincial assembly, mostly PUSA leaders, was appointed. But the PUSA élite now needed official confirmation of these *ad hoc* moves, initially from the new federal 'United States of Indonesia' of December 1949; and then, after August 1950, from its successor, the unitary Republic of Indonesia.

It was the failure to achieve these goals through their alliance strategy that led the PUSA *ulama* towards a communal rebellion, and the failure of their negotiations is explainable in terms of the factional struggle for power at the centre.

In 1946 the PUSA *ulama* had allied with the newly formed Islamic nationalist party, *Masjumi*.[74] In terms of its popular support base, *Masjumi* was probably the strongest of the political parties, and it was well represented in the parliamentary cabinets formed from 1949 to 1953.[75] The Acehnese PUSA leaders were hopeful, therefore, that the alliance with *Masjumi* at the centre would result in government accession to their demands. However, the influence that the PUSA leaders had with the central élites was inhibited both by the social gap between themselves and the Dutch-educated Javanese *priyayis* who predominated in Jakarta, and also by the outcome of the factional rivalries amongst the central political élites, in which *Masjumi*'s influence was steadily eroded.

Factional disunity at the centre: the collapse of the Acehnese PUSA's alliance strategy

The progressive marginalization of the Islamic élite factions in central government, together with the pressures towards administrative centralization, reduced the government's willingness and ability to accommodate the calls of the Acehnese *ulama* for provincial autonomy. The Ministry of Religion, dominated by Javanese 'administrators' unsympathetic to regionalist 'solidarity makers', responded to Acehnese demands for the recognition of Sjariah courts by 'for years . . . replying that nothing could be done because the revolutionary Islamic courts did not have sufficient legal basis.'[76] Moreover, the Hatta cabinet of 1949–50 was similarly dominated by 'administrators' who sought to defuse divisive ethno-regional affiliations by creating ten large multi-ethnic provinces. Thus Aceh was to be incorporated within the North Sumatra Province with its capital in Batak Medan. This was followed up, during 1950 and 1951, by the army rationalization programme which included the disbandment of the Acehnese division of the Indonesian National Army, and the posting of a non-Acehnese unit to Aceh.[77]

For the PUSA leaders, the loss of provincial status would directly threaten their personal interests as salaried officials and their influence as the communal patrons of their Islamic Acehnese clientele. For the *uleebalang* remnant groups, however, it offered an opportunity for removing the PUSA leaders from power positions in Aceh, so that the *uleebalang* began attempts to influence the government in this direction, and to turn public opinion in Aceh against PUSA.[78] For the central government leaders, either a concession to Aceh or an Aceh rebellion could provide a precedent stimulating unrest in other dissatisfied regions. Each group therefore sought to gain advantage through negotiations between 1950 and 1953. From the outset, the PUSA leaders recognized the weakness of their bargaining position *vis à vis* the centre, and sought to compensate for this by pressure tactics. They responded to the plan to incorporate Aceh within the North Sumatra Province by stating their loyalty to Indonesia, reiterating their call for provincial status, and threatening the resignation of all PUSA leaders from Aceh's administrative positions.[79] In response, various government leaders visited Aceh to try to persuade them that Aceh could not be made an exception to the provincial rationalization. Hopes were raised in Aceh by the change of government in August 1950, which brought a *Masjumi* dominated cabinet to power, and an Acehnese delegation immediately went to Jakarta to negotiate. But the *Masjumi* leaders were paralysed by administrative considerations and factional rivalries, and failed to respond.[80]

In January 1951, when the provincial reorganization was due to take effect, Prime Minister Natsir (the Chairman of *Masjumi*), came to Aceh and:

> pledged his personal authority, which commanded great respect from PUSA *ulamas*, and Masjumi's power, which time would show was not that impressive, to press Aceh's claim for provincial status .... For his part, Teungku M. Daud Beureueh acceded to Natsir's request for compliance, and, for the time being, withdrew the threat of large-scale resignations from government service.[81]

The rebellion occurred, then, after it became clear to PUSA that Natsir and *Masjumi* lacked sufficient influence at the centre to implement this 'pledge'. Between 1950 and 1953 the government proceeded to appoint non-Acehnese, mainly Javanese, to administrative positions in Aceh,[82] and at the end of July 1953 a new cabinet was formed which, for the first time, excluded *Masjumi* from government. By August the new PNI Prime Minister announced that the elections originally scheduled for early 1954, which *Masjumi* and the Acehnese PUSA believed would strengthen their positions, would not now be held until 1955. The PUSA leaders had hitherto relied upon *Masjumi* as their only ally at the centre. When *Masjumi* proved unable even to deliver the election 'which they thought would establish the ideological hegemony of Islam', the PUSA leaders 'no longer listened to the arguments of *Masjumi* leaders that a little more patience would reap great rewards'.[83] The Aceh PUSA *ulama* perceived that the central government was now completely closed to further efforts at alliance.

The strategy of communal mobilization: Acehnese rebellion

So long as the PUSA élite believed that an independent Indonesia would recognize their positions as Acehnese leaders, so that they could promote their communal goal of an Islamic Aceh, they had an interest in commitment to the Indonesian Republic rather than in rebellion against it. As Daud Beureueh noted in 1949:

> There are no regional feelings in Aceh; thus we have no intention of establishing a Great Aceh state as we are republi-

can spirited . . . . The loyalty of the people to the Republic of Indonesia is neither pretended nor fabricated but rather is honest and sincere loyalty which comes from pure heart-felt commitment as well as from firm calculations and considerations.[84]

But now that attempts at negotiation with the centre had failed, the PUSA leaders moved towards the mobilization of communal support as a radical means of putting pressure on the centre. This involved mobilizing communal grievances against the centre on a wide range of issues relating to the loss of provincial status. These included the government's imposition of a ban on direct trading with Malaya and Singapore, the downgrading of Acehnese in favour of non-Muslim Bataks in administrative positions, the disbandment of the Acehnese army unit, the increase in 'un-Islamic' activities, such as gambling and beer drinking, which allegedly accompanied administration by non-Acehnese officials, and the apparent neglect of Aceh in funding allocations in such areas as education, road repairs, and irrigation.[85] Daud Beureueh concluded that Sukarno and the proponents of the *Panca Sila* state had betrayed the goal of an Islamic Indonesia in general, and the goal of an Islamic Aceh in particular.[86] In March 1953 when once again Sukarno visited Aceh, he was greeted by banners with the slogan 'We love the President but we love religion more'.[87]

Daud Beureueh launched the regional rebellion in the hope that it would force a government concession. He had several reasons for hoping that this radical form of pressure would succeed. First, the Wilopo Cabinet had conceded to regionalist pressures in the 1952 armed forces rebellions, and had granted enhanced autonomy to areas of Kalimantan, Sulawesi and the Moluccas.[88] Second, PUSA believed that they had the resources with which to maintain such a rebellion, in the armed and trained *Pemuda* PUSA who had led the violent social revolution against the *uleebalang*. Third, Daud Beureueh believed that the Acehnese demands would be acceded to, not because of Acehnese pressure alone, but because of the spread of the *Darul Islam* movement in other regions.

PUSA thus began mass mobilization activities; organizing youth, women's and veterans groups.[89] Daud Beureueh sought the support of Acehnese administrative and military officers, and in September the rebellion was launched as part of the Kartosuwirdjo's *Darul Islam* movement in West Java and South Sulawesi.[90] Pamphlets justifying the rebellion argued that:

> If in reality the Republic's laws guaranteed religious freedom for Muslims, then religious law would already have been implemented in Aceh [but] . . . not a single Acehnese request has been granted by the government. Aceh has been prevented from standing on its own, from having its own province, even though it was stated that this would have been in the context of a unitary state . . . . We do not want to separate ourselves from our brothers and sisters in other regions . . . but at the same time we refuse to be treated as stepchildren or left to live like slaves.[91]

The Acehnese rebellion thus reflected the intense commitment of the Acehnese and of their leaders to the goal of an Islamic Aceh. But that same commitment had generated, a few years earlier, a strong alignment with the Republican Indonesian cause. The shift from national integration to national disintegration occurred only when the alliance strategies of the central and regional élites ceased to coincide. Once élite cohesion at the centre gave way to an élite factionalism in which *Masjumi* leaders began to loose power, then the Acehnese PUSA leaders lost their hope of access to the resources and power of the centre.

Elite cohesion at the centre: the resolution of the rebellion

Although government troops were able to regain control of the main towns by 1954, much of Aceh's countryside remained under guerrilla control, and a military stalemate developed. The rebellion ended only when the rebuilding of élite cohesion at the centre led to the opening up of new alliance options for the Acehnese leaders.

The failure of the 1955 elections to resolve the deadlock in the parliamentary cabinets provoked the shift from parliamentary democracy towards 'guided democracy', with power gravitating to President Sukarno and to the military commander, General Nasution. But this attempt at the centralization of power in turn helped to provoke the 'regionalist' mutinies and rebellions of the late 1950s. In this new situation, 'Aceh enjoyed greater leverage with Jakarta because of the center's preoccupation with growing dissidence elsewhere'.[92]

Specifically, when faced with 'regionalist' opposition from the North Sumatran Regional Commander, Colonel Simbolon, General Nasution sought to undercut him by appointing an Acehnese, Major Sjammaun Gaharu, to command the subordinate Aceh regiment within North Sumatra.[93] When Simbolon staged his regionalist rebellion so as to avoid removal from his command by Nasution in December 1956, Gaharu pursued his own career interest by bypassing Simbolon and establishing his Aceh regiment as a Regional Military Command directly responsible to army headquarters.[94] Gaharu's position as an 'administrative' military officer and also as an Acehnese who was unaligned either with the *uleebalangs* or PUSA, then led him to a strategy of co-opting Acehnese to accept central authority by giving them civilian and military responsibilities in Aceh's administration. This would erode support for the rebellion and would also enhance Nasution's central military power *vis à vis* both the cabinet and Colonel Simbolon.

After the onset of the Acehnese rebellion, the central government had sought to restore administrative order to Aceh by turning to PUSA's opponents, the orthodox *ulama* and the *uleebalangs*, to man the vacated administrative posts, and this coincided with the *uleebalangs'* concern to revive their influence in Aceh and to make alliances at the centre. Reportedly, 80 per cent of Aceh's administrative appointments went to *uleebalangs*.[95] Nevertheless, Aceh's position as part of the North Sumatran province continued to mean that many of these Acehnese were posted to Medan, and that many non-Acehnese occupied posts within Aceh.

Gaharu now proposed that Aceh be granted provincial status, that some Acehnese army officers be returned to Aceh under his command, and that some of the respected PUSA *ulamas* who had been imprisoned, be returned to positions as Aceh's religious, judicial and educational officials. This strategy offered the central government a way of dividing the Acehnese rebels from Simbolon's North Sumatran rebellion of December 1956, and of promoting internal dissension amongst the PUSA leaders. Accordingly, at the end of 1956 Aceh was granted provincial status; Ali Hasjmy, an administrative official who had actively supported PUSA in the early stages of the rebellion, but who had a history of rivalry with Daud Beureueh, was appointed Governor.[96] Nasution then instructed Gaharu to begin negotiations for an end to the rebellion, and a cease-fire was agreed in April 1957.

The impact of these developments upon Aceh were crucially influenced, however, by the opening up of an alternative option in the form of the dissident Revolutionary Government of the Republic of Indonesia (PRRI) of February 1958. The further erosion of *Masjumi*'s position after the 1955 elections had impelled its leaders to join forces with the rebel regionalist officers in West Sumatra, and they appealed to the *Darul Islam* rebels in Aceh to join the PRRI. The PRRI was too divided and weak to offer an immediately useful alliance for the PUSA leaders, but its opposition to Jakarta and its pro-Islamic element did persuade some PUSA leaders, notably Daud Beureueh, to continue the struggle to establish an Islamic state in Aceh; and he therefore aligned himself with the short-lived 'United Republic of Indonesia', which the PRRI leaders proclaimed in 1960.[97]

The net result, therefore, of the changed situation of the late 1950s, was to provoke a split within the PUSA leadership, between the *ulama* who gave primacy to their Islamic goals, and the *zuama* elements who adhered to the goal of an Islamic Aceh, but saw themselves as political realists, with a personal interest in assuming administrative positions in a restored Aceh province.[98] Alongside this cleavage, the negotiations between the government and the PUSA leaders also served to provoke the opposition of the *uleebalang* and the orthodox *ulama*, who had expected that they themselves, as PUSA's opponents, should be recognized as Aceh's representatives.

The division between these religious and regionalist formulations of Acehnese communalism was expressed most clearly in the split within PUSA between Daud Beureueh and his military leader, Hasan Saleh. Hasan Saleh, with a majority of the PUSA leadership, formed a revolutionary council to negotiate with the government; while Daud Beureueh continued his military rebellion, limited now to East, North and Central Aceh. In May 1959, negotiations between the government and Aceh's revolutionary council began, with the Acehnese leaders demanding an amnesty for themselves so that they could be integrated into the administrative services, and a guarantee that Jakarta would not interfere in the local judiciary.[99] The negotiations resulted in Aceh being recognized as the 'Islamic Republic of Aceh', a 'special region' having 'extensive' autonomy in religion, education and customary law. But this ambiguous formulation fell short of Daud Beureueh's demand for a specific government recognition of Aceh's right to implement Islamic law. The government sought a final end to the rebellion, but despite defections and the ending of the PRRI movement, Daud Beureueh maintained his demand for such a statement. The government finally conceded this, in April 1962, by means of a decree from Aceh's martial law administrator, authorizing the implementation of 'elements of Islamic Law' in Aceh.

From the perspective of 1962, therefore, it appeared as if the strategy of mobilizing Acehnese communalism to put pressure on the governing élites had achieved some success. Acehnese communalism had been mobilized in support of the Indonesian revolution so long as the PUSA leaders believed that their alliance with *Masjumi* would give them access to the resources and power of the state which they needed so as to lead Aceh in an Islamic direction. The Acehnese rebellion had occurred when the linkages between the state and Aceh were broken by the weakening of the alliances between administrators and solidarity makers, between republican élites and Islamic élites, between PNI and *Masjumi*, and between Sukarno and the political parties. The result was that Daud Beureueh and the PUSA leaders in Aceh were left with no-one at the centre to act as their patron. The end of the rebellion occurred only when this vacuum was filled; when a new patrimonial linkage was temporarily created, from Nasution through Gaharu, to Hasan Saleh and the revolutionary council in Aceh.

While the linkage between Aceh and the centre was rebuilt only because of the shift from élite factionalism at the centre to the cohesion (albeit temporary) of 'guided democracy'; it was such as to generate, in turn, a return to élite factionalism within Aceh itself; with the result that the end of the rebellion did not mean the onset of effective central-regional integration.

The impact of the New Order on factionalism in Aceh

Despite their apparent success in gaining special regional status, the Acehnese *ulama* found themselves unable to make any significant progress towards their goal of an Islamic Aceh in the absence of co-operation from the centre. One consequence of this was the relative decline of the Islamic schools as secular education expanded, and this in turn contributed to the emergence, in the 1960s, of a new generation of secular-educated Acehnese whose interests were located more in the socio-economic development of the region than in its Islamic development. The neo-patrimonial New Order government sought to use *Golkar* to engineer an alliance with this secular educated élite in Aceh; but it was not successful in preventing their rivals, the *ulama*, from once again mobilizing oppositionist communalism against the centre. Moreover, not all Aceh's secular educated élites saw alliance with the pro-Javanese centre as a fruitful strategy, and some of them responded to their perceived exclusion from state patronage by trying to mobilize Acehnese support for a new political autonomy insurrection. Only with the 1987 election, which saw a shift from a strategy of coercion against the *ulama* towards one of co-optation, did *Golkar* make sufficient progress to gain a small electoral majority in Aceh.

Aceh's politics during the New Order period have thus been marked by internal disunity; and it is the élite rivalries underlying this, and the centre's manipulation of these rivalries, which must be examined if this politics is to be explained. These élite rivalries involved, as before, the tension between regionalist and religious forms of Acehnese communalism; but they entered a new phase with the emergence of a new generation of Acehnese 'technocrats'.

Factional disunity in Aceh: the ulama *versus the 'new* uleebalang' *versus the 'alienated professionals'*

The defeat of the *uleebalang*, and the *ulamas'* assertion of Islamic Acehnese communalism against the centre, had engendered a high degree of élite cohesion and communal consensus in Aceh during the rebellion. This was evident in Aceh's 1955 election results. Even though the election could not be held in the Aceh Besar, Pidie and East Aceh districts where the PUSA *ulama* retained control, 77 per cent of the voters in the remaining districts voted for the Islamic parties which the *ulama* had encouraged their followers to support,[100] with 64 per cent voting for *Masjumi*.[101] By the end of the rebellion, however, the consensus was eroding.

The rise of élite dissensus within Aceh was in part a response to the rapid changes in Aceh's social and economic circumstances since the 1960s. The major priority of the New Order régime, from the outset, was to promote politically stable economic development, and this ensured a particular concern with Aceh. By the mid-1970s Aceh had emerged as a major exporter of oil and natural gas, so that it has become one of the richest regions of Indonesia with the fastest growth rate.[102] But Aceh itself has received almost no share of the revenues accruing from its exports, which were used partly to promote development in poorer regions, and partly as contributions to general central government revenues.[103] Thus 'Clearly, at the national level the benefits [of the oil boom] have been enormous . . . But the benefits to the local community have been much smaller and the cost-benefit calculus more problematic.'[104]

These economic changes have indeed brought significant progress in Aceh's socio-economic amenities and in its interactions with the rest of Indonesia, but increasing interaction does not of itself generate a sense of integration.[105] The gap between the development of Aceh's resource revenues and the standard of living of the ordinary Acehnese people has been growing rapidly,[106] so that despite the low incidence of absolute poverty, there has developed a widepread perception of Aceh's relative regional deprivation. These rapid changes in Aceh's economic position have served to increase the salience of the 'regionalist' dimension of Acehnese communalism, which focuses on the goal of economic interests, in contrast to the vision of an Islamic Aceh which had hitherto been dominant. But this in turn has raised the dilemma of whether regional economic development can best be promoted through a strategy of alliance with the centre, or through opposition to the centre.

The PUSA *ulama* had achieved their goal of provincial autonomy and the right to implement 'elements of Islamic law'. They therefore set about, after 1962, implementing the goal of achieving an Islamic society, and they established a representative assembly which enacted, in 1968, a regional regulation to enable the implementation of Islamic law. This was followed by an attempt to promote the *madrasah* schools by integrating them with the primary schools under the control of the Ministry of

Education and Culture. In both cases, however, the Acehnese leaders failed to get the necessary approval from Jakarta. By 1969, ten years after the attainment of 'provincial autonomy', it was becoming clear that central control was in fact much more pervasive than in the past, and that no significant progress had been made towards implementing the Islamic goal.[107] Thereafter, the prospects became even worse, as the New Order régime adopted an increasingly restrictive stance towards *santri* Islam.[108]

This of itself would probably not have eroded the *ulamas'* communal influence within Aceh, since the religious élite could, as before, direct resentment against the centre. However, the failure to make progress on the Islamization programme meant that secular education in Aceh flourished, and contributed to the rise of a new social group who could seek communal influence precisely by arguing that the efforts to achieve an Islamic Aceh were not only futile, but were also directly detrimental to their alternative development-oriented vision of Acehnese communalism.

By the mid-1960s secular education was well developed in Aceh, with the Syah Kuala University being established in 1961. This, together with the access of some Acehnese to education in Jakarta and overseas, produced a new secular-educated aspiring élite. In the belief that the New Order régime would be more amenable to Acehnese interests, this new generation of Acehnese youths responded to the violent events of 1965–6 by organizing themselves into 'action fronts' directed against the enemies of the New Order: communists, then Chinese, and then Sukarno's Indonesian Nationalist Party.[109] By the early 1970s many of this generation had attained positions as army officers in Aceh, as Aceh's administrative officials, and as academics. Such wealthy and secular-educated individuals might well have been regarded by the wider Acehnese community as simply a self-interested class lacking communal influence within the Islamic-oriented society. But once the option of alliance with the centre was made available, they could aspire to positions as communal patrons.

Elsewhere in Indonesia, the central 'technocrats' sought to promote their control over the regions by relying upon either traditional deference, allying with traditional élite groups; or upon resource-patronage, using their provincial-level appointees to dispense amenity resources in return for political support. In Aceh, however, neither of these routes towards central control sufficed. First, the combined impact of colonialism and the 'social revolution' had irrevocably weakened the *uleebalang* traditional élites. Second, Aceh was regarded, increasingly, as a resource-rich province whose resources were necessary to finance government revenues at the centre, so that a net outflow of resources, rather than any net inflow to the Acehnese populace, was indicated. The central government therefore sought an alternative means of extending their control over Aceh: by co-opting Aceh's secular educated administrative élite, and promoting them as communal influentials. In terms of both their role as agents of central government, and their rivalry with the *ulama*, they constituted Aceh's 'new *uleebalang*'.[110]

Thus, instead of manning Aceh's administration with Javanese, as was the case in most other regions, the central government deliberately built a 'technocratic development linkage'[111] between the centre and Aceh, and sought out those educated Acehnese who, in their background and secular education, provided a local leadership group whom the centre could employ against Aceh's Islamic *ulama*.[112] 'What was unique about Aceh was the purposeful nurturing and emergence of a new leadership group which came to assume a far more prominent role than was the case for civilian groups in other regions.'[113]

Once this group had been co-opted by the centre, they could claim 'that their position derived from presumed expertise'[114] and designate themselves as Aceh's 'technocrats' alongside those who dominated central government. They could then attempt to persuade the Acehnese people of the validity of their regionalist development goal by arguing that the apparent paucity of central expenditure in Aceh had arisen, not from any internal-colonial exploitation by the centre arising from its Javanese bias, but rather from Aceh's social backwardness and isolation, which could be corrected by communal support for the technocrats. The central government's failure to invest in Aceh was thus blamed not so much on central government itself, as on Aceh's lack of influence at the centre and its parochial insularity, engendered by adherence to fanatical Islam.

The distinction between the two Acehnese élites competing for communal influence had thus become, by the 1970s, a particularly clear one. The co-opted technocrats articulated the goal of Acehnese regional development through a strategy of alliance with the centre, and saw *santri* Islam as the cause of the community's backwardness, while the religious leaders expressed the goal of an Islamic Aceh, defending itself against the un-Islamic centre. Each leadership group articulated a version of Acehnese communalism which had widespread potential support in various parts of Acehnese society. But there emerged also a third élite group in Aceh who offered a different diagnosis and prescription for Aceh, and who sought to appeal both to the regionalist and to the religious concerns of the community.

During the 1970s, some of Aceh's younger secular-educated men began to doubt the wisdom of the strategy of allying with *Golkar*. As the gap grew between Aceh's contribution to Indonesia's economy and Jakarta's contribution to Aceh's economy, the technocrats' argument that alliance with the centre was the way to increase Aceh's bargaining power, began to seem less convincing. The alternative possibility was to argue that the centre's Javanese bias in resource distribution implied an 'internal colonial' relationship to Aceh which would only be corrected by Aceh moving towards a political autonomy in which it could retain control over its own resource revenues. This diagnosis was reinforced by the personal interests of these younger educated Acehnese, who perceived that their prospects for promotion were blocked not only by the Javanese bias of the régime,[115] but also by those Acehnese technocrats who had been co-opted by the centre so as to achieve leadership positions in Aceh, and who had then become a closed Acehnese oligarchy enjoying exceptional privileges from which other educated and qualified men were excluded. Moreover:

> Leading [Acehnese] technocrats found it increasingly difficult to keep the political support of a succeeding generation of university educated professionals who saw the accommodation with the center to be inherently compromising in view of the restraints placed on political activities . . . . The emphasis on Aceh's marginality and development had not in fact served to bring the center and periphery closer together; rather it had laid the basis for true regionalist sentiment.[116]

Since this diagnosis of Aceh's problems put the blame on central government rather than on Acehnese society itself, it could accommodate also the grievance of the Islamic Acehnese that, during the 1970s, the government had become increasingly antagonistic to Aceh's Islamic leaders. By appealing both to religious and to regionalist grievances, the alienated professionals sought to articulate a goal of Acehnese political autonomy which could gain widespread communal support.

Competing strategies: electoral support, electoral opposition, and insurrection

The impact of central government upon the attempts by these three Acehnese élite groups to mobilize communal support during the 1970s and 1980s can be understood through an examination of the centre's election strategies in Aceh, and their treatment of the 'Free Aceh' insurrection movement.

The results of the five elections between 1971 and 1992 indicate that most Acehnese have voted on locality and district communal lines, following the lead of their community patrons. The Aceh Besar, Pidie and Aceh Utara districts, where *ulama* influence had been strongest in precolonial times and where the PUSA *ulama* were clustered, returned the highest votes for the Islamic party, the PPP; while those areas where most non-Acehnese resided, and where *uleebalang* influence had traditionally been stronger (Aceh Tengah, Tenggara and Timur), voted more for *Golkar*.

All of Aceh's leaders, including the *ulama*, were under strong pressure to support *Golkar*, since it offered the only chance of access to state resources:

> The switch to Golkar covered the range from village headman to the highest provincial officers. A threat often employed was that reluctance to go along with Golkar would result in posting to an isolated part of South Aceh. In the interests of preserving an institutional pocket for Islam, a number of religious leaders also came to terms with Golkar.[117]

Those who acceded to the pressures to support *Golkar* were rewarded with career advancement, while those who refused 'were blocked from attaining important positions or playing a policy role'.[118]

Nevertheless, in the 1971 election Aceh divided almost down

the middle, with *Golkar* getting 49.71 per cent of the vote and the Islamic parties getting 48.89 per cent; and thereafter the *Golkar* vote steadily declined (41.17 per cent in 1977 and 36.39 per cent in 1982), and the PPP vote increased (57.28 per cent in 1977 and 59.56 per cent in 1982). This steady increase in the vote for the PPP at a time when the rest of Indonesia was giving increasing support to *Golkar*, can be interpreted as a growth in support for the Islamic *ulama* in the face of the central government's dominant strategy of coercion and intimidation against them, detaining and prosecuting party leaders, and cancelling their campaign rallies. 'By the mid-1970s public forums no longer existed for proponents of Islamic law to give expression to their demands. Even sermons of the Friday mosque meetings were inhibited for fear of detention'.[119]

The government's strategies against the Islamic leaders who supported the PPP can be illustrated by its treatment of the most influential of these, Daud Beureueh. After 1962 he had returned to his village and his mosque in Pidie, but had continued to travel around Aceh giving speeches. During the 1970s however, the government increasingly restricted his activities. One form of coercion, noted by Morris, was, 'that if invited Teungku M. Daud Beureueh would be allowed to speak, but, following his departure, the army would detain members of the committee extending the invitation'.[120]

In 1971 the government sent him away 'on a world tour' during the campaign, so as to prevent him mobilizing support for the Islamic parties, and prior to the 1982 elections they again sent him away to Jakarta. In 1977, however, they attempted to employ his influence to their own advantage by engineering a meeting in Pidie between him and the Indonesian Foreign Minister, Adam Malik. But this plan backfired when the chairman of *Golkar* in Aceh banned the meeting at the last minute, so that the impression was given that *Golkar* had 'insulted Aceh's leading *ulama*'.[121]

By the mid-1980s the negative impact of the government's oppressive stance towards Acehnese Islam, together with economic discontent exacerbated by a cut-back in Aceh's development budget, had provoked a rethinking as to *Golkar*'s strategies.[122] *Golkar*'s leaders decided to give top priority in the 1987 and 1992 elections to reversing its 1982 defeat in Aceh, since they were determined to show that it could carry all

Indonesia's provinces; and they shifted from a strategy of coercion against the PPP, to one of conciliation and co-optation.

This new strategy began in 1984 with the appointment of an Islamic *ulama* who was also a senior *Golkar* official, to liaise with Aceh's Muslim leaders. In addition, several prominent Acehnese central officials were sent on visits to Aceh.[123] The crucial initiative, however, was the 1986 appointment of Ibrahim Hasan, an Acehnese from Pidie, as governor of Aceh.[124] He was careful to show respect and support for Islam, to show humility and approachability in his campaign meetings, and to promise increased development aid if the province voted for *Golkar*.[125] He sought to persuade PPP supporters that 'there were no longer any significant religious differences between the two parties, thereby making it easier for them to switch their support to Golkar in this election',[126] and he was probably crucially helped in this by the statement which Daud Beureueh made, shortly before his death in June 1987, saying that he 'does not mind' should *Golkar* win the coming elections, since it would promote Aceh's development.[127]

As King and Rasjid have argued, therefore, the 1987 Aceh election result, in which *Golkar* got 51.8 per cent of the vote and PPP got 42.8 per cent, is thus explainable not in terms of Aceh's increased socio-economic integration into Indonesia, or of a decline in the strength of its commitment to Islam, but rather in terms of Aceh's new leverage with the centre and the centre's new strategy of conciliation. This linkage with the centre was personified in Ibrahim Hasan's ability to persuade Islamic leaders that *Golkar* was now more pro-Islamic, and to persuade secular educated leaders that *Golkar* would now increase development expenditure. Accordingly, 'some local government officials as well as traditional leaders urge[d] their followers to temporarily change their party preference and support Golkar'.[128] This successful strategy was apparently maintained for the 1992 elections, when Ibrahim Hasan succeeded in further increasing the *Golkar* vote.[129]

An erosion of the distinction between regionalist concerns with development and religious concerns with Islam can also be discerned in the insurrection movements which have occurred in Aceh in the late 1970s and again in the early 1990s. These attempts by alienated Acehnese professionals to mobilize support from both *ulamas* resentful of the government's treatment of Islam and from various Acehnese groups resentful of Javanese political and economic domination, have been inhibited by the swift action of the armed forces. The army has sought to prevent the insurrection leaders from gaining communal influence by branding the insurrections as criminal non-political actions, and by implementing swift and ruthless coercion so as to inhibit any attempts at mass mobilization. While it is possible that there may be widespread sympathy for the insurrectionists, and that this may indeed have been further promoted by the ruthlessness of the military actions in Aceh, government action has probably ensured that the insurrections fail to develop into effective secession movements and so remain small guerrilla groups.

The Free Aceh Movement (GAM) was launched by a small group of Acehnese professionals in 1976 who sought support from *ulama* who had allied with the 1950s rebellion, including apparently Daud Beureueh.[130] The movement was forced underground in May 1977 when its insurrection plans were apparently prematurely disclosed to the authorities. It was led by Hasan Tiro, an Acehnese businessman previously resident in the USA, who sought to revive ideas of Acehnese autonomy through his descent from the famous war hero against Dutch colonization, Teungku Chik di Tiro;[131] but the imagery of the movement was primarily that of internal colonialism, thus Hasan Tiro's 'Redeclaration of Independence' of December 1976 asserted that:

> During the last thirty years, the people of Acheh, Sumatra, have witnessed how our fatherland has been exploited and driven into ruinous conditions by the Javanese neo-colonialists . . . Acheh, Sumatra, has been producing a revenue of over 15 billion US dollar yearly for the Javanese neo-colonialists, which they used totally for the benefit of Java and the Javanese.[132]

This insurrection seemed to have been effectively crushed by the Indonesian armed forces by 1979, but Hasan Tiro has subsequently claimed responsibility for the renewal of unrest, attributed to the 'Acehnese National Liberation Front', which has occurred since 1989 or early 1990.[133] This renewed insurrection seeks to build on various sources of discontent in Aceh, both Islamic and economic, gaining some support from criminal elements, from farmers suffering from the collapse of clove prices and from a clampdown on marijuana production, from unemployed or poor workers dislocated by the influx of non-Acehnese workers in Aceh's new industrial enclave; as well as from the professionals who had formed the core of the GAM. The government initially dismissed the unrest as a terrorist movement (GPK),[134] but has more recently admitted that it is indeed a separatist movement seeking to establish an Islamic Aceh state.[135]

These recent insurrections are clearly neither an attempt by potential Acehnese leaders to seek alliance with central government, nor an attempt to put pressure on the centre for a 'better deal'. They are indeed unique in Aceh's history, in that they are the first articulation of political opposition which asserts a secessionist rather than a regionalist goal. These insurrections do not then conform to the patterns of neo-patrimonial politics which have been examined; but they are nevertheless explainable as one of the outcomes of such politics in that they reflect an alienation on the part of those who have repeatedly failed to gain access to advantageous patrimonial alliances, and who see the patrimonial system as increasingly biased against them.

It has been the purpose of this chapter to show how Aceh's politics have been influenced by the neo-patrimonial character of the Indonesian state, in that the élite factionalism, Javanese *abangan* bias, and communal political mobilization have engendered, unintentionally, political opposition and disunity within Aceh. The impact of the factional rivalries at the centre in promoting an increasing bias in favour of Javanese *abangans* in both élite recruitment and resource allocation has been to generate discontent amongst Outer Island *santris* in general, and amongst Acehnese in particular. This discontent encompassed Aceh's growing economic contribution to Indonesia's development and also the apparent decline in its political leverage at the centre since the Indonesian revolution. Acehnese communalism has indeed manifested itself in different ways during the New Order period, as under the Old Order, but this can be coherently explained by showing how the contentions between communal patrons have been manipulated by the neo-patrimonial élites at the centre.

From the neo-patrimonial perspective then, ethnic consciousness develops and is politicized, not on the basis simply of objective cultural attributes, but rather as a response to the 'definitions of the situation' offered by competing élites seeking positions as communal patrons. Thus it is not the objective features of the social structure which of themselves threaten national integration, but rather the personalist character of the neo-patrimonial state in which élite cohesion is inherently fragile. As Gerald Heeger has noted:

> Communalism . . . is not a lingering vestige of the past, comprehensible in terms of traditional political behaviour. Rather, it is inseparable from the political process of the underdeveloped state as a whole, defined by the personalism of élite interaction and feuding as well as by the segmentation of society. Communalism is only one characteristic of a shift from élite cohesion to élite dissensus.[136]

Chapter 5

Internal colonialism and ethnic rebellion in Thailand

The internal colonial characterization of the state is one variant of the more general argument that it is economic disparities which are the root cause of political tensions.[1] The central proposition is that when the state promotes the economic development of a core region at the expense of the development of its periphery, then the peripheral regional community will develop a reactive ethno-regional consciousness which may be articulated in the form of an ethno-regional autonomy movement, directed against the state.

The problem facing such an argument, as Walker Connor has noted, is that most ethno-regional unrest has occurred in situations where clear inter-regional economic disparities have coincided with clear cultural distinctions between the regional communities, with the result that it is difficult to test whether it is the economic or the cultural cleavage which constitutes the root cause of the ethnic movement, or whether it is the accidental correlation of the two which provides the necessary conditions.[2]

Thailand has experienced unrest in each of its peripheral regions – amongst the Muslim Malays in the southern Pattani region, amongst the Northern hill tribes, and amongst the Isan people of the Northeastern region. Whereas both the Pattani Malays and the Northern hill tribes exhibit clear cultural differences from the majority Thai Buddhist community, the Northeastern Isan people do not. Their region is populated by various Thai-Lao groups whose objective cultural attributes do not differ significantly from those of the Central Thais. The communist insurgency in the Northeast, which persisted from the early 1960s to the early 1980s, was explained by several commentators as arising out of the political disaffection of the

Isan people, who sought some form of autonomy from Bangkok. Their ethno-regional consciousness was depicted, moreover, as arising out of the impoverishment of the Northeast which contrasted sharply with the economic development of Bangkok and the Central Plains.[3]

The purpose of this discussion, therefore, is to critically examine the internal colonial argument by looking at this one case of ethno-regional unrest where the regional economic disparities do not coincide with a clear cultural distinction.

INTERNAL COLONIALISM THEORY

The theory of internal colonialism involves a two-stage argument. First, it seeks to explain the causes of uneven economic development between different regional communities within a state. Second, the theory argues that such disparities are the fundamental cause of the emergence of ethnic nationalist movements amongst cultural groups located in peripheral regions.

The theory developed, as its name implies, as an analogy of international colonialism and the anti-colonial nationalist responses which that evoked. But the internal colonial argument thereby also inherited much of the ambiguity relating to the attempts to characterize colonialism and anti-colonialism. Chaloult refers to 'the concept's unsystematic theoretical basis, which has not been sufficiently structured and worked out to permit a logical and precise selection of descriptive and analytical variables'.[4]

Charges of ambiguity have been focused on three major issues. First, on the conceptualization of colonialism and specifically its relationship to the class structures arising from capitalism; second, on the characterization of ethnic groups and their status either as autonomous features of the society or as derivatives of class relations; and third, on the causal status to be accorded 'uneven development' in the explanation of ethnic nationalism. There has also been disagreement amongst economists as to whether the theory can be stated in quantitative terms so as to measure regional or class exploitation.[5]

Despite, or perhaps because of, such areas of ambiguity the concept has been applied by various writers to a wide range of situations.[6] It has clear links with Frank's formulation of metropolis–satellite relationships, and with the wider literature on dependency and underdevelopment, and it has been applied, for example, to the situation of various ethnic minorities in South Africa, the USA, Canada, Australia, Yugoslavia, Israel, France and the UK.

The attempt to apply the same conceptual argument to such diverse states, and the sheer variety of the formulations of the theory, add to the impression that 'one factor is being asked to do far too much work'.[7] But much of the criticism is based on the misguided argument that internal colonialism theory fails if it does not identify all necessary and sufficient conditions for all cases of ethnic nationalism;[8] whereas its proponents claim only that it locates the necessary conditions of one particular class of ethnic nationalism.

Recently, various commentators have defended the theory and argued that it can be formulated in ways that offer both precision and coherence.[9] There is certainly no consensus as to its meaning and implications, but it is possible to identify some core propositions. No attempt will be made here to assess those formulations of the theory which have referred to non-territorial ethnic movements and to ethnic unrest in economically dominant regions.[10] The focus will be on the situation of subordinate ethnic communities occupying peripheral underdeveloped regions within a state, and on the character of the state which perpetuates and exacerbates the economic exploitation, political oppression and cultural domination of such groups. Such an initial outline of the focal points of the theory immediately raises the problem as to the relationship between the structure of the internal colonial state, and these processes of economic exploitation, political oppression and cultural domination. If the term 'colonialism' is to have precision, it might be explained as the political institutionalization *either* of the class disparities arising from the capitalist production process, *or* of the regional disparities arising from relationships of unequal trade, *or* of the cultural (or racial) distinctions inherent in imperialism. But since the concept is employed precisely to refer to all three aspects, it can only remain coherent if it is able to specify the relationships between each of them.

Of the various attempts to refine and tighten the concept, those by Harold Wolpe and Michael Hechter are particularly significant.[11] In order to begin to resolve the ambiguities evident in some early characterizations of internal colonialism,[12] Harold

Wolpe argued that the concept of colonialism could only be given precision if it referred to the spread of capitalist modes of production, rather than, as in Frank's formulation, the spread of the capitalist market system. Colonialism can thus be stated to involve, in essence, a system of class exploitation in which the subordinate class is exploited by the extraction of surplus from the producers. As the core of the state develops economically, the capitalist mode of production employs the resources of other non-capitalist modes of production in the peripheral regions. The capitalist core seeks to sustain the non-capitalist mode of production in the periphery in that it relies on the extraction of raw material and agricultural commodities produced by such non-capitalist production. But, in varying degrees, capitalist development also has an inherent tendency to erode the very non-capitalist production sector upon which it relies. The latter sector is undermined either by the extraction of its labour supply, or by the pressure for increasing raw material output, or by the spread of capitalist investment directed towards the capitalist sector but located in the non-capitalist sector. Colonialism then becomes the means employed by the state to conserve the non-capitalist modes of production and social organization in the periphery which are crucial for the development of capitalism in the core regions, but which are being undermined by that same capitalism. In order to facilitate this, the state will express its domination, not in class exploitation terms, but rather in ethnic terms:

> It is in part the very attempt to conserve and *control* the non capitalist societies in the face of the tendency of capitalist development to disintegrate them and thereby to undermine the basis of exploitation, that accounts for political policies and ideologies which centre on cultural, ethnic, national and racial characteristics. In certain circumstances, capitalism may, within the boundaries of a single state, develop predominantly by means of its relationship to non-capitalist modes of production. When that occurs, the mode of political domination and the content of legitimating ideologies assume racial, ethnic and cultural forms.[13]

If the state depends on the cheap labour, raw material or foodstuff production of the non-capitalist sector, then it must protect the source of these by portraying that sector as a coherent society with its own social, economic and cultural system distinct from and subordinate to that of the capitalist sector. It must imbue the subordinate society with an ideology of ethnic deference. State education might involve the teaching of the culture of the core community, but the intention is not assimilationist, it is rather the culturally imperialist goal of inculcating awareness of the superiority of the core culture and the inferiority of the distinctive periphery culture. By promulgating such an ideology the state inhibits the disintegrative spread of capitalism and promotes its development in the core.

Wolpe's argument thus begins to specify the relationship between the existence of different modes of production in different regions, the form of class exploitation, and the emergence of ethnic ideologies. However, the development of ethnic nationalist movements remains difficult to explain so long as ethnic consciousness is portrayed solely as a state ideology, since a nationalist reaction to internal colonialism might, on the face of it, imply also a rejection of the ideological myths propagated by the state. We need therefore, to explain why, and in what form, ethnic consciousness develops amongst the peripheral communities. This is illuminated by Hechter's elaboration of the 'cultural division of labour'.

Hechter begins with the assumption that cultural variations exist between core and peripheral regional communities in most states.[14] Even minor cultural variations might become politically salient: 'Groups need not speak separate languages or adhere to different religions in order to be considered 'culturally distinctive'. Initially such cultural differences may merely reflect rural/urban or highland/lowland distinctions.'[15] Hechter thus notes that such cultural variations would not of themselves provide a basis for politically salient ethnic consciousness. This would develop, however, if the core regional community were to employ the machinery of the internal colonial state so as to reserve for themselves the social roles of high status, and to correspondingly restrict the social and occupational mobility of the peripheral community.

> This . . . cultural division of labour contributes to the development of distinctive ethnic identification in the two groups (core and periphery). Actors come to categorize themselves and others according to the range of roles each may be

expected to play. They are aided in this categorization by the presence of visible signs, or cultural markers, which are seen to characterize both groups.[16]

Although Hechter initially introduces the concept of the cultural division of labour as a status distinction, it becomes clear that he conceives it as involving the restriction of the occupational mobility of the peripheral community. They cluster in those subordinate occupational positions which either sustain the non-capitalist economy of the peripheral region, or which, in the form for example of migratory cheap manual labour, sustain the development of the capitalist core.

The theory of internal colonialism has frequently been attacked for simply assuming that class and cultural groupings will coincide,[17] but this is not what Hechter is arguing. He is referring not to an end-state, but to a process in which class relationships between regional communities lead to the clustering (but only the clustering) of members of the peripheral cultural group in low status and subordinate class positions. Such clustering is not sufficient to cause the convergence of class and cultural groupings, but it is sufficient to generate the *belief* on the part of members of the peripheral cultural group that they are being treated as a subordinate class. It is not the objective identity of class and cultural groups which is being asserted, merely the subjective perception of class cleavages in ethnic terms. If a rebellion occurs then, it will not be based on class consciousness; rather, 'the disadvantaged group will, in time, reactively assert its own culture as equal to or superior to that of the relatively advantaged core. This may help it conceive of itself as a separate "nation".'[18]

This conclusion, that the economic and social disparities promoted by internal colonialism will engender ethnic consciousness rather than class consciousness amongst the peripheral community, is sustained, for Hechter, by three distinct arguments. First, it is argued that the establishment of a hierarchical cultural division of labour promotes high ethnic consciousness because it is a system in which 'individuals are assigned occupations solely on ascriptive criteria':[19] ethnicity becomes politically salient in that one's life chances are seen to depend upon one's ascribed cultural attributes. Second, ethnic consciousness will be promoted among the subordinate regional community because of 'the extent to which members interact wholly within the boundaries of their own group'.[20] Since the cultural group is restricted by the internal colonial state to particular types of occupation and status positions, and occupies also a particular geographical territory, it is likely to develop what Hechter terms 'interactive group formation'.

The third argument offered by Hechter refers to the emergence of élites from the peripheral community as 'ethnic leaders' who employ ethnicity as a resource whereby they can mobilize support for ethnic nationalist political movements. Ethnic consciousness thus develops when it is articulated in the form of an ethnic nationalist ideology.[21] The emergence of an ethno-nationalist movement thus depends crucially on the availability of indigenous political élites within the peripheral community, and this is itself dependent upon the form of political control employed by the internal colonial state.

The concept of internal colonialism is often criticized on the grounds that it seeks to explain ethnic nationalist movements solely as responses to economic deprivation. But the internal colonial state is the state which institutionalizes such economic disparities by erecting systems of political control over the deprived peripheral communities, and such political control itself plays a crucial role in influencing the emergence of ethnic nationalist responses. We have already noted Wolpe's argument that the internal colonial state pursues policies intended to conserve the integrity of the pre-capitalist societies at the periphery so as to counteract the disintegrative impact of capitalist development. This would correspond to the attempts by international colonialism especially in its British variant, to employ the strategy of 'indirect rule' in various parts of Africa and Asia. This involved administrative devolution to indigenous élites so as to prop up traditional systems of government whose authority was being steadily undermined by the emergence of the new educated bourgeoisies created by capitalism and colonialism. Hechter has noted that where the state does adopt such a policy towards its peripheral regions, allowing them to retain their cultural distinctiveness and their political institutions, it thereby enhances the possibility of a strong ethno-regional movement developing, since such a situation provides the resources – the regional organizational structures, the indigenous leadership, the cultural and ideological bases – upon which an effective political movement can build.[22]

In several internal colonial states, however, the circumstances of state-formation were such as to involve the suppression of indigenous political structures in the periphery, and the subsequent imposition of administrative centralization. In such cases the likelihood of an ethno-national movement in the peripheral regions would seem to depend on the degree of effectiveness of such central control, the kind of strategies employed, and the timing of central penetration initiatives.[23] If ethno-regional unrest already exists, then central attempts to suppress indigenous political élites or to reduce political autonomy will themselves be perceived as new grievances which can further fuel ethno-national unrest, and which can foster the emergence of new radical élites to replace the regional leaders whose positions are threatened by the centre.

It should be stressed that the impetus for ethno-regional unrest is the socio-economic deprivation of the peripheral region and of its cultural community. The initial goal of the ethno-regional movement is therefore likely to be that of the more efficient and more autonomous management of its own resources. The extent to which such a movement radicalizes towards violent rebellion and outright separatism, would seem to depend both on the resources of the movement and on the nature of the state's responses to the initial demands.

It is clear therefore that ethnic nationalism is not an inevitable response to internal colonialism. Were the state to be fully effective in its attempts at regional deprivation, cultural division of labour and political domination, then the effect on regional political consciousness in the periphery would be to produce a colonial mentality of economic, cultural and political inferiority in relation to the more advanced core community. The political implication would be for a response of deferential acquiescence. The test of the theory is thus not to prove that all cases of internal colonialism engender ethnic nationalist reactions, it is rather to examine whether political unrest in an economically deprived region can indeed be explained as an ethnic nationalist response to the internal colonialism of the state.

Internal colonialism in Thailand

Thailand has been cited as the paradigmatic case of a 'neo-colonial' economy undergoing 'ersatz' industrialization.[24] Initially locked into the international economy as an exporter of raw materials, the state has functioned to promote industrial development based on foreign capital import-substitution investment, and more recently on export-oriented industrialization.

As Kevin Hewison has argued, however, the role of the Thai state has not been simply that of passive intermediary of international capital. Particularly since 1958, it has implemented credit and investment policies which have promoted the emergence of a national bourgeoisie based primarily on banking and large-scale industries.[25] The earlier development of Bangkok as the commercial import-export hub of the Thai economy has thus been extended by its development as an industrial centre, with the result that economic disparities between the urban metropolis and its rural hinterland have increased and become, by any standards, extreme. This, together with the increasing penetration of successive central governments into the peripheral rural areas, would seem to offer *prima facie* grounds for an examination of Thailand in terms of the internal colonialism argument. If the state has indeed acted as the agency of international and national capital in promoting investment in Bangkok so as to neglect or exploit the rural areas of Thailand, then it becomes at least feasible to ask if this has, in turn, promoted political disaffection amongst the hinterland communities.

The increasing disparities between the 'primate city' of

Table 5.1   Per capita income in Thailand (baht, in current prices)[26]

	1960	1970	1980	1983
Whole country	2,106	3,849	14,743	18,770
Bangkok metropolis	5,630	11,234	41,300	51,441
Central Plains	2,564	4,662	15,646	24,002
South	2,700	3,858	13,745	16,148
North	1,496	2,699	9,866	12,441
Northeast	1,082	1,822	6,012	7,146

Bangkok and its rural hinterland have resulted in the relative underdevelopment of the agricultural regions of the North, Northeast and South.[27] The widening economic disparities are evident in the data on per capita income shown in Table 5.1. Each of these three regions might thus be regarded as 'internal colonies', and examined accordingly. The focus here will be on the case of the Northeast, but a brief comment on the North might be useful both as a general comparison and as an indication of the kind of variations in economic situation and ethnic reaction which the concept seeks to relate.

The state's policy towards the North remained one of neglect rather than active political and economic intervention until the early 1950s. Since then the proclaimed government policies have been to promote the economic development and national integration of the Northern communities. In practice, however, the relative underdevelopment of the region and the political subordination of its communities have intensified. Despite the diversified economy of the North and its rich timber, mineral and agricultural resources, its contribution to the national product and the per capita income of Northerners, relative to the national average and to those in Bangkok, have continued to decline.[28] Although in aggregate terms the region is not quite as poor as the Northeast, the intra-regional rural income disparities are probably greater and hide pockets of more intense absolute poverty.[29] This has had various implications for ethnic consciousness and for politics in the region.[30] In general terms it has been argued that the subordinate positions of the Northern regional communities within the Thai state have engendered strong regional and ethnic consciousness, and a weak sense of national identity.[31]

Amongst the various Thai groups who occupy the lowland areas there has developed a Northern Thai (*Khon Muang*) ethno-regionalism which has remained of low political salience.[32] There has also developed some sense of 'Northernness' which encompasses both the lowland Thais and the various 'tribal' minorities who predominate in the highlands.[33] However, the most politically salient manifestation of the economic, cultural and political subordination of the North has been the intensification of the ethnic consciousness of the upland tribal communities, and its emergence in confrontations with the state, and to a lesser extent in inter-tribal tensions.[34]

These ethnic responses can be related to internal colonialism in that they correspond to different aspects of the cultural division of labour. While the *Khon Muang* are primarily involved in lowland wet-rice agriculture, the various hill tribes perform different roles in the highland dry-rice and opium economies. These occupational disparities imply some situations of economic rivalry between hill tribes and *Khon Muang*, and between different hill tribe communities, which generate inter-ethnic tensions. The distinctions between the various hill tribe groups are sustained not only by their clustering in specific occupations and by their cohesive communal cultures in frequently remote villages, but also by the state strategies towards them. Alongside the overall policy of inculcating admiration of Thai culture into the tribal minorities, the state has recently, since the 1960s, taken various initiatives which accept the legitimacy of the tribal communities and their cultures, and expressed a concern over disintegrative trends. This is evident in much of the work of the Tribal Research Centre, but is most dramatically expressed in the patronage activities of the Thai royalty, which Nicholas Tapp has interpreted as an attempt to restore a traditional dependency relationship between the ethnic minorities and the state. Tapp pinpoints three processes which have served to promote ethnic consciousness and discontent amongst one particular hill minority which has been involved in opium production, the White Hmong.[35]

First, the Thai government has taken various initiatives to reduce opium production. This arises partly from international pressure, but also from the security and economic problems emanating from the Golden Triangle trade and the private armies it finances, and from the government's concern to conserve or exploit the natural resources of the region. Government attempts to end opium production have involved resettlement programmes, rural development projects, and the imposition of fines, but not, apparently, the provision of viable alternatives. Government interventions have posed a fundamental threat to the Hmong traditional economy of shifting cultivation. Since they are not the only group involved in opium production, but have been singled out as the main culprits by the government, the Hmong interpret government actions as evidence of 'a fundamental ethnic hostility and antagonism towards them'.[36] This has led to various clashes, most notably the Hmong rebellion of 1967 which lingered on until 1973, and led to the bombing of Hmong villages and to an estimated 15,000 refugees.[37]

Second, the impoverishment of Northern Thai peasants has led to increasing landlessness and indebtedness, and thence to their migration into upland areas in search of new farming land. This has increased the pressure on land for the Hmong, and led to clashes between the two communities.[38]

The third factor involves efforts at acculturation into Thai society, through education, missionary activity and government propaganda, which are often disintegrative rather than assimilationist in their impact, because they have not been seen as opening up avenues for upward socio-economic mobility. As Keyes noted with reference to the Karen, those who feel the constraints of their subordinate position but who reject acculturation, have responded by ethnic rebellion or by resurgences of millenarianism.[39] Alternative responses have included fleeing into communist sanctuaries, and assertions of 'a very strong sense of autonomy'.[40]

The Hmong, as well as other hill tribe groups, have given varying degrees of support to the Communist Party of Thailand (CPT) since the mid-1960s, mainly because:

> In extreme cases of conflict or trouble with the government . . . CPT-controlled areas provided an alternative sanctuary . . . Most of the Hmong interviewed had joined the CPT to avoid economic ruin, or to escape for some reason from the Thai authorities.[41]

It is important to note, however, that support for the CPT did provide a channel through which tribal autonomy aspirations could be promoted, since at least until 1970 the CPT mobilized support in the North explicitly by promising tribal group autonomy from 'oppression by the Thai officials'.[42]

The general picture then, is that the political articulation of ethnic consciousness in the North can be explained as a response to the ways in which the state has promoted the economic, cultural and political subordination of the Northern communities. Such an argument might similarly be applied to the ethnic unrest amongst Pattani Malays in Southern Thailand, in that they also constitute an economically deprived regional community who have been subject to a hierarchical cultural division of labour and who have experienced political and cultural domination within Thailand.

The case of the Northeast is of particular interest, as has been noted, because of the lack of a culturally distinctive population. But it also offers a good test case for at least the most basic version of the internal colonial argument – that ethnic rebellion is most likely amongst the most exploited regional community – in that it is the most impoverished part of the country. Moreover, the Northeast is an interesting case because it appears almost, but not quite, to conform to the internal colonial model. It therefore offers a test as to whether the model should be regarded as misleading, or whether it can provide its own explanations of 'exceptions' without losing its coherence.

THE NORTHEASTERN REGION

The history of the Northeastern region, as a peripheral border area between Lao and Siamese kingdoms, and subject to repeated waves of migration, is reflected in its cultural composition, with 'a multiplicity of tribes and groups of different origin, language and habits'.[43] As is the case with most of Thailand, however, the linguistic and cultural variations within the region are relatively minor. Most of the groups, perhaps two-thirds of the population, belong to dialect groups within the Thai-Lao family. The main sub-group distinctions are between the Lao Wieng in the north, west and south-east of the region; the Lao Kao in the north and south-east; the Lao Pan in the centre; and the Thai Korat, of Siamese-Khmer origin. There are, in addition, several minority groups clustered near the Mekong, with co-ethnics across the river. These include Puthai, Yuai, So, Saek and Kaleung. Other groups include the Kha Brao of southern Laos origin, the Khmer and the Khmer-speaking Kui, and the hill tribe Chaobon. Many of these minority groups are in the process of being assimilated. The region also contains Chinese and Central Thais, and recent migrant groups such as Vietnamese refugees.[44]

Just as there are variations of language and culture among the different groups within the Northeast, so also are there variations between the people of this region and the Lao people across the Mekong. They are 'closely related culturally (but) variations . . . have developed due to a long period of local autonomy and the greater impact of Khmer culture upon the people of the Northeast.'[45] There is more social distance between northeasterners and the Central Thais, but the actual cultural differences are again minor; they are variations of dialect and life style which have developed amongst people with a common origin. Linguistically, the position is that:

> The main Isan [Northeastern] dialect is similar to the Lao language but there are a few differences of words and tone. It differs more from Central Thai vocabulary, pronunciation and tone, but the dialects of Isan and Central Thai are mutually intelligible.[46]

The peopling of the Northeastern region by the cross-migrations of distinct but related groups meant that politically it remained divided into competing localist principalities until well into the present century. When Central Thai control over the area began to be established from the late 18th century onwards, Bangkok apparently built upon this political localism by using the village-group principalities as the administrative units (*huamyang*), and it is likely that the indigenous élites of these principalities were progressively replaced by rulers (*Cao myang*) appointed from Bangkok.[47] Such political and administrative localism was reinforced by the economic structure of the region, which was, until recently, a predominantly subsistence farming area, with poor communications between small village communities which were to a large extent self-sufficient.

The general picture of the Northeast, then, is of a region which lacked internal cultural homogeneity in that it consisted of a variety of related dialect and cultural groups, and also lacked clear cultural distinctiveness from its neighbours. The objective cultural attributes thus offered no basis for an overarching sense of ethnic or regional communal identity, and communal consciousness remained focused at the village, kin group and locality level.

In economic terms, the Northeast is characterized by poverty and low productivity. The region contains one-third of the country's population (i.e. nearly 16 million in 1980) and about one-third of its land area, but it only produces one-eighth of the gross national product (1986). Its low agricultural output is explained in part by poor soils and erratic rainfall, but partly also by the continued out-migration of farm workers. Agricultural productivity is further reduced as less fertile deforested lands are used for crops, and as the resultant soil erosion progresses. Most crop land is still used for glutinous rice production, which is mainly for subsistence use within the region,[48] but output of non-glutinous rice for export, and of non-rice crops, is rising.[49] The Northeast used to be a major source of timber for Thailand, and in 1957 it provided 34 per cent of the country's net forestry product.[50] However, the forest cover has declined fast. In 1961 forest comprised 42 per cent of the region's land area, and by 1985 it comprised 13 per cent. This rapid deforestation is due partly to encroachment for conversion to crop land, and partly to the expansion of the timber industry resulting from the improved accessibility of the region after the 1958 opening of the 'Friendship Highway' from Bangkok.

Various different explanations have been offered as to the poverty of the Northeast. First, that it is poor for natural environmental reasons. Second, that it has been neglected by a state élite which focuses its attention on the development of Bangkok. Third, that the dynamics of capitalist development have not, as predicted by conventional economics, 'trickled down' to Bangkok's hinterland and the rural poor, but have instead had the effect of increasing the economic vulnerability of the peripheral regions. Finally, that the poverty of the Northeast occurs because it has been exploited and discriminated against by the state.

Several writers have noted that a full explanation would need to take account of all of these factors, but this is probably because they are not really distinct or alternative explanations at all, but are interrelated. Thus the dynamics of capitalist development imply a focus of investment on Bangkok and the Central Plains precisely because of the natural advantages of their location and fertility when compared with the environmentally-induced low productivity of the Northeast. The state élite seek to foster and promote the economic development of Bangkok because that is their main constituency and power base. This focus on Bangkok implies the neglect of the peripheral regions, especially the distant and unproductive Northeast. But it also implies the exploitation of the periphery in various respects: the centre's need for cheap labour from the Northeast, over-allocations to Bangkok in development and budget funding and the consequent under-allocation of the Northeast, the promotion of infra-structure development by the state which has had Bangkok as its focal point,[51] and the distribution of profits from the Northeast produce of timber, agricultural products and manufacturing mainly to Central Thais rather than to Northeasterners.

If the poverty of the Northeast is indeed connected with the development of capitalism and with the policies of the state, then it becomes necessary to examine the specific mechanisms which have promoted uneven regional development, and which have connected such economic disparities to the development of an ethno-regional consciousness.

INTERNAL COLONIALISM IN THE NORTHEAST

In order to examine the nature of internal colonialism in the Northeast it is necessary to see it in historical perspective. Prior to the late nineteenth century the peripheral regions of present-day Thailand had remained semi-autonomous of the Thai state, subject to intermittent tribute. In the 1890s, formal political control was established and between the 1890s and the 1930s the peripheral regions were subjected to increasingly effective administrative control from the centre.[52] The extent and nature of state penetration of the peripheries has progressively increased, and two major phases may be distinguished.

From the early twentieth century until the late 1950s Bangkok sought sufficient control over the peripheral communities to extract the taxation revenues and labour which were needed for the expansion of the metropolis. This involved the incorporation of the peripheral regions into the centralized administrative system and the introduction of education in the Central Thai language. Such interventions did not, however, involve any attempt to actively change the local economies and internal cultures of the peripheral communities. In the economic, political and cultural realms, the peripheral communities were treated as subordinate and inferior, so that the policies pursued by the state involved a combination of neglect and extraction.

During this period the peripheral regions were under-allocated in national budgets and in state and private invest-ment. The importance of these regions as pools for cheap labour increased when Chinese immigration was restricted after 1949. This led to increased migration from the periphery to Bangkok, and thence to increasing awareness on the part of North-easterners of their relative deprivation, the hierarchical cultural division of labour, and the incidence of discrimination. Moreover, by the 1950s various other factors were promoting change in the centre–periphery relationship. The transition to the second stage of Bangkok's industrial development required expanded investment, which implied the need for increased supplies of labour, raw materials, and foodstuffs from the peripheries. Further central intervention was also indicated by the spectre of communist insurgency, which was fostered by events in China, Laos and Vietnam.

From the late 1950s until the present, the autonomy of the peripheral communities has been increasingly eroded by state interventions and by the spread of the capitalist economy. State interventions have arisen from the concern of the state to pursue policies of 'rural development' so as to improve the infrastructure of the regions, promote agricultural diversification and productivity, and promote industrialization. In adopting such rural development policies the state has had two main concerns. First, agriculture in the periphery has hitherto been of low productivity and has been oriented largely towards subsistence. Thus, if diversification and productivity increases can be achieved, then the regions can contribute more to the urban area of Bangkok and to the national economic revenues. Second, it was widely argued by American aid donors amongst others, that the poverty and deprivation of the peripheral rural communities, found most clearly in the Northeast region, was the fundamental cause of the support which the CPT received from the early 1960s. The argument was that policies of rural development would increase living standards and would therefore reduce support for communist subversion.

It is significant that the emergence of a concern for rural development in the peripheral regions was based not so much on welfare considerations as such, but rather on the economic, political and security needs of the Bangkok-centred state. In this sense, the rural development policies which ensued 'may be described as a sort of neo-parasitism, tempered by increased centrifugal flows, but still reflecting the dominance of the center's needs in determining what aid is given to the periphery.'[53]

Moreover, the shift towards rural development policies did

not actually lead to any significant reduction in relative peripheral deprivation during the period from the late 1950s up to the early 1980s. It seems likely that in several respects the state policies actually exacerbated both economic disparities and political discontent, and so further promoted regional unrest. In order to examine this rural development form of internal colonialism in the Northeast, and thereafter to relate it to the articulation of ethno-regional consciousness, the different aspects of its impact will be outlined.

It will be argued that the political consciousness of the Northeasterners was influenced in four distinct ways by the impact of internal colonialism. First, uneven regional development led to perceptions of relative deprivation. Second, the prevalence of absolute poverty and of intra-regional economic disparities provided a basis for class-based grievances. Third, the experience of migration promoted perceptions of cultural discrimination, while the experience of state education promoted images of cultural inferiority. Fourth, the experience of increasing but inefficient central political control prompted assertions of autonomy. Each of these experiences contributed, it will be argued, towards the development of a politically salient sense of ethno-regional communal identity in the Northeast.

Uneven regional development and relative deprivation

Although the Northeast is 'naturally' a poor region when compared to Bangkok and the Central Plains, it is clear that the economic development of Thailand, which has been particularly marked in the post-war period, has been accompanied by an increase rather than a decrease of regional economic disparities. This is, to a large extent, the outcome of the rational decisions of economic managers to invest in those locations which offered higher profits. The comparative advantage of different locations is not, however, something that arises simply out of differentials in natural resources; it is crucially influenced by fiscal, investment and other policies of the state. In Thailand, the state has pursued policies which have favoured Bangkok as the focal point of development. Even when the state began announcing and implementing policies explicitly aimed at the development of the peripheral regions, these policies were either insufficient to counteract other state policies favouring Bangkok, or were indirectly of primary benefit to Bangkok and its environs.[54] The outcome of uneven regional development provided the basis for the emergence, amongst Northeasterners, of their perception of relative deprivation.

The poverty of the Northeast was perpetuated during the first half of this century by the state's policies of neglect, but the subsequent change to rural development policies has served, in some respects, to increase the region's relative economic deprivation.[55] Its contribution to the gross national product has declined steadily, falling from 19.1 per cent of GNP in 1960, to 17.8 per cent in 1966, 14.7 per cent in 1976, and 13.89 per cent in 1986. The data on income disparities produces a similar picture. In per capita terms, Northeastern incomes have declined from 51 per cent of the national average in 1960, to 38 per cent in 1983,[56] and the Northeast remains, in all measures, by far the poorest of the regions.

In some respects the Northeast did benefit from the overall development of Thailand, but the regional disparities remained significant. Thus, in 1968 the Northeast had 0.71 per cent of households with TV compared with 52.37 per cent in Bangkok. By 1983 there had been an influx of cheap Japanese TVs and 17.3 per cent of Northeastern households had one as compared to 78.5 per cent in Bangkok. The disparity had indeed decreased, but whereas in 1968 the Northeast figure was higher than those for the North and South, by 1983 the Northeast figure was easily the lowest.[57]

The government made some efforts at counteracting regional disparities from the late 1950s by trying to attract private investment to the Northeast, and by increasing its own infrastructural development there. It is important to note, however, that the increased allocations of government funds and foreign loans to the Northeast, which peaked in the mid-1970s, never came near to reflecting its weightage of 34 per cent of the population. Between 1967 and 1971 the Northeast received 20.7 per cent of total allocations in development budgets, and almost a quarter of this Northeast allocation was for security-related projects.[58] From 1972 onwards the allocations to the Northeast began to decline, and under the third development plan, 1972 to 1976, the Northeast's share of the budget fell from 28 per cent to 18 per cent . In addition, there was a reduction of foreign aid to Thailand and a withdrawal of the American presence.[59] By the end of the 1970s, according to Fuller:

> Considerably less is spent per head in the Northeast, already the poorest part of Thailand, than in any other region; expenditure per head in Bangkok is over three times higher than in the rest of the Central Region, and almost six times higher than in the Northeast.[60]

The rise in government expenditure in the Northeast between the early 1960s and the late 1970s had been primarily intended to encourage private investment in the region, and in particular to encourage the development of industry.[61] This increased industrial investment in the Northeast did not, however, lead to any significant improvement in its economic situation. Despite having nearly one-third of manufacturing firms, the Northeast only produced 5.6 per cent of value added from manufacturing in 1970, and by 1978 this fell to 3.6 per cent. In contrast, Bangkok with one quarter of manufacturing firms, provided 51.2 per cent of value added from manufacturing in 1970, rising to 54.3 per cent by 1978.[62]

The shift of government policies towards the promotion of development in the peripheral regions failed to reduce regional economic disparities since the government was in fact pursuing incompatible policies. Its commitment to a private enterprise and import substitution strategy of development implied policies which continued to favour Bangkok, and thus outweighed the commitment to rural development. Moreover, this imbalance was exacerbated by the central state's perception of peripheral region development primarily in terms of central security and development. The relative deprivation of the Northeastern region thus remained as great as it had been under the earlier 'parasite' phase of internal colonialism, but as interactions between the Northeast and the central state and economy increased, so did the Northeasterners' awareness that they constituted a regional community, defined in terms of their common experience of relative deprivation.

Absolute deprivation in the Northeast

While the primary basis for the internal colonial argument is undoubtedly that the policies of the state serve to exacerbate the relative deprivation of peripheral regions, the incidence of absolute deprivation in such regions is also relevant. Absolute poverty occurs, says the argument, not because of the persistence of 'traditional backwardness', but rather because of the penetration of state-promoted capitalism into the peripheral regions; this increases the dependence of vulnerable groups on the vagaries of the market and promotes intra-regional class disparities. Thus an overall decline in inter-regional disparities may well hide an actual increase in absolute deprivation levels amongst some sections of the regional community, who constitute, therefore, the main potential site of political unrest. The incidence of intra-regional economic disparities is also significant in the internal colonial argument in influencing the form in which political unrest manifests itself: as class consciousness or as ethnic consciousness, or as some combination of the two.

In Thailand as a whole there has been a significant reduction of poverty since the early 1960s, as the economy has maintained a growth rate of nearly 8 per cent per annum. Estimates vary, but according to one measure, the percentage below the poverty line halved between 1962/3 and 1975/6, from 52 per cent to 25 per cent.[63] All regions of Thailand have benefited from this economic growth, though in varying degrees. In the Northeastern region, the official statistics show a dramatic improvement from a 1962 figure of 75 per cent below the poverty line in the rural Northeast, to a figure of 38 per cent for 1975. However, other estimates of poverty do not coincide with the official statistics, and throw doubt on the argument that there has been a significant decline in absolute poverty there (see Table 5.2). Whatever the exact figures, it is clear that more than half of those in absolute poverty reside in the Northeast. Moreover, several reports indicate increasing disparities and thence the increasing impoverishment of some groups alongside the prosperity of others. If existing trends in prices, population, and agricultural output continue, the prospects are for a further increase in absolute poverty in the rural Northeast in the 1990s.[64]

It appears that this perpetuation of poverty in the Northeast is related to the development of new intra-regional economic disparities as the region becomes progressively integrated into (or penetrated by) the developing capitalist economy of Thailand. Urban–rural disparities in the Northeast are greater than in

Table 5.2   Estimates of percentage of the rural Northeastern population below the poverty line[65]

1962	1968	1969	1971	1975	1979	1984
		73.2a	74.7a			
				38b		
		64c		45c		
						59.6d
77e	68e			48e	67e	
					82.9f	
75g	60g			38g		

other regions,[66] and within the rural areas there are indications of increasing class disparities.[67] In a case study of villages in Buriram Province of the Northeastern region, Chou Meng Tarr pinpointed the mechanisms involved. The average size of land-holdings in the Northeast is over 5 hectares, which is larger than in other regions, and has been increasing as less fertile lands have been brought into use.[68] However, Chou found that this average concealed large and increasing disparities, with over 53.3 per cent of his sample having less than 3.2 hectares, while a small number of large landowners (6.7 per cent) had over 9.6 hectares. The disparities were even greater when yield and the proportion of cultivated land were taken into account, since the poorer peasants tended to have the least fertile land.

This disparity in size of landholding was closely related to the incidence of tenancy and landlessness.[69] Over two-thirds of peasants operated less than 2.4 hectares of land and had to rent land, buffalo or rice storage space from rich peasants; while peasants who lacked any access to rice land comprised 21.9 per cent in one village and 7.5 per cent in another. Such households sometimes had no option but to migrate for work, to rely on income from child labour, or to become dependent upon the rich peasants. The problem of indebtedness was widespread. The increasing monetization of the economy meant that even 'subsistence' households were increasingly dependent upon money for purchasing processed foods and medical goods, or for paying taxes; and over half of Chou Meng Tarr's sample claimed to be in debt, with an average debt of 8,300 baht. The poor peasants, lacking collateral, had to borrow from village moneylenders or urban merchants charging high interest rates, and such borrowing implied the further risk of loss of land.[70]

But the problems of rural poverty cannot be attributed simply to the dynamics of capitalism. The state continued to promote these changes by its conservative land ownership laws, its credit policies, its taxation system, and its rural development campaigns. Rural farmers have also been subject to extortion and other corrupt practices from officials.[71] The state's primary reliance on highly regressive indirect taxation, rather than on the more difficult to collect progressive direct taxation, serves to exacerbate existing income disparities and thus enhance the relative deprivation of the Northeast.[72] Hans Luther discussed the impact of the rural development activities organized by the Mobile Development Units (MDUs) in the 1960s and 1970s. He found that these campaigns did achieve some infrastructural developments which benefited the peasants, but the government's underlying aims were to promote security and to 'expand the volume of exports and state revenues'.[73] Aid was thus channelled to the more productive and 'loyal' farmers, while the poor farmers were bypassed and found that 'the price for fertilizer increased while income from paddy production stagnated'.[74] In the absence of any genuine land reform,[75] the overall impact was that:

a traditionally self-contained subsistence economy had been gradually eroded and turned into a fragile and market-dependent form of capitalist economy. Although this transformation may have partially increased productivity – but only to a limited extent and under optimal conditions – it has as well resulted in higher debts due to unequal 'terms of trade' between villages and cities, rising income disparities, land concentration, and impoverishment. The stated aim of the reform program was to reduce income disparities . . . [instead] the rural income gap has widened and poverty increased.[76]

The argument is, then, that the majority of rural Northeasterners continued to be in a situation of absolute deprivation during this period, and that their position probably worsened as intra-regional disparities increased. This absolute poverty of the Northeast is related to regional low productivity and to capitalist penetration, but both these factors are in turn related to the internal colonial role of the state, whereby the interests of each of the peripheral regions, but especially the Northeast, have been subordinated to the interests of Bangkok-focused development and the central state. While it is possible that the Northeastern peasants have a high cultural tolerance of poverty and inequalities within the village,[77] it is likely that they are less tolerant of 'exploitation' when it is perceived as coming either from the 'small urban based merchant with whom they establish their closest connection',[78] or from the Bangkok-focused state. Moreover, class tensions within the village communities are probably mitigated by kinship and social affinities, so that 'members of the rich peasantry may to a certain extent sympathize with, support and share common interests with poorer peasants, especially in opposition to the depredations of official strata and some urban elements.'[79]

Thus, although the intra-regional economic disparities may promote class tensions, the more likely initial response would be, as Turton notes, for grievances to be directed outwards towards the Central Thai 'official and upper classes' who have exhibited 'prejudiced and racial perceptions of the minority peoples' inclusive of Northeasterners.[80] One possible alternative to articulating such grievances might appear to be the strategy of migration. But migration might itself promote a sense of political grievance if it generates increased perceptions of such prejudice.

Migration, education and the perception of discrimination

Keyes has argued that the main factor promoting the emergence of a Northeastern ethno-regional communal consciousness, denoted by the term 'Isan', was the escalation in the migration of Northeasterners to Bangkok and the Central region, which accompanied the postwar expansion of the Thai economy and particularly the restriction on Chinese immigration after 1949:

Among those who poured into Bangkok were large numbers of northeastern peasants in quest of wage-labor in order to supplement the subsistence endeavors of their families . . . . Most of the migration of Isan villagers to Bangkok was (and is) 'temporary'. That is, migrants came to Bangkok only seasonally, between harvest and planting times, or at most spend only a few years in Bangkok before returning to settle permanently in their home villages.[81]

This stream of out-migration from the Northeast to Bangkok dramatically increased during the 1960s and 1970s. Northeast gross migration to Bangkok rose from 26,947 in 1955–60, to 66,813 in 1965–70, to 119.661 in 1975–80; and in the 1980s almost half of the recent immigrants to Bangkok came from the Northeast.[82]

On arrival in Bangkok, Northeastern migrants reported that 'the Central Plains people look down on them . . . . The Bangkok people [are] unfriendly.'[83] Keyes and others have indicated that the Northeastern migrants to Bangkok were clustered in lower class positions. 'Not only were they employed in lowly occupations, but they also discovered that Bangkok Thai thought of them as unsophisticated and uncultured provincials.'[84] The position of the Northeasterners, both as glutinous rice farmers within their region, and as pedicab drivers and servants in Bangkok, conforms closely to that indicated by Hechter's concept of the hierarchical cultural division of labour; a cultural community clustered into particular occupations and with restricted social mobility. The impact of this, as Keyes noted, was that:

> From his experiences in Bangkok the returned migrant carried home with him feelings of class and ethnic discrimination directed towards him as a Northeasterner by Central Thai inhabitants of Bangkok and an enhanced awareness of the common culture and problems which all Northeasterners share. In brief, the pattern of increasing temporary migration of northeastern villagers to Bangkok beginning in the postwar period greatly spurred the development of 'we-they' attitudes among Northeasterners.[85]

Migration did of course reflect a perception of Bangkok as a magnet; an attractive potential source of material wealth peopled by a high status Central Thai community. Resentment at exclusion from the benefits of this metropolis thus coexisted with a widespread admiration. This is significant because it implies that the political consciousness of Northeasterners would be unlikely to take an overtly separatist direction which would ensure exclusion from the potential benefits of Bangkok.

Rather, the experience of economic and cultural discrimination implied that the goal of Northeasterners would be that of gaining respect from the Central Thais as a distinct, autonomous and equal constituent community of Thailand.

In this respect, the experience of migration probably had a similar impact to that of state education. Given the low integration of the Northeast with the rest of Thailand, and its linkages with Lao across the Mekong, the central state has been concerned to employ educational and propaganda resources so as to promote the sense of loyalty and identification with the Thai state. At least since the time of King Chulalongkorn (1868–1910), Thai governments have regarded education as a major avenue to national integration. The integration of the Northeast was to be achieved by an educational curriculum which was, on the face of it, an assimilationist one; but which was designed in fact to promote a 'cultural imperialism', ensuring the deference of Thai-Lao speaking villagers to a Central Thai culture portrayed as high status. Thus the socio-economic mobility of rural Northeasterners appears to have been restricted by their low school enrolment beyond the lower primary level,[86] but also, crucially, by the fact that state education has been provided through the medium of Central Thai. While educated Northeasterners speak a version of Thai-Lao which is 'like Thai with a slight accent', the rural villagers speak a version which 'is so different as to be incomprehensible'.[87] This means that the rural Northeastern children are educated in a dialect in which they are not fluent and which is not used at home.[88]

The result is not only that they perform poorly in the examinations, but also that they come to associate Central Thai with 'government, education and the élite, it is considered to have high status and prestige'. By contrast, they come to perceive their own language as having low status, 'a hay-haw language'.[89] State education thus becomes an agency for 'linguistic deprivation' serving to restrict, rather than promote, occupational mobility, and serving to enhance perceptions of cultural distinctiveness and inferiority, rather than promoting assimilation and integration. As Keyes notes, the experience of state education

> began to make Northeasterners realize that their local culture and patterns of living were considered inferior to those of the Central Thai. Such was apparent in the attitudes of the new

government officials and in the content of the educational curriculum.[90]

The extension of political control

The internal colonial argument indicates that the economic distinction between core and peripheral regions will tend to be paralleled, and maintained, by decentralized and indirect-rule forms of administration, so as to maintain the cohesion of the peripheral community and economy. If the alternative strategy of centralized administrative control is employed however, as has been the case in Thailand, the political impact of the regional disparities will depend crucially upon whether the state has sufficient administrative capability to implement such central control effectively. If the state were to attempt such administrative interventions in an inefficient and disruptive way, then these interventions could themselves become a focus for discontent in the peripheral community, and could thereby provide a focus for the emergence of a reactive communal consciousness.

Thailand has developed as a 'bureaucratic polity' with a centralized administrative system as a result of the combined impact of the extensions of state control under King Chulalongkorn and the political prominence of the military in successive governments. The regional, provincial (*changwat*) and subordinate administrative units do not, therefore, provide arenas for the articulation of popular demands, or potential organizational bases for political autonomy. Even at the base level, the village headman is a government official whose job is primarily that of conveying government orders.[91]

In normal circumstances villagers would have few direct relationships with government officials, but once the government began rural development and counter-insurgency initiatives, the impact of government officials on village life in the Northeast became much more intrusive. From the mid-1960s onwards Northeasterners were subject to anti-communist propaganda campaigns which stressed loyalty to the King and the unity of the Thai people. Apart from any beneficial economic effects of the associated rural development programmes, the political effect was to increase the scope of central control over village affairs. The aim was to establish 'an organizational network in the countryside whose members are loyal to government and have pledged to stop subversion and infiltration by communists'.[92] Luther has argued that these attempts to extend central control and to establish a 'tightly controlled rural society' were to some degree counter-productive, in that they served to reinforce perceptions of the Thai state as an oppressive 'other', and thus promoted the alienation of the Northeastern peasantry, and thence their sympathy for communist rebels.[93] One reason for this was the corruption and inefficiency of state officials; vividly captured in the saying quoted by Luther: 'Floods, fires, drought and corrupt officials from Bangkok, these are the four evils which make life for us so difficult.'[94]

The arrival of more and more officials to combat communism in the region was unlikely to be effective in reducing an unrest which had its origins, in part, in discontent at 'excessive' central control. Even if some of these officials sought to promote genuinely democratic organizations for rural development, such initiatives came only 'from the top down' and were motivated primarily by central security concerns. Moreover, it would seem that appeals to national loyalty would have been effective as anti-communist propaganda only if the rural Northeasterners had indeed been intending secessionist rebellion. If, however, as seems more likely, they were primarily demanding a better deal within Thailand, the calls for loyalty were probably regarded as irrelevant or as irritating central interventions in local affairs.

In general then, it seems likely that although the state's expansion of central control in the form of national loyalty campaigns and other community campaigns run by central officials were intended to reduce the unrest in the Northeast, they may in fact have had a reactive impact, and have themselves become grievances which added to the discontent.

THE EMERGENCE OF ISAN CONSCIOUSNESS AND ITS POLITICAL MANIFESTATIONS

Relative deprivation, absolute deprivation, the experience of discrimination in Bangkok, 'culturally imperialist' education, and the disruptive impact of increased political control have all combined to increase the sense, amongst Northeasterners, of a specific ethno-regional identity.

Charles Keyes undertook his fieldwork in Northeastern Thailand in the early 1960s. He found that many villagers still considered local distinctions to be significant, but that above and beyond this, there had developed 'a supra-village identification';[95] a new sense of ethnic identity as 'Isan' people.

> Within recent years the term Isan, already used by people of other regions to indicate the people of the Northeast, has been taken up by a growing segment of the northeastern population to indicate their own ethnic identity. Northeasterners have begun to speak of themselves as being *khon isan* or *phu isan* ('Isan people'), as using *phasa isan* (lit. Isan language) and as living in *phak isan* ('Isan region'). The increasing usage of 'Isan' by Northeasterners bespeaks their growing sense of regional/ethnic identity.[96]

Thus the term 'Isan' has come to be adopted by the majority of the Northeasterners to refer to the common elements in their culture and language, and to 'a common cause and a common tradition which ramified throughout the region'.[97]

> These people have a specific regional identity that is neither Lao nor Thai but genuinely 'Northeastern' (*khon pakh isan*), and they say that they have other customs, eat other food (sticky rice, in Thai, *khao niuw*), wear different clothes, and speak another language compared to the people in Bangkok and the central plains of Thailand.[98]

Moreover, although some Northeasters retained an identification as 'Lao', and had kinship and other attachments across the Mekong, the main significance of the 'Lao' designation was that it served to distinguish the villagers from the Central Thai.[99] A 1967 study of village attitudes in Khonkaen Province of the Northeast makes it clear that the perception of affinity with the Lao arises from the perception of discrimination by the Central Thais; and does not imply secessionism or any desire to live in Laos rather than Thailand.[100]

The significance of this development of an ethno-regional identity designated as Isan or Lao, lies both in the fact that it is of 'very recent origin',[101] and also in the fact that it constitutes a distinctive ethnic consciousness defined in terms of distance from the 'dominating other', the Central Thais. It involves an acceptance of Thai citizenship and an identification with the

Thai state, but it comprises an assertion of ethno-regional distinctiveness within that state. The potentiality for ethno-regional political organization thus existed, since: 'One of the foundations upon which such organization might rest is, of course, cultural similarity, or the perception of a distinctive *ethnic identity* in the peripheral group.'[102]

The articulation of Isan regionalism

The initial imposition of administrative control and taxation from the central Thai (Siam) state, provoked a widespread millenarian rebellion in the Northeast during 1901–2. The rebellion involved a coalition of localist uprisings under messianic leaders, and occurred during a period of particular economic hardship and starvation.[103] It was not however until after the introduction of the constitutional monarchy in 1932 that there was any evidence of the development of an ethno-regional Isan consciousness, and any channels through which such consciousness could be articulated.

The administrative centralization of Thailand has offered few institutional channels through which indigenous élites could emerge as political spokesmen for their communities, but one partial exception to this has been the elections to the National Assembly which have been held since 1932. Elections and military coups have been interspersed in Thailand's history, but up to 1958 the military were sufficiently committed to democracy that the coup leaders changed only the governments in power, but did not abolish the constitution. Elections continued to be held, and after 1946 political parties were allowed to function, although their roles in parliament were limited by the presence of appointed members of the assembly.[104] Thus there were at least some channels through which the people of Thailand could articulate their demands. Although various observers have portrayed the Thailand peasantry as politically apathetic or deferential, it has also been widely noted that those in the Northeast have constituted something of an exception, and have had a history of supporting and electing radical and oppositionist politicians.

To some extent this reputation for political oppositionism arose because of the predisposition of successive Bangkok governments to identify the Northeast as a centre for communist activities. This image of the Northeast probably had its origin in the fact that Vietnamese communists used the Northeast as a sanctuary on various occasions from the late 1920s onwards.

Another factor promoting the image of the Northeast as 'oppositionist', was the alignment of many of the region's MPs in the 1930s with Pridi Phanomyong. The first elections were held in 1933, 1937 and 1938 (the 1933 election was indirect) and were dominated by the rivalry between Pridi, a liberal lawyer, and Phibun Songkram, a military officer. Keyes has argued that many of the Northeastern MPs aligned with Pridi because of their social background as men of 'humble origin' who had risen through access to education, and who supported the liberal parliamentarian against the army officer because:

> Their political strength did not lie with whom they knew in Bangkok, at least not initially, but with the peasantry who had elected them. To enhance their position they needed to espouse, dramatically if possible, programs and policies which would both increase their popularity in the countryside and bring them to the attention of the national leadership.[105]

Between 1933 and 1938, it was the Northeastern MPs who articulated the most vocal criticism of the government; and when Phibun Songkram emerged victorious over Pridi and maintained that dominance for most of the period until 1957, it was inevitable that the Northeastern MPs would align with 'the opposition'.[106] When Pridi led the secret Free Thai Movement against Phibun's pro-Japanese government, Northeastern MPs played a leading role; and also they played a key part in bringing about the defeat of Phibun in 1944.[107] With the return to power of Phibun after the 1947 coup, the leading supporters of Pridi, including the most vocal of the Northeastern MPs, were accused of subversive plots and arrested.

During the late 1940s and early 1950s, Northeastern MPs sought to mobilize support amongst temporary Northeastern migrants to Bangkok, who were becoming increasingly highly politicized. These MPs mobilized regional support and articulated the growing sense of regional identity by accusing the government of neglecting the Northeast and discriminating against Northeasterners. They called for increased development expenditure on the Northeast region and also criticized 'bur-

eaucratic centralization', calling for increased regional autonomy to reduce both the inefficiency and the discrimination
which seemed to accompany central control.[108] During the
1950s opposition to Phibun continued to be expressed primarily
by 'leftist' MPs from the Northeast,[109] and the government
responded by accusing the Northeastern MPs of being in
alliance with the Viet Minh.[110]

In late 1958, however, Sarit reintroduced military rule, so that
the articulation of Northeastern demands through legitimate
channels was blocked from then until the early 1970s. The 1973
student uprising resulted in a brief restoration of democracy,
and in the 1975 elections over 80 per cent of the seats won by the
Socialist United Front party and the Socialist Party of Thailand
were from the Northeast.[111]

David Wilson has interpreted such Northeastern support for
opposition politicians as indicating an 'ideological' oppositionism
in that region;[112] but this does not seem to fit with the portrayal
of Northeasterners as sharing in the 'avoidance of confrontation' culture of other Thai groups.[113] Keyes suggests that what
appears as 'oppositionism' was simply the concern of Northeasterners to return representatives who would further the regional interests of Isan.[114]

Although the Bangkok governments have repeatedly branded
Northeastern political activists as separatists advocating the
secession of the Northeast from Thailand and its unification
with Laos, there is little evidence of such a movement, and even
less of mass support for it. The main source of such allegations
has been the various contacts between Northeastern political
leaders and the leaders of the Pathet Lao and Viet Minh
communist/nationalist movements, contacts which have involved
support, for example, for the idea of a Southeast Asian Union
based on the vision of a united Indo-China.[115] There undoubtedly has been discontent amongst villagers adjacent to the right
bank of the Mekong at the fracturing of their close kinship and
economic ties across the river, and the government has made the
connection between its opposition to the regional autonomy
demands of its Northeastern critics, its awareness of the porousness of the border, and its anti-communism. These have been
conflated so as to raise the spectre of 'Communist separation-
ists'.[116] There seems to be no evidence, however, for such a link
between Thai communism and Isan separatism.

The suppression of Isan leadership

Internal colonial theory does not predict that all peripheral regional communities will experience ethnic nationalist movements – only those which possess the requisite resources for their organization. One crucial resource is the availability of indigenous élites who possess both the authority and the opportunity to mobilize mass support. If no such effective leadership were available, then ethno-regional consciousness would not manifest itself in the form of a viable nationalist movement, but might be articulated in some other way. The change in the leadership situation in Northeastern Thailand is therefore a crucial factor influencing the form in which communal discontent was manifested.

The 1947 coup against the Pridi government was legitimated by Phibun's accusations that Pridi and his supporters had been involved in subversive plots. As the possibility of arresting Pridi was thwarted by his exile abroad, the charges began to be focused more specifically on the Northeasterners. Northeastern MPs were accused of plotting a separatist movement – an accusation which was based on their involvement in Pridi's 'Southeast Asian Union' with communist-nationalist movement leaders of Laos and Vietnam – and in 1949 three of the Northeastern MPs who had been in Pridi's cabinet were killed by the police.[117] Two other Northeastern leaders were tried on charges of separatism. They were later released, but one of them, Tiang Sirikhin, another ex-cabinet member, later disappeared and was presumed killed by the police.

> The elimination of these men had lasting repercussions in the Isan region. Northeasterners had taken pride in the accomplishments of local men who had risen to cabinet level. This pride was severely injured when these men were killed. Moreover they were killed not only because they had been followers of Pridi, but, more damaging, because they had been Northeasterners . . . . In the subsequent period these four men became symbols of the growing sentiments shared by a large part of the northeastern population that they were discriminated against as a whole by the Central Thai and the central government. The death of these prominent north-

eastern leaders was a major catalyst in the development of Isan regional political identity.[118]

Such suppression of the articulation of Northeastern interests continued through the 1950s. In mid-1958, Sarit forced the resignation of the two major Isan representatives in the cabinet because of their opposition to government policies, and in October 1958, when Martial Law was declared, many left wing Northeastern MPs were accused of being communist or pro-communist and were either arrested or went into exile.

By 1958 therefore, the National Assembly was no longer available as a channel for the articulation of Northeastern interests, and the main spokesmen for the Northeast had been silenced. Moreover, between 1958 and 1963, the Northeastern problem was redefined by the government from a minor issue into a major threat to Thailand's unity and existence. This arose from the communist threats in Laos and Vietnam, and the strategic location of the Northeast on the Laotian border.

It was believed that the success of the Viet Cong and/or Pathet Lao would bring hostile and expansionist governments to power near the borders of Thailand. If some of the regional opposition in the Isan region was sympathetic to or controlled by these powers, then Thailand itself would be threatened by internal insurrection or external attack supported by a 'fifth column' in the exposed Northeast. All northeastern political dissent, since it was not permitted to be channeled within legitimate forums, was viewed by the Thai government as part of a larger Communist-led conspiracy to overthrow the pro-Western government of Thailand. Consequently, such dissent must, in the government's belief, be ferreted out and eliminated.[119]

It was this perception by government which led to the 1961 arrest and execution of former pro-government MP Khrong Chanthawon as a communist ringleader. The Northeastern MP Thongpan Suthuom was also executed. Luther asserts that both of these were leaders of a Northeastern 'Solidarity Movement'.[120] In 1961 the government also organized raids on several Northeast towns and arrested alleged communist agents.

After Sarit's death in 1963 the Thnom government continued to suppress Isan political dissent, and increased its troops in the

Northeast. By the mid-1960s therefore it was clear that: 'No provision exists for the expression of legitimate regional grievances, and desires cannot be expressed through any existing group of political representatives sanctioned by the central government.'[121]

In the absence of legitimate political channels and indigenous political élites, the articulation of ethno-regional unrest appeared to be blocked. If political discontent were to be expressed, then it would have to take a different form.

The development of the CPT in the Northeast

Between the mid-1960s and the early 1980s there was an 'insurgency' in Northeastern Thailand which gained some support from the poor peasantry of the region. But should this be understood as a manifestation of ethno-regional consciousness, or of class consciousness?

Since the late 1920s, Vietnamese communists used the Northeastern region of Thailand as a base and a sanctuary, and 'were particularly effective in finding sympathizers among the Thai Vietnamese, overseas Chinese, and Thai students' in the Northeast.[122] Similarly, the pro-communist Free Thai Movement against the Japanese in the 1940s concentrated its activities in the North and Northeast.

After the end of the war, the Thai Communist Party attempted on several occasions to cooperate with politicians and to work through parliamentary means; but when the Phibun Songkram government intensified its repression against the communists, the renamed Communist Party of Thailand (CPT) made the decision to focus its activities on building mass support in rural areas. Until the early 1960s the anti-communist activities of successive governments kept the communist groups on the defensive, and their activities were restricted to building up their organization and infrastructure. In 1961, at the CPT's third congress, held in the Northeast, the decision was made to prepare for armed rural insurgency:

> To this end, a new front organization was established- the Democratic Patriotic Front. This new organization sought territorial acquisition through protracted warfare in suitable areas of provincial Thailand. From 1961 to 1964, the

Democratic Patriotic Front concentrated its efforts in Northeastern Thailand . . . . The overall strategy of the CPT . . . was to avoid direct confrontation with government troops and provincial officers while concentrating its resources exclusively upon the formation and training of effective fighting units.[123]

The early concentration of communist activities in the Northeastern region occurred partly because of the difficulty of sustaining activities in Bangkok where government suppression was most effective; but also because the Northeast was particularly attractive with its tradition of mass-based opposition to the central governments, and its strategic location and porous boundary with Laos.

The main communist bases were established in the remote mountain areas of Nakhon Phanom and Sakon Nakhon provinces, and communist activities were concentrated there and in the Loei, Ubon Ratchathanie, Kalasin, Udon Thani and Nong Khai provinces. Initially, the active insurgents in the Northeast numbered only a few hundred. By 1967 the official estimate was about 1,000, and by the mid-1970s they numbered about 3,000.[124] From the late 1960s onwards, communist insurgents were active in the North and South, as well as in the Northeast. The estimates of insurgents vary greatly, but Ladd Thomas estimates that the peak of communist activities was reached in 1978, when: 'There were nearly fourteen thousand armed insurgents operating in fifty-two of the seventy-two provinces. There were also twelve thousand unarmed village militia and perhaps as many as seventy thousand other active supporters.'[125]

The extent of involvement of the local Northeast population in the communist rebellion is difficult to gauge. Most of the village level cadres in the Northeast were recruited from the villages, and as Luther notes:

probably the majority of the insurgents in 1967–68 were members of desperate local groups of wretched peasants who had lost all their land, joined by other peoples without income who had previously tried other channels of dissent but were persecuted or could not find any response to their socio-economic problems.[126]

It is clear 'the majority of villagers living in the so-called "sensitive areas" were not communists'[127] in that they were neither ideological Marxists nor CPT members; but clearly communist insurrection in the Northeast was sustained for so long partly because the communists were able to mobilize 'sufficient popular support in the major insurgent areas to generate sources of manpower, food, shelter, and finances (in part through local tax levies) , and to develop an effective intelligence network.'[128]

The extent of mass-based support for communist insurrection in the Northeastern region is most easily and satisfactorily explained as a response to the widespread incidence of poverty and deprivation. The evidence for this is not only the circumstantial evidence that the main communist base was in the economically most deprived region, but also in the evidence which exists as to the means by which the communist cadres mobilized their support. The reports on communist recruitment activities in the Northeast show quite clearly that recruitment and mobilization efforts focused on appeals to the class interests of the poorer peasants, with the Thai government depicted as a 'capitalist' government exploitative of the farmers.

> The Thai government cooperates with America to oppress the people. The RTG [Royal Thai Government] never pays attention to the people and never helps the poor. People are arrested for cutting down trees to build their houses and clear their land for farming. Even though taxes are collected every year, the government has never stopped trying to extort more money from us. Farmers have to sell rice for a low price because the capitalists or middlemen set the price as they please since the price has never been controlled by the government. It lets the merchants take advantage of the farmers all the time . . . . These mean that the government is fascist and not a democratic government.[129]

The deprivation of the region was not depicted as an inevitable consequence of the region's ecology, but was rather attributable 'to government neglect, disinterest and administrative failing'.[130]

What is particularly significant about this communist mobilization strategy, is that there is no evidence from the available documentation of any attempt to portray the identity of the

Northeastern villagers in ethno-regional terms, as an Isan, Northeastern, community; whereas such appeals to ethnic consciousness were central to communist mobilization activities amongst the Northern hill tribes and the Pattani Malays.[131] In other words, despite the suggestion by various observers that support for communism in the Northeast was at least partly an articulation of Isan or Lao ethno-regional identity, there is no evidence either that such ethnic consciousness played a significant part in motivating the Northeastern villagers, or that the CPT ever appealed to such identities as a means of mobilizing support.

If Keyes is correct in saying that by the early 1960s the Northeasterners had developed a sense of Isan ethno-regional consciousness, then why did the CPT not make use of this by specifically proclaiming the goals of ethnic and regional autonomy for the Isan people and the Northeastern Region, as they did in the case of the Northern hill tribes and the Southern Malays?

Two main factors seem to have been involved in the CPT decision to rely on class identities rather than on ethno-regional identities in the Northeast. The first factor was that of the rivalry between the CPT leadership and the Pathet Lao and Vietnamese Communist Parties. It has been argued, for example by Robert Zimmerman, that:

> The predominantly Lao population in all of the Mekong River border provinces adjoining Laos provides a base for irredentism and hence a potential cause which the Communists can exploit with the objective of detaching the Lao portions of the Northeast from Thai rule.[132]

The evidence for this does not come from the CPT however, but rather from Vietnamese and Pathet Lao sources. In 1975 the Bangkok Post published a stolen North Vietnamese document which:

> revealed the general strategy of Hanoi towards Thailand. Part of this strategy is aimed at increasing the level of conflict in Northeast Thailand in order to establish a liberated area 50–100 kilometres deep along the Mekong River, particularly in the vicinity of Vientiane, which can become a protectorate of both the unified Vietnamese nation and Laos.[133]

Similarly, stories of Laotian attempts to 'liberate' Thailand's Northeast in 1977 by forming a new Indochinese Federation, came from a former Pathet Lao defector.[134]

The idea of Laotian irredentism is one which has been actively promoted by both the Vietnamese and Laotian Communist parties; but it is not one which the CPT has ever espoused. Indeed, as Stuart-Fox has noted, the issue of Laotian irredentism has been one of the causes of tension and estrangement between the Thai communists and their neighbours.

> If such is the Vietnamese-Lao intention, then it is certain to be strenuously opposed by the CPT as potential inheritors of the present Thai state, and must count as of considerable importance in affecting relations between the Thai and Lao communist parties.[135]

The concern of the CPT to distance themselves from this Laotian irredentist position has meant that they avoided any specific support for Isan regional autonomy, despite their awareness of the attractiveness of such a stance amongst the populace. Stuart-Fox noted that the distinction between separatism and autonomy is one which has managed to escape the Bangkok government.[136] It is also one which the Isan peasantry are likely to be unclear on, since they probably had an ideal in which autonomy and Lao irredentism blur in a vision of a trans-Mekong Lao community which has autonomy and equality within a reformed Thailand.[137] The CPT thus not only failed to mobilize support by building on Isan regionalism, it in fact actively campaigned against it, seeing it as a manifestation of a dangerous pan-Lao consciousness: 'The CPT is apparently wary of the effect Lao nationalism may have in the Isan region. Cadres are quick to correct any dangerous tendencies towards pan-Laoism instilled into Isan trainees by their PL instructors.'[138] These tensions increased after the Pathet Lao takeover in Laos in 1975, and by 1978 it was evident that there was growing estrangement between the CPT and the Vietnamese and Laotian Communist parties; tensions which were caused, in part, by this issue of Lao irredentism.[139]

The second factor inhibiting any CPT exploitation of the Isan autonomy issue, has been the Central Thai composition of the party leadership. Although a few Northeasterners did attain senior positions in the CPT, the bulk of the leadership were of

Sino-Thai or Central Thai origin. This directly influenced their perception of the nature and goals of the Northeastern peasantry who supported them. The Isan claim to ethnic distinctiveness was based on the argument that they were a sub-group of the Thai family who had been treated by the Central Thais as inferior, second-class Thais. For the Central Thai leaders of the CPT therefore, the solution to this lay in the recognition of the Northeasterners as fully equal and integrated Thais. Whereas they could accept that Malays, Hmong or Karens who had suffered discrimination could seek to rectify this by stressing their distinctiveness from the Thais and by asserting their right to parity of ethnic status and autonomy, the CPT leaders could accept no such notion of 'separate but equal' ethnic identity with regard to the Northeastern Thais. While non-Thai communities could claim legitimate distinctiveness, the cultural variations within the Thai community were not so regarded. For the CPT leadership therefore, the Isan assertions of ethnic distinctiveness offered no basis for their political mobilization.

How are we to relate the CPT's mobilization strategies, focusing on class deprivation rather than on ethno-regional distinctiveness, to the facts of its support base in the Northeast? The Northeast was undoubtedly the major base for the CPT. By 1979: 'The north-east, with 4,800 CT (Communist Terrorists), remained the best organised CPT region with a Regional committee, and five subordinate committees, controlling some 450 villages.'[140]

However, as several observers have noted, most villages in the Northeast remained outside communist control or influence, and by the mid-1970s it was clear that they were failing to generate or maintain sufficient active mass support.[141] This was no doubt partly because of the effectiveness of the government's suppression activities, partly because of intensified government development activities in the region, and partly the result of various organizational limitations of the CPT. Some writers have argued, moreover, that communism failed in Thailand because of the particular cultural attributes shared by all Thais. Thailand is portrayed as being resistant to communism either because it has a deeply entrenched free-enterprise and materialistic culture,[142] or because it has the opposite – an other-worldly fatalism.[143]

But there might be one more specific reason for the decline in support for communism in the Northeast in the later 1970s. It appears that after the student revolt of 1973 there was an influx of Central Thai students and intellectuals into the ranks of CPT cadres in the Northeast.[144] By 1977 this meant that not only the leadership positions but now also village-level cadre positions were manned by recently arrived Central Thai youths who did not recognize the legitimacy of Isan identity or aspirations. Thus the Northeastern villagers found it increasingly difficult to see the CPT rebellion as a vehicle for their regionalist goals. The failure of the CPT to provide a vehicle through which Isan ethnic consciousness could be articulated thus emerges as a possible explanation for the limited support given to the communist insurgency. Since the main mobilization strategy of the CPT focused on the economic grievances of the poor peasants, thus articulating class consciousness rather than ethno-regional solidarity, it remained an 'instrumental' or pragmatic form of mobilization which could go into reverse gear if the peasants felt that co-operation with government offered more rewards than co-operation with the CPT. This is implied in John Girling's argument:

> Only a small minority of the villagers in the Northeast have taken to the hills. For the Thais are practical people. Better living conditions are what they want and they do not care how they get them . . . . Disillusionment with the communists' ability to produce quick results breeds disaffection . . . . The great majority of Northeasterners, far from seeking the armed overthrow of the Government, as claimed by communist propaganda, instead want the Government to do more for them.[145]

There is no doubt that the Northeast was vulnerable to communist insurgency because that region had been subjected to various governmental policies of internal colonialism. It seems clear, moreover, that it was the experience of such internal colonialism which generated a new Isan ethno-regional identity; an identity which manifested itself in the form of widespread electoral support for regional political activists demanding regional development and administrative autonomy. But it does not follow that the Northeastern support for communist insurgency should itself be regarded as a manifestation of Isan consciousness. Indeed, it was precisely because the Isan people had been deprived of the indigenous leadership and the organizational structures through which Isan demands could be articulated, that they 'resorted' to support for communist rebellion. Thereafter, the CPT's decision to rely on class rather than ethno-regional consciousness in its mobilization activities probably played a significant part in ensuring that the insurgency in the Northeast remained limited in its mass support base.

The post-communist Northeast

Just as the communist insurrection in the Northeast developed in the early 1960s as a reaction to the economic policies of the state; so has the modification of those policies during the 1980s in turn helped to change the level and form of that political unrest. The ironic impact has been that the most anti-military and pro-communist region has become, since the mid-1980s, the most pro-military of all Thailand's regions.

The recognition that economic deprivation was a root cause of the communist insurrection, and that the CPT could not be defeated solely by military means, led in the early 1980s, to a willingness, on the part of central government, to consider modifying its rural development strategy in the Northeast. This involved a shift towards a more 'bottom-up' approach with greater private sector and NGO participation, which stressed local community action, and which was focused specifically on the most poverty-stricken and politically alienated sections of the community. While this shift of strategy did not tackle the fundamentals of regional economic disparity in Thailand, it did serve apparently to raise the self-confidence of the poor and to reduce the salience of resentment against the state in some specific localities of the Northeast.[146] But there was also a second change in the 1980s which has had the opposite effect, raising the level of political discontent in particular localities. Thailand's economic boom since 1986 has probably exacerbated the unevenness of its development and has had a disastrous impact on those at the vulnerable margins.[147] In particular, various extractive industries, most notably timber and salt, have had a progressive effect on environmental degradation leading to new crises of land alienation and rural impoverishment.

The combined impact of these changes has been twofold. Firstly, there has been a shift towards smaller scale and more localized forms of political resistance. Economic interests have been articulated in part through village level Buddhist and indigenous cult channels;[148] and in part through an upsurge in various kinds of agitation, defiance and criminality.[149] Secondly, the re-opening of democratic electoral politics in 1980–82 brought new options for the articulation of discontent. In the absence of regionalist leaders and organization, this discontent was manifested in the form of electoral corruption, with impoverished Northeasterners willing to sell their support to the vote canvassers (*hua khanen*) of the wealthy military-backed political parties anxious for the populous Northeastern vote in return for cash, and the promise of a 'better deal' for the region. The Northeast has thus became 'Thailand's biggest election battleground', and 'The combination of poverty and a large voting base has for years made the Northeast a prime target of any party rich enough to buy itself into power.'[150]

The outcome was that in the September 1992 election, when the rest of Thailand gave majority support to the 'angel' anti-military parties, it was the Northeast which provided the main support base for the 'devil' pro-military parties.

The decline of communist insurrection in the Northeast occurred then, partly because of peasant disillusion with the CPT's ability to offer tangible benefits, and partly because of the emergence of more uneven and localized economic issues. The failure of the 'rebellion route' towards a better deal for the Northeastern regional community has given way to new options: anomic unrest and vote selling.

CONCLUSIONS

The case of Northeast Thailand conforms to the Internal Colonial model in several respects. First, it appears that the region has remained relatively deprived as a result of a combination of policies relating to trade, labour, credit, investment and taxation, which have resulted in net outflows of resources. The regional disparities have led to low socio-economic status and low mobility for the regional community, so that a hierarchical cultural division of labour has developed. This deprivation of the regional community can be explained in terms of the role of the state in promoting the capitalist development of the core region, focused on Bangkok. Second, the deprivation of the

regional community has resulted in an ethno-regional consciousness. This Isan identity does not rest on any strong cultural homogeneity and distinctiveness, but rather arises
reactively, out of the perception of the state as an agency of
Central Thai economic domination. Third, this Isan consciousness was articulated through demands for regional development
and autonomy so long as the necessary resources for this were
available. The key resources involved access to elections, political
parties and parliament, the emergence of indigenous élites willing to articulate the regionalist demands, and the ability to
employ Isan ethno-regional identity for the mobilization of
support.

How are we to evaluate, though, the fact that the Northeastern support for communist rebellion from the mid-1960s
onwards was not an expression of Isan ethno-regional consciousness, but was rather a manifestation of class consciousness
on the part of the poor peasantry concentrated in the region?

At first glance, this appears to contradict the major proposition of the model that the political reaction to internal colonialism would take an ethnic rather than a class form; but the
proponents of the model have tried to incorporate clauses which
would account for apparent 'exceptions'. These elaborations of
the basic model, which have attracted the accusations of ambiguity and looseness, were intended precisely to 'tighten' the
concept by specifying necessary conditions.

The literature on internal colonialism appears to offer three
explanations as to why an ethnic consciousness reaction might
give way to a class consciousness reaction. First, as Wolpe pointed
out, it is intrinsic to the process of the development of capitalism
in the core region that capitalist features also expand into, and
progressively erode, the non-capitalist economy of the peripheral
region. One likely corollary of this is the increase of economic
disparities within the region as the capitalist demands for surplus
extraction intensify. Although not phrased in class terms, Frank's
model of metropolis–satellite relations also indicates a similar
process of increasing economic disparities within the underdeveloped satellite region. The metropolis–satellite disparities are
repeated within the peripheral region in 'a whole chain of
constellations', and the disparities increase as incorporation into
the world capitalist system intensifies.[151]

When such increasing economic disparities occur within the

peripheral region between urban and rural areas, and within the rural community between landowners, commercial farmers, traders and money lenders, as well as amongst the impoverished peasantry, they necessarily reduce the extent of the occupational clustering among the regional community, which Hechter refers to as the cultural division of labour. If it is indeed this cultural division of labour which promotes the emergence of ethnic consciousness in preference to class consciousness amongst the deprived regional community, then the dilution of the cultural division of labour would in turn open the way for dilution of ethnic consciousness in favour of the emergence of class consciousness. In the case of Northeastern Thailand, it would thus make sense to argue that while the early 'parasitic' phase of internal colonialism promoted a hierarchical cultural division of labour which led to the emergence of an Isan ethno-regional identity, the later 'regional development' phase of internal colonialism served to promote new economic disparities which fostered the perception of class cleavages, within the rural Northeast, upon which communist mobilization could build.

The second way of explaining the shift from ethnic to class consciousness in the Northeast, is to focus on the nature of the cultural distinctions between the Isan and the Central Thais. It is central to Hechter's initial argument that ethnic consciousness in the peripheral region is not a product of cultural distinctiveness, but rather a response to the common experience of exploitation by the core regional community. Hechter explicitly indicates that even minor cultural variations will be sufficient to act as symbols around which an ethnic consciousness can develop.[152] This argument does not sit easily with Hechter's later formulations of the internal colonialism model, where he explains that a strong ethno-regional movement cannot emerge and mobilize mass support unless it can build upon a strong and distinctive culture. Indeed he asserts that 'the most important determinant of the intensity of the ethno-regional movement is the existence of the culture on which the ethnoregion is based'.[153] The clear implication is that only a 'strong' cultural distinctiveness can generate a 'strong' ethnic consciousness upon which a political organization can build its ideology.

But the contradiction is more apparent than real, since Hechter shifts towards arguing the importance of cultural distinctiveness primarily in order to explain that ethno-regionalism is most likely in those cases where the state tolerates cultural diversity and thereby promotes the autonomy and organizational infrastructure which a political movement needs. This connects with Wolpe's argument that internal colonialism involves the articulation of an ideology which stresses cultural distinctiveness precisely to legitimate its political domination intended to conserve the pre-capitalist society in the periphery.

The implication of this for the Northeastern Thailand case is that the Isan ethno-regional movement failed to survive the state oppression of the 1950s and 1960s, not because of any weakness in ethno-regional consciousness arising from the lack of a culture which was clearly distinctive, but rather because of the relationship of Isan identity to the ideological character of the state. Although the Central Thais recognized the Isan as a distinct community characterized by regional location, inferior status and a 'bush' dialect and culture, they saw Isan as referring intrinsically to a low-status sub-group of the Thai people rather than to a non-Thai category. Moreover, even though the Isan self-perception rose in a specific attempt to assert a distinction from the Central Thai, it remained of little use as a mobilizing ideology, since Northeasterners were inhibited from adopting an overtly Lao-oriented identity which would more clearly distinguish them from the Thai by their own perceptions of the need to distance themselves from those across the Mekong. While the state could portray the Northern hill-tribes as *both* low status and distinctive in their non-Thai-ness, and could thus promote their sense of autonomy in ways which might provide resources for an ethnic nationalist reaction, it could only portray the Isan as low status. Thus, while Isan-ness might provide a strong basis for ethnic consciousness, it was less effective in providing an ideological justification for political autonomy which could be useful as a means of putting pressure on the state.

There is, finally, a third argument provided by internal colonialism as to why ethno-regionalism gave way to a 'class' support for communism. The key factor influencing a shift from deferential 'colonial mentality' in the peripheral region towards a reactive assertion of ethnic nationalism is, according to Hechter and others, the availability of suitable organizational resources. If the state employs an ideology of ethnic distinctiveness and promotes administrative decentralization, then the ethno-regional movement can build on the existence of indigenous élites, regional cultural associations and political organizations. By the late 1960s the state had in fact removed most of the resources upon which an Isan movement could build, by removing the indigenous élites and the parliamentary channels upon which they relied, and by pursuing policies of progressive centralization. At the same time, however, the discontented peasantry of the region were faced with the new infrastructural resources which were provided by the communists. Leaders, organizational structures, and ideologies, were all provided as new channels through which political discontent could express itself. There is here a sense in which it is the nature of the organizational options which determine the nature of group consciousness: so long as the élites and organizations necessary for an ethnic movement existed, then ethnic consciousness developed and became politically salient in the Northeast. When those options closed, however, so that it was only the communist leadership and organizations which were available, then class consciousness developed and became politically salient. Such an assertion indicates that we should perhaps understand the experience of internal colonialism as one which in this case offered several potential forms of communal consciousness additional to existent localist identities: deferential low-status Thai identity, reactive Isan identity, and class identity. The implication is that the political response to internal colonialism is a variable one: whether or not relative deprivation produces political discontent, and what form that discontent takes, depends upon the type of resource options which are available. As Rudolph and Thompson have recently commented: 'What has been neglected in the literature is a full consideration of what makes people think political action is a possible avenue for resolving their problems.'[154]

The significance of the internal colonialism model is, therefore, that it focuses attention on the character of the state as the crucial factor in explaining ethno-regionalism. But the state is crucial in two respects: first as the agency for the promotion of uneven development and thence of the perceptions of relative deprivation which in turn generate a reactive ethno-regional consciousness, and second as the institutional structure which influences the political resource options available for ethno-regional political movements. In the case of Northeastern

Thailand, the peripheral regional community has suffered progressive economic, political and cultural subordination, which has provoked political unrest. But the very tendency towards the centralization of power that provoked this political unrest, has also deprived the peripheral communities of the kind of leadership, organizational and ideological resources necessary for the building of effective ethnic nationalist movements.[155]

The implication is that if the internal colonial model is to be coherent, it must recognize explicitly two distinct scenarios. Where the internal colonial economic relationship between core and periphery regions is sustained by a cultural strategy promoting ethnic ideologies and by an administrative strategy promoting regional 'indirect rule', then ethno-regional consciousness is likely to be manifested in a coherent ethno-national autonomy movement. However, in those cases where the core-periphery regional economic relationship is not so sustained, then the dynamics of capitalist penetration of the periphery act to promote the disintegration of social and political cohesion in peripheral communities. This would generate, not a coherent ethnic nationalist autonomy movement, but rather the politics of non-communal political unrest, manifested through whatever class, religious, criminal, migratory or insurgency opportunities present themselves.

The internal colonial characterization of the state thus indicates the need to distinguish between different functions of ethnic consciousness. While even a minor cultural variation may provide a symbolic marker around which ethnic consciousness can develop, the absence of historical myths of distinctive origin and destiny may prove decisive in inhibiting the emergence of an effective ethnic nationalist movement. Such legitimatory myths can of course be created by leaders able to generate and articulate them, but this will not happen if, as in the Isan case, there are no such indigenous élites available.

Chapter 6

Class, state and ethnic politics in Peninsular Malaysia

It has been noted that one of the ambiguities in the internal colonial explanation of ethnic nationalism concerns the relative roles of cultural distinctions and economic disparities in the formation of ethnic consciousness. To what extent is ethnicity a reactive response to economic inequalities and to what extent is it an autonomous expression of the cultural map? This issue is pursued more systematically in the debates as to the nature and manifestations of class consciousness. If ethnicity were to be portrayed as a derivative manifestation of class, then what kind of characterization of ethnic politics, and of the role of the state, would be implied?

The purpose of this chapter is therefore to see how a characterization of the state in terms of its relationship to the class structure might generate an explanation of ethnic politics. The discussion is conducted through an examination of ethnic politics in Malaysia, since Malaysian politics has attracted a significant literature influenced by the class perspective that offers, at least potentially, an alternative to the mainstream primordialist portrayal which takes for granted the political salience of Malaysia's racial and cultural pluralism. Whereas most class explanations of Malaysian ethnic politics have focused on the manipulation of ethnicity by the dominant class, the purpose here is rather to show how ethnicity offers an ideological channel which is employed for antithetical purposes by various contending class and class-fraction groups. While it is the class character of the state which explains the development of the ethnic ideologies in Malaysia, the resultant politics is such that the state increasingly functions, not just as the manipulator of ethnic ideologies, but also as the arena in which the contending ethnic ideologies must be problematically balanced.

Each of the main racial groups in Malaysia – the Malays, Chinese and Indian Tamils – is dispersed throughout the class hierarchy; and for social and political purposes Malaysians have an overwhelming tendency to cluster with co-ethnics from different class groups rather than affiliating on a class basis across communal lines. In such circumstances, where the patent strength of ethnic affiliations contrasts with the obvious weakness of class ties, it might be argued that an analytical perspective asserting the primacy of class and the derivative nature of ethnicity would be both inappropriate and misleading. The more straightforward approach is undoubtedly to argue simply that racial communities necessarily possess a group loyalty and affiliation which is intrinsically stronger than that generated by the socio-economic affiliations of class.

There are, however, other ways of formulating the relationship between class and ethnicity. One possibility is to see racial and cultural categories as constituting a set of 'vertical' pillars of society, which are likely to be cross-cut, to varying degrees, by the 'horizontal' distinctions between the different socio-economic strata relating to income, status and occupation. If racial attributes necessarily generate ethnic attachments, and if economic attributes necessarily generate class attachments, then the individuals in such a society will be faced with competing affiliations, either ethnic or class. Such an approach has frequently been adopted, but it does make systematic analysis difficult, there being no *a priori* way of knowing which affiliation will predominate, since this depends on the situational options available to the actors at any particular time.[1]

The more theoretically tight argument which will be developed and explored here, and the one which merits designation as a distinctively class approach, is that in which the ethnic affiliation to racial-cultural community is explained as arising out of the structure of the economy, and specifically as a manifestation of class relationships. At its simplest, the ethnic affiliation is seen as the specific form, the clothing, in which class interests manifest themselves under particular conditions of economic inequality in culturally plural societies. In other formulations, ethnic consciousness constitutes a distorted ideological manifestation of class consciousness which, in that it involves an inaccurate comprehension of the real economic structure of the society, has sometimes been designated as a 'false consciousness' ideology. In these perspectives, therefore, ethnic affiliations are explained as manifestations of the class structure rather than as autonomous bonds arising from the cultural or racial structure.

Perhaps the most frequent criticism of class analysis is that it too often becomes complex, thereby mystifying where it claims to illuminate. The potential for confusion is particularly high in the discussion of dependent and underdeveloped societies where classes are depicted as weak and fractured; with the complexity of the incipient class structure frequently begetting a corresponding obscurity in class analysis. Much of the class literature on Malaysia does exhibit this problem, but the intention here is not to summarize or review that literature; rather to build on it so as to offer a coherent class explanation of three crucial aspects of ethnic politics in Malaysia: the formation of ethnic political parties in the late 1940s and early 1950s, the outbreak of ethnic rioting in the late 1960s, and the trend towards an Islamic resurgence which was evident during the 1970s and 1980s.

The attractions of class analysis are as apparent as are its potential problems. It is clear to Marxists and non-Marxists alike that economic disparities and occupational rivalries frequently play an important causal role in ethnic tensions. It is clear, moreover, that the state constitutes a central actor in the politics arising from economic disparities in that it influences the economic structure of society, it constitutes the arena within which the resultant economic tensions are played out, it comprises the main object and prize of these contentions, and it offers crucial resources to promote the interests of whichever socio-economic groups might 'capture' the state. Thus a characterization of the state which specifies the relationships between the class structure and the state institutions offers a potentially powerful insight into the ways in which economic tensions might generate ethnic rivalries.

The term 'class' refers to the economic relationships which arise out the production process, and thence to the crucial distinction, in capitalism, between the dominated class of producers who provide labour, and the dominating class of capitalists who expropriate the resultant surplus value generated by that labour. The two major problematical ambiguities of the concept relate to the notions of class consciousness and of class fraction. Since the interests of contending classes are deemed to be antithetical, it might be expected that the economic groupings designated as classes would 'normally' organize politically as classes and would develop explicit and overt class consciousness. This is by no means inevitable, however, and indeed is a development which is likely to occur only in specific and dramatic conflict situations: the 'crises of capitalism'. For most periods, 'objective' class groups might exhibit only a low level of class awareness, so that class interests might be expressed through a variety of ideological forms other than that of class consciousness.

Such an outcome is particularly likely where there exist significant distinctions, relating to occupational categories and working conditions, within a class strata. In such a situation, class unity is compromised by the divergent interests of competing class fractions. It is thus clear that politics and consciousness may reflect in part the contention between classes, and in part also the intra-class contention between class fractions.

Though these points might appear to fatally compromise any claims to a scientifically testable class theory, they do open the door to a potentially illuminating discussion of ethnicity. Specifically, racial and cultural structures may function as one type of situational factor influencing the relative significance of inter-class relations and intra-class (fractional) relations; and ethnicity may also function as one of the ideological manifestations of class interests which are employed by contending classes and class fractions. The particular form of the relationship between ethnic consciousness and class structures depends, however, upon the character of the state.

The core Marxist proposition concerning the state is that, in capitalism, the dominant economic class is able to influence and potentially to gain control of the state so that it functions as 'a committee for managing the common affairs of the whole bourgeoisie'.[2] This proposition sits rather uneasily alongside the other Marxist perspective, which recognizes that the state has 'relative autonomy' from society and from the dominant class in that it constitutes an administrative entity with interests and purposes of its own, particularly those of mediating between the competing classes and fractions so as to promote capitalist economic development.[3] While the first perspective indicates that the state will promote class contention by acting to promote the exploitation of the subordinate classes, the second view implies that the state will ameliorate such contention, maintaining the stability of capitalist development by eliciting the consent of the dominated classes.

The tension between these two perspectives emerges in the literature on the nature of the state in non-industrialized societies at the periphery of the world capitalist system. Such a state is 'fundamentally Janus-faced' in that it must act to promote the international division of labour most conducive to the development of world capitalism, while at the same time reflecting the balance of class forces within the peripheral society.[4] It has been argued that the class structure in such peripheral societies frequently has a 'Bonapartist' character in that no one class is sufficiently developed and cohesive to exercise effective control over the state, so that the state has the independence to mediate between the class fractions amongst the bourgeoisie. In Poulantzas's terms, the state, even in industrialized societies, acts as the 'condensation of the balance of forces within the power bloc'.[5] If the 'balance of forces' within the bourgeois power bloc is uneven, then the state will act primarily in the interests of the more dominant class fraction. The state both expresses the contradictory relations between the different fractions within the power bloc; and also acts as a factor for the cohesion of the power bloc.

In the discussions concerning the 'overdeveloped' state in post-colonial societies, Alavi, Saul and others have argued that the absence of a strong indigenous capitalist bourgeoisie means that it is the ownership and control of the 'overdeveloped' state machinery which provides the means towards the accumulation of capital. The state bureaucracy thus emerges as the dominant fraction of the bourgeoisie, and has sufficient autonomy to promote 'bureaucratically directed economic activity in the name of promoting economic development'.[6] The state bureaucrats employ their control of the state and thence of society in order to promote their own interests and development, so that they cease to be merely one fraction within the bourgeoisie, but emerge rather as a newly formed dominant class, the bureaucratic bourgeoisie.[7]

This stress on the state as the instrument of the bureaucratic bourgeoisie is challenged by the argument that the peripheral state, since it functions in the interests of international capitalism, must seek both to promote the penetration of the capitalist mode of production, and also to lock pre-capitalist production into the world market system.[8] In order to maintain both capitalist and pre-capitalist elements, which are in tension with each other, the state must mediate the interests of the various classes and fractions. The state bureaucrats must employ the state machinery, therefore, in ways which are responsive to these various class groups, rather than simply in ways which promote their own interests.[9]

The picture that emerges is of the state bureaucrats attempting a 'balancing act'; employing the state machinery so as to promote their own interests and their emergence as the dominant class, but also willing to compromise their own interests in order to promote international capital, and to mediate between the other bourgeois class fractions and also between the other dominant and subordinate classes. It is not suggested here that such a 'balancing act' is unproblematical. Indeed it is the dynamics inherent in the politics of this venture, which provide the major explanatory focus for the analysis of political change.

The pattern of political development which perhaps most clearly illustrates these dynamics, and that which will be examined for its ethnic implications in the Malaysian case, may be summarized as follows.[10] During the colonial period, the state was characterized as the agency of British capitalist interests, mainly those in plantation and mining, so that state expenditure was focused on the infrastructural developments necessary to promote primary product exports.[11] During the next period, from Independence up to 1969, the state acted to mediate between competing classes and between the class fractions amongst the bourgeoisie, and this was reflected in the institutionalization of a governing alliance between the various bourgeois class fractions. After 1969, the bureaucratic bourgeoisie gained predominant control of the state machinery and used this to attain progressive dominance within the governing alliance, and to acquire access to commercial and industrial capital. As the state became more clearly the agency of the bureaucratic bourgeoisie, the stability of the alliance was threatened both by fractional rivalries as the other bourgeois class fractions were marginalized, and by class tensions as state-based industrial development exacerbated disparities between the bourgeoisie as a whole and the subordinate classes. The bureaucratic bourgeoisie then sought to employ the machinery of the state so as to contain and mediate the resultant tensions. They did this partly by granting political concessions, but primarily through the manipulation of ideology. One such available ideological theme, and that which predominated, was the ideology of ethnicity.

If ethnicity constitutes a form of communal consciousness in which actors perceive that the possession of common cultural attributes (relating to race, religion or language) implies a politically salient group loyalty, then it necessarily constitutes, from the perspective of class analysis, a form of 'false consciousness' in the sense that it signifies a failure to perceive the reality of objective class interests. But it has been frequently objected, by Marxists and well as non-Marxists, that such a designation is problematical both in that it appears to belittle the real power of the ethnic bond, and also in that it does not in fact constitute an explanation of ethnicity unless it is accompanied by an elucidation of how such an ideology is generated and implemented.

Marx's discussions of class make it clear that he conceived of mature class consciousness as implying more than just the awareness of a common relationship to the means of production. It involves also the sense of community arising from the sharing of a common mode of life, common interests, and common culture distinct from those of other classes.[12] This view of class as a communal group with a common culture accords with the structure of early European industrial societies in which members of a common class frequently inhabited particular localities and towns, and so comprised territorially-based communities with high levels of internal social interaction. It was not, therefore, simply common economic interests which provided potential for the generation of class consciousness, but also the situational context in which the economic group could become an interactive community with a common culture. The implication is that the form class consciousness takes will be related to the way in which the everyday social communities in a society overlap with and are modified by the development of economic groupings. There has been increasing recognition of the fact that class consciousness may assume diverse forms depending upon the kind of situational options and cultural values available to individuals in their everyday life. The character of the post-colonial state, the nature of the peripheral capitalist economy, and the racial structure of society, combine to generate situations quite distinct from those generated in metropolitan capitalism. The result is a corresponding distinctiveness in the relationship between class development and its manifestation in political consciousness.

The colonial situation generated a distinctive type of relationship between class and ethnicity in two major respects. First, colonialism facilitated the process whereby pre-capitalist modes of production were progressively transformed by incorporation into a world capitalist system. This involved the emergence of an international division of labour in which different racial groups (and religious and linguistic groups) were subjected to distinct forms of class exploitation by the metropolitan bourgeoisie, so that each subordinated racial group was recruited into a particular occupational category. This coinciding of race with class fraction fostered the perception by the exploited classes that it was their racial attributes which determined their class position. Thus, the defence of their class position could be perceived and articulated in terms of the mobilization and politicization of their racial identity. Ethnic ideologies thereby 'give coherence' to class objectives, rather than acting as 'false consciousness' to undermine them.[13] Ethnicity becomes the form in which class consciousness is manifested, so that it may be denoted by the term 'ethno-class consciousness'.[14] So long as the racial division of labour remains intact, this ethno-class consciousness would be politically salient: it would only give way to an explicitly class consciousness should the racial division of labour erode, either through the dynamics of capitalist development, or through the deliberate interventions of the state.[15]

The second distinctive aspect of colonialism refers to the decolonization process. This implied the formation of a comprador commercial sector and of a state bureaucratic sector which together could maintain a neo-colonial relationship between the metropolis and the newly independent state. The post-colonial state thus developed as a partnership between the state functionaries and the emergent commercial bourgeoisie, who allied together to inherit power from the colonialists. Such a state had a clear interest in maintaining the social order of which the allied commercial and bureaucratic bourgeois fractions were the major beneficiaries. One of the main strategies employed by emergent bourgeois groups seeking to acquire or maintain state power has been to employ ethnicity as, in Richard Sklar's words, 'a mask for class privilege'.[16] Their employment of ethnicity as an ideology for state legitimation has been particularly significant in the Malaysian case, where this development was facilitated by three interrelated factors.

First, the colonial state was able to make use of the prevalent ethno-class consciousness which had been generated by the racial division of labour under colonialism. The ethnic consciousness of the emergent racial class fractions was employed as the basis for a 'divide and rule' strategy towards the subordinate classes, so as to inhibit the emergence of an incipient class consciousness which transcended racial lines and which posed a potential threat to orderly decolonization.[17]

Second, the institutional form of the alliance between the commercial bourgeoisie and the bureaucratic bourgeoisie, which formed the basis for the decolonization agreement, was that of the ethnically consociational state. The alliance between bourgeois class fractions was implemented through the political institutions of an 'alliance' between racial groups, in which subordinate racial class fractions were persuaded to ally with dominant racial class fractions within patronage parties structured on avowedly ethnic communal lines.

Third, although colonialism generated a racial division of labour during the first stages in the development of peripheral capitalism, by the decolonization period the processes of industrialization and urbanization were sufficiently well advanced so that the 'watertight' compartmentalization of each racial class fraction began to erode. This generated increasing rivalry between racial class fractions, as they came into contact with each other in conditions of unequal competition for jobs and resources. These tensions lent apparent credibility to the ethnic ideology promulgated by the state élites.

The combined impact of these three factors was thus to promote the political salience of the ethnic ideology articulated by the state, which was portrayed in racial terms as a consociational partnership between racial patrons who alone had sufficient skill to contain the racial tensions threatening the society. The net result of this ethnic ideology was that overtly class-based political movements were suppressed by the colonial and post-colonial state, and were redesignated as ethnic communal movements so as to be politically neutralized.[18]

Once the ethnic ideology has been promoted by the state, in order to attain hegemonic status, it becomes available for a variety of purposes. If the post-colonial state may function either to legitimate the dominance of the emergent bourgeoisie as a whole, to promote political stability by inhibiting class tensions, or to promote the interests of the state bureaucratic fraction, then the ethnic ideology might be employed, correspondingly, to promote any of these goals. Thus the political analysis of the post-colonial state can be approached through an examination of the shifts in the employment of the ethnic ideology: as a 'divide and rule' ideology for maintaining the bourgeois alliance, as a 'garrison' ideology to promote political unity and stability by engendering a siege mentality, and as an ideology of racial superiority which could legitimate the political dominance of one racial class fraction within the bourgeoisie. Moreover, the ethnic ideology also becomes available to be employed by subordinate class groups wishing to challenge the state, with the result that ethnicity becomes the language of a subtle political contention between the various class groups in society.

The class analysis of Malaysian politics, and specifically of the ethnic factor, involves, therefore, an examination of the relationship between the two forms of consciousness: the ethno-class consciousness which derives from the racial division of labour in the economy, and the ethnic ideology which derives initially from the state. The interweaving of these two aspects forms the focus for the more detailed discussion that follows.

RACIAL CLASS FRACTIONS IN MALAYSIA

Any discussion of ethnic politics in Malaysia must seek to explain two countervailing aspects; first the almost unique success of the Malaysian state in maintaining a high degree of political stability and a form of parliamentary democracy in a system where political parties are organized very largely upon ethnic lines; and second, the increasing tendency in the direction of a Malay/Muslim-oriented state, and the consequent politically salient tension between Malay and non-Malay communities.

The starting point for such a discussion involves an examination of the economic impact of colonialism upon the way in which Malaysians responded politically to the issues posed by decolonization. It is clear that by the time of Malaysia's Independence in 1957, all the political parties which competed or co-operated for the inheritance of power were communally based in terms of their membership, their ideologies, and their appeal. But this outcome does not of itself show the innate priority of primordial racial ties, since it is explainable from a class perspective. This involves three related propositions. First, that colonialism engendered the emergence of racial-class groups which sought to organize themselves politically for the defence of their ethno-class interests. Second, that the colonial state promoted an ethnic ideology as the dominant paradigm for comprehending Malayan politics. Third, that the bourgeois racial-class groups were able to sustain their class dominance by employing this ethnic ideology to portray themselves as racial patrons.

The ethnic-based political parties of the 1950s had their origins, then, in the racial division of labour engendered by the circumstances of British economic and political domination. The concern of British colonialism was to modify the structure of the Malayan economy away from one focused on subsistence agriculture and localist and regional trade, towards one focused upon the export to Britain (and to the USA) of raw materials – mainly tin, rubber and timber – and the importation of consumer goods.[19] The primary beneficiaries of this transition were the European commercial interests and the colonial administrators themselves.[20] In order to promote this restructuring, the British encouraged the immigration of labour. From the early 19th century onwards the development of the Straits Settlements as trading centres attracted increasing numbers of Chinese traders. When demand for tin escalated in the 1850s, Chinese labour and capital moved into Perak and Selangor, where Chinese mining settlements developed. In the early 20th century world demand for rubber escalated, and the colonial government subsidized the importation of labour from the Indian colony, mainly for European-owned rubber plantation companies, so that by 1938 Indians constituted 80.4 per cent of the estate labour force.[21] The reluctance of Malays to leave their peasant communities for lower real incomes in the mines and plantations, when contrasted with the docility of the vulnerable

Indian immigrant labourers and the enforced industriousness of the impoverished Chinese workers, gave rise to the British colonial ethnic stereotypes of Malay laziness, Indian docility, and Chinese enterprise; so that the beginning of the racial division of labour was accompanied, from the outset, by a legitimatory ethnic ideology.[22]

The expansion of Chinese and Indian labour necessitated a significant increase in rice production and importation.[23] The colonial régime responded, in the 1930s, with various measures designed to encourage rice production amongst the Malay peasantry, but to also discourage non-Malay rice-planting. There is debate as to whether the resultant clustering of Malays in rice farming arose primarily from British responsiveness to the economically rational preferences of each communal group, or from a deliberate policy of racial occupational stereotyping.[24]

The net result was, however, the clustering of the different racial groups in specific occupational and territorial areas. Chinese clustered in urban commerce and in tin-mining communities, Indians clustered in rubber plantation labour, Malays clustered in the rice-farming peasantry. Moreover, the British colonial government, committed to an ideology of primordial racial incompatibility, welcomed and fostered the compartmentalization of society along racial-occupational lines, so that there existed only limited interactions between the various racial-occupational groups. The result of this situation was, therefore, a racially compartmentalized society in which each occupational category comprised a particular racial group.

This racial compartmentalization was exacerbated by the colonial education policy whereby the majority of Malays (with the exception of the Malay aristocracy), were provided with only an elementary vernacular education, 'practically oriented so as to stress the educational value of manual labour and not give rise to any dissatisfaction with the peasants' humble lot'.[25] They were thus under-represented in the English-medium secondary and tertiary institutions located in the urban areas, and were thereby also excluded to a large extent from the colonial administrative services and from management positions. The British education system, in effect, favoured the Chinese and Indians in the urban areas, and the few members of the Malay aristocracy who were offered English-medium education as part of their grooming for administrative élite positions.[26] Although the British opened the Malayan state bureaucracy to Malay recruitment as early as 1902, the number and proportion of Malay administrators remained small until after Independence.[27]

The resultant socio-economic compartmentalization of society on racial lines is reflected in various ways in the available aggregate data on occupational categories and income distribution. By 1957, 97.5 per cent of rice farmers were Malays, while 69 per cent of those in market gardening were Chinese; 48 per cent of Indians were involved in rubber production and they comprised 40 per cent of rubber estate labourers;[28] 66 per cent of those in commerce and 72 per cent of those in mining and manufacturing were Chinese. In terms of occupational category, 62.4 per cent of administrative and managerial workers, and 66.1 per cent of sales and related workers were Chinese, whereas 62.1 per cent of agricultural workers were Malays.[29] The data on employment status shows a similar racial clustering. Thus, in 1947, 69 per cent of all employers were Chinese, while 61.8 per cent of own-account workers and 79 per cent of unpaid family workers were Malays.[30] Within the professions, the Chinese comprised 89.1 per cent of dentists, 80.9 per cent of architects, 65.45 of accountants, and 71 per cent of engineers; with Malays comprising, respectively, 3.1 per cent, 4.3 per cent, 6.8 per cent, and 7.3 per cent.[31] Finally, data on incomes show that in 1957, mean Chinese household incomes were perhaps twice as high as Malay incomes.[32]

Although the structure of the Malaysian economy has undergone significant changes since the colonial period, particularly in the shift from rural agriculture to urban manufacturing and service industries, the racial division of labour established by the time of Independence has remained remarkably intact. It is certainly the case that government's preferential recruitment policies have promoted Malay entry into government, defence and public enterprise employment. Malay participation in professional and technical occupations, in the service, transport and communications sectors, and in production labouring, increased significantly from 1970 to 1980. But these changes have modified rather than fundamentally eroded the racial division of labour. Malay predominance in agriculture remains intact (falling from 72 per cent in 1970 to 67.7 per cent in 1980), and Malay predominance in government-protected employment is counterbalanced by non-Malay predominance in non-government protected employment.[33] Moreover, it appears that the racial segregation of employment establishments remains intact.[34]

Despite some differences in terminology, most attempts to extrapolate a class framework from the occupational, income and racial structure of the economy, have been in broad agreement. Martin Brennan's classification is one of the more recent and systematic.[35] In his terminology, the dominant ruling class comprises a 'dependent and subservient [national] bourgeoisie which relies upon international capital for its existence'. It comprises four main class fractions: the Malay aristocracy,[36] the Malay landlords, the predominantly Malay state bureaucracy, and the predominantly Chinese comprador capitalists.

Below them, urbanization has fostered the growth of a petit-bourgeoisie comprising 'middle-level bureaucrats, teachers, workers in the social agencies, professionals, and small-scale capitalists mainly in retailing and distribution'. This class is dependent upon the dominant class for patronage. It is a multi-racial class, but divides into two main class fractions, the predominantly Chinese private business sector, and the predominantly Malay government service.

The dominated classes comprise three main class groups, the predominantly Malay peasantry, the rural proletariat of plantation and mine workers – mainly Indian and Chinese respectively – and the urban proletariat which was previously Chinese, but has become increasingly multiracial. This urban proletariat remains fragmented, however, in racially segmented employment establishments.

Each of these classes and class fractions sought to defend their interests during the decolonization period; but they did so in ways which resulted, by the time of Independence, in the institutionalization of ethnicity. How did this occur?

Racial class fractions and political parties

The major political parties of the decolonization period, the Malayan Communist Party (MCP), the United Malays National Organization (UMNO), the Partai Islam (PAS), the Malayan Chinese Association (MCA), and the Malayan Indian Congress (MIC), each grew out of attempts by the various racially-clustered class fractions, from the 1930s onwards, to defend their ethno-class interests in the situational context of the decolonization process.

Prior to the late 1940s, such movements varied in their ideological manifestation, some taking an overtly ethnic form, some proclaiming themselves in class and ideological terms, and some appearing as pragmatic single-issue alliances. From that time onwards, however, they became increasingly institutionalized in explicitly ethnic terms, proclaiming themselves not as class movements which were racially clustered, but rather as ethnic movements which happened to be dominated by particular occupational groups. There were two major reasons for this shift towards the ethnic institutionalization of class-based political movements. The first relates to the strategies of decolonization adopted by the British. They had initially opted for an 'indirect rule' approach which built on the traditional Malay authority structure. Immediately after the war, however, they attempted to shift to a 'Malayan Union' plan to hand over power to the emergent multi-ethnic bourgeoisie.[37] The resentment of the Malay aristocracy at this 'betrayal', and the concern to combat the anti-colonial rebellion of the MCP led the British to revert to an ethnic 'divide and rule' strategy.

It was thus the way in which the British colonialists posed the question as to who should inherit state power, which ensured the political salience of the ethnic ideology. Faced with their 'betrayal' in the Malayan Union plan, the Malay aristocracy could effectively respond only through mobilizing a coalition based on a Malay nationalist platform. Similarly, the subsequent British proposal for a Malayan Federation constituted a direct threat to Chinese citizenship rights, which prompted the Chinese bourgeoisie, who saw this as a threat to their economic interests, to oppose it through the appropriate Chinese communal response.

The second factor promoting the shift towards explicitly ethnic institutions arose out of the need for the political movements to adopt mass mobilization strategies in the context of the electoral politics of the 1950s. If the bourgeois class groups were to inherit power from the colonial régime, then they would have to demonstrate, in the elections, that they could mobilize the support of the subordinate class groups. They therefore had to portray themselves as the prospective patrons of the subordinate classes. This was accomplished by the adoption of overtly communalistic programmes in which the bourgeois classes of each racial group could portray themselves as communal élites, able to channel state resources to their communal clienteles in return for electoral support. The electoral factor thus gave rise to political parties whose support and platforms reflected a communal appeal transcending class positions. Nevertheless, an examination of their origins, leadership and key policies reveals their essential character as vehicles for the interests of the racially clustered class fraction who formed their core.

These two factors, the situational options posed by the British strategies of decolonization and by the imperatives of electoral mobilization, ensured that the racial class fractions, concerned to defend and promote their interests in the decolonization process, would have to articulate those interests by employing the language of ethnicity, rather than that of class.

It is sometimes argued that the failure of those political movements which were not communally based proves, of itself, the 'naturalness' of Malaysia's ethnic-oriented political culture. The two main non-communal political organizations were probably the AMCJA-PUTERA coalition of 1947–8, and the Independence of Malaya Party (IMP) of 1951–3, but the failure of both movements could be explained adequately in terms of the weakness of their class base, rather than as a result of their multiracial composition. Both movements failed because they comprised inherently fragile alliances between competing class groups which could not be held together by patronage.[38]

Perhaps the most important of the political movements which 'failed' was the Malayan Communist Party. The MCP began life in the early 1930s defending the interests of poor workers, most of them Chinese, who were hit by the Depression. It organized demonstrations, strikes and later trade unions amongst the impoverished mine and estate workers, and was thus explicitly a movement of the emergent proletariat. From 1937 onwards it began to articulate the interests of Chinese, mainly workers, against first the Japanese, and then subsequently the British. By the end of 1941 it had become 'the strongest political force in the country with a membership estimated at 5,000', and by 1945, in its armed resistance wing, the Malayan Peoples Anti-Japanese Army (MPAJA), it had an organized armed force of 10,000.[39]

After the war, when the British authorities refused to recognize the MCP as a legitimate political movement for the purposes of decolonization negotiations, it put forward a platform demanding democratic self-rule and sought to appeal to Malayans of all races. This platform demanded widespread support, as was evidenced by the success of its January 1946 nationwide strike and the February demonstrations.[40] By 1947 the MCP, through its trade union wing, the Pan Malayan Federation of Trade Unions, had mobilized mainly Chinese workers so as to gain control of 80 per cent to 90 per cent of all unions in Malaya, and had a membership of 50 per cent of the industrial workforce.[41]

It was the withdrawal by the British of the Malayan Union scheme and its replacement by the agreement with UMNO offering a 'special position' to the Malays and imposing restrictions on Chinese citizenship, which pushed the MCP, once more, towards defence of Chinese interests; though it continued, in its programmes, to appeal to Malayans 'irrespective of race'.

These basic facts regarding the MCP allow three possible interpretations: that it was essentially a class movement of the Malayan proletariat which happened, because of the racial division of labour in the economy, to be primarily Chinese; that it was essentially an anti-colonial nationalist movement which, because of Malay support for the pro-Malay decolonization settlement, again happened to be primarily Chinese; or that it was essentially a Chinese ethnic-nationalist movement, constituting thereby a serious threat to Malayan national integration.[42]

The 'class' and 'anti-colonial' perspectives are compatible in that they stress the contingent nature of Chinese predominance in the MCP. Both Hua Wu Yin and, more recently, Frank Furedi, have argued that by the late 1940s the MCP constituted a radical nationalist movement with strong support amongst the predominantly non-Malay working class, but also with support amongst some Indians and, increasingly, amongst Malays.[43] It was in order to prevent the further growth of such a class-based anti-colonial movement that the British administration took its initiative in proclaiming a 'Moscow plot', imposing the state of emergency, and playing down Malay involvement in the insurrection so that it could be portrayed as a communal insurrection amongst the Chinese:

The British authorities depicted any threat to colonial rule as subversive, and exaggerated the ethnic or communal character of popular revolt to undermine its claim to nationalist status. At the same time, to win the approval of Washington, the Colonial Office sought to link anti-colonial resistance to the influence of Moscow.[44]

The depiction of the MCP as essentially a Chinese racial movement, rather than as the movement of an anti-colonial proletariat, was thus the manifestation of a classic 'divide and rule' strategy employed by the colonial régime to limit and to undermine the rebellion. The British suppression of the MCP was paralleled by their attempts to suppress those political organizations through which the subordinate Malay racial-occupational groups sought to defend their interests.

The interests of the Malay peasantry were primarily articulated through the Malay Nationalist Party which emerged out of the Young Malays Association (KMM) formed in the late 1930s by rural-based primary teachers. By mid-1947 it had a similar membership to that of UMNO (60,000–100,000), but it was suppressed by the British at the onset of the communist insurrection. The youth wing of the MNP was banned in mid-1947, and many of its activists arrested. The MNP itself was banned in 1950. As Funston notes:

> Members responded differently to the party's proscription, a minority joining forces with the Communist Party in open revolt, some continuing the struggle through the medium of literature, and larger numbers joining UMNO; most, however, appear to have been without any initial political mooring, and drifted into the various anti-UMNO groups that emerged during the 1950s.[45]

One such anti-UMNO group, which became the most effective channel for the interests of the subordinate Malay classes, was the Partai Islam (PAS). This developed out of the Islamic wing of the MNP and out of the Pan Malayan Supreme Religious Council (MATA), which was formed in 1947. Its activists were primarily Islamic-educated religious teachers and officials who in many cases were also middle and lower ranking civil servants, and who came from what Funston terms a 'rich peasant' background. In class terms, therefore, PAS was primarily the voice of the Malay peasants moving out of the traditional economy into the lower and petit-bourgeois ranks of the colonial-capitalist system. Its grassroots activists were the village religious leaders, the *ulama* and *pondok* teachers; and its support base was the discontented peasantry.[46] PAS has been the only party articulating the interests of subordinate racial-occupational groups to have survived from the colonial period, and for most of its history it has played an oppositionist role. But the political parties which flourished, and which co-operated to inherit political power from the British, were those representing the bourgeois class fractions.

The political division between PAS and UMNO reflected the class divisions within Malay society:

> At the top echelon of party leadership for instance, UMNO members were drawn from the traditional aristocracy or those identifying with it, received a tertiary English education (in Britain), and gained employment in the upper ranks of the public service; PAS leaders on the other hand, came generally from a rich-peasant background, received a tertiary Islamic education (often at institutions in Indonesia or the Middle East identified with a modernist interpretation of Islam) and became Islamic teachers, or occasionally, lower ranking bureaucrats, small businessmen or journalists . . . . Linked with these different class backgrounds, the parties adopted quite different ideologies.[47]

The Malay traditional aristocracy had initially articulated their interests through various literary associations and Malay Unions in the 1930s and later revived these conservative movements after the Japanese surrender, culminating in the formation of UMNO.[48]

UMNO began in March 1946 as a protest at the British administration's proposal for a Malayan Union which would almost completely strip the Malay Sultans of their powers, and would open Malayan citizenship to non-Malays with few restrictions. It was thus, from the outset, a coalition of explicitly Malay organizations to protect Malay interests. It is equally clear, however, that in its roots and its political programmes, it represented primarily the interests of the Malay feudal aristocracy and the land-owning class, who were concerned to maintain their dominant position during and after the decolonization process. This class character was reflected from the outset in the leadership of UMNO:

Dato Onn, a high ranking aristocrat, was promoted from chairman to President with the inauguration of UMNO, and using his presidential powers to select his own executive committee surrounded himself with leading Malay aristocrats and bureaucrats of the highest order.[49]

Until the 1970s, the leadership of UMNO remained firmly in the hands of the older generation of Malay aristocrats (born before 1920), who had career backgrounds in the state bureaucracy. Thus, Tunku Abdul Rahman, its President from 1951 to 1970, was the son of a Kedah Sultan who had risen through the senior bureaucracy to the post of Superintendent of Education; while Tun Abdul Razak (UMNO Deputy President, and President from 1970 to 1976) was the son of a major Pahang chieftain who held senior ranks in the Pahang state bureaucracy.[50]

The predominant role of the Malay aristocracy within UMNO was closely related to their attainment of dominant positions as 'administocrats' within the state bureaucracy.[51] The British had recruited the aristocratic graduates of the Kuala Kangsar Malay College into the élite Malayan Civil Service. Since the colonial system was an essentially undemocratic one, in which the senior administrators played the dominant role in policy making as well as policy implementation, this 'fusion of politics and administration'[52] resulted in the senior civil servants dominating the Malay nationalist movement of UMNO, as well as, in their executive role, exerting a major influence on state policies and planning.[53] Malay aristocrats thus comprised the political élite, with the same individuals and families dominating UMNO (thence the alliance government), and the senior bureaucracy. UMNO was thus led at all levels by government employees, but so long as the state bureaucracy was itself dominated by the Malay aristocrat-landowners, the class basis of UMNO remained intact. It functioned as an agency for the promotion of the interests of the Malay aristocracy and landlords, expressed through a Malay nationalism which depicted the aristocrats as communal patrons.

The parallel political organization for the Chinese commercial fraction of the bourgeoisie was the Malayan Chinese Association (MCA). This was formed in 1947 at the urging of the British administration who sought the help of the Chinese commercial bourgeoisie in creating a Malayan Chinese organization which could mobilize Chinese support against the MCP, and so help to defeat the rebellion. This goal coincided with the concern of those businessmen who had earlier organized the Straits Chinese British Association and the Chinese Chambers of Commerce to develop 'an organization to protect Chinese capitalist interests in anticipation of a period of economic and political rehabilitation in [post-war] Malaysia'.[54]

The proposal for the Malayan Federation constitution, with its drastic restriction of Chinese citizenship rights, provided a specific impetus for the organization of a movement to protect the 'Chinese mercantile class'.[55] The class identity of the MCA was reflected also in the composition of its leadership in the 1949–57 period. As Heng's analysis shows:

> The majority of MCA national leaders were Malayan-born, English-educated, wealthy businessmen and/or professionally qualified men who held positions in government bodies as well as Chinese associations and multiracial organizations . . . . All the . . . leaders were men of considerable wealth, and some were certainly among the wealthiest in Malaya. These men derived their fortunes mainly from tin mines, rubber and other agricultural estates, banking, shipping, real estate development, import-export agencies, wholesale and retail trading, and other commercial enterprises and small scale manufacturing industries.[56]

These national leaders acted as the patrons for the state-level activists of the MCA, who were mainly businessmen and merchants. The grassroots activists were also mainly merchants, teachers or clerks who constituted the 'power brokers' in the small towns and new villages of Malaya.[57] The party's mass support base came mostly from lower income groups who regarded the businessmen as their prospective patrons.

The third of the successful bourgeois parties was the Malayan Indian Congress. Despite its name, it was not led by the activists of radical Indian nationalism, which had been articulated through the Independence League and the Indian National Army prior to 1945. These political activists were effectively dispersed by the British after the war, or drifted into movements allied to the Malayan Communist Party. It was thus the political conservatives, anxious for a channel through which to articulate their views on the decolonization negotiations, who came to dominate the MIC. From the outset it was essentially a 'middle and upper class bod[y] with little or no mass backing. The leadership reflected the heterogeneity of the professional and commercial groups who were their chief supporters.'[58]

MIC meetings were held in English, thereby excluding the mass of Tamil speaking Indians in Malaya; and the professional and commercial profile of the early MIC is clear from the proliferation of lawyers, journalists, teachers and businessmen amongst its leaders.[59] Initially the MIC opposed any stance of Indian communalism. Even though it did eventually accept the need for communalism as an electoral mobilization strategy, its leadership continued to comprise bourgeois professionals concerned to protect their own interests. These leaders were those most acceptable to, and were to some extent chosen by, the Malay UMNO leadership.[60]

These brief discussions of the major political parties show that in each case they developed as channels for the articulation of the interests of a particular racial class fraction. In the case of the bourgeois parties, they developed support across class lines by proclaiming that the bourgeois racial-class fractions were communal patrons for the subordinate class groups. This did not necessarily indicate any dilution in the class character of the parties, which continued to be determined by the material interests of the class fraction who comprised the parties' core leadership.

The essentially bourgeois class character of these avowedly communal parties also implied their overriding common interest in co-operating both with the colonizing power and with each other, to defend their positions of class domination during the decolonization process:

> Political independence was granted only after the colony had been rendered firmly dependent economically on the metropole, and this required collaboration of local ruling classes whose own interests to extract surplus value from the masses coincided with that of the élites in the metropole.[61]

In order to maintain this collaboration, the British administration had to find a form of government that would maintain the political dominance of the indigenous bourgeoisie. Their first decolonization strategy of the Malayan Union proposal had been for a 'Malayan Malaya' in which political institutions would be non-communal and national in character. When this proposal was rejected by the Malay aristocracy and bureaucrats, the British were impelled to accept the need to work with overtly communal political parties. A similar process of rethinking occurred amongst the Malayan bourgeoisie. Dato Onn's efforts to move UMNO in a non-communal direction, and his attempt with Tan Cheng Lock to develop the IMP, both failed. This led the two main bourgeois racial class fractions – the Chinese commercial bourgeoisie and the Malay aristocracy – to pursue their common interest in maintaining bourgeois domination in an independent Malaya through the formation of an alliance which was clothed in an overtly communal institutional form.

The result of these revised strategies, which initially took the form of an UMNO–MCA electoral pact in the 1952 Kuala Lumpur municipal elections, was the Alliance Party, comprising UMNO, MCA and MIP. The Alliance easily won the 1955 General Election and attained governmental power in an independent Malaya in 1957. It was organized on an ethnically consociational basis, in which each political party represented one racial-communal segment of the society. The political élites of each communal group governed by co-operating in a grand coalition 'with the deliberate aim of counteracting disintegrative tendencies'.[62]

The proponents of the concept of consociationalism have argued that it represents the only effective way of organizing democracy in an ethnically plural society. Nevertheless, they admit that the kind of democratic institutions it generates have certain features which are intrinsically anti-democratic. Decision-making is by secret negotiations within the grand coalition, the various communal élites are careful to exclude issues relating to the values and interests of each ethnic segment from the area of public political debate, and élite co-operation is maintained primarily by the existence of an imminent threat of instability. In that decision-making is monopolized by an élite coalition, consociational democracy contains significant elements of élite control.

Such an image of consociationalism, in which democracy may become something of an institutional and ideological facade for élite oligarchy, can be more effectively characterized in class terms. The consociational Alliance reflected a 'class compromise' in which the state had sufficient autonomy to mediate between the various fractions of the bourgeoisie. 'The post-colonial governing stratum was committed to defending the interests of the British bourgeoisie in Malaya, while permitting the local, predominantly Chinese capitalists to consolidate and further strengthen their position.'[63]

The inter-communal Alliance was thus the institutional form for the maintenance of bourgeois class domination, which allowed the bourgeois class fractions to disguise the defence of their own class interests as the protection of communal interests. The communal composition of the political parties allowed each bourgeois fraction to claim the role of communal patron *vis-à-vis* its co-racial subordinate classes, and thus to promote the formation amongst the latter of a deferential clientelist consciousness, rather than a class consciousness of their exploited position.[64] Thus, particularly at election time, the parties of the Alliance sought to deliver sufficient benefits to the subordinate classes so as to maintain their political support. UMNO in particular functioned as a patronage machine, promising and distributing government largesse to local communities in return for the vote.[65] The MCA, for its part, gained the support of the poorer Chinese in the mid-1950s by ensuring government policies beneficial to them, so that:

> The Alliance pledges on education and citizenship gave the MCA the support of Chinese voters from different class and social backgrounds. The Manifesto's economic platform appealed to Chinese capitalist interests, and the agrarian and labour platforms attracted the sympathy of the Chinese rural and urban proletariat.[66]

It was, then, the very strength of inter-communal co-operation amongst the dominant bourgeois class which ensured the dominance of ethnic communal consciousness over class consciousness at the level of the subordinate classes.

The class approach to Malaysian politics at the time of Independence thus provides two main themes which may be employed in the analysis of the political changes which occurred thereafter. The first theme is that politics comprises the articulation of the interests of racially clustered class fractions, which are expressed increasingly in ethnic, rather than in overtly class, terms. The second theme, which emerges after the defeat of the proletarian rebellion led by the MCP, is that the political domination of the emergent bourgeoisie is maintained and legitimated by the employment of an ethnic ideology. The resultant situation, the effective control of the state by the consociational Alliance, was not, however, a stable or static situation for two main reasons: first because of changes in the structure of the economy arising from the dependent development generated by neocolonialism, and second because of the tensions between the various bourgeois class fractions arising from their rivalry for access to state resources. It is to these two dynamics which we must turn in order to explain the origins of the political tensions which emerged in the violence of 1969.

THE 1969 RIOTS

The 13 May riots were precipitated by the general election campaign in which each political party appealed overtly to communal affiliations and prejudices in order to mobilize support, and also by the results of the election, which allowed both the Alliance parties (who won a much reduced majority of seats) and their opponents to perceive and to claim victory. The 'victory procession' of Chinese DAP and Gerakan supporters, which taunted Kuala Lumpur Malays that 'The Malays have fallen', provoked an UMNO counter-demonstration by Malays, ending in rioting between lower-class Malays and Chinese which continued for several days. The official figures were that 196 people died, 9,143 were arrested, and 753 buildings were damaged or destroyed by fire.[67] Gordon Means was no doubt right in asserting that:

> What happened . . . was not the expression of overt economic grievances or of class animosities. Rather, in the atmosphere of crisis and with the irrational mechanisms of crowd psychology, primal emotions surged in uncontrollable waves combining racial antipathies, anger, fear, hatred, and self-justifying rationalizations for barbarous behaviour.[68]

But it is necessary to distinguish between the 'primal . . . racial antipathies' which motivated behaviour in the riots, and the causes of that consciousness. The immediate focus for the manifestation of racial antipathies related to cultural and political issues: the fear of the Chinese communities that their language and culture were under threat from a Malaysian state increas-

ingly under Malay control, and the fear of the Malay communities that their political dominance was now being threatened by
the rise of opposition parties at federal and state level which
were overwhelmingly Chinese-based. But these cultural fears of
the Chinese and political fears of the Malays in turn arose out
of more fundamental economic grievances. The Malay bourgeoisie, petit-bourgeoisie and peasantry had each become aware
that since Independence they had a declining share of the
nation's wealth. There was a widespread perception that the
various government schemes to help the Malays had not been
effective. There was evidence for this in the higher rates of
Malay unemployment in the urban areas, and in the overall
decline of Malay incomes relative to Chinese incomes, from a
ratio of about 1:2 in 1958, to one of 1:2.5 in 1967.[69] The various
Chinese class groups, for their part, were aware that the increasing Malay dominance in the Alliance and in the senior civil
service was accompanied by increasingly overt attacks on
Chinese education and on their dominance in commerce and
industry, which were beginning to constitute a real threat to the
security of their economic position in Malaysia.

These ethnic perceptions of zero-sum economic rivalry had
their origin in changes in the structure of the economy which
manifested themselves first in the growth of intra-racial economic disparities and thence of intra-racial class tensions. Second,
they developed from the process of urbanization and thence the
growth in interactions and rivalries between the racial class
fractions. Third, they involved a change of the class character of
the state, which led to shifts in the nature and role of the state's
ethnic ideology. In discussing each of these developments,
their cumulative impact in generating ethnic conflict can be
elucidated.

Intra-racial disparities

During the 1950s and 1960s there was a fundamental change in
the economic structure, which involved the growth in the wealth
and size of the national bourgeoisie on the one hand, and
the declining living standards of rural and urban workers
on the other. In the late 1940s the national bourgeoisie was still
extremely weak. Only 1.27 per cent of the workforce (24,220
persons) were classified as employers.[70] Over two-thirds of the

economy was in foreign (European and to a lesser extent Chinese) hands,[71] and as of 1950 only 21.4 per cent (31 individuals) in the senior Malayan Civil Service (MCS) were Malayans.[72]

It was the increased integration of the Malayan economy into the world capitalist system which generated the rapid growth of this domestic bourgeoisie.[73] In the case of the bureaucratic bourgeoisie, the expansion occurred because of the changes in the role of the state and the indigenization of the state machinery precipitated by decolonization. Between 1957 and 1970 the percentage of those employed in professional and technical categories increased from 2.8 per cent to 4.8 per cent. Malayan Chinese businesses in banking, property development, manufacturing and trading all expanded, and Malay involvement in manufacturing expanded rapidly.[74] By 1969 the top three divisions of the federal and state public services employed nearly 76,000 persons, with 4,744 in the higher civil service and 696 in the élite MCS.[75]

This expansion of the commercial, industrial and bureaucratic bourgeoisies was accompanied by a moderate growth in the Malaysian economy, with an average annual GDP per capita growth rate of 3.3 per cent between 1958 and 1969.[76] In line with the predominant western and World Bank philosophies, it was assumed by the Alliance government that *laissez-faire* and open-door economic policies would result in this economic growth 'trickling down' to benefit the subordinate classes; and the government largely restricted its role to one of providing infrastructural and financial incentives to encourage import-substitution investment. In fact no such trickle down occurred, and the economic data indicates that the expansion of the bourgeoisie was accompanied both by a marked widening of income inequalities between the urban wealthy and the urban and rural poor, as well as by an absolute decline in living standards both for the rural peasantry and proletariat, and for the increasing number of urban poor and unemployed. To some extent this impoverishment of the subordinate classes was a reflection of a general decline during the 1960s in world prices for Malaysia's main exports of rubber, tin and iron ore; but state policies ensured that it was the workers and peasants, rather than the bourgeois class groups, who experienced the deprivation.

The escalation of both relative and absolute deprivation

amongst the subordinate classes during this period is reflected in three sets of data. The increase in income disparities meant that while the wealthiest 20 per cent of the population increased their share of total income from 48.6 per cent to 56.1 per cent, the share accruing to the poorest 40 per cent fell from 15.9 per cent to 11.2 per cent.[77] Estimates of absolute poverty indicate that while the percentage of the population below the poverty line did decline very slightly between 1957/8 and 1970 (from 51.2 per cent to 49.3 per cent), the extent of poverty of those below the line worsened.[78] Finally, the data on unemployment levels shows an increase from 6 per cent in 1962 to 8 per cent in 1970.[79] Moreover, this increase was concentrated in the urban areas (from 8.09 per cent in 1962 to 9.73 per cent in 1967) and amongst young men, so that: 'one of two young men between the ages of 15 and 19 and one of four between the ages of 20 and 24 actively sought but could not find employment in 1967'.[80]

The formation of the Alliance in the early 1950s had been based on the claim, and the assumption, that the political leaders of each of the three Alliance parties would act as communal patrons, delivering first the benefit of Independence, and subsequently the benefits of national economic development, to the subordinate class groups who gave them their popular support. But by the end of the 1960s, it was becoming increasingly evident that the net result of government economic policies was the redistribution of wealth, within each racial community, from the poor to the rich. Between 1957 and 1970, intra-racial income disparities (measured by the Gini ratio) grew by 36.2 per cent for the Malays and by 21.6 per cent for the Chinese.[81] By this latter date, nearly 90 per cent of overall income inequality was due to differences within racial groups, rather than to differences between them.[82] Between 1957 and 1970 the wealthiest 20 per cent of Malays increased their share of total income from 42.5 per cent to 52.5 per cent, while the share accruing to the poorest 40 per cent fell from 19.5 per cent to 12.7 per cent. The figures for the Chinese show a similar, though somewhat less dramatic trend. While the top 20 per cent increased their share of income from 45.8 per cent to 52.6 per cent, the bottom 40 per cent reduced their share from 18 per cent to 13.9 per cent.[83] Clearly then, the bourgeois leaders of UMNO and of MCA were no longer delivering on their promise to act as communal patrons for the subordinate classes of each race. Indeed, the growing economic disparities suggest rather that the bourgeois racial class fractions were increasingly exploitative of the subordinate classes.

The political impact of this increase in intra-racial economic disparities was, therefore, to prompt significant sections of the subordinate classes in each racial group to withdraw their support from the Alliance parties, and to seek alternative channels for articulating their interests. This is reflected in the significant decline in electoral support for the Alliance; from 79.6 per cent of the vote in 1955, to 51.5 per cent in 1959, up to 58.5 per cent in 1964, and then down to 48.5 per cent in 1969. Meanwhile, the opponents of the Alliance gained in popularity, with the beneficiaries being mainly PAS, the Democratic Action Party (DAP), and the Gerakan.

This move in political allegiance should not be interpreted as a shift from communal consciousness and its replacement by class consciousness, but rather as primarily a search for alternative and more effective communal patrons on the part of the racially clustered subordinate class fractions.

In the case of the MCA, by the mid-1960s its leadership was put in the position of having to choose whether to give priority to their identification with the bourgeoisie or their identification with the mass of their supporters who were Chinese workers:

> The majority of MCA leaders were *Laukeh towkey* (wealthy businessmen of early immigrant descent) whose economic interests were a major factor in weighing the consequences of political actions. For these businessmen-cum-political leaders, continued membership in an MCA which belonged to the ruling coalition was a much better proposition than being cast out into the political wilderness.[84]

The growing disaffection of Chinese subordinate classes from the MCA leadership meant that the MCA suffered a 10 per cent decline in electoral support between 1959 and 1969. The Alliance did retain 40.4 per cent of the non-Malay vote, but the DAP got 30 per cent, the Gerakan got 17.8 per cent, and the Peoples Progressive Party (PPP) got 8.6 per cent.[85] These parties sought to mobilize the support primarily of the poorer and unemployed Chinese by arguing that they could promote their economic interests through a defence of Chinese education as the main channel of upward socio-economic mobility.[86]

It is significant that, unlike the Alliance parties, these opposition parties did not campaign on an overwhelmingly ethnic platform. In fact, the three main 'Chinese' opposition parties gained nearly 10 per cent of their support from Malays; and the Gerakan succeeded in defeating the Alliance in Penang by avoiding communal appeals to voters and 'garner[ing] votes by emphasizing socio-economic rather than ethnic issues'.[87] Nevertheless, the perception that the interests of the subordinate classes could best be promoted through access to bourgeois patronage was sufficiently strong to ensure that the only party which did espouse an explicitly anti-bourgeois and non-communal programme, the Partai Rakyat, did much worse than the communal parties, receiving only 1.2 per cent of the vote.

A similar trend of political disaffection arising out of disillusion with the bourgeois leadership's claim as communal patrons is evident amongst Malay supporters of UMNO. Most of the poor Malays who deserted UMNO went to PAS, which increased its share of the total vote from 14.6 per cent in 1964 to 23.8 per cent in 1969. Amongst the Malays, PAS now got 40.2 per cent of the vote. PAS was of course an explicitly communal party based on an ideology of Malay nationalism and Islam, but it mobilized support, not so much by appeals to religious solidarity, as by pointing to the economic inferiority of the Malay-Muslims, so that it had 'instant appeal to the mass of the peasantry, for whom independence had been associated with a stagnant or deteriorating economic position'.[88] Wherever possible, for example as the state government of Kelantan, PAS also employed development patronage as a way of mobilizing support from the poor.

By 1969, therefore, there was widespread discontent amongst both the Chinese and the Malay subordinate classes that their bourgeois 'patrons' had failed to defend their interests, and had instead furthered their own bourgeois interests. But the growth of intra-racial economic disparities and political disunity does not, of itself, explain the growth of antipathies between members of the two racial groups; unless it were to be argued that discontent against the bourgeois élites might be deflected, through a non-rational process of cathartic racial scapegoating, on to the other community.[89] There is, however, a simpler explanation connecting the intra-racial cleavages with the inter-racial tensions; one which assumes behaviour based on perceptions of rational class fraction interests.

Inter-racial economic rivalries

In the late 1940s Malayan society had conformed closely to Furnivall's description of a plural society 'with different sections of the community living side by side, but separately within the same political unit. Even in the economic sphere there is division of labour along racial lines.'[90]

By the end of the 1960s the racial division of labour was still very much intact, but the impermeability of the racial-occupational compartments had declined. It was the growth of the urban areas, and the growing interactions between Chinese and Malays within those urban areas, which constituted the decisive change. So long as, and to the extent that, the members of each racial group had not significantly interacted with each other, there could be no conflict or dispute between them. Only with the increase in interactions could economic rivalries develop and generate political tensions.

The rate of urban expansion had been rapid in Malaya up to Independence, with the proportion of the population residing in urban areas over 10,000, rising from 15.9 per cent in 1947 to 26.5 per cent in 1957. Thereafter, however, the rate of urbanization slowed down, rising only to 28.7 per cent by 1970. The exception to this was the rapid expansion of the largest metropolitan areas, especially Kuala Lumpur, which expanded by 40 per cent during this period and also generated a large conurbation around itself. Most of the urban growth was due to natural increase, but about one-quarter was due to rural–urban migration, mainly of Malays. Choo Keng Kun has calculated that the rate of Malay urbanization was three times higher than that of the non-Malays.[91] Indeed, there was a net loss of Chinese and Indian males from urban areas:

> The loss of Chinese and Indian males may be explained by the urban Chinese and Indian youths having been pushed out by growing unemployment rates and rising competition for the limited available employment possibilities from the Malay immigrants, who have 'privileged status'.[92]

The result was a significant shift in the racial composition of the urban areas. In 1947 over 92 per cent of the urban population were non-Malay. By 1970 the proportion of Malays had nearly doubled, to 14.9 per cent, while the proportion of Chinese fell from 46.2 per cent to 40.8 per cent.[93] In the case of Kuala Lumpur, between 1957 and 1970 the proportion of Malays rose from 14.86 per cent to 25.15 per cent, while that of the Chinese fell from 62.1 per cent to 54.7 per cent.[94] By 1975 83 per cent of the Malay population of Kuala Lumpur was born outside the city.[95]

Some observers have postulated that the development of a multiracial proletariat would engender a corresponding growth of pan-racial class consciousness.[96] It seems, however, that the Malays and non-Malays in the urban areas did not interact with each other on an equal basis, so that their interactions tended to promote mutual distrust and resentment rather than integration. Thus, almost all urban occupational categories were racially 'crowded', Malays being clustered, for example, both in the higher paying public service occupations, and also in clerical and labourer categories. Moreover, urban employees were segregated by race in different establishments.[97] Malays earned less than Chinese, primarily because of differences in education level.[98] For the poor, mostly the underemployed and unemployed, the racial differences were extremely significant, with the incidence of urban poverty among Malays (22.9 per cent) being twice that among the Chinese (11.5 per cent).[99] Moreover, both the rate and the duration of unemployment were significantly higher for Malays than for Chinese.[100]

The growth of Malay migration into the urban areas coincided with, and was partly responsible for, the rise in unemployment and the relative decline in the position of the urban poor.[101] This promoted the perception on the part of the non-Malay natives that the Malay migrants, who tended to be better educated, were their rivals for employment, and had a 'privileged status' because of the various government programmes giving preferential quotas for education, the public service, and for business and commercial licences. Malay migration appeared to lengthen the 'queue' for the 'attractive but infrequent modern sector jobs';[102] and thus seemed to reduce the prospects for upward socio-economic mobility for long-time urban dwellers, who were mostly Chinese.

For their part, the Malay migrants entered the urban areas

with expectations far higher than those of the Chinese;[103] this was partly because of the message from the Malay political élites that 'the special position of the Malays' entitled them to a 'rightful share' of resources. The experience of encountering unemployment and low earnings, while the employed urban Chinese were in relative prosperity, therefore engendered perceptions of inter-racial economic rivalry.

The predominantly migrant Malay workers and the predominantly native Chinese workers thus had markedly different occupational and income experiences within the urban areas. In the context of the urban rivalry for employment and resources, they comprised competing class fractions whose interactions failed to reduce or modify the high incidence of racial stereotyping,[104] and whose divergent interests generated enhanced ethnic consciousness. There was thus an economic rationality behind the growth of resentment between the Chinese and Malay fractions of the urban proletariat. This does not imply, however, any inevitability as to the outbreak of violence and political conflict between the two groups. In order to explain such occurrences, it will be necessary to show how a conducive political situation could develop, and how those involved acquired an ideological legitimation for their behaviour.

Ethnic ideologies

The outburst of inter-ethnic animosities in 1969 had its roots in the combination of increasing class disparities within each racial group, and the increasing rivalries between racial class fractions of the proletariat. It was precipitated, however, by the structure of the 1969 elections, and it was legitimated by the type of ethnic ideological myths propounded by political activists both in the campaign, and in the preceding period.

The ethnic ideologies that emerged in the late 1960s differed markedly from those which had prevailed in the 1950s, and they indicated a growing tension between the shifting balance of forces within the bourgeoisie and the institutional structure of the state. It is, therefore, the shift in the position of the dominant class fractions, and the impact of this upon the state, which constitutes the final stage in the explanation of the ethnic violence.

We have noted that at Independence state power was inherited by the Alliance of the Malay aristocrat-landowners who promoted their interests through their domination of the senior civil service and the UMNO political party; and the Chinese commercial bourgeoisie, who defended their economic interests through their control of the MCA. The 'bargain' underlying this Alliance was reiterated by Tunku Abdul Rahman in the 1969 election campaign:

> The Malays have gained for themselves political power. The Chinese and Indians have won for themselves economic power. The blending of the two with complete goodwill and understanding has brought about peace and harmony, coupled with prosperity to the country.[105]

By this time, however, the 'bargain', and its institutionalization in the Alliance, were no longer congruent with the underlying class structure which had given rise to them in the early 1950s. This incongruence precipitated the instability of 1969 and the resultant restructuring of the government in 1970.

Decolonization had implied the need to expand the role and size of the state bureaucracy. The introduction of the quota system had ensured the predominance of Malays, but the need for increasing numbers of educated Malays implied the opening up of civil service recruitment to those from subordinate class groups. Between 1950 and 1957 the number of Malays in the senior bureaucracy quadrupled, and by 1970 it had doubled again,[106] so that Malays comprised 603 in the élite MCS (86.6 per cent of the total), 1,863 in the higher civil service (39.3 per cent of the total), and 48,946 (64.5 per cent) in the civil service as a whole. These Malay civil servants now came predominantly from rural backgrounds (53.4 per cent). They had fathers who were uneducated or had only primary education (70.2 per cent), and who worked in agriculture, blue collar jobs, or sales and clerical jobs (67.9 per cent). The large majority came then, from 'lower and middle level socio-economic backgrounds'.[107]

The effect of this was to change the class character of the bureaucratic bourgeoisie. Instead of articulating the interests, and indeed constituting an arm, of the Malay aristocracy and landowning class, by the latter half of the 1960s they were beginning to act as an independent class group. This involved increasing efforts to assert their independence from the more conservative Malay aristocrats who dominated UMNO. They sought to assert the autonomous role of the state bureaucracy in economic development, thus challenging the economic independence of the private sector dominated by the Chinese commercial bourgeoisie. While neither the aristocratic leadership of UMNO nor the dominant *laissez-faire* stance of the state were decisively restructured until after the events of 1969, it was the increasingly vociferous and strident pressure in these directions which provoked those events.

Despite the *laissez-faire* philosophy, the state bureaucrats did achieve some shift of emphasis towards economic interventionism, though mainly in the agricultural sector. This was evident in the Second Five Year Plan (1961–65) and the First Malaysia Plan (1966–70). Direct state intervention in urban enterprises was more limited. Nevertheless, as James Jesudason notes:

> An important departure took place in the government's role in the economy in the mid-1960s. It modified its previous policy of not engaging in direct commercial and industrial activities in the modern sector because of urban Malay pressures for greater Malay progress in business. The Malay middle class, comprising aspiring businessmen, politicians, and administrators, wanted parity with rich Chinese entrepreneurs. Lacking capital and expertise, these groups turned to the state for help.[108]

The earliest manifestations of this shift were the holding of the first *Bumiputra* Economic Congress in 1965, in which Malay bureaucrats and politicians expressed their economic aspirations in primarily racial terms;[109] and the establishment, in the same year, of the Bank Bumiputra, and of MARA ('Council of Trust for the Indigenous People') to finance and organize Malay projects.[110]

During the 1960s, these changes were beginning to be felt within UMNO. Bureaucrats and professionals from subordinate class backgrounds had by then become influential within the middle ranks of the party. An early manifestation of the cleavage between this group and the 'old guard' leadership was the 1962 cabinet crisis, which led to the dismissal of Aziz Ishak, the Minister of Agriculture and Co-operatives, who favoured more overtly pro-Malay policies.[111] The 'state bureaucracy' group began to campaign, especially within UMNO Youth, for a shift of UMNO's policies, and were branded, variously, as extremists, racialists, 'ultras' or 'Young Turks'.[112] They argued in favour of state intervention in economic development so as to foster the entry of poor rural Malays into entrepreneurial activities, and they were critical of the 'feudal attitudes' within UMNO, arguing that, 'UMNO's activities are not compatible with the present political conditions'.[113] In proposing such ideas, they were articulating their own ethno-class interests, as Malays, as state bureaucrats, and as men from predominantly rural and lower socio-economic backgrounds.

The call for state help for aspiring Malay businessmen could have been defended either by the claim that this would be in the self-interest of the Malay bureaucratic bourgeoisie, or by the claim that it would ultimately benefit the mass of rural, poor Malays. In terms of public legitimacy, the latter argument was undoubtedly the most ideologically powerful. However, its articulation implied a significant departure from the ethnic ideology proclaimed by the Malay political élites up to the mid-1960s. Hitherto, the state had promulgated an ethnic ideology designed to legitimate the racial power-sharing which was institutionalized in the Alliance. It stressed that, while the Malays were the indigenese, the *Bumiputras*, and so had a rightful claim to predominant governmental power, such power should not be used so as to interfere in the capitalist economy or the plural social structure in ways detrimental to the welfare of the other races.

The new ethnic ideology of the emergent Malay bureaucratic bourgeoisie interpreted the 'special position' of the Malays in a more insistent way.[114] It initially took the form of assertions of linguistic nationalism, focusing on discontent over the Alliance compromise of the 1967 National Language Act. Thereafter, it developed into broader assertions that the Malays were in danger of being 'overwhelmed' in their own country by being left behind in the process of development and modernization, unless decisive action was taken. The ideological groundwork for such demands already existed in the inherent ambiguity of UMNO's position, in which a commitment to racial integration coexisted uneasily with an assertion of *Bumiputra* priority.

The attempts by the 'ultras' to shift the balance more towards Malay dominance than towards integration caused increasing disunity within UMNO during the mid-1960s, and this was evident in the August 1966 UMNO General Assembly:

> What is UMNO's ideology? What is the government's economic creed? While there was no outright rejection of the present economic system there was clear evidence that many delegates were disturbed at some of these failings . . . . There seemed to be a growing feeling that unless the economic basis is fairly laid, the ra'ayat's standard of living will stagnate at its present level. [What is needed is] greater initiative on the part of the government in commerce and industry to assure the people of a fairer deal . . . . There is no doubting the first breath of the wind of change.[115]

During the 1969 election campaign, the UMNO leadership adhered to the ideology of ethnic balance, but many of the middle ranking and grassroots activists espoused the more radical ideological theme of Malay dominance, which posed a direct threat to the security of the non-Malays, and which therefore served as a justificatory basis for the violence that followed.

The communal chauvinism which developed during the election campaign did not just come, then, from the opposition parties. It was granted legitimacy by the demands of the UMNO 'ultras' that state power be employed overtly for pro-Malay purposes. Perhaps the classic case was the advice from Dr. Mahathir to his Chinese constituents in Kedah, that they should 'not vote for him, as he would not represent their interests in Parliament'.[116]

The 1969 riots were thus the communal manifestation of class tensions. These involved the growing alienation of subordinate class groups from the bourgeois class fractions who claimed to be their communal patrons, the growing rivalry for urban employment between poor Malays and poor Chinese, who comprised competing proletariat class fractions, and the efforts of the emergent Malay bureaucratic bourgeoisie to legitimate their class interests through an ideology of ethnic dominance. By the end of the 1960s these changes in the class structure of Malaysian society were generating various tensions relating to the character of UMNO and the governing Alliance, the role of the state, and the relationships between the main racial groups. The eruption of these tensions in 1969 proved crucial for Malaysian politics in several ways. It paved the way for a restructuring of the state institutions, and thereafter for two initiatives which have dominated the subsequent politics of Malaysia. The government committed itself, in its New Economic Policy (NEP), to using state power to generate a Malay commercial and manufacturing bourgeoisie. This was accompanied by a shift towards a much more ethnocentric stance, whereby Malay-Muslim dominance became increasingly the main legitimatory ideology of the state.

ISLAMIC RESURGENCE AND THE NEW ECONOMIC POLICY

After 1969, the Malay state bureaucrats emerged as the dominant 'reigning' class,[117] and this was reflected in the shift towards a state-led strategy of economic development. This shift in the role of the state, embodied in the New Economic Policy, gave the Malay bureaucrats direct and privileged access to capital. Nevertheless, the restructuring of the state was itself a response to the class tensions which had generated the 1969 riots, so that the state bureaucrats were impelled to employ the state machinery in ways which would ameliorate those tensions. Thus, in addition to the use of coercion, policies were formulated which sought to reduce the alienation of the subordinate classes and to conciliate the various bourgeois class fractions. Again, therefore, politics consisted of the attempt at a balancing act in which the state served the interests of the dominant class group, but only to the extent that this remained compatible with the imperative of political stability and capitalist economic development.[118]

The claims by the 'Young Turks' of UMNO that the party was 'feudal' in its outlook and its leadership, and out of touch with the realities of post-colonial Malaysia, were apparently vindicated by the riots. This was reflected in the retirement of Tunku Abdul Rahman as UMNO leader and as Prime Minister in September 1970. Thereafter, the new generation of UMNO activists, mainly men with bureaucratic career backgrounds and from rural and subordinate class families, moved progressively into leadership positions. The 'changing of the guard' was completed with the election of Dr. Mahathir to the UMNO Presidency in 1981, and the subsequent shift of style towards a more activist and 'efficient' orientation to policy-making.

The shift of power within UMNO was paralleled by a shift of power in the governing coalition. It was argued that 'Malay backwardness' had generated the riots, and therefore that the Malay dominance in government had to be more firmly and effectively institutionalized than was the case in the Alliance. In the immediate aftermath of the riots, governmental control passed from the Alliance cabinet to the National Operations Council, which was dominated by bureaucrats (the heads of the police, armed forces, public service and foreign service) and by Malays (with seven Malays to two non-Malays). Thereafter, the Alliance was progressively enlarged by the co-option of opposition parties, thereby reducing the influence of each of these parties except for UMNO itself. By 1973 the restructuring was complete, and the Barisan National emerged. As Diane Mauzy has noted: 'Although UMNO was the dominant party in the Alliance, it is even more hegemonic in the Barisan . . . . After 1969 it was clear to everyone that the Malays led by UMNO were in charge.'[119]

The third stage of the post-1969 transition was to restructure the relationship between state and economy. Since it was argued by the UMNO leaders that the ethnic riots had been generated by the economic backwardness of the Malay community, it followed that the solution was the decisive employment of state power to rectify that imbalance. The theme of 'Malay special rights' would be translated into a radical affirmative action programme to improve the economic position of the *Bumiputras*.[120]

Initially, great care was taken, for example in the promulgation of a national ideology (*Rukunagara*), to stress the goal of national unity and justice; and to use this language to legitimate positive economic discrimination in favour of the Malays. Rather than openly labelling this as ethnocentric, the government proclaimed that its goal was the ethnically neutral one of 'reducing racial economic disparities'. Increasingly, however, the language of ethnic neutrality began to be supplemented by explicit justifications of Malay dominance.

The programme of economic restructuring designated as the National Economic Policy was implemented from 1971 with the onset of the Second Malaysia Plan. It was a programme of economic development which gave the leading role, for the first time, to government:

Government was . . . assigned a multiple role of statesman, innovator and catalyst in the efforts to restructure the society . . . . In other words, the government, including State Economic Development Corporations, statutory bodies and other government agencies, would pave the way for Malay entry into the modern sector [of the economy] in terms of employment and ownership.[121]

The eventual aim was that individual Malays would purchase shares and run businesses, but it was argued that their lack of experience, credit, etc. necessitated the proliferation of state enterprises, run by 'bureaucratic entrepreneurs' who would, in theory, hand over to individual businessmen after a few years.[122] The NEP involved, therefore, a rapid expansion in the size and range of government departments and quasi-public corporations. In terms of personnel recruitment, these new state employment opportunities were reserved overwhelmingly for Malays. Between 1970 and 1977 they gained 68 per cent of the 162,000 newly created jobs, and by 1979/80 they comprised 93 per cent of new employees. Similarly, in the armed forces and the police, their share of employment went up from 70 per cent in 1969/70 to 86 per cent in 1979/80.[123] It should be noted that the cohesion of this emergent 'bureaucratic entrepreneur' class is potentially compromised by the differing interests and circumstances of, for example, share-owners, salaried bureaucrats, public enterprise managers and private enterprise directors, etc., and also by the tension between comprador and Malay nationalist interests. But the unifying element, and the defining characteristic of the Malay bureaucratic bourgeoisie, remains their reliance upon state power as the basis for their class position.[124]

The direct participation of the government in commercial and industrial activities thus benefited Malays in two respects: by giving them public sector employment in the expanded state machinery, and by providing incentives and assistance for them to enter industrial and commercial activities, in the form of the provision of equity capital, loan finance, education and training.[125]

The resultant growth in employment and investment opportunities favoured educated Malays, those who had funds to invest, and those who had business connections.[126] Thus it was the Malay bureaucrats and politicians who became the main beneficiaries of the NEP, using their control of the state to become also 'bureaucratic capitalists'.[127] During the 1980s, UMNO itself became 'an avenue for wealth expansion':

> With political power in UMNO's hands, government licences, contracts, finances, and other concessions could easily be awarded in the party's interest or to individuals aligned to it. The government apparatus could thus be used to secure income, not just for the party, but also for personal interests, establishing a base for accumulation of corporate wealth by the ruling élite.[128]

The impact of the NEP, proclaimed as a programme to benefit all Malays and to narrow the income and occupational disparities between Malay and non-Malay, was therefore to further increase the income and occupational disparities within the Malay community. It is certainly the case that the gap between the average Malay incomes and the average non-Malay incomes began to decline after 1970, but at the same time, the gap between the mean and median Malay incomes increased between 1970 and 1984.[129] As Yukio Ikemoto noted in 1985, 'The NEP . . . neglected the inequality within each race and the total inequality in 1979 is still as high as in 1970. Thus the inequality within races is becoming more important.'[130] In the urban areas, for example, the impact of the NEP was that the well-educated Malays now earned more than the well-educated Chinese, while the poor Malays earned less than the poor Chinese.[131] The NEP might well have the impact, therefore, of increasing rather than reducing urban racial tensions, since: 'Commonly placed in subordinate and competitive relationships to non-Malays, the newly urbanized Malay proletariat may be more rather than less conscious of its relative inferiority *vis-à-vis* other races.'[132]

The effect of the NEP in fostering the growth of a Malay state bourgeoisie – 'those who command the state as its privileged instrument for the accumulation of wealth',[133] would seem likely to lock them in a direct confrontation with the Chinese bourgeoisie, discriminated against by the NEP state policies and subjected to the expansion of state regulatory legislation and procedures. This scenario has been outlined by Chandra Muzaffar:

The largely Malay government is committed to the creation of a Malay middle and upper class. This class and its aspirations have brought it into direct conflict with an established non-Malay middle and upper class which grew out of the colonial era. An emerging Malay middle and upper class backed by, indeed an extension of, what is perceived as a Malay state *versus* an established non-Malay middle and upper class deriving its strength from what is essentially a market economy linked to international capitalism – this is the scenario of the post-69 period that has influenced the entire pattern of ethnic relations in the country.[134]

But what is remarkable is that the Chinese bourgeoisie has not come into overt confrontation with the Malay bourgeoisie. Despite the marginalization of the MCA within the Barisan, the political co-operation of the two bourgeois class fractions has been maintained. The most obvious explanation for this is that the NEP has been implemented so as to minimize its adverse impact upon the Chinese commercial and business sectors, and indeed to ensure their continued prosperity. As James Jesudasan has noted, the larger Chinese businessmen had to face new constraints from the implementation of NEP policies, but they were able to employ various accommodation devices so as to maintain their profits. Moreover, the NEP did allow for the expansion of non-Malay share-capital from 23.5 per cent to 40 per cent, and this allocation was already exceeded by 1982.[135] In a study of the directorates of the largest corporations in Malaysia, Lim Mah Hui concludes that:

> The New Economic Policy has brought about increasing partnership between state, foreign and local Chinese capital. Among the large corporations, the consequences of this policy have not been as problematic as it has been for the small firms. Hence the protest from big Chinese and foreign capital has been less strident compared to that from middle-level Chinese businesses.[136]

Various forms of *ad hoc* co-operation developed between Chinese businessmen, Malay businessmen and the state, including the common practice of 'Ali-Babaism',[137] and the investment of state capital into Chinese-controlled businesses. Specific instances of such co-operation include the accommodations between the MCA's 'Multi-Purpose Holdings' company and *Bumiputra* organizations in the 1980s,[138] and the government's concession to foreign and non-Malay capitalist pressures in amending the 1975 Industrial Co-ordination Act.[139] The net result has been that while the poor Chinese have got poorer under the NEP, the wealthy Chinese have been able to increase or maintain their wealth.[140]

There has been a fundamental shift in the class character of the state, from representing an alliance of bourgeois class fractions towards acting more as the instrument of a new dominant 'bureaucratic capitalist' class. This has had the actual impact of hurting the economic position of the mass of poor Malays more than it has hurt the wealthy Chinese, with the result that the political disunity of the Malays has been exacerbated.[141] In order to camouflage this economic impact and to remedy this political effect, the state has had to strengthen the countervailing myth of Malay ethnic unity and Malay cultural superiority. It has been able to do so by employing the resurgent ideology of Islam. This is not to say that the Islamic resurgence is simply an ideological weapon of the dominant class. Indeed, the dynamics of contemporary Malaysian politics can only be understood if it is recognized that Islam has been employed as the ideology of several different class groups, who have sought to use it for purposes which are mutually antithetical.

The ideology of Malay-Muslim dominance

The growth and radicalization of Islam in Malaysia must be seen as part of a global phenomenon affecting numerous Third World countries and arising from their progressive incorporation into the world capitalist system. This involved the 'neo-colonial' investment of metropolitan and indigenous capital for the development of industry and commerce in such countries, and the consequent process of rapid urbanization. The cultural impact of industrialization and urbanization is an alienating one, in the Marxist sense, in that it involves the domination of human beings by machines, and thence the estrangement of the individual from others, from work and from his potential self. The alienating impact of urbanization is particularly strong when it involves the rapid uprooting of individuals from traditional or feudal pre-capitalist societies. From this perspective then, the fundamental explanation for the Islamic upsurge is that it offers a new sense of security by offering a sense of individual identity and communal solidarity which appears as a resolution to the problem of alienation and social dislocation. From a Marxist perspective, the retreat to religion is of course simply a retreat from one form of alienation to another, but this is not to deny its emotional appeal. This is argued specifically for Malaysia by Chandra Muzaffar:

> Many of the urban migrants . . . turn to religion for solace and comfort. They perform faithfully the various rituals prescribed by their faith. They put on Islamic attire. Some modifications are made to their pattern of living. By this time they will have joined some Muslim organization. Through enthusiastic participation in its activities a group spirit develops. A new solidarity is thus created and a sense of belonging is provided.[142]

For some specific class groups amongst the urban Malay populace, the appeal of Islam was particularly strong in that it seemed to offer, in addition to a sense of psychological and social security, a resource through which economic and career interests might be promoted. This applied particularly to the new generation of Malay students who were recruited into the universities in the early 1970s, and who constituted an emergent petit-bourgeois class fraction destined to man the expanding middle ranks of the public service and teaching professions.

Islam and the petit-bourgeoisie

The NEP indicated the need for a rapid increase in the numbers of educated Malays, and accordingly Malay-language universities were set up from 1970 onwards. Educational quotas were also introduced after 1971 to rectify the Chinese dominance in tertiary education, so that between 1969 and 1980 the proportion of Malays registered for local degree courses rose from 35.6 per cent to 66.7 per cent.[143]

The large majority of these Malay students were from poor, rural backgrounds. Their limited command of English, which was still in the early 1970s the main language on the campuses and in administration and business, together with their lower educational qualifications, meant that they could not compete on equal terms either with earlier generations of Malay students or with Chinese graduates.[144]

Their perception of inferiority generated high levels of anxiety, and the appeal of radical Islam was partly that it could resolve such anxieties by offering moral certainties and legitimating an unthinking rejection of new ideas. But the demand for an Islamic society in which Malay-Muslims would have definite preference also offered the promise of a protective barrier against economic competition from non-Muslims, so that: 'The religion became a tool, an instrument to serve their own interests. They have a vested interest in seeing that their type of Islam triumphs.'[145]

The appeal of radical Islam for Malay students at the Malaysian universities was paralleled by its appeal for those who attended foreign universities and who reacted against the alienation of immigrant life in the West. Several of these returned to Malaysia as academics, and Islam offered a route to career advancement:

> By projecting themselves as champions of Islam in a situation where Islam is on the upsurge, they hope to be promoted to senior positions within the university. Sometimes university administrators, afraid that they will be chastised for being 'un-Islamic', succumb meekly to the manipulations of these so-called 'defenders of the faith'.[146]

The Islamic study groups that developed in the universities in the early 1970s (widely designated as *dakwah* groups) provided one of the few channels through which students could articulate grievances against what they considered the corrupt and self-aggrandizing behaviour of the bourgeois Malay politicians. The first major organization to emerge was the Muslim Youth Movement of Malaysia (ABIM), co-founded by Anwar Ibrahim at the University of Malaya in 1972. In the later 1970s, more radical Islamic movements developed amongst Malaysian students studying in England, influenced by Middle Eastern and Pakistani groups there. They formed the Malaysian Islamic Study Group, and various breakaway groups including the *Suara Islam* (Voice of Islam) and the Islamic Representative Council.[147]

It has been estimated that by the late 1980s, some 60 to 70 per cent of Malay students had some commitment to *dakwah*, either in the sense of adopting Islamic dress, or in the more political sense of campaigning for an Islamic state. Of the various *dakwah* groups, the largest was the Islamic Republic Group, influenced by the Iranian revolution and with close ties to PAS.[148] Other groups, notably the *Tabligh* groups and the *Darul Arqam* movement, had extensive rural as well as urban support, but were less overtly political in their goals.[149]

Thus, while the appeal of the *dakwah* movement has been widespread, its momentum came from the class grievances and aspirations of the expanding Malay petit-bourgeoisie, who were increasingly frustrated by the employment and promotion bottleneck within the Malay bureaucracy, and who reacted against the corruption and materialism of the Malay élite to which they sought entry.

Islam and the peasantry

The emergent Malay bureaucratic bourgeoisie formulated the NEP policy with the primary aim of promoting the entry of Malays into the urban commercial and industrial bourgeoisie. They were aware, however, that such a programme would have to be legitimated in the form of a commitment to the economic betterment of all Malays; and that this could not remain only a rhetorical ideology. It would necessitate the expansion of rural development programmes in addition to the new focus on urban industrial development.[150]

This concern to alleviate rural Malay poverty was to a large extent a response to the 1969 riots, which were seen as resulting from the urban migration of poor rural Malays. While the Malay bureaucratic bourgeoisie wished to alleviate poverty and the political discontent this generated, their commitment to the poor Malays did not extend to any willingness to undertake fundamental land reforms, since this would involve alienating the landowners who were still an influential class fraction within UMNO. The rural development programme was translated, therefore, into an expansion of expenditure on rural infrastructure development, the subsidizing of resettlement projects, and the provision of agricultural resources, including irrigation schemes, so as to increase productivity and generate a 'green revolution'.

This programme of state intervention had the effect of fundamentally altering the rural economy and the position of the poor
farmers in that economy. The 'green revolution' involved
attempts to increase productivity in various areas, but efforts to
promote rice production were given particular stress. This was
because the rice-farming Malays comprised both the poorest
segment of the community and also the one most politically
alienated from the UMNO government.

Rice farming is concentrated in the four northern states of
Kelantan, Trengganu, Perlis and Kedah. These states are predominantly Malay (ranging from about 75 per cent in Kedah to
about 95 per cent in Trengganu), with about 84 per cent of the
Malays employed as paddy farmers.[151] In many respects the
programme to promote rice productivity and reduce the
poverty of these farmers has been remarkably successful. Rice
productivity increased dramatically during the 1970s with the
provision of fertilizers, farm machinery, etc., and the introduction of double cropping through enhanced irrigation. By the
mid-1980s Malaysia was near to achieving self-sufficiency in rice
production.[152] Moreover, the price subsidies on rice served to
raise the incomes of rice farmers, so that there was a significant
drop in the incidence of poverty, with the percentage below the
poverty line falling from 88.1 per cent in 1970, to 50.2 per cent
in 1987.[153]

These figures on declining poverty and rising productivity are
somewhat misleading, however. The improvements were heavily dependent on the maintenance of state subsidies, so that in
1984 69 per cent of estimated net annual income from rice
cultivation was the result of price subsidy.[154] Moreover, various
studies have argued that the decline of aggregate poverty levels
amongst rice farmers camouflaged an increase in rural inequalities; so that those below the poverty line, while declining in
overall numbers, were probably more deeply impoverished.[155]
As Jomo Sundaram notes:

> Big farmers, who produce large surpluses of rice for sale, and
> large landowners, who qualify for larger input subsidies on
> the basis of land owned, tend to gain proportionately greater
> benefits from such government intervention.[156]

This process, and its detrimental impact upon the poorer
farmers, is explained more graphically by James Scott. He

recognizes that state interventions have raised average real incomes, but argues that 'the distribution of income is now more skewed than it was previously'.[157]

> The rich have got richer and the poor have remained poor or grown poorer. The introduction of huge combine-harvesters in 1976 was perhaps the coup de grace, as it eliminated two-thirds of the wage-earning opportunities for smallholders and landless labourers.[158]

Moreover, he argues that:

> By the very logic of its policy, the state displaced both the private sector and to some degree even the weather as the crucial factor in farm incomes . . . . The state was once largely a bystander or mediator . . . . It is now a direct partici-pant, decision maker, allocator, and antagonist in nearly all vital aspects of paddy growing. Most of the buffers between the state and rice farmers have fallen away, thereby vastly increasing both the role of politics and the possibilities for direct confrontation between the ruling party and its peasantry.[159]

Scott's discussion of the Northern Malay rice farmers stresses that their class struggle is articulated primarily through eclectic or symbolic resistance, rather than through the emergence of overt class consciousness and class rebellion. Nevertheless, the rice farmers in the Muda irrigation project did stage a major mass protest in 1980 to demand higher rice prices, and there have been several such instances of 'class' protest by rural Malays.[160] But the most sustained way of articulating protest has been through political support for PAS, which has consistently gained between 35 per cent and 50 per cent electoral support in the four Malay paddy farming states.

The assertion that PAS gains its main support from the most impoverished section of Malay society does not of itself justify the claim that support for PAS is the articulation of class con-sciousness rather than religious or communal consciousness. Indeed, such a distinction appears to be misleading. PAS, like UMNO, builds upon the local patron–client relationships through which, in peasant societies, class relations are articu-lated.[161] The primary motivation for supporting PAS is as a protest against economic deprivation. But awareness of an economic grievance does not necessarily imply recognition of a viable economic solution, since such a solution may not be conceivable within the prevalent cultural values. The resultant politics is thus one in which awareness of economic deprivation is articulated through the available cultural norms. Support for PAS is explainable then, not as false consciousness, but rather as an expression of ethno-class consciousness, in which the class grievances of a racially clustered group are articulated in terms of racial-religious cultural values.[162]

Islam and the state bureaucratic bourgeoisie

If the UMNO bourgeoisie were to try to regain the political support of the subordinate Malay classes at the same time as promoting policies which involved their economic exploitation, they would have to promulgate a powerful ideology of communal unity. Such an ideology was particularly necessary in order to legitimate state coercion against workers, peasants and students who protested at such exploitation.

One ideological strategy, which was employed after 1969, was the attempt to generate unity behind the new Barisan government through the generation of a siege mentality, in which political support for the Barisan leaders could be engineered by arguing that it was the only way to avoid 'a return to May 13th'. The spectre of racial conflict was thus employed repeatedly as an ethnic ideology to promote support for the incumbent bourgeois political leaders.[163] The more long-term strategy, however, was to articulate a coherent ideology of Malay unity which could rebuild support for UMNO.

The basis for such an ideology did exist in the well-established kinship myth that all Malays were indigenes whilst all non-Malays were immigrants. This distinction between *Bumiputra* (sons of the soil) and non-*Bumiputra* gained prominence as a unifying myth in the post-Independence period, when the UMNO leaders were trying to frame legislation to institutionalize the 'special position of the Malays' enshrined in the Constitution.[164] The major focus of these efforts had been on the issue of language. The dominant unifying argument was that education offered the key to upward socio-economic mobility, and that once Malay became the language of education (and of administration) the Malay community as a whole would benefit and its 'special position' *vis à vis* the non-Malay speakers would be assured.

This *Bumiputra* ideology needed modification by the early 1970s if it was going to provide an adequate state ideology for the new Malay bourgeoisie. It would need to detract Malay attention from the escalating intra-ethnic inequalities, legitimate the more strident discrimination against non-Malays embodied in the NEP, and reassert Malay political support for UMNO after its decline in the 1969 elections.

The shift of emphasis in state ideology, from the issue of the Malay language to that of the Islamic religion, occurred for two major reasons. First, by 1970 the issue of the Malay language and its role in education had been settled, with the progressive introduction of Malay as the language of instruction in all state schools, to culminate in 1982. This meant that it was no longer either an emotionally powerful rallying cry or a suitable symbol for Malay unity, as non-Malays became educated in the language. An alternative unifying symbol was therefore needed.[165] Second, it was already clear by 1969 that the consociational Alliance with non-Malay political parties made the UMNO élite vulnerable to outbidding by more explicitly communal parties, which could mobilize mass support unconstrained by the need for coalition compromises. The major such party was undoubtedly PAS. The response of the UMNO leadership was first to incorporate PAS into the governing alliance in the form of the new Barisan, and second to co-opt its ideological themes, so as to win back its supporters. By this time, 1972, PAS was beginning to shift its emphasis from one in which the language of Islam was used to legitimate particularist Malay nationalism (*asabiyyah*), towards one in which the absolutist tenets of Islam received primary stress.[166] UMNO has responded by asserting its own legitimacy as an Islamic movement, and adopting an Islamization programme which has included the establishment of an Islamic University, Islamic Bank, Islamic insurance scheme, etc., all designed to take the steam out of the more radical Islamic movements.

The Islamic element in the state ideology is designed to re-unify the Malay community behind UMNO by strengthening the *Bumiputra* myth, thus camouflaging the bourgeois character of the UMNO-led government policies:

The Bumiputra/non-Bumiputra dichotomy . . . has become much stronger with the implementation of the New Economic Policy (NEP) of the Government. For the NEP is in reality a strategy designed to accommodate, entrench and extend the interests of the Bumiputra middle and upper classes. It is a policy whose actual aim is to enhance and expand the wealth and power of these classes within the Bumiputra community. For this purpose, the Bumiputra/non-Bumiputra dichotomy has to be maintained, indeed reinforced, at all costs. Since the State, given its capitalist orientation, reflects the interests of the middle and upper classes, and since the interests of these classes dominate society, society as a whole lives and breathes through this Bumiputra/non-Bumiputra dichotomy.[167]

There are clear tensions then, between the attempts by the Malay petit-bourgeoisie to employ Islam as a tool to facilitate their own upward mobility into the dominant class, the attempts by poor rural Malay peasants to oppose that class through the medium of Islam, and the employment of Islam by the dominant class itself as a Malay unifying myth and as a state ideology. The tensions emerge in the continued rivalry between UMNO and PAS, and in the factional rivalries within UMNO itself.

CONCLUSION

The dominant role of racial, religious, linguistic and cultural issues in Malaysian politics, which tends to be treated as a common-sense and self-explanatory fact precisely because of that dominance, is explainable in terms of the class structure of the economy and of the state. Its origins lie in the racial recruitment policies of the colonial state, and thence in the racially clustered class fractions which sought to protect their interests during the process of decolonization. Thereafter, the shifting balance of forces within the bourgeois power bloc, towards the Malay state bureaucrats, has constituted the dominant factor maintaining the politicization of ethnicity. During the period of the NEP, the state has not restructured the society and the economy so as to promote the socio-economic mobility of all Malays in the way the ethnic ideology claimed. This is perhaps the reason for the lower profile, in the New Development Plan launched in 1990, of the 'racial restructuring' goal, though the pro-*Bumiputra* policies remain intact.[168] The state has, however, had sufficient restructuring capability to promote the acquisition of capital by the expanding Malay state bourgeoisie.

The politics of ethnicity in Malaysia is complex, not just because class interests are expressed through ethnic forms, but also because they are so expressed in two distinct but intertwined ways. They are articulated as the ethno-class consciousness of racially clustered class fractions, and also as the ethnic ideologies of the dominant class, which seeks to unify the class-divided Malays by asserting and institutionalizing Malay–Chinese rivalry. Thus, the shifting balances between contending classes and class fractions are worked out, in the culturally plural context of Malaysia, in the ideological language of ethnicity.

In the previous chapters, the varying impact of the state upon ethnicity has been explainable, in part, in terms of differences in the 'strength' of the state, such that it has had a reactive impact on ethnicity in the Burmese and Thailand cases, a largely responsive impact in the Singapore case, and a largely manipulative impact in the Indonesian case. But in the Malaysian case, the relationship between state and ethnicity appears to be, in this respect, more subtle, with reactive, responsive and manipulative elements interwoven. The dominant class is able to promote a 'divide and rule' ethnic ideology so as to achieve a responsive impact on ethnicity and thence to maintain UMNO and Barisan rule. But subordinate class groups have at the same time been able to manipulate this ideology to their own class-fractional advantage; and in some respects, as with the rise of PAS, the ethnic ideology has at times been employed reactively, to oppose the state and the dominant class. The class perspective on ethnicity thus offers the basis for a subtle understanding of contemporary Malaysian politics, including the emergence of contending interpretations of the meanings and implications of the Malay-*Bumiputra*-Islam identity.

Chapter 7

Ethnicity, nationalism and democracy

In the foregoing examinations of the differing characterizations of the state, ethnicity has been depicted as related, variously, to the collapse of traditional authority structures, to the state's managerial institutions, to the factional rivalries amongst political élites, to regional economic disparities, and to the class structure of society. Clearly, if each or any of these features of the political, social and economic environment were intrinsic to the nature of ethnicity, then the discussion would contain a central inconsistency. It has been argued here, however, that these aspects of the environment are only contingently related to ethnicity; while what is intrinsic to ethnicity is its ideological character – as a psychological and political kinship myth. Both the type of cultural attributes to which this myth attaches, and the kind of economic, political or social mechanisms by which it is engendered are, it has been argued, crucially influenced by the character of the state.

Thus the discussions have had two purposes: to offer explanations of the various patterns of ethnic politics in Southeast Asia, and to explore different models of the state so as to make explicit some of their ethnic implications. The intention has been to narrow the perceived gap, frequently evident in Southeast Asian studies, between the recognition and description of the unique politics of each country, and attempts at comparative and conceptual analysis. The resultant argument has been in two stages: that ethnic consciousness constitutes an emotionally powerful ideological response to the pattern of insecurities generated by the power structure of the state, and therefore that the character of the state constitutes the dominant influence upon the character of ethnic politics. The exploration of the different perspectives on the state thus offers a series of differing scenarios as to the development of ethnic consciousness and its relationship to state nationalism. The resultant explanations are distinct in that they employ the markedly different languages relating to class, corporatist, ethnocratic, clientelist or internal colonial models, but are comparable in terms of their common reference to the causal impact of the character of the state. It has not been suggested that the perspectives used for the examination of ethnicity in each country are of general validity; merely that they provide, in each case, an illuminating angle from which to examine some facets of that country's ethnic politics.

Such an approach begins to offer a basis for tackling the crucial question as to why countries which have many similarities in the cultural pluralism of their societies should nevertheless vary greatly in the character and consequences of their ethnic politics. Why is there endemic ethnic violence in Burma, fragile but generally non-violent ethnic relations in Malaysia, and generally harmonious ethnic relations in Singapore?

One crucial factor influencing the relative success of the different states in implementing their ethnic strategy relates to the capacity of the state. Whereas the Singaporean state has sufficient administrative and ideological capability to implement its ethnic management strategies in a reasonably competent way, the Burmese state has no such capacity, and merely has a disruptive impact upon the targeted communities. But to say that the state's ability to manage ethnicity depends on its capacity to manage ethnicity is clearly not very profound. The intention here, therefore, is to draw together some themes as to the relationship between the character of the state and the nature of ethnic politics which have been implicit in the discussions of the different types of state. The discussion will be limited to two factors which seem to have influenced the politics of each of the Southeast Asian states so as to inhibit the effective management of state–ethnic relations. These factors relate to the ambiguities evident in the states' portrayals of the nation, and to the role played in ethnic–state relations by the ideology of democracy.

There is no inevitable clash between the claims of ethnicity and the claims of state nationalism, and each of the models of the state which have been discussed offers a potentially feasible formula for achieving their reconciliation through state management of the ethnic-state relationship. But there is no denying that such efforts at ethnic management rarely seem to have been fully successful, though there are, as we have noted, major variations in the extent and form of the ethnic tensions which such failures have engendered.

The way in which ethnicity and state nationalism relate to each other depends in part upon the type of state nationalism adopted in a particular country. We have previously noted the distinction, deriving from Meinecke and Kohn, between the idea of the political nation, and the idea of the cultural nation.[1] In the first formulation – the political nation – the state claims that its people constitute a nation because they have willingly come together to form a community of equal citizens irrespective of their racial, religious or linguistic backgrounds. They are a nation because they wish and believe themselves to be a nation; and nationhood is defined in terms of the equal duties, rights and status of all citizens. Such a formulation of a political nation might seem to be particularly appropriate for societies, like those in Southeast Asia, which contain several ethnically conscious cultural communities. It would seem to imply, most clearly, a depiction of the nation as an overarching ethnically neutral community in which ethnicity is regarded as politically irrelevant to the national politics of meritocratic, democratic or universalistic procedures which are employed to define citizenship rights. Alternatively, the idea of the political nation may accommodate the idea of a community comprising ethnic components, with each component enjoying equal status, power, and access to resources, according to some formula of 'unity in diversity', consociationalism, or federalism.

The alternative formulation of the nation is as the cultural nation: the community which constitutes a distinct people with its own language, way of life, history and homeland. When a state claims to constitute such a cultural nation it is seeking to arrogate to itself the power of the kinship myth by portraying the whole society as an ethnic community. The claim to cultural nationhood allows the state to demand the allegiance of its people in ways that echo the imperative of ethnic loyalty. The nation is depicted as offering identity, security and authority to its members such as the family offers the child, and in return the nation demands the loyalty and allegiance the child owes to the family. The more that the state can point to, or itself generate, the common cultural attributes which define the cultural nation, the more claim it has to the allegiance of its members. Similarly, the more clearly an individual possesses the cultural attributes which define the national community, the more fully does that individual deserve the citizenship rights accruing to membership of the nation.

The distinction between the political nation and the cultural nation was originally intended and employed to refer to different types of nation-state. But what is apparent in the foregoing discussions of Southeast Asian politics is that instead of these states fitting neatly into one or other category, they each seek, in different ways, to employ both formulations. They claim somehow to offer equal citizenship rights to all citizens irrespective of cultural attributes, but they also define the nation in cultural terms so as to give priority of some kind to those possessing the attributes of cultural nationhood. It is this ambiguity or incoherence in the designation of the nation-state which hinders the effective management of ethnic–state relations.

The origin of this ambiguity in the definition of the nation is quite clear. The state élites consider cultural nationalism to offer a stronger basis for political cohesion and societal loyalty than does political nationalism; and indeed political nationalism is perceived to be both western in origin and colonialist in its connotations. Despite their cultural pluralism, each of the Southeast Asian societies can derive, from their pre-colonial history, an image of a set of dominant cultural attributes and values which form the core for the definition of contemporary nationhood. They therefore seek to portray the culturally plural society as one which is potentially culturally homogeneous, and which already has a cultural core around which nationhood can develop. For Burma this cultural core is Burman, for Singapore it is the idea of consensual Asian values, for Indonesia it is embodied in *Panca Sila*, for Malaysia it is the *Bumiputra* attribute, for Thailand it is the Central Thai monarchy and culture.

The employment of two different languages of nationhood leads to two incompatible definitions of citizenship. Those groups in society which do not possess, or do not fully possess, the attributes of cultural nationalism are nevertheless told by various clauses in their constitutions and laws, and by political leaders, that they inhabit a political nation which gives equal citizenship status and rights to all. But they are also told, in other clauses, laws, speeches and policies, that they are in some sense of lower status than those who possess the prescribed cultural attributes; that they are, in effect, second-class citizens. This produces a sense of confusion and grievance amongst those who perceive themselves as unfairly culturally marginalized by the state. The political implication of this is that such minority cultural groups become in varying degrees alienated from the state.

Clearly this clash is greatest in the Burmese case where the state has discriminated against those who have not assimilated into Burman culture, but it has produced varying degrees of resentment against the state amongst Indonesia's *santri* Muslims, Malaysia's non-Malays, and Thailand's non-Thai citizens. In Singapore it emerges as a confusion amongst those whom the state suggests are 'too westernized' or who possess Asian attributes other than those fostered by the state, but who have expected equal consideration in an avowedly ethnically neutral meritocracy. In such circumstances, the capacity of the state to manage state–ethnic relations is undermined by the extent of these resentments.

The ambiguities generated by the mixing of the two languages of political nationalism and cultural nationalism provide one element in explaining the problematical nature of ethnic politics in Southeast Asia, and the variations in the intensity of such problems. But there is another factor emerging out of the previous discussions which concerns the relationship between ethnic and state nationalism on the one hand, and the ideology of democracy on the other.

Solutions

The claims of ethnic nationalism and of state nationalism are potentially negotiable and manageable so long as each party recognizes the legitimacy of the other's claims. In some respects, it might be expected that the impact of the dominant legitimatory argument of the twentieth century – the democratic argument – would be such as to promote the prospects for reconciliation between ethnic and state claims, since democracy appears to promise the politics of negotiation and compromise rather than the politics of confrontation and violence. But the way in which the democratic ideology has been repeatedly employed in the politics of ethnicity in Southeast Asia has been such as to reduce the possibilities for compromise and accommodation.

The most obvious way in which this occurs is in the argument frequently employed by state élites, that they wish to promote democracy in their societies but are inhibited from doing so, in varying degrees, by the ethnic pluralism which they portray as inherently anti-democratic in its implications. This argument is formulated in various ways. The 'siege' formulation of the argument portrays ethnicity in terms of the spectre of chaos; as an anti-democratic, irrational and absolutist tie which makes some variant of authoritarian rule an unfortunate necessity. Once this spectre of ethnic chaos is raised, it follows that all rational citizens will resist it and will voluntarily, and democratically, choose the option of unity, development and stability which is offered by the state. Democracy thus becomes redefined by the state as rational support for the state's restriction on the politicization of anti-democratic ethnicity. At its most extreme, this argument is used to justify the continuation of oppressive military rule in Burma, but it has also been used to legitimate the 'soft authoritarian' democracies of Malaysia, Thailand, Indonesia and Singapore.

A second formulation of ethnicity as anti-democratic portrays the state as the embodiment of a consensual Rousseauean general will, and then depicts attachments to the subnational ethnic community as partial, self-interested attachments which threaten to undermine the national consensus and thence divide the nation. A third way of counterposing the democratic state with the undemocratic ethnic attachment is the frequent employment of the majoritarian principle. This was intended in democratic theory to refer to situations where individuals move between majorities and minorities on different issues as the balance of non-ascriptive opinions and interests repeatedly shifts. But it has been applied in culturally plural societies to legitimate the dominance of ascriptive cultural majorities. By this means the democratic argument is employed in the service of the majority cultural group claiming to represent the whole nation-state, which is therefore 'democratically' free to ignore the interests of the cultural minorities.

By such means, the state which claims to be democratic can promote its own claim precisely by depicting ethnicity as an anti-democratic and therefore illegitimate claim. Since there is immense pressure in the twentieth century for all states to claim such democratic legitimacy, there is a corresponding pressure to employ such a claim to reduce the bargaining power of ethnicity.

This tendency for the democratic argument to polarize state–ethnic relations is exacerbated by the parallel tendency for ethnic élites to similarly use the democratic argument to strengthen their claims against the state. The democratic argument that the individual has a right to the achievement of self-realization through taking a full and active part in public decision making, does not of itself imply that any particular grouping of individuals – in this case the ethnic community – has any corresponding right to self-determination. The ethnic nationalist claim to political autonomy cannot, in other words, be derived from the democratic argument about the political 'rights of man'. Nevertheless, the ethnic nationalist argument has frequently sought to make such a connection by means of analogy. In other words, minority cultural groups have frequently argued that, just as democracy grants the citizen the right of rebellion against an authoritarian state, so do a people – an ethnic nation – have a democratic right to assert their autonomy against the central state, which is depicted as alien and undemocratic. Thus, the ethnic minority portrays itself as the guardian of legitimate democracy, and the state as the alien and illegitimate opponent of democracy.

This use of the democratic argument both by the state and by the ethnic élites so as to portray each other as the illegitimate opponents of democracy, is one which does not necessarily produce confrontation between the state and ethnicity. None of the states examined have condemned all manifestations of ethnicity as threats to democracy; and not all ethnic élites have asserted their claims by denigrating the democratic credentials of the state. Nevertheless, it has generated suspicion and resentment in each case. The articulation of ethnic interests becomes inherently hazardous in such circumstances since it risks being labelled by the state as anti-democratic communalism. The danger has been, in each of the Southeast Asian states, that ethnic interests have been deemed democratically legitimate by the state only when they have been supportive of the incumbent régime. Ethnicity thus inhabits a shadow world – liable to be designated as subversive communalism at one moment, but applauded as the legitimate articulation of cultural values and interests at another.

The problem then, is not that ethnicity constitutes a primordial loyalty which inevitably attaches to fixed ascriptive cultural attributes and is necessarily absolutist and overwhelming, but rather that it is frequently perceived in such a way by state élites who portray it as a primitive and threatening force to be suppressed, subverted or tamed. It has been argued here that it is not the cultural attributes themselves which define and generate the ethnic attachment, but rather the variable patterns of status, power and economic insecurities in the social environment. Ethnic consciousness is indeed 'irrational' in the sense that it is a response to emotional needs for identity, security and authority. But it fulfils these needs in part by providing an ideological myth of continuity and permanence which facilitates the adaptation of individuals to changing situations of insecurity. If the contemporary state intervenes in society sufficiently to influence the cultural attributes, political options, and security threats with which members of the multicultural societies are faced, then it becomes clear that the form, political manifestations and political consequences of ethnicity are not fixed, but depend to a significant extent upon variations in the character of the state.

Notes

Introduction

1 For an outline survey of the primordialist position, see James McKay 'An exploratory synthesis of primordial and mobilizationist approaches to ethnic phenomena', *Ethnic and Racial Studies*, 1982, vol. 5, no. 4.

2 Clifford Geertz *The Interpretation of Cultures: Selected Essays*, New York, Basic, 1973, p. 259.

3 John F. Stack 'Ethnic mobilization in world politics: the primordial perspective', in Stack (ed.) *The Primordial Challenge: Ethnicity in the Contemporary World*, New York, Greenwood, 1986, p. 8.

4 The terms 'primordial image' and 'archetype' are treated as synonymous by Jung. There is a close relationship between the primordial image and the instincts, thus 'the primordial image might suitably be described as the instinct's perception of itself . . . . Just as the conscious apprehension gives our actions form and direction, so unconscious apprehension through the archetype determines the form and direction of instinct'. From C. C. Jung *The Structure and Dynamics of the Psyche*, extracted in Joseph Campbell (ed.) *The Portable Jung*, Harmondsworth, Penguin, 1976, p. 56. Jung apparently derived the term 'primordial' from Jacob Burckhardt.

5 Katherine M. Noonan 'Evolution: a primer for psychologists' in Charles Crawford, Martin Smith and Dennis Krebs (eds) *Sociobiology and Psychology: Ideas, Issues and Applications*, Hillsdale, Lawrence Erlbaum, 1987, p. 49. The implications of sociobiology for the study of race are outlined in Irwin Silverman 'Race, race differences, and race relations', in the same volume. Sociobiological theories are outlined and placed in the context of alternative approaches in Vernon Reynolds, V. Falger and I. Vine (eds) *The Sociobiology of Ethnocentrism*, London, Croom Helm, 1987; Robert A. Levine and Donald T. Campbell *Ethnocentrism: Theories of Conflict, Ethnic Attitudes and Group Behaviour*, New York, Wiley, 1972, Chapter 6, 'Evolutionary Theories'; and James G. Kellas *The Politics of Nationalism and Ethnicity*, London, Macmillan, 1991, Chapter 1.

6 Antony Black *State, Community and Human Desire*, Hemel Hempstead, Harvester-Wheatsheaf, 1988.

7 J. S. Furnivall *Colonial Policy and Practice*, Cambridge, Cambridge University Press, 1948; M. G. Smith *The Plural Society in the British West Indies*, Berkeley, University of California Press, 1965; Alvin Rabushka and Kenneth A. Shepsle *Politics of Plural Societies*, Columbus, Merrill, 1972. Smith's formulation of the plural society model is discussed in Chapter 2.

8 Dick Robison and John Girling 'Southeast Asian area studies political science methodology: four essays', in *Asian Studies Association of Australia Review*, 1985, vol. 9, no. 1, p. 8, and the similar comment in the same piece by Harold Crouch.

9 This stress on the unresponsiveness of the state to societal (including ethnic) influences is surveyed in the case of Indonesia in Andrew MacIntyre *Business and Politics in Indonesia*, Sydney, Allen and Unwin, 1990, Chapter 2.

10 For a perceptive discussion of the inconsistencies in Karl Deutsch's argument, from a primordialist standpoint, see Walker Connor 'Nation-building or nation-destroying', *World Politics*, 1972, vol. 24, no. 3.

11 For a review of such 'conflict modernization theorists' see Saul Newman 'Does modernization breed ethnic political conflict', *World Politics*, 1991, vol. 43, no. 3.

12 Walker Connor 'Ethnonationalism' in Myron Weiner and Samuel P. Huntington (eds) *Understanding Political Development*, Boston, Little Brown, 1987.

13 Walker Connor 'Prospects for stability in Southeast Asia' in Kusuma Snitwongse and Sukhumbhand Paribatra (eds) *Durable Stability in Southeast Asia*, Singapore, Institute of Southeast Asian Studies, 1987; A. D. Smith, 'State and homelands: The social and geopolitical implications of national territory', *Millenium: Journal of International Studies*, 1981, vol. 10, no. 3.

14 D. Ronen *The Quest for Self-Determination*, New Haven/London, Yale University Press, 1979. On situationalism see also N. Kasfir *The Shrinking Political Arena: Participation and Ethnicity in African Politics*, Los Angeles, University of California Press, 1976; C. Young *The Politics of Cultural Pluralism*, Madison/London, University of Wisconsin Press, 1976. For a survey of the situationalist approach see Jonathan Y. Okamura 'Situational ethnicity', *Ethnic and Racial Studies*, 1981, vol. 4, no. 4.

15 It is indicative that Michael Hechter, who outlined a situationalist explanation of ethnic nationalism as a response to economic disparities, cultural division of labour and internal colonialism (discussed in Chapter 5), progressively developed his theory until it emerges as an overtly 'rational choice' theory of individual behaviour. The shift is evident in M. Levi and M. Hechter 'A rational choice approach to the rise and decline of ethno-regional political parties' in E. A. Tiryakian and R. Rogowski (eds) *New Nationalisms of the Developed West*, Boston, Allen and Unwin, 1985. Hechter's mature 'rational

choice' approach is summarized in his 'Rational choice theory and the study of race and ethnic relations', in John Rex and David Mason (eds) *Theories of Race and Ethnic Relations*, Cambridge, Cambridge University Press, 1986. Rational choice theory is also proposed in Michael Banton *Racial and Ethnic Competition*, Cambridge, Cambridge University Press, 1983, Chapters 9 and 10.

16 For an explanation of nationalism, including ethnic nationalism, on these lines, see Leonard W. Doob *Patriotism and Nationalism: Their Psychological Foundations*, New Haven, Yale University Press, 1964.

17 Robert H. Taylor 'Perceptions of ethnicity in the politics of Burma', *Southeast Asian Journal of Social Science*, 1982, vol. 10, no. 1; Charles F. Keyes (ed.) *Ethnic Adaptation and Identity: The Karen on the Thai Frontier with Burma*, Philadelphia, Institute for the Study of Human Issues, 1979; J. A. Nagata 'What is a Malay?': Situational selection of ethnic indentity in a plural society', *American Ethnologist*, 1974, vol. 1, no. 2. Liddle uses the language of primordialism, but his analysis is primarily in situational terms, see R. William Liddle *Ethnicity, Party, and National Integration: An Indonesian Case Study*, New Haven/ London, Yale University Press, 1970.

18 For discussion of the possibility of synthesizing the two approaches, see McKay 'An exploratory synthesis', and George M. Scott 'A resynthesis of primordial and circumstantial approaches to ethnic group solidarity: towards an explanatory model', *Ethnic and Racial Studies*, 1990, vol. 13, no. 2.

19 D. L. Horowitz *Ethnic Groups in Conflict*, Los Angeles/London, University of California Press, 1985. See also Walker Connor 'A nation is a nation, is a state, is an ethnic group, is a . . .', *Ethnic and Racial Studies*, 1978, vol. 1, no. 4.

1 Ethnicity and the state

1 For a useful discussion of various formulations as to the state's impact upon ethnicity see the introductory chapter by Paul Brass (ed.) *Ethnic Groups and the State*, Beckenham, Croom Helm, 1985.

2 For an examination of various formulations as to the relationship between ethnicity and nationalism, see James G. Kellas *The Politics of Nationalism and Ethnicity*, London, Macmillan, 1991.

3 See the 'Symposium' articles by G. A. Almond, E. A. Nordlinger, T. J. Lowi, and S, Fabbrini in *American Political Science Review*, 1988, vol. 82, no. 3.

4 Joseph Rothschild *Ethnopolitics: A Conceptual Framework*, New York, Columbia University Press, 1981, Chapter 7.

5 For a discussion of variations in the penetrative capability of the state, which stresses the tendency in Third World countries towards the weakness of the state in relation to societal groups, see Joel S. Migdal *Strong Societies and Weak States: State Society Relations and State Capabilities in the Third World*, New Jersey, Princeton University Press, 1988. For a discussion of state autonomy and capacity in the Southeast Asian context see Donald K. Crone 'State, social élites,

and government capacity in Southeast Asia', *World Politics*, 1988, vol. 40, no. 2.

6 Leo Suryadinata *Pribumi Indonesians, The Chinese Minority and China*, Singapore, Heinemann, 1992.

7 Migdal *Strong Societies.*

8 Psychological (especially psychoanalytic) interpretations of politics are sometimes regarded with suspicion. One suggestion is that the thoughts of individuals may be determined not by their own wills, but rather by the ideological, cultural or linguistic systems which they inhabit; so that it is the system rather than the subject of the system, which warrants examination. But such a dismissal of the individual psyche would be problematical if it could be shown, as psychoanalysis in particular seeks to do, that it is the mechanisms and structures of the unconscious mind which provide the link between the individual will and the cultural system, and which therefore warrant examination. The psychological and social dimensions would then offer complementary, rather than antithetical, perspectives. Rather few psychologists have explicitly examined ethnicity, but psychoanalysis in particular offers insights as to how individuals respond to perceptions of insecurity. The shift from a focus on the individual to the discussion of ethnicity as a group phenomenon is also sometimes regarded as problematical. 'We proceed [however] on the commonsense view that it is difficult to conceive of a psychology of human groups that is unrelated to the psychology of the individual.' Group for the Advancement of Psychiatry *Us and Them: The Psychology of Ethnonationalism*, Report no. 123, New York, Brummer/Mazel, 1987.

9 Henry Tudor *Political Myth*, New York, Praeger, 1972, pp. 17 and 139.

10 Nicholas Tapp *Sovereignty and Rebellion: The White Hmong of Northern Thailand*, Singapore, Oxford University Press, 1989, pp. 167–79.

11 When Franz Fanon employed psychoanalysis as the basis for his examination of colonized societies in Africa and the Antilles, he did so by arguing that the Oedipus complex and its related neuroses were not indigenous to negro society. They arose only out of the colonial situation. It was not the real parents who gave rise to the Oedipus complex, it was the colonizers. Franz Fanon, *Black Skins, White Masks*, London, MacGibbon and Kee, 1968. A similar position is adopted, though within a radical critique of the Oedipus myth, by Gilles Deleuze and Felix Guattari *Anti-Oedipus: Capitalism and Schizophrenia*, London, Athlone, 1984, pp. 166–84. For indications that the Oedipus complex is relevant to at least some Third World societies, see Manisha Roy 'The Oedipus complex and the Bengali family in India (a study of father-daughter relations in Bengal)', in Thomas R. Williams (ed.) *Psychological Anthropology*, The Hague, Mouton, 1975.

12 Group for the Advancement of Psychiatry *Us and Them*, p. 7.

13 Stephen Frosh *The Politics of Psychoanalysis: An Introduction to Freudian and Post-Freudian Theory*, London, Macmillan, 1987, p. 269.

14 Frosh *The Politics*, p. 125. See pp. 113–29 for an outline of Klein's arguments.
15 David Holbrook *Human Hope and the Death Instinct*, Oxford, Pergamon, 1971, p. 212.
16 Group for the Advancement of Psychiatry *Us and Them*, p. 115. The Group does recognize, however, the pathological and destructive potential of ethnicity. Indeed, they indicate (p. 56) a division within the Group between those who stress the 'normality' of ethnicity and those who argue that ethnicity is a 'quasi pathological' process which emerges 'to compensate for and alleviate some of the developmental problems the ego may be having in other areas, for example, differentiating self from mother'. For discussion of the biological (especially neurological) bases for object relations development, see pp. 29–36.
17 For discussions of Lacan's arguments and their implications for politics, including racism, see Frosh *The Politics*, pp. 129–38; and also Stephen Frosh 'Psychoanalysis and racism', in Barry Richards (ed.) *Crises of the Self: Further Essays on Psychoanalysis and Politics*, London, Free Association Books, 1989, pp. 142–56, 227–49.
18 There are parallels with Claude Levi-Strauss's depiction of primitive ideology or 'mythic thought', whereby, 'reality is given to human subjects in the form of social and natural conditions which they experience: the thought of these subjects, governed not by the will nor by conscious intention . . . but by unconscious structures, selects specific elements from this reality and transforms them into imaginary representations of it'. Alan Jenkins *The Social Theory of Claude Levi-Strauss*, London, Macmillan, 1979, p. 151.
19 Fanon *Black Skin, White Masks*, p. 161 footnote.
20 Frosh 'Psychoanalysis', p. 241.
21 Ego psychology posits the existence of the ego as intrinsically autonomous from the id, and influenced in its development predominantly by early social experiences. For ego psychology, adaptation to the environment promotes personal development, whereas for Freud it involved repression and possibly neurosis. Ego psychology is associated particularly with the work of Anna Freud, Heinz Hartmann and Erik Erikson.
22 Erik H. Erikson *Dimensions of a New Identity*, New York, Norton, 1974, p. 87.
23 Erikson *Dimensions*, pp. 70 and 78.
24 Erikson *Dimensions*, pp. 94–8.
25 These quotations from Erikson are reprinted in Calvin S. Hall, Gardner Lindzey, John Loehlin and Martin Manosevitz *Introduction to Theories of Personality*, New York, Wiley, 1985, p. 90.
26 The reference is to Erich Fromm *Escape From Freedom*, New York, Rinehard, 1941, published in the UK as *The Fear of Freedom*, London, Allen and Unwin, 1942. The subsequent quotations are from Erich Fromm *The Same Society*, New York, Fawcett, 1955, p. 43.
27 Fromm *Sane Society*, p. 45.

28 Fromm *Sane Society*, pp. 59–60.
29 Philip Rieff *Freud: The Mind of the Moralist*, Chicago, University of Chicago Press, 1979, p. 223.
30 T. W. Adorno, E. Frenkel-Brunswick, D. J. Levinson and R. N. Sanford *The Authoritarian Personality*, New York, Harper and Row, 1950. In the 'authoritarian personality' the individual fails to resolve the Oedipus complex adequately and develops an extreme and compulsive submission to authority and an aggression against outgroups. See Lasswell 'The selective effect of personality', in Richard Christie and Marie Jahoda (eds) *Studies in the Scope and Method of the 'Authoritarian Personality'*, Glencoe, Free Press, 1954.
31 Rieff *Freud*, pp. 235 and 237.
32 The classic work on ethnic prejudice remains Gordon Allport *The Nature of Prejudice*, Boston, Beacon, 1954. The approach is primarily that of social psychology, but Allport does employ several psychoanalytic insights, most notably in the discussion of the displacement of aggression on to external objects. For a discussion on similar lines see Pettigrew's discussion of prejudice in G. M. Pettigrew, G. M. Fredrickson, D. T. Knobel, N. Glazer and R. Ueda *Prejudice*, Cambridge, Belknap/Harvard University Press, 1982.
33 Various formulations of the 'frustration-aggression-displacement' argument, and the 'compensatory masculinity' variant of this argument are summarized in Robert A. LeVine and Donald T. Campbell *Ethnocentrism: Theories of Conflict, Ethnic Attitudes and Group Behaviour*, New York, Wiley, 1972, Chapters 8 and 9.
34 The implication of this for ethnic politics are discussed in Chapter 7.
35 Christopher Lasch *Haven in a Heartless World: The Family Besieged*, New York, Basic, 1977; see also Herbert Marcuse *Eros and Civilization*, Boston, Beacon, 1955, Chapter Four 'The dialectic of civilization'.
36 For the argument that a myth of ethnic nationalism is a crucial component element for all state nationalisms, see Anthony D. Smith *National Identity*, London, Penguin, 1991, Chapter 2.
37 The intellectual progression from ideas of individual self-determination to those of national self-determination, stressing the contributions of Kant and Fichte, is traced in Elie Kedourie *Nationalism*, London, Hutchinson, 1960, revised 1986.
38 Erik Erikson *Identity: Youth and Crisis*, London, Faber and Faber, 1968, pp. 247 and 246.
39 Claude Levi-Strauss *The View From Afar*, Harmondsworth, Penguin, 1985, p. 10.
40 Anthony D. Smith *The Ethnic Origins of Nations*, Oxford, Blackwell, 1986, pp. 175 and 176.
41 K. R. Minogue *Nationalism*, London, Batsford, 1967, p. 32.
42 Fromm *Sane Society*, p. 45.
43 Fromm *Sane Society*, p. 43.
44 A. D. Smith 'State and homelands: The social and geopolitical implications of national territory', *Millenium: Journal of International Studies*, 1981 vol. 10, no. 3, p. 191.

45 Walker Connor 'Prospects for stability in Southeast Asia: the ethnic barrier', in Kusuma Snitwongse and Sukhumbhand Paribatra (eds) *Durable Stability in Southeast Asia*, Singapore, Institute of Southeast Asian Studies, 1987, p. 34.

46 Rousseau is often quoted as the spiritual father of nationalism, but his own concern was primarily with individual freedom. It is primarily the very abstractness and ambiguity of his 'general will' which facilitated its subsequent translation, by Hegel for example, into the idealizing of the spirit of the nation.

47 Crone 'State, social élites'. Useful discussions on both these general tendencies and on variations between particular states were offered by James Mackie and Harold Crouch in their papers on 'Analysing Southeast Asian political systems' at the conference on 'New Directions in Asian Studies', February 1989, Singapore, organized by the Asian Studies Association of Australia, Institute for Southeast Asian Studies, Singapore, and Centre for Advanced Studies, Singapore.

48 Quoted in Julien Freund *The Sociology of Max Weber*, Middlesex, Penguin, 1966, p. 60. Note the distinction between Weber's position and the contemporary intepretive hermeneutic approach which rejects the distinction between objective truth and subjective evaluation.

49 It should be noted that the 'bureaucratic polity' view of the state is dealt with here as an aspect of the neo-patrimonial perspective, the bureaucratic-authoritarian approach is incorporated within the corporatist perspective, and the consociational view of the state is discussed in the context of the class perspective. The most obvious views of the state not dealt with here are those which would depict it in terms of military rule or of democratic pluralism, or in explicitly 'modernization' terms.

2   The ethnocratic state and ethnic separatism in Burma

1 Esman offers a useful definition of ethnic separatist movements: 'movements to achieve or regain effective political, cultural and often economic control over their homeland. Their strategy is to struggle within the rules of the system where possible, by civil disobedience and violence where necessary, for autonomy from the political center ranging from federal or quasi-federal status to separation and independence. Their ideology is likely to be the powerful modern doctrine of self-determination of peoples, the illegitimacy of rule by foreigners.' Milton J. Esman 'Two dimensions of ethnic politics', *Ethnic and Racial Studies*, 1985, vol. 8, no. 3, pp. 438–40. For a survey of Southeast Asian ethnic separatist movements see R. J. May 'Ethnic separatism in Southeast Asia', *Pacific Viewpoint*, 1990, vol. 31, no. 2.

2 In a preliminary version of this chapter, the cases of the Moro of the Philippines and the Pattani Malays of Thailand were discussed alongside those of the Karen and the Shan, and were explained as

arising out of the ethnocratic state tendency, common to the three states. The present discussion is limited to the Burmese case study so as to facilitate the clear presentation of the core argument. David Brown 'From peripheral communities to ethnic nations: separatism in Southeast Asia', *Pacific Affairs*, 1988, vol. 61, no. 1.

3 The term 'Burman' is here used to refer to the ethnic group, and the term 'Burmese' to the state. Note that there is no consensus as to this usage.

4 The official Burmese figures, for 1983, which are of questionable accuracy, state that Burmans constitute 69 per cent of the population, Shan 8.5 per cent, Karen 6.2 per cent, Arakanese 4.5 per cent, Mon 2.4 per cent, Chin 2.2 per cent, Kachin 1.4 per cent, Kayah 0.4 per cent and others 0.1 per cent. From David I. Steinberg *The Future of Burma: Crisis and Choice in Myanmar*, Lanham, University Press of America, 1990, p. 66. The 1931 census, the last complete one, lists fourteen language groups within four broad linguistic categories, but subdivides these fourteen groups into 139 sub-groups.

5 For the most detailed account of the history of the various insurgencies, and their current state, see Martin Smith *Burma: Insurgency and the Politics of Ethnicity*, London/New Jersey, Zed, 1991. This chapter was written before Smith's book became available. While his material does stress the need to explain the interweaving of ethnic with communist unrest, it is otherwise compatible with the explanatory framework suggested here. His examinations of Karen and Shan rebellions are indicated in the relevant endnotes below. On the international dimensions of the conflicts, in relation to the Thailand, Chinese and Indian borders, see Bertil Lintner 'The internationalization of Burma's ethnic conflict', in K. M. de Silva and R. J. May (eds) *Internationalization of Ethnic Conflict*, London, Pinter, 1991.

6 On this general theme, that ethnic identities and their relationship to political alignments were fluid and porous in pre-colonial Burma, see Victor B. Lieberman 'Ethnic politics in eighteenth century Burma' *Modern Asian Studies*, 1978, vol. 12, no. 3; Edmund R. Leach *Political Systems in Highland Burma*, Boston, Beacon, 1954; Frederick K. Lehman 'Who are the Karen, and if so, why', in C. F. Keyes (ed.) *Ethnic Adaptation and Identity: The Karen on the Thai Frontier with Burma*, Philadelphia, Institute for the Study of Human Issues, 1979; Ronald D. Renard 'Minorities in Burmese history', in K. M. De Silva, Pensri Duke, Ellen S. Goldberg and Mathan Katz (eds) *Ethnic Conflict in Buddhist Societies: Sri Lanka, Thailand and Burma*, London, Pinter, 1988. See also the discussion by Robert H. Taylor 'Perceptions of ethnicity in the politics of Burma', *Southeast Asian Journal of Social Science*, 1982, vol. 10, no. 1, pp. 7–22.

7 Lieberman 'Ethnic politics'; Taylor 'Perceptions of ethnicity', p. 120.

8 Taylor 'Perceptions of ethnicity', p. 13.

9 David J. Steinberg *Burma: A Socialist Nation of Southeast Asia*, Boulder, Colo., Westview, 1982, p. 47.

10 Taylor 'Perceptions of ethnicity', p. 8.

11 M. Weiner 'Political change: Asia, Africa and the Middle East', in

M. Weiner and S. P. Huntington (eds) *Understanding Political Development*, Boston, Little Brown, 1987, pp. 36–7.

12 Lucian W. Pye *Politics, Personality and Nation Building: Burma's Search for Identity*, New Haven/London, Yale University Press, 1962, pp. 17–18.

13 Cynthia Enloe 'Ethnic diversity: the potential for conflict', in Guy L. Pauker, Frank H. Golay and Cynthia H. Enloe *Diversity and Development in Southeast Asia*, New York, McGraw Hill, 1977, p. 143.

14 For a characterization of the post-1962 Burmese state as an autonomous bureaucratic agency which claims legitimacy on the basis of an ethnically neutral Burmese socialism, and so tends to dominate and unify society, see Robert H. Taylor *The State of Burma*, London, Hurst, 1987.

15 Steinberg *The Future of Burma*, p. 75.

16 M. G. Smith *The Plural Society in the British West Indies*, Berkeley, University of California Press, 1965, p. 86.

17 Smith *Plural Society*, pp. 86 and 91.

18 Josef Silverstein *Burmese Politics: The Dilemma of National Unity*, New Brunswick, Rutgers University Press, 1980, p. 25.

19 Steinberg *The Future of Burma*, pp. 49–50.

20 Steinberg *Burma*, p. 36.

21 Furnivall argues that British rule created a plural society which not only 'stimulated sectional particularism' by its administrative structures, but which also led to social dislocation. 'Even within the village the social ties of the community were unable to withstand the strain of competitive individualism. This process of social disintegration was expedited by the extension of central authority through the village system.' J. S. Furnivall *The Governance of Modern Burma*, New York, Institute of Pacific Relations, 1958, pp. 22–3.

22 Silverstein *Burmese Politics*, pp. 10–11. Silverstein's discussion is here based primarily on the work of Furnivall.

23 Steinberg *Burma*, pp. 36–7.

24 David J. Steinberg (ed.) *In Search of Southeast Asia: A Modern History*, Sydney, Allen and Unwin, 1987, p. 282.

25 Steinberg *In Search of Southeast Asia*, p. 286. The *Wunthanu Athin* ('own race societies') were promoted by the General Council of Burmese Associations (GCBA), which had developed out of the YMBA. See below.

26 Steinberg *In Search of Southeast Asia*, p. 284. Effective British administration of the north was not established until after 1885. From this time onwards the educated Lower Burmans came into rivalry with educated Burmans from the north, as well as government functionaries recruited from India.

27 Steinberg *Burma*, p. 14.

28 Steinberg *Burma*, p. 43.

29 Steinberg *In Search of Southeast Asia*, p. 287.

30 Steinberg *Burma*, p. 42.

31 Andrew Selth *The Anti-Fascist Resistance in Burma, 1942–1945: The Racial Dimension*, Occasional Paper 14, (undated), Centre for

Southeast Asian Studies, James Cook University of North Queensland.

32 Silverstein *Burmese Politics*, p. 61.
33 Robert H. Taylor *An Undeveloped State: The Study of Modern Burma's Politics*, Centre of Southeast Asian Studies, Working Paper No. 28, 1983, Monash University, Clayton, Australia.
34 Frank N. Trager *Burma: From Kingdom to Republic*, New York, Praeger, 1966, Chapter 3.
35 Hugh Tinker *The Union of Burma*, London, Oxford University Press, 1967, p. 22.
36 Tinker *The Union*, p. 67.
37 Tinker *The Union*, pp. 76–7.
38 Silverstein *Burmese Politics*, pp. 134–44.
39 Silverstein *Burmese Politics*, p. 151.
40 The 1940 figures are given in Steinberg *Burma*, p. 60.
41 Cynthia H. Enloe *Ethnic Soldiers: State Security in Divided Societies*, Athens, University of Georgia Press, 1980, pp. 136–7.
42 Barry Buzan *People, States and Fear: The National Security Problem in International Relations*, Brighton, Wheatsheaf, 1983, p. 67.
43 This pattern of expansion of 'core cultural states' generating 'cultural mobilisation of the periphery' is one which is applied to Asia in general, and particularly to Thailand and Burma, in Crawford Young *The Politics of Cultural Pluralism*, Madison, Wisconsin University Press, 1976, pp. 507–11. The distinction is largely ignored by Milton Esman when he asserts that 'by far the most common and most significant [pattern of communal politics in Southeast Asia] is the centre-periphery pattern'. Milton Esman 'Communal conflict in Southeast Asia', in Nathan Glazer and Daniel P. Moynihan *Ethnicity: Theory and Experience*, Cambridge, Harvard University Press, 1975, p. 393.
44 Clifford Geertz 'The integrative revolution', in Clifford Geertz (ed.) *Old Societies and New States: The Quest for Modernity in Asia and Africa*, New York, Free Press of Glencoe, 1963, p. 136.
45 Silverstein *Burmese Politics*, p. 220.
45 From a speech by Ne Win to the Fourth Party Seminar, 1969, quoted in Robert H. Taylor 'Burma's national unity problem and the 1974 Constitution', *Contemporary Southeast Asia*, 1979, vol. 1, no. 3, p. 238. Taylor argues, however, that the 1974 Constitution reflects a significant shift towards an accommodationist approach to national unity, and reduces the political salience of ethnic distinctions. For an alternative view, which argues that the 1974 Constitution reflects and consolidates Burman dominance and exacerbates Burman-minority tensions, see David I. Steinberg 'Constitutional and political bases of minority insurrections in Burma', in Lim Joo-Jock and Vani S. (eds) *Armed Separatism in Southeast Asia*, Singapore, Institute of Southeast Asian Studies, 1984.
47 Steinburg 'Constitutional and political bases', p. 65.
48 Silverstein *Burmese Politics*, p. 221.
49 Silverstein *Burmese Politics*, pp. 224–6.

50 Taylor *The State of Burma*, p. 372.
51 Silverstein *Burmese Politics*, p. 239.
52 Josef Silverstein 'Ethnic protest in Burma: Its causes and solutions', in Rajeshwari Gose (ed.) *Protest Movements in South and South-East Asia: Traditional and Modern Idioms of Expression*, Hong Kong, Centre of Asian Studies, University of Hong Kong, 1987, p. 86.
53 William M. Sloan 'Ethnicity or imperialism', *Comparative Studies in Society and History*, 1979, vol. 21, no. 1, p. 124.
54 It should be noted, however, that these myths of unity do not of themselves imply the emergence of political ethnic unification movements. In line with the argument presented here, such movements would only be expected where the authority structure has been disrupted. On the absence of a unification movement among the Thailand Karen, see Ananda Rajah, 'Ethnicity, nationalism and the nation-state: the Karen in Burma and Thailand', in Gehan Wijeyewardene (ed.) *Ethnic Groups Across National Boundaries in Mainland Southeast Asia*, Singapore, Institute of Southeast Asian Studies, 1990.
55 See for example J. Stone 'Ethnicity versus the State' in Donald Rothchild and Victor A. Olorunsola (eds) *State Versus Ethnic Claims: African Policy Dilemmas*, Boulder, Colo, Westview Press, 1983, p. 90.
56 For a discussion of the relationship between the opium trade, Shan separatism and communist insurgency, see Bertil Lintner, 'The Shans and the Shan State of Burma' in *Contemporary Southeast Asia*, 1984, vol. 5, no. 4, pp. 403–50.
57 Silverstein *Burmese Politics*, pp. 18–19.
58 The role of the 1947 Constitution in promoting minority ethnic demands is stressed in Taylor 'Burma's national unity problem'.
59 Lintner 'The Shans', p. 412.
60 Taylor 'Perceptions of ethnicity', p. 12.
61 See John Cady *A History of Modern Burma*, Ithaca, Cornell University Press, 1958, pp. 42–3. Karen factional disunity continued through the mid-nineteenth century; see Constance M. Wilson 'Burmese-Karen warfare, 1810–1850: a Thai view', in De Witt C. Ellinwood and Cynthia H. Enloe *Ethnicity and the Military in Asia*, New Brunswick, Transaction, 1981.
62 The People's Volunteer Organization was formed by Aung San in 1946 out of the members of the disbanded Burma National Army who did not register for the new regular army. By 1948 the government was seeking to disband the PVO, but most of them 'went underground'. See Tinker *The Union of Burma*, pp. 34–48.
63 This stage of ethnic consciousness – the sense of being a distinctive but low status ethnic minority – would seem to be a more intense version of that which Keyes notes as characteristic of the Karens in northern Thailand. 'The identity of the Karen derives not only from their cultural belief in being speakers of the same language, but also from myths and folk history that define them as different from other neighbouring groups. Common to these myths and histories is the cultural belief, constantly reiterated, that 'the people' are in

some way (in power, in wealth, in knowledge), inferior to the dominant lowland people.' Keyes, *Ethnic Adaptation*, p. 11.

64 But note Lanternari's argument that this of itself could develop, 'go into reverse', and produce a separatist rebellion. Vittoria Lanternari, 'Ethnocentrism and ideology', *Ethnic and Racial Studies*, 1980, vol. 3, no. 1, p. 262.

65 Taylor 'Perceptions of ethnicity', p. 15.

66 It is the educated youth, the intelligentsia, who are seen by Smith as the main mobilizers of ethnic nationalism in the Third World. The role of traditional élites is largely ignored. See Anthony D. Smith *The Ethnic Revival*, Cambridge, Cambridge University Press, 1981, Chapter 7, 'State integration and ethnic schism'.

67 Silverstein *Burmese Politics*, pp. 189–92.

68 Lintner, 'The Shans', p. 411.

69 Chao Tzang Yawnghwe argues that the Shan *sawbwa* did themselves recognize the need to give up their hereditary rights, and willingly handed over their powers to the Shan State Government; the only controversy being about the extent of the compensation offered in 1959. Chao Tzang Yawnghwe 'The Burman military: holding the country together?', in Joseph Silverstein (ed.) *Independent Burma at Forty Years: Six Assessments*, Ithaca, Cornell Southeast Asia Program, Cornell University, 1989, pp. 95–6.

70 Lintner 'The Shans', p. 416.

71 Chao 'The Burman military', p. 94.

72 Jon A. Wiant 'Insurgency in the Shan State', in Lim and Vani *Armed Separatism*, p. 90.

73 Taylor 'Perceptions of ethnicity', p. 16.

74 Lintner 'The Shans', p. 413.

75 Lintner 'The Shans', p. 430.

76 Later renamed the Shan State Peasants Organization.

77 Taylor *An Undeveloped State*, pp. 21–2.

78 Smith *Burma*, pp. 190–4.

79 Lintner 'The Shans', p. 430.

80 There was a long history of Burman action against the Karens, but hitherto they had 'endure[d] heavy taxation and oppression with a kind of dull indifference'. Cady *A History*, p. 42.

81 There seem to be no precise figures available as to the ethnic composition of the civil service, apart from the 1931 statistic that the public administration comprised 37.4 per cent Burman and 25.2 per cent 'other indigenous'. The implication, then, is that the Karens were over-represented within the 'other indigenous' category. See the table reproduced in Taylor *The State of Burma*, p. 130.

82 Rajah 'Ethnicity, nationalism and the nation-state', p. 121.

83 Cady *A History*, p. 138.

84 Smith *Burma*, pp. 50–2. See also Smith's discussion of the Karens' constitutional 'betrayal' in 1947, pp. 83–7, and of the events of the Karen uprisings, pp. 110–21 and Chapter 8.

85 Tinker *The Union of Burma*, p. 76.

86 Cady *A History*, p. 550.

87 Cady *A History*, p. 551.
88 Trager *Burma*, pp. 102–7.
89 Taylor 'Perceptions of ethnicity', pp. 15 and 18.
90 For details of the 1949 rebellion see Smith *Burma*, pp. 110–18 and Chapter 8.
91 Donald L. Horowitz *Ethnic Groups in Conflict*, Berkeley, University of California Press, 1985, p. 176.

3 Ethnicity and corporatism in Singapore

1 This is a revised and extended version of David Brown, 'The corporatist management of ethnicity in contemporary Singapore', in Garry Rodan (ed.) *Singapore Changes Guard: Social, Political and Economic Directions in the 1990s*, Melbourne, Longman Cheshire, 1993. I am grateful to Peggy Lim Chai Yean for thought provoking discussions on Singapore's ethnic politics during supervision of her undergraduate Academic Exercise in Political Science, *Ethnic Strategies in Singapore Politics*, National University of Singapore, 1990.

2 Chew Sock Foon *Ethnicity and Nationality in Singapore*, Ohio, Center for International Studies, Ohio University 1987; R. Betts *Multiracialism, Meritocracy and the Malays of Singapore*, PhD thesis, Massachusetts Institute of Technology, 1975; Chan Heng Chee and Hans-Dieter Evers 'Nation-building and national identity in Southeast Asia', in S. N. Eisenstadt and Stein Rokkan (eds) *Building States and Nations*, Vol 2, Beverly Hills/London, Sage, 1973.

3 This is rarely publicly acknowledged; but see the comments by the PAP MP, Abdullah Tarmugi in *Straits Times*, 6 March 1990: 'There is a certain formality in the relationship between races. There is not enough spontaneity and relaxed feeling in our relations, which appear almost contrived in some cases . . . . Chauvinism exists even among the highly educated sections in our society . . . [The government's drive to promote the ethnic cultures] is good . . . . However I do concede the argument by some quarters that it accentuates our ethnic and cultural differences and makes us more conscious of our different cultural backgrounds. This is not the intention. Of course, the drive can be misapplied by some to emphasise differences and can give chauvinists and bigots an excuse to peddle their outlook and attitudes . . . . For a Malay to make good, he has to run a gauntlet of prejudices and stereotypes.'

4 Given the high salience of the issues of Chinese and Malay ethnic identities in Singapore, it is these two communities which will be focused on in this paper. The relevance of the analysis to the Indian community, particularly the Tamils and the Sikhs, is however discussed briefly.

5 For useful discussions see P. J. Williamson *Varieties of Corporatism: A Conceptual Discussion*, Cambridge, Cambridge University Press, 1985; P. C. Schmitter 'Still the century of corporatism?' in Schmitter and G. Lembrucht (eds) *Trends Towards Corporatist*

Intermediation, London, Sage, 1979; and S. Schwartzman, 'Corporatism and patrimonialism in the Seventies' in James M. Mallow (ed.) *Authoritarianism and Corporatism in Latin America*, Pittsburgh, University of Pittsburgh Press, 1977.

6   Schwartzman 'Corporatism and Patrimonialism', p. 91.

7   See the seminal articles by Hamza Alavi, 'The State in post-colonial societies: Pakistan and Bangladesh', and by John Saul, 'The State in post-colonial societies: Tanzania' in Harry Goulbourne (ed.) *Politics and State in the Third World*, London, Macmillan, 1979.

8   See especially Guillermo O'Donnell *Modernization and Bureaucratic-Authoritarianism*, Berkeley, University of California, 1973.

9   The inclusionary-exclusionary terminology is that offered by Guillermo O'Donnell 'Towards an alternative conceptualization of South American politics' in Peter F. Klaren and Thomas J. Bossert (eds) *Promise of Development: Theories of Change in Latin America*, Boulder, Colo., Westview, 1986. The state-societal terminology is that employed by Philippe C. Schmitter in 'Still the century'. Williamson refers to a similar distinction by the terms 'authoritarian-licenced corporatism' and 'consensual-licenced corporatism', Williamson *Varieties of Corporatism*.

10   Williamson *Varieties of Corporatism*, p. 3.

11   Williamson *Varieties of Corporatism*, p. 4.

12   Williamson *Varieties of Corporatism*, p. 8.

13   Williamson *Varieties of Corporatism*, pp. 20–1.

14   Schmitter 'Still the century', p. 13.

15   S. M. Lipset *Political Man*, New York, Doubleday, 1960. The main recent proponent of this view has been Francis Fukuyama *The End of History and the Last Man*, New York, Free Press, 1992.

16   The quotations are from pp. 85–7 of Chan Heng Chee 'The PAP and the structuring of the political system', in K. S. Sandhu and P. Wheatley (eds) *Management of Success: The Moulding of Modern Singapore*, Singapore, Institute of Southeast Asian Studies, 1989.

17   The government's graduate student survey conducted in 1980 showed 38.3 per cent employed in the public sector. See Inland Revenue Department *Report on the Survey of Employment of Graduates*, Singapore, 1980. National University of Singapore's graduate surveys show the proportion of NUS graduates entering the public sector was 54.5 per cent in 1975, 47.5 per cent in 1980, 58.2 per cent in 1985, and 34 per cent (for NUS and NTI) in 1990.

18   The change from the 'depoliticization' of the 1970s to the increased 'consultation' of the late 1980s and early 1990s is seen here, therefore, more as a change of governmental strategy than one of political culture.

19   Ho Wing Meng, 'Value premises underlying the transformation of Singapore', in Sandhu and Wheatley *Management of Success*, p. 678.

20   Ho 'Value premises', pp. 685–6.

21   Frederic C. Deyo *Dependent Development and Industrial Order: An Asian Case Study*, New York, Praeger, 1981; Carry Rodan *The Political Economy of Singapore's Industrialization: National State*

and International Capital, London, Macmillan, 1989; and V. Anantaraman *Singapore Industrial Relations System*, Singapore, Singapore Institute of Management/McGraw-Hill, 1990. See also 'The Corporate State vs the Autonomy Model', *Business Times*, 4 August 1989.

22 Stephen Milne 'Corporatism in the ASEAN countries', *Contemporary Southeast Asia*, 1983, vol. 5, no. 2.

23 Milne 'Corporatism', p. 178. Milne's other example, of the relationship between the government and the trade union organization, the NTUC, is indeed characterized by 'the overriding authority of the political leadership' (p. 178), but the NTUC is surely a classic 'Schmitterian' corporatist institution, developed by the government to replace the 'disruptive' STUC. For a discussion of the role of the NTUC in Singapore's 'state corporatism', see Rodan *Political Economy*, pp. 92–3.

24 Guillermo O'Donnell, 'Corporatism and the question of the State' in Malloy *Authoritarianism and Corporatism*, pp. 48–9.

25 For a brief discussion of corporatism and ethnicity in the context of the USA, see Michael Walzer 'Pluralism in political perspective' in M. Walzer, E. T. Kantowicz, J. Higham and M. Harrington *The Politics of Ethnicity*, Cambridge/London, Belknap, Harvard University Press, 1982.

26 The tendency of modern corporatist writers to see corporatism as excluding territorial or ethnic groups is partly related to their focal interest in the economic realm, but it also arises from the attempt to distinguish between the idea of the organic state which might be built out of feudal estates, and the modern corporatist state, built out of functional associations. The point seems to be that the corporatist state might be one variant of the organic state, but that it is built out of interest associations rather than 'loyalty groupings'. Such a distinction between ethnic interests and ethnic loyalties, is therefore central to the present attempt to relate corporatism to ethnicity.

27 PAP organizations which subsequently performed corporatist functions include the People Association (formed 1959), the Community Centres (formed 1959), and the Citizens Consultative Committees (formed 1965).

28 Chew *Ethnicity*, pp. 124–32.

29 On the idea of the 'administrative state' see Chan Heng Chee, 'Politics in an administrative state: where has all the politics gone?', in Seah Chee Meow (ed.) *Trends in Singapore*, Singapore, Singapore University Press, 1975.

30 Ismail Kassim *Problems of Elite Cohesion: A Perspective from a Minority Community*, Singapore, Singapore University Press, 1974, pp. 23–8. 'Ethnic balancing' was evident in the appointment of a Malay as the first President, in the inclusion of one Malay, one Indian and one Eurasian in the first (1959) Cabinet; and in the ethnic proportions of the PAP candidates in the 1959 and 1963 elections, with 66.7 per cent Chinese and 33.3 per cent non-Chinese in both cases. See

Shee Poon Kim, *The PAP in Singapore, 1954–1970: A Study in Survivalism of a Single-Dominant Party*, PhD thesis, Indiana University, 1971, p. 130. Note that after 1965 the proportion of Chinese in the Cabinet and Parliament tended to rise.

31 Seah Chee Meow and Linda Seah 'Education reform and national integration', pp. 240–2, in Peter S. J. Chen (ed.) *Singapore Development Policy and Trends*, Singapore, Oxford University Press, 1983; and Kassim *Elite Cohesion*, pp. 77–80.

32 Ethnic accommodation was evident, for example, in the appointment of one Chinese, one Malay and one Eurasian to the Legislative Council in 1924, and in the 1946 nomination of the leaders of the Chinese, Indian and Singapore (European) Chambers of Commerce to the Legislative Council.

33 This is embodied in the Constitution as Article 152, section 2, which requires the government to recognize the special position of the Malays as the indigenous people of Singapore, and to protect their interests in specified areas, including educational and economic areas, but it does not specify the policy implications.

34 During the 1950s Malays were under-represented in the higher occupational categories, but otherwise the facts did not support 'the popular image of Malays as economically backward'. This 'myth' was widespread at the time, but Tania Li shows that it was only after 1959 that the economic position of the Malays relative to the Chinese began to decline. Tania Li *Malays in Singapore: Culture, Economy and Ideology*, Singapore, Oxford University Press, 1988, pp. 100–8.

35 It should be noted however that Singapore was ejected from the Malaysian Federation in 1965 precisely because the PAP was perceived as functioning at the federal level as a pro-Chinese and anti-Malay political party. See Shee Poon Kim 'The evolution of the political system', pp. 9–10, in Jon S. T. Quah, Chan Heng Chee and Seah Chee Meow (eds) *Government and Politics of Singapore*, Singapore, Oxford University Press, 1987.

36 Betts *Multiracialism*, pp. 123–86.

37 Betts *Multiracialism*, p. 184.

38 In varying degrees, the PAP Malay MPs also accepted the predominance of their 'national role'. The impact was that 'all of the non-PAP Malay leaders [believed that] the PAP Malay leaders were ineffective in representing the interests of the Malay community'. Kassim *Elite Cohesion*, pp. 115–16.

39 By 1965 the Housing and Development Board (HDB) had completed its first Five Year Plan to relieve the housing shortage. The explicit criterion for rehousing was 'first come first served'; but the acknowledged impact was to replace ethnically segregated neighbourhoods with ethnically integrated public housing estates. Hassan found an increased level of inter-ethnic contacts and an improvement in inter-ethnic relations. See Riaz Hasan *Families in Flats: A Study of Low Income Families in Public Housing*, Singapore, Singapore University Press, 1977, pp. 75–9. On the integrative

impact of government policies, up to 1980, see Chiew Seen-Long, 'The socio-cultural framework of politics', in Quah, Chan and Seah, *Government and Politics*.

40 The promotion of Malay began in 1959 with the 'Learn Malay Drive', and was followed up by 'National Language Week/Month' campaigns in 1962, 64, 65 and 1966. The last such campaign was held in November 1966. During the 'Meritocracy' period of the 1970s no further language campaigns were conducted. In 1979 the first 'Speak Mandarin Campaign' began. Tham Kok Wing *National Campaigns in Singapore Politics*, Academic Exercise, Political Science, National University of Singapore, 1983. The policies to promote the use of English were in fact implemented with great subtlety and skill. See Chan Heng Chee, 'Language and culture in a multi-ethnic society: a Singapore strategy', paper prepared for the MSSA International Conference on Modernization and National Cultural Identity, Kuala Lumpur, 10–12 January, 1983.

41 S. Gopinathan 'Education' in Quah, Chan and Seah *Government and Politics*, p. 217.

42 Shee Poon Kim 'The Evolution of the Political System', in Quah, Chan and Seah *Government and Politics*, p. 7–9.

43 Rodan *Singapore's Industrialization*, pp. 71. See also Deyo *Dependent Development*, pp. 37–8.

44 The legislation included the 1966 Trade Union (Amendment) Act and the Trade Union Ordinance, the 1968 Employment Act, and the 1969 Industrial Relations (Amendment) Act. The legislation was accompanied by the adoption of the 1965 'Charter for Industrial Progress', and the 1972 introduction of the National Wages Council. The corporatist implications of these measures are spelled out in Deyo *Dependent Development*, Chapter 3, 'The emergence of bureaucratic-authoritarian corporatism in labor relations'.

45 David Gibbons 'The spectator culture: a refinement of the Almond and Verba model', *Journal of Commonwealth Political Studies*, 1971, vol. 9, no. 1, pp. 19–35.

46 Chan and Evers 'Nation-building', p. 304.

47 See Michael Leifer 'Communal violence in Singapore', *Asian Survey*, 1964, vol. 4, no. 10. The only previous significant riot was the 1950 Maria Hertog riot directed against European Christians. In 1969, there were relatively minor ethnic disturbances in Singapore as a 'spillover' of the 13 May riots in Malaysia.

48 The four racial/cultural categories are Chinese, Indian, Malay and Eurasian. John Clammer *Singapore: Ideology, Society, Culture*, Singapore, Chopmen, 1985, Chapter 9, 'The institutionalizing of ethnicity in Singapore'.

49 Geoffrey Benjamin 'The cultural logic of Singapore's multiracialism', in Riaz Hassan (ed.) *Singapore: Society in Transition*, Singapore, Oxford University Press, 1976.

50 The Baba Chinese community are also referred to as Straits Chinese or *Peranakan*, and are descended from early Chinese

migrants who adopted many of the Malay and British colonial cultural attributes associated with the new environment.

51 Benjamin 'Cultural logic', p. 124.

52 Note that such a distinction between cultural and political identities is not in fact necessary to Chew's argument, which rests on the claim that ethnic and national identities can constitute complementary *levels* of identity. Chew's model is thus probably even more applicable to the 'Asian communitarian' Singaporean identity of the 1980s. Chew *Ethnicity and Nationality*.

53 Chan and Evers 'Nation-building', p. 315.

54 Chan Heng Chee *The Politics of Survival 1965–1967*, Singapore/Kuala Lumpur, Oxford University Press, 1971, pp. 48–54.

55 Shee 'Evolution of the political system', p. 16–17.

56 'Day of decision' editorial, *Straits Times*, 2 September, 1972. Such portrayals of the PAP's political opponents are, of course, often accurate.

57 Election campaign speech by S. Rajaratnam, Foreign Minister, *Straits Times*, 31 August, 1972.

58 Editorial *Straits Times*, 31 August, 1972.

59 In the 1980 General Election, the PAP won all seats and 77.7 per cent of total valid votes. In 1981, in the Anson by-election, the opposition won a parliamentary seat for the first time since 1968. In the 1984 General Election, the PAP won 64.8 per cent of total valid votes; a drop of 13 per cent since 1980.

60 Rodan *Political Economy*, Chapter 5.

61 Tania Li *Malays in Singapore*, Chapter 7, 'Malays in the national economic and education system'. See Tables 7.4 and 7.13. The latter shows that the percentage of Chinese attaining upper secondary education or beyond was 15.1 per cent for those aged 30–9, 16 per cent for age 25–9, and 16.8 per cent for age 20–4. The same figures for the Malays were, respectively, 4.6, 3.9, 4.1

62 Li *Malays*, p. 179.

63 In 1966, as in 1961, the government detained Malays on the grounds that they were extremists plotting to incite racial hatred in Singapore. Shee 'The evolution of the political system' in Quah, Chan and Seah *Government and Politics*, p. 15.

64 Kassim *Elite Cohesion*, pp. 121–2; Betts *Multiracialism*, pp. 243–89; Chan and Evers 'Nation-building', p. 312.

65 Chan and Evers 'Nation-building', pp. 312–14.

66 The main occasion for the articulation of this argument was the Internal Security Act detention of the Marxist conspirators in 1987, and the associated tensions between the Prime Minister and some of the Catholic priests.

67 There were two arguments. First, that there was a general revival of interest in religion, especially in Buddhism, Christianity and Islam, as a response to the sense of anomie engendered by westernization and modernization. Second, it was argued that Christianity had spread amongst the educated youth precisely because they were most directly susceptible to western ideas,

including western religion. The concern that a religious revival might both promote inter-ethnic tensions and might provide a platform for political opposition culminated in the introduction of the Maintenance of Religious Harmony Bill in January 1990.

68 Rodan *Political Economy*, p. 143. The economic and political measures involved in this transition are discussed in Chapter 5, 'Second industrial revolution'.

69 Lee Kuan Yew, speech to NTUC Seminar, 6 November, 1979, quoted in Rodan *Political Economy*, p. 156.

70 Lee Kuan Yew's speech to NTUC Seminar, 6 November, 1979, quoted in Rodan *Political Economy*, pp. 156–61.

71 Rodan *Political Economy*, pp. 161–5.

72 Rodan *Political Economy*, p. 170.

73 The phrase was first used by Lee Kuan Yew in late 1982, see *Straits Times*, 23 December, 1982. The full argument for fostering 'responsible' opposition was made by the Prime Minister in the parliamentary debate on the non-constituency MP proposal, see *Straits Times*, 25 July, 1984.

74 Tan Teng Lang *The Evolving PAP Ideology: Beyond Democratic Socialism*, Academic Exercise, Political Science, National University of Singapore, 1983, pp. 77–9.

75 See the case studies examined in Tan Peng Chuan *Advisory Committees and Policymaking in Singapore*, Academic Exercise, Political Science, National University of Singapore, 1990.

76 Quoted in *Straits Times*, 1 April, 1989.

77 Quoted in *Far Eastern Economic Review*, 15 September, 1988, p. 16.

78 Most recently during the 1991 election, with the PAP's focus on the danger of communal violence being aroused by the appeal of the Workers Party candidate, Jufrie Mahmood, to Malay grievances.

79 Government of Singapore *Singapore: The Next Lap*, Singapore, Times, 1991, p. 139.

80 W. E. Willmott 'The emergence of nationalism' in Sandhu and Wheatley *Management of Success*. The Institute of Policy Studies (1989) survey showed 84 per cent 'positive' or 'very positive' about being Singaporean (with the Malays and Indians scoring higher than the Chinese); 85 per cent never having considered the possibility of emigrating; 70.4 per cent seeing the national anthem as 'very important'; and 87.9 per cent stating that 'There is a future for me in Singapore'. Institute of Policy Studies *The Singaporean: Ethnicity, National Identity and Citizenship*, Press Release, Singapore, 1990. The survey was organized by Chiew Seen Kong and Tan Ern Ser.

81 Both Goh Chok Tong and Lee Kuan Yew have specifically cited the arguments to this effect put forward in George Lodge and Ezra Vogel (eds) *Ideology and National Competitiveness*, Cambridge, Harvard Business School Press, 1987. The consensual culture is, either explicitly or implicitly, associated with Confucianism. See for example, the speech by Gob Keng Swee (then Deputy Prime

Minister) quoted in *Straits Times*, 4 February, 1982.

82 See the Prime Minister's National Day speech of 1978, and other related speeches quoted and discussed in Clammer *Singapore*, pp. 22–3.

83 Some of the implications of the promotion of Mandarin are discused in Nirmala Puru Shotam 'Language and linguistic policies', in Sandhu and Wheatley *Management of Success*, pp. 512–14.

84 See Li *Malays*, pp. 168–77. Li notes that this portrayal of the Malays was of long standing, but was renewed and promoted in the late 1970s and the 1980s, by both government leaders and by the Malay élite.

85 Li *Malays*, p. 175.

86 Li *Malays*, p. 176. The role of Islam in promoting social control and cohesion was enhanced by the establishment in 1968 of MUIS, the Council for Muslim Religion, to promote the administration of Muslim Law. MUIS acts as the supreme Islamic religious authority. Its President and up to five members are appointed directly by the government, the rest are appointed by the Singapore President on the advice of various religious organizations. One of its roles is to 'advise the Government on matters relating to Muslim affairs.' Ministry of Communications and Information *Singapore 1989*, Singapore, p. 29.

87 *Straits Times*, 29 October, 1988.

88 In response to comments during 1988 and 1989, a fifth value was subsequently added, that of 'community support and respect for the individual'. Government White Paper, Cmd 1 of 1991 *Shared Values*; *Straits Times*, 16 January, 1991.

89 See for example Lee Kuan Yew's remarks in an interview with Christopher Lockwood of the British *Daily Telegraph* reproduced in *Sunday Times* (Singapore), 22 October, 1989, p. 20.

90 The course was implemented in 1984. Students studied Confucianism, Islamic studies, Bible studies, Buddhist studies, Hindu studies, Sikh studies or world religions.

91 B. G. Lee, quoted in *Straits Times*, 31 January, 1990.

92 From the ministerial statement of Dr. Tan, Minister of Education *Straits Times*, 7 October, 1989, p. 1 and pp. 22–4.

93 The proposal for a bill to lay out the 'ground rules' of relations between religion and politics, was initially announced by the President in January 1989. It was discussed again in Parliament during the discussion on the introduction of civics in the schools. See *Straits Times*, 7 October, 1989, p. 1. The bill was outlined in a white paper published in January 1990.

94 Schmitter 'Still the century', 1979, p. 13.

95 The Malay association, Mendaki, and the Indian association, SINDA, are both discussed below. The government's increased concern to be seen to tackle the grievances of poor Chinese preceded the 1991 election, but their interpretation of those election results as reflecting a move away from the PAP by these poorer Chinese added impetus to the call for a Chinese Mendaki.

96 The CDAC was thus in part a response to the emergence of an Indian version of Mendaki (SINDA) which had been approved by the government. The PM's suggestion was that Chinese community leaders should initiate the project, but that if they did not do so, he would 'gather Chinese MPs to get it off the ground'. He then appointed two government members to pursue the idea, and by November, the Federation of Chinese Clan Associations and the Chinese Chamber of Commerce had 'received the nod from the government' to establish the Council. *Straits Times*, 8 July and 15 November, 1991. On the CDAC's organizational structure, see *Straits Times*, 28 April and 13 May, 1992.

97 See speech by Lee Kuan Yew *Straits Times*, 9 August, 1989; and speeches by S. Dhanabalan, Minister for National Development, *Straits Times*, 20 August and 31 August, 1989. The related issue of Hong Kong immigration was raised by the Prime Minister in his speech quoted in *Straits Times*, 21 August, 1989. For a discussion of Chinese discontent at this proposal, see *Far Eastern Economic Review*, 7 September, 1989.

98 Discontent about the pressure upon Chinese children to learn Mandarin as a second language arose mainly from the fact that it was a compulsory advanced level subject for those wishing to enter university from the junior colleges. One of the main debates on this issue was again initiated by the Prime Minister's National Day speech in August 1989 when he discussed the reasons for emigration. Several letters on this subject appeared in the 'Forum' page of the *Straits Times* in September. The most influential and poignant of these was the letter, 'Family going because son cannot cope with Chinese', *Straits Times*, 26 September, 1989.

99 For example, in January 1987 the Institute hosted an international conference on 'Confucian Ethics and the Modernisation of Industrial Asia'. In January 1990 it held one on 'Confucian Humanism and Modernisation: The Institutional Imperatives'.

100 In the 1988 election, which Mr. Lee saw as an endorsement of the 'new guard', and Mr. Goh (then First Deputy Prime Minister) saw as a mandate for his style of leadership, the PAP vote was 63.1 per cent, a drop of 1.7 per cent since the 1984 election. In the 1991 election, when the dominant issue, according to Goh Chok Tong, was again that of his style of leadership, the PAP vote fell by a further 2.1 per cent to 61 per cent.

101 Mr. Zainul Rashid currently (1991) acts in both capacities. He is also an editorial consultant of the Malay language paper, *Berita Harian*, which is part of the monopolistic Singapore Press Holdings.

102 *Straits Times*, 9 October, 1991.

103 The relationship between AMP and Mendaki, which is at present an uncomfortable one (*Straits Times*, 26 October, 1991), does not as yet fulfil the corporatist requirement for a concompetitive institution with a representational monopoly.

104 Preliminary data from the 1990 Census *Straits Times*, 28

November, 1992.

105 An alternative interpretation suggests that the impact of the GRC scheme might be, in some respects, to discourage 'minority' MPs from acting as spokesmen for their own ethnic communities, since their position as MP arises from their selection as one of a multi-ethnic team elected by primarily Chinese votes. Behaviour as a minority ethnic representative, rather than as a national leader, would thus endanger election as a GRC team member. I am grateful to Dr. Hussin Mutalib for this point.

106 Quoted in *Straits Times*, 11 August, 1987.

107 *Straits Times*, 11, 19 and 26 September, 1988. The allegation was accompanied by a warning that the government might not proceed with the plan to upgrade and strengthen Mendaki. For the resultant affirmations of support for the PAP see *Straits Times*, 18 September, 1988. For the Feedback Unit Forum on this issue, see *Straits Times*, 28 September, 1988.

108 *Straits Times*, 2 September, 1987.

109 *Straits Times*, 19 May, 1989.

110 The Malay students organizations of the National University of Singapore held a Forum which voted 22 for and 175 against the proposal. A survey conducted by them found 54 for and 196 against. See *Straits Times*, 7 August, 1989. For Mendaki's acceptance of the proposal, see *Straits Times*, 24 January, 1990.

111 No attempt is made here at a systematic and full discussion of the Sikh and Tamil situations; but I am indebted to Dr. A. Mani and Dr. Bilveer Singh, both at the National University of Singapore, for giving me the benefit of their expertise on the two communities.

112 Sikh studies was introduced into the school syllabus in 1984, and the government approved Punjabi as an examinable second language from 1990.

113 For a historical outline of the Sikh community in Singapore, and a discussion of the threats to their communal cohesion, see Kernial Singh Sandhu, 'Historical role of the Sikhs in the development of Singapore', in *Seminar Report on Sikh Youth and Nation-Building'*, Singapore, Sikh Advisory Board, 1989.

114 The Sikh Advisory Board is similar in structure and scope to the MUIS which was established for Muslims.

115 The Sikh Research Panel was established in 1989 under the auspices of the Sikh Advisory Board. Its aims and concerns were articulated in the seminar which it organized on 'Sikh Youth and Nation-Building' in March 1989, which constituted a classic case of corporatist interest articulation. It provided a forum in which the Government Law Minister, Professor Jayakumar could stress the need for Sikh commitment to Singapore, and in which Sikh spokesmen could also articulate 'constructive' recommendations to deal with the perceived problems facing the community. See *Seminar Report on Sikh Youth*.

116 It might be argued that 'consummatory' value systems such as

those espoused by Sikhs or Muslims, in which cultural, religious, political and homeland identities are intertwined, are particularly resistant to such attemps at 'compartmentalization'.

117 Indians account for 16 per cent of emigrants from Singapore, while comprising 6 per cent of the population; so it is perhaps the case that emigration comprises an alternative form of grievance expression.

118 See the Action Committee for Indian Education *Report of the Action Committee on Indian Education: At the Crossroads*, Singapore, 1991.

119 *Straits Times*, 15 August, 1989.

120 See for example the complaints articulated at the conference organized by the Tamil Language and Literature Society in Singapore, on the problems facing the Indian community, including the poor performance of Indians in the primary schools. The conference was attended by the Indian MP, Chandra Das. *Straits Times*, 21 August, 1989.

121 See the comments by Goh Chok Tong, *Straits Times*, 24 January, 1990. These comments were extracted from interviews with Raj Vasil, conducted in 1989, for a second edition of his *Governing Singapore*, Singapore, Eastern Universities Press, Singapore, 1984.

122 The prayers were held in April 1989, and apparently continued despite police warnings. See the report 'Sikh member calls for checks on two temples', *Straits Times*, 26 February, 1990.

123 The problem of distinguishing expressions of legitimate ethnic interest and illegitimate political loyalty was also evident in the case of Mohamed Jufrie Mahmood, an official of the Social Democratic Party, when he suggested the possibility that the ratio of Chinese to non-Chinese in Singapore might eventually shift to 50:50. Since the PAP regarded the present ratio of 78:22 as sacrosanct, Jufrie was promptly accused of trying to 'undermine racial harmony'. See *Straits Times*, 5 and 19 August, 1989, and *Sunday Times*, 13 August, 1989.

124 The clash of views between the government and some sections of the Catholic Church was spelled out in July 1986 when the government gave the Catholic Archbishop a list of social issues, including poverty, upon which Catholic publications and organizations should refrain from comment and involvement. *Far Eastern Economic Review*, 5 October, 1986, p. 16. For the comments of the Catholic Archbishop on the Maintenance of Religious Harmony Bill, see *Far Eastern Economic Review*, 18 January, 1990, pp. 20–1.

125 See Goh Chok Tong's speech stating the government's role in these terms, *Straits Times*, 24 October, 1991.

126 Goh Chok Tong, *Straits Times*, 5 March, 1990.

127 Thus in April 1992 the Indian Muslims launched a Federation of Indian Muslims, chaired by the Minister of State for Education, to promote their community welfare in ways which would supplement, but not interfere with, the work of Mendaki and SINDA. In June 1992 the Eurasian community accounced plans to launch its own community association.

4 Neo-patrimonialism and national integration in Indonesia

1 For a useful review of the literature on the 'unresponsive' Indonesian state, see Andrew MacIntyre *Business and Politics in Indonesia*, Sydney, Allen and Unwin, 1990, Chapter 2. On the unresponsiveness of the state to Islam see Ruth McVey 'Faith as the outsider: Islam in Indonesian politics' in J. Piscatori (ed.) *Islam in the Political Process*, Cambridge, Cambridge University Press, 1983. Both MacIntyre and Harold Crouch argue that the Indonesian state has become increasingly unresponsive to pressures 'from below', but that it is becoming increasingly receptive to pressures 'from above', that is from the business groups. H. Crouch *Domestic Political Structures and Regional Economic Cooperation*, Singapore, Institute of Southeast Asian Studies, 1984, pp. 75–89.

2 For a focus on élite competition and its impact on group formation, see Paul Brass (ed.) *Ethnic Groups and the State*, Beckenham, Croom Helm, 1985, pp. 24–49.

3 For an overview of these fluctuations, and an analysis in terms of the shifting balance of centrifugal and integrating factors, see J. A. C. Mackie, 'Integrating and centrifugal factors in Indonesian politics since 1954' in J. J. Fox, R. Garnaut, P. McCawley and J. A. C. Mackie (eds) *Indonesia: Australian Perspectives* (Volume 2), Canberra, Australian National University, 1980.

4 Max Weber *The Theory of Social and Economic Organization*, New York, Free Press, 1957, p. 341.

5 By the same token, the leader who falls from power must have similarly deserved his fate.

6 On contemporary patrimonial or neo-patrimonial states, and their relationship to patron–client linkages and ethnicity, see Christopher Clapham 'Clientelism and the State', in Christopher Clapham (ed.) *Private Patronage and Public Power: Political Clientelism in the Modern State*, London, Pinter, 1982; Christopher Clapham *Third World Politics: An Introduction*, London, Croom Helm 1985, Chapter 3; J. D. Powell 'Peasant society and clientelist politics', *American Political Science Review*, 1970, vol. 64, no. 2; J. C. Scott, 'Patron–client politics and political change in Southeast Asia', *American Political Science Review*, 1972, vol. 66, no. 1; R. Theobald 'Patrimonialism', *World Politics*, 1982, vol. 34, no. 4; R. Lemarchand 'Political clientelism and ethnicity in tropical Africa: competing solidarities in nation-building', *American Political Science Review*, 1972, vol. 66, no. 1.

7 Gunther Roth 'Personal rulership, patrimonialism and empire-building in the new states', *World Politics*, 1968, vol. 20, no. 1; S. N. Eisenstadt *Traditional Patrimonialism and Modern Neo-Patrimonialism*, Beverly Hills/London, Sage, 1973.

8 MacIntyre *Business and Politics*, p. 8. MacIntyre cites Karl Jackson, Harold Crouch, John Girling, Ruth McVey and Jamie Mackie as the main writers who have adopted this approach, which he specifically associates with the 'bureaucratic polity' approach deriving

from the work of Fred Riggs. For a critical comment on the approach, and its applicability to Indonesia see D. Y. King, 'Indonesia's New Order as a bureaucratic polity, a neo-patrimonial regime or a bureaucratic-authoritarian regime: what difference does it make?' in B. Anderson and A. Kahin (eds) *Interpreting Indonesian Politics: Thirteen Contributions to the Debate*, Ithaca, Cornell Modern Indonesia Project, Cornell University, 1982.

9 Anderson builds upon Schrieke's portrayal of the pre-colonial Javanese kingdom in Weberian patrimonial terms. See B. Schrieke *Indonesian Sociological Studies 1*. The Hague/Bandung, Van Hoeve, 1955.

10 B. R. O'G. Anderson 'The idea of power in Javanese culture' in Claire Holt (ed.) *Culture and Politics in Indonesia*, Ithaca, Cornell University Press, 1972, p. 13. A classic example would be Sukarno's NASAKOM ideological slogan, claiming to reconcile nationalism, Islam and communism.

11 Anderson 'The idea of power', pp. 35–6.

12 K. D. Jackson 'The political implications of structure and culture in Indonesia', in K. D. Jackson and L. W. Pye (eds) *Political Power and Communications in Indonesia*, Berkeley, University of California Press, 1978, p. 34.

13 Patron–client linkages and factionalism, in the Indonesian context, are discussed in A. Gregory *Recruitment and Factional Patterns of the Indonesian Political Elite: Guided Democracy and the New Order*, PhD thesis, Columbia University, 1976, pp. 431–57.

14 Roth 'Personal rulership', p. 205. But Roth continues by stressing the fragility of such 'integration'.

15 *Aliran*, ethnicity, patron–clientage and geographic units are also, as Kahn observes, the main ideological perspectives through which Indonesians perceive social reality. J. S. Kahn 'Ideology and social structure in Indonesia', in Anderson and Kahn *Interpreting Indonesian Politics*.

16 C. Geertz *The Religion of Java*, Chicago, University of Chicago Press, 1960. The *aliran* distinctions refer specifically to Javanese society, but have come to be employed as a model for Indonesian society as a whole.

17 H. Feith *The Decline of Constitutional Democracy in Indonesia*, Ithaca, Cornell University Press, 1968, pp. 31–2.

18 This means for example that within the military the distinctions between regionally-based army divisions have in most cases coincided with the main ethno-linguistic distinctions, and this has significantly influenced the pattern and intensity of rivalries within the military. This has been modified by recent territorial reorganizations of the military, particularly that of 1985.

19 Clapham 'Clientelism and the State', p. 12.

20 H. T. Silalahi 'The 1977 General Elections: The results and the role of traditional authority relations in modern Indonesian society', *Indonesian Quarterly*, 1977, vol. 5, no. 3.

21 H. T. Silalahi 'The 1987 Election in Indonesia', *Southeast Asian*

Affairs 1988, Singapore, Institute of Southeast Asian Studies, 1988, p. 100. Proponents of a class perspective have argued that capitalism has the effect of breaking the traditional and personal patron-client linkages, so that class consciousness may emerge. This is argued by W. F. Wertheim 'From aliran to class struggle in the countryside of Java', *Pacific Viewpoint*, 1969, vol. 10, no. 1. The state apparatus may function as a patrimonial machine so as to inhibit subordinate class consciousness, but its capacity for maintaining this is inhibited by the emergence of technocratic bureaucrats committed to promoting industrialization through a more effective state apparatus. R. Robinson *Power and Economy in Subarto's Indonesia*, Manila, Journal of Contemporary Asia Publishers, 1990, Chapter 3.1.

22 A. R. Zolberg *Creating Political Order: The One-Party States of West Africa*, Chicago, Rand McNally, 1966, pp. 141–2.

23 K. D. Jackson 'A bureaucratic polity: a theoretical framework for the analysis of power and communications in Indonesia', in Jackson and Pye *Political Power*.

24 G. A. Heeger *The Politics of Underdevelopment*, London, Macmillan, 1974, pp. 83, 91.

25 Feith *The Decline*, pp. 113–22.

26 Feith *The Decline*, p. 325. The *Panca Sila* are the five principles of Indonesia's national ideology, namely belief in one God, nationalism, humanism, democracy and social justice.

27 The seeds of the cleavage were sown in 1945, when Sukarno supplemented the *Panca Sila* statement with his Jakarta Charter (*Piagam Djakarta*) which offered the *santris* a constitutional preamble and article committing the state to allowing Muslims to practice Islamic law and specifying that the President be a Muslim. Since *santri* Muslims were under-represented amongst the nationalist leadership, Sukarno came under increasing pressure to rescind this promise. The *santris* reluctantly agreed to accept this withdrawal on the argument that it would disrupt national unity. In compensation, they achieved the formation of a Ministry of Religion under the control of Islamic officials. D. S. Lev *Islamic Courts in Indonesia: A Study in the Political Bases of Legal Institutions*, Berkeley, University of California Press, 1972, pp. 41–5.

28 Parliamentary and constituency elections had been long delayed, but the Elections Act was passed in April 1953, and the Minister of the Interior stated at that time that elections would be held within ten months. Feith *The Decline*, p. 280 and footnote 100.

29 Feith argues that it was the PNI which was mainly responsible for the delays, since it believed it had most to lose from elections, and that *Masjumi* was a prominent advocate of early elections. Herbert Feith *The Wilopo Cabinet, 1952–1953: A Turning Point in Post-Revolutionary Indonesia*, Ithaca, Cornell University, Modern Indonesia Project, 1958, pp. 156–8.

30 Quoted in Feith *The Wilopo Cabinet*, p. 159.

31 Feith *The Decline*, pp. 135–8.

32 In 1945 Sukarno and Hatta had proposed a unitary constitution, but the need to overcome the divison between regions which had been brought back under Dutch control in the Federated BPO (Federal Consultative Assembly), and those which had remained under Republican control, led them to agree by 1950 to a federal formula for Indonesian independence. Hatta recognized that the federal system was preferable for the building of an élite coalition form of national unity. Feith *The Decline*, p. 72.

33 Feith *The Decline*, p. 114.

34 For a list of Indonesia's uprisings, including the regionalist rebellions, see K. J. Dorodjatun and T. A. M. Simatupang 'The Indonesian experience in facing non-armed and armed movements: lessons from the past and glimpses of the future', in Kusuma Snitwongse and Sukhumbhand Paribatra (eds) *Durable Stability in Southeast Asia*, Singapore, Institute of Southeast Asian Studies, 1987, pp. 108–16.

35 R. McVey 'Separatism and the paradoxes of the nation-state in perspective' in Lim Joo-Jock and S. Vani (eds) *Armed Separatism in Southeast Asia*, Singapore, Institute of Southeast Asian Studies, 1984, p. 10.

36 This is evident within the New Order régime itself, in the tension between the technocrats concerned to promote universalistic administrative practices and those who are themselves practitioners or recipients of patrimonial practices.

37 J. F. Medard 'The underdeveloped state in tropical Africa: political clientelism or neo-patrimonialism', in Clapham *Private Patronage*. For a classic allegation of corruption against the New Order régime in terms of the neo-patrimonial clash between universalistic claims and the practice of favouritism, see Heri Akhmadi *Breaking the Chains of Oppression of the Indonesian People: Defense Statement at his Trial on Charges of Insulting the Head of State*, Bandung, June 1979, Ithaca, Cornell Modern Indonesia Project, Translation Series, Cornell University, 1981.

38 Leo Suryadinata 'Government policy and national integration in Indonesia', *Southeast Asian Journal of Social Science*, 1988, vol. 16, no. 2, p. 113. The exception to this formula is the Chinese community, which has been subjected to assimilationist policies designed to promote their absorption into the indigenous culture.

39 R. Robison *Power and Economy*, Chapter 8; D. K. Emmerson 'The military and development in Indonesia', in Soedjati Djiwandono and Yong Mun Cheong, (eds), *Soldiers and Stability in Southeast Asia*, Singapore, Institute of Southeast Asian Studies, 1988, pp. 123–4; Adam Schwartz 'All is relative: Suharto family businesses face mounting criticism in Indonesia', *Far Eastern Economic Review*, 30 April, 1992, pp. 54–8.

40 According to Yasunaka, the proportion of Javanese was 52.8 per cent in the Cabinets of 1945–50, 44.3 per cent in those of 1950–7, and 54.8 per cent in those of 1957–64. Akio Yasunaka 'Basic data on Indonesian political leaders', in *Indonesia*, 10 October, 1970,

pp. 107–43. See also H. W. Backtiar *The Indonesian Nation: Some Problems of Integration and Disintegration*, Singapore, Institute of Southeast Asian Studies, 1973. Backtiar documents this claim with reference to the first three cabinets.

41 Gregory *Recruitment and Factional Patterns*, Table 5, p. 109.

42 B. R. O'G. Anderson 'Current data on the Indonesian military élite', *Indonesia*, Ithaca, Cornell Southeast Asia Program. The percentage seems to have stabilized at 'roughly 80 per cent'. The listings consulted are in various issues of *Indonesia*.

43 A. Gregory 'The influence of ethnicity in the evolution of the Indonesian military élite' in D. C. Ellinwood and C. H. Enloe (eds) *Ethnicity and the Military in Asia*, New Brunswick/London, Transaction Books, 1981, pp. 267, 269.

44 Anderson 'Curent data', No. 45, 1988, p. 138.

45 Gregory 'The influence of ethnicity', p. 281. The ethnic issue played a part in the tensions between Sukarno and the military leadership. Sukarno's distrust of his army Chief of Staff, Nasution, arose in part from his desire to replace Nasution with 'an officer more amenable to his own influence, perferably a Javanese'. Nasution's successor, Yani, was a Javanese whò was 'more at east in Sukarno's palace circle . . . As a Javanese he tended to treat Sukarno with the respect due to a 'Bapak.'' H. Crouch *The Army and Politics in Indonesia*, Ithaca, Cornell University Press, 1978, pp. 52–3.

46 Gregory *Recruitment and Factional Patterns*, p. 47.

47 R. McVey 'Nationalism, Islam and Marxism: the management of ideological conflict in Indonesia', Introduction to Soekarno, *Nationalism, Islam and Marxism*, Ithaca, Cornell University Press, 1970, p. 7.

48 R. W. Liddle 'Ethnicity and political organization: three East Sumatran cases', in Holt *Culture and Politics*, p. 148. See R. W. Liddle *Ethnicity, Party and National Integration: An Indonesian Case Study*, New Haven/London, Yale University Press, 1970.

49 On patron-client pyramids see Powell 'Peasant society', pp. 411–26.

50 Liddle 'Ethnicity', pp. 172, 178.

51 For a patrimonial explanation of how the short-term stability of the New Order (compared to the instability of Guided Democracy) was threatened by the impending problem of mass participation, see H. Crouch 'Patrimonialism and military rule in Indonesia', *World Politics*, 1979, vol. 31, no. 4.

52 J. M. Boileau *Golkar: Functional Group Politics in Indonesia*, Jakarta, Centre for Strategic and International Studies, 1983, pp. 113–4.

53 Aceh (sometimes spelt more phonetically as 'Atjeh' or 'Acheh') is in northern Sumatra. Its population of about 3 million is roughly 90 per cent ethno-linguistic Acehnese.

54 E. E. Morris *Islam and Politics in Aceh: A Study of Center-Periphery Relations in Indonesia*, PhD thesis, Cornell University, 1983, pp. 11–12.

55 There are two full-length studies in English of Acehnese politics, both focusing on the 1953 rebellion. The most useful is the excellent PhD thesis by Morris, and the following discussion relies heavily on this source. Morris's analysis in terms of the relations between contending Acehnese leadership groups and the centre is compatible with Feith's study of the impact of élite rivalries at the centre upon Indonesian politics inclusive of the Aceh case. Nazaruddin's book, derived from his Monash PhD thesis, lays stress on the uniqueness of Aceh, but sees its centre-regional linkages in ethnic terms, and thence as illustrating the argument that national integration depends on central responsiveness to ethnic interests. See Morris *Islam and Politics*; Nazaruddin Sjamsuddin *The Republican Revolt: A Study of the Acehnese Rebellion*, Singapore, Institute of Southeast Asian Studies, 1985; Feith *The Decline*.

56 Morris *Islam and Politics*, p. 45.

57 On the dual position of reformist *ulamas* as village authorities and also as representatives of the wider Islamic Acehnese community, see J. T. Siegal *The Rope of God*, Berkeley/Los Angeles, University of California Press, 1969, pp. 48–67.

58 On the village influence of the *ulama*, and mobilization for the rebellion, see Nazaruddin, *Republican Revolt*, pp. 172–80. On the similar process of mobilization for the *Darul Islam* rebellion among the Sundanese in West Java, see K. D. Jackson and J. Moeliono 'Participation in rebellion: the Dar'ul Islam in West Java', in R. W. Liddle (ed.) *Political Participation in Modern Indonesia*, New Haven, Yale University Press, 1973, pp. 12–57.

59 On the position of the *uleebalang* in pre-colonial Aceh see Morris *Islam and Politics*, pp. 24–41, and Siegal *Rope of God*, Part 1.

60 On the erosion of the *uleebalang*'s position as *adat* figures and territorial administrators under Dutch rule, see Siegal *Rope of God*, pp. 84–97.

61 For a biography of Daud Beureueh, see Nazaruddin *Republican Revolt*, pp. 180–4.

62 Morris stresses that the goals of the PUSA leaders transcended Aceh, and involved the wider concern to attain an Islamic Indonesia. This is certainly the case, but it did not make their goal any the less a communalist one since, as he notes, 'PUSA leaders believed an Islamic state of all of Indonesia would come closer to realization if the Acehnese were left alone to manage their society according to the dictates of Islam'. Morris *Islam and Politics*, pp. 181–2.

63 Morris argues that the rivalry between *ulamas* and *uleebalangs* dates not so much from the pre-colonial period, as from the 'Aceh War' against the Dutch, when the *uleebalangs* began to co-operate with the Dutch so as to protect their trade and administrative powers, so that the *ulama* emerged as the leaders of resistance. Morris *Islam and Politics*, pp. 54–61.

64 Nazaruddin *Republican Revolt*, Chapter 1. Nazaruddin stresses that

each of the cleavage lines were, in practice, rather fluid, with numerous cases of individuals 'crossing' the factional lines.

65 On the position of the *uleebalang* under Dutch rule, and their overthrow in the 'social revolution', see A. Reid *The Blood of the People: Revolution and the End of Traditional Rule in Northern Sumatra*, Kuala Lumpur, Oxford University Press, 1979. The position of the *uleebalang* was further weakened by Japanese rule, but with the ending of Japanese rule they sought to revive their administrative and judicial powers. See Morris *Islam and Politics*, Chapters 4 and 5.

66 On Aceh's Islamic courts see Lev *Islamic Courts*, pp. 75–92. In 1944 the Japanese had sought to placate the *ulamas* by reorganizing Aceh's judicial system and establishing a separate system of Islamic courts, with jurisdiction over issues relating to marriage, divorce, inheritance and religious taxes and trusts. The Japanese also granted official recognition to the *madrasah* schools. Morris *Islam and Politics*, pp. 102–11.

67 Lev *Islamic Courts*. pp. 80–1, footnote 26. While the goal of an 'Islamic Aceh' had an inherent vagueness, it involved, as a minimum, the securing of a system of Islamic courts and the further strengthening of the *madrasah* schools. See Morris *Islam and Politics*, pp. 154–65.

68 Lev *Islamic Courts*, p. 254.

69 During the Dutch offensives, the Republican leaders in Java were unable to exercise any effective control over events in Aceh, which was not re-occupied by the Dutch.

70 The Governor was an Acehnese *uleebalang*, Teuku Muhammad Hasan, and he sought to control 'a wild situation in Aceh' by authorising Islamic courts throughout Sumatra. The PUSA leaders took this as authority to extend further the scope of the Acehnese Islamic courts. See Lev *Islamic Courts*, pp. 81–2; and Morris *Islam and Politics*, p. 162.

71 Also, in November 1948 the Sumatran Governor supported PUSA against the incipient opposition group in Aceh who urged prosecution of those who had attacked the *uleebalang* in the socal revolution. See Morris *Islam and Politics*, pp. 167–8.

72 Nazaruddin *Republican Revolt*, pp. 29–30. Nazaruddin adds that, according to Daud Beureueh, Sukarno also promised that Indonesia would be based on Islamic principles, and that it was only on that assurance that Daud Beureueh agreed to support the Republic. See p. 30, note 30.

73 Morris *Islam and Politics*, pp. 169–70. According to Nazaruddin the decision was not announced until 5 December, three days after the Hatta cabinet, in which Sjafruddin was Deputy Prime Minister, had resigned. Nazaruddin *Republican Revolt*, pp. 35–6.

74 Though some, including Ali Hasjmy, later allied with PSII (Indonesian Islamic Unity Party), when it broke away from *Masjumi*; 'the rationale being that if there were to be another Islamic party it should be under PUSA's control as well'. Morris *Islam and Politics*,

p. 123, note 16. Nazaruddin links the *Masjumi*–PSII division with the factional rivalry within PUSA between the *ulama* and the *zuama*. Nazaruddin *Republican Revolt*, p. 7.

75 The first cabinet which excluded *Masjumi* was that formed in July 1953 under Ali Sastroamidjojo. *Masjumi* was involved in the subsequent cabinets up to 1957, but it was progressively weakened by internal rivalries, the rivalries with the other parties, and the general eclipse of the influence of political parties. Feith *The Decline*, Chapter 10.

76 Lev *Islamic Courts*, p. 81, note 28. The government had however recognized similar courts set up in East Sumatra.

77 Nazaruddin *Republican Revolt*, pp. 54–5. Also, in December 1951 the government placed economically detrimental restrictions on Aceh's direct trade with Malaya and Singapore. The only positive response from central government was its recognition of the *madrasah* schools, but the resultant government subsidies were 'insignificant'. Morris *Islam and Politics*, p. 189–90.

78 Nazaruddin *Republican Revolt*, pp. 45–63. Nazaruddin suggests that the *uleebalang* 'directed' the 1951 army raids on PUSA leaders, which were part of a nation-wide search for arms.

79 Morris *Islam and Politics*, p. 180.

80 Nazaruddin *Republican Revolt*, pp. 43–5.

81 Morris *Islam and Politics*, pp. 182–3. Natsir's visit was a response to Daud Beureueh's threat to resign as Governor. Nazaruddin *Republican Revolt*, p. 47.

82 Nazaruddin *Republican Revolt*, pp. 52–3.

83 Morris *Islam and Politics*, p. 197.

84 Quoted in Eric Morris 'Aceh: social revolution and the Islamic vision', in Audrey R. Kahin (ed.) *Regional Dynamics of the Indonesian Revolution: Unity from Diversity*, Honolulu, University of Hawaii Press, 1985, p. 99. This was in response to a Dutch suggestion of 1949 that the Acehnese leaders should support a Dutch-backed federal system.

85 Feith *The Decline*, p. 345, and Nazaruddin Sjamsuddin 'Regionalism and national integration in Indonesia: the Acehnese experience' in Jamie Mackie, Herb Feith, Nazaruddin Sjamsuddin and Hamish MacDonald *Contemporary Indonesia: Political Dimensions*, Melbourne, Centre of Southeast Asian Studies, Monash University, 1978, p. 25.

86 Morris *Islam and Politics*, pp. 198–9.

87 Feith *The Decline*, p. 346. Note also that in April Daud Beureueh acted as chairman of the All Indonesian Conference of Ulama, supported by *Masjumi*, to prepare for elections by formulating a constitutional framework for 'a state based on Islam'. Feith *The Wilopo Cabinet*, pp. 158, 162.

88 Feith *The Wilopo Cabinet*, p. 200.

89 Feith *The Decline*, p. 346.

90 The events of the rebellion are discussed in Nazaruddin *Republican Revolt*, Chapter 3. An overview of the rebellion, based on Nazaruddin, can be found in R. J. May 'Ethnic separatism in

Southeast Asia', *Pacific Viewpoint*, 1990, vol. 31, no. 2, pp. 34–40.
91 'Political Manifesto' circulated in Aceh in September 1953, from S. M. Amin, *Disekitar Peristiwa Berdarah*, quoted in Morris *Islam and Politics*, p. 201. I wish to thank Siti Mariam for her translation help with this and other Bahasa Indonesia sources.
92 Morris *Islam and Politics*, p. 222. On the negotiations between the rebels and the government, between 1953 and 1956, see Nazaruddin *Republican Revolt*, pp. 144–56.
93 Gaharu's background was unusual in that he was one of the few non-*uleebalang* Acehnese to acquire a secular education during the colonial period. He had been appointed the Aceh commander for the Republican Army in 1946, and was removed from this position by the PUSA leaders in the 'social revolution'. Most of his fellow officers were *uleebalangs*, but he played a mediating role in the revolution and apparently owed his life to a PUSA *ulama*. Morris *Islam and Politics*, pp. 127, 133–4.
94 Nazaruddin *Republican Revolt*, pp. 256–60.
95 Morris *Islam and Politics*, p. 207 and note 56; Nazaruddin, *Republican Revolt*, pp. 130–6.
96 Hasjmy had led the PUSA Pemuda in the 1946 revolution. As a *zuama* he had joined the PSII and had opposed the ending of Aceh's provincial status and had helped plan the revolution. He was put in detention for this, but subsequently appointed an official at the Ministry of Social Affairs in Jakarta. Nazaruddin *Republican Revolt*, pp. 153, 191, 261.
97 It was proclaimed in February 1960 and collapsed in August 1961.
98 Nazaruddin *Republican Revolt*, pp. 216–30.
99 Nazaruddin *Republican Revolt*, pp. 292–4.
100 Nazaruddin *Republican Revolt*, p. 147.
101 The statistics are from *Tempo*, 18 April 1987, p. 17, note 54. They do not fully tally with the information in Morris *Islam and Politics*, p. 206: 'The elections . . . produc[ed] the results the rebels desired: Masjumi took roughly three-quarters of the vote, winning every *kabupaten* except South Aceh where Perti, the conservative Islamic party, won.'
102 Between 1976 and 1980 Aceh had by far the fastest growth rate of all regions, at 31.4 per cent. C. Drake *National Integration in Indonesia: Patterns and Politics*, Honolulu, University of Hawaii Press, 1989, p. 170.
103 Revenues from oil and natural gas, because they occur in the form of royalties and involve relatively little labour, have by their very nature little impact on the general welfare level of the region in which they are located. Nevertheless, Aceh did in fact receive large foreign investments for development in the oil and natural gas industries. Drake *National Integration*, p. 298.
104 Dayan Dawood and Sjafrizal, 'Aceh: the LNG boom and enclave development', in H. Hill *Unity and Diversity: Regional Economic Development in Indonesia since 1970*, Singapore, Oxford University

Press, 1989, p. 115. Thus they note also that, 'Despite its status as an energy-rich province, less than 10 per cent of Aceh's villages have a steady supply of electricity.' (p. 122).

105 Despite qualifications, Drake sees socio-economic integration as promoting political integration, thus: 'It appears that real progress has been made both in developing Aceh's economic resources and in integrating this province, with its peripheral position, its fanatical Muslim character, and its history of continuous rebellion against any outside power, whether Dutch or Javanese, into the national whole'. Drake *National Integration*, p. 220.

106 In 1980 Aceh's per capita GDP was the fourth highest of the 27 provinces, while on a household welfare index score it ranked 21st, 'lower even than . . . the very poor province of West Nusa Tenggara'. I. J. Aziz 'Key issues in Indonesian regional development', in Hill, *Unity and Diversity*, p. 61 and Table 2.5.

107 On the attempts at Islamization between 1962 and 1970 see B. J. Boland *The Struggle of Islam in Modern Indonesia*, The Hague, Martinus Nijhoff, 1971, pp. 174–85.

108 McVey 'Faith as the outsider'.

109 Morris *Islam and Politics*, p. 247. For a discussion of student involvement in the killing of communists in Aceh, and the links with Acehnese communal consciousness, see J. Siegal *Shadow and Sound: The Historical Thought of a Sumatran People*, Chicago/London, University of Chicago Press, 1979, pp. 271–82.

110 The phrase is quoted in Morris *Islam and Politics*, p. 259.

111 Morris *Islam and Politics*, p. 255.

112 Morris notes that their backgrounds were diverse, and some were from *ulama* families, but, 'Even though many of those who received a higher secular education were from the village, once they had taken their place in the development bureaucracy they were no longer of the village.' Morris *Islam and Politics*, p. 259.

113 Morris *Islam and Politics*, pp. 255, 258.

114 Morris *Islam and Politics*, p. 255.

115 One indication is that within the military the increase in Javanese domination in senior positions was paralleled by the decrease in Acehnese representation. Between 1967 and 1973 the Aceh Regional command was manned by sometimes one and sometimes two Acehnese senior officers, though no Acehnese reached other senior positions. Since 1974 (until 1989) no Acehnese have appeared in the listings of senior military officers. Anderson 'Current data'.

116 Morris *Islam and Politics*, pp. 267–8.

117 Morris *Islam and Politics*, p. 291.

118 Morris *Islam and Politics*, p. 291.

119 Morris *Islam and Politics*, p. 277.

120 Morris *Islam and Politics*, p. 286, note 32.

121 Morris *Islam and Politics*, p. 296. According to one report he was also sent away from Aceh before the 1977 election, 'forced to take an overseas medical trip'. *Far Eastern Economic Review*, 25 June,

1987, p. 38. There is also an account of him being sent away by the government to Jakarta in May 1978, in order to combat his possible influence in favour of GAM, discussed below. See M. Nur El Ibrahimy *Tengku Muhammad Dadu Beureueh: Peranannya dalam pergolakan di Aceh*, Jakarta, Gunung Agung, 1982, p. 237.

122 D. Y. King and M. Ryass Rasjid 'The Golkar landslide in the 1987 Elections: The case of Aceh', *Asian Survey*, 1988, vol. 28, no. 9.

123 King 'Golkar landslide', p. 919.

124 He is an economics professor who was appointed deputy leader of the National Logistics Board and head of *Golkar*'s 'intellectual group at the centre'. See King 'The Golkar landslide', p. 919.

125 According to one source, Ibrahim Hasan concentrated on mobilizing support in the rural areas, while Bustanil Arafin, the Acehnese who was Minister of Co-operatives in the government, and who was also extremely active in the campaign, concentrated on winning over the secular educated élites. See *Pelita*, 6 April, 1987, p. 36.

126 King 'Golkar landslide', p. 924. Note that according to one source, the PPP had supported Ibrahim's appointment as Governor. 'We did not choose Golkar, we chose Ibrahim Hasan', *Tempo*, 2 August, 1986, p. 21.

127 *Tempo*, 15 March 1986, p. 15. The Malay phrase is 'tak keberatan'. Note also that Daud Beureueh's son-in-law was one of the campaigners for Golkar in 1987.

128 King 'Golkar landslide', p. 923. King notes that William Liddle, amongst others, has disagreed, arguing that there has been a fundamental socio-economic shift towards Aceh's integration.

129 Preliminary results indicate that *Golkar* succeeded in winning six of Aceh's ten House of Representatives seats, including Aceh Besar (where *Golkar* got 48 per cent), North Aceh (where *Golkar* got 50.6 per cent), and Pidie. No analysis is presently available.

130 GAM is the acronym for Gerakan Aceh Merdeka (Free Aceh Movement). Daud Beureueh apparently refused to support the movement because it did not give sufficient prominence to the Islamic goal, see Nazaruddin Sjamsuddin 'Issues and politics of regionalism in Indonesia: evaluating the Acehnese experience', in Lim and Vani *Armed Separatism*, p. 125. In order to pre-empt the possibility of Daud Beureueh endorsing the movement, he was reportedly sent by the government to Jakarta in May 1978. See Nazaruddin Sjamsuddin *Integrasi Politik di Indonesia*, Jakarta, Penerbit PT Gramedia, 1989, p. 86.

131 For the beginnings of the movement see Nazaruddin 'Issues and politics'. Hasan Tiro had supported the 1953 rebellion but had spent most of this life in the USA. Tiro probably fled to Singapore in 1979.

132 Hasan M. di Tiro *The Price of Freedom*, National Liberation Front of Acheh, Sumatra, Norsborg, Sweden, 1981, p. 26.

133 For reports that the 1990 unrest was organized from Libya by Hasan Tiro, see *Far Eastern Economic Review*, 28 June, 1990. On the

organization and leadership of the movement see e.g. *Tempo*, 14 July and 17 November, 1990, 23 March and 30 March, 1991.

134 'Gerombolan Pengacau Keamanan', *Tempo*, 30 March, 1991, pp. 17–18; *Economist*, 8 September, 1990. The estimates of Acehnese killed by the military in 1990 vary from 3,000 according to insurrectionist sources, 1,000 according to Asia Watch, 200–400 according to Jakarta Human Rights sources, and 20–30 according to the armed forces. *Far Eastern Economic Review*, 24 January, 1991, p. 20. For other reports of harsh military action see *Far Eastern Economic Review*, 28 June, 1990 and 11 October, 1990; and *Economist*, 15 December, 1990.

135 *Tempo*, 20 March, 1991, p. 17.

136 Heeger *Politics of Under-Development*, p. 94.

5 Internal colonialism and ethnic rebellion in Thailand

1 For various formulations of this argument see Mark Irving Lichbach, 'An evaluation of "Does economic inequality breed political conflict?" studies', *World Politics*, 1989, vol. 41, no. 4.

2 Walker Connor 'Eco- or ethno-nationalism?', *Ethnic and Racial Studies*, 1981, vol. 7, no. 3.

3 For this view of support for communism in the Northeast, as deriving at least in part from ethno-regionalism, see for example Robert F. Zimmerman 'Insurgency in Thailand', *Problems of Communism*, 1976, vol. 25, no. 3; Frank C. Darling *Thailand: New Challenges and the Struggle for a Political and Economic Take-Off*, Bangkok, American–Asian Education Exchange, 1969; and Charles F. Keyes *Thailand: Buddhist Kingdom as Modern Nation-State*, Boulder, Colo./London, Westview, 1987, p. 108.

4 N. B. Chaloult and Y. Chaloult 'The internal colonialism concept: methodological considerations', *Social and Economic Studies*, 1979, vol. 28, no. 4, p. 87.

5 J. L. Love 'Modeling internal colonialism: history and prospect', *World Development*, 1989, vol. 17, no. 6; Chaloult, 'The internal colonialism concept'.

6 For a critical survey of the literature, focusing upon differences in the usage of the concept, see Robert J. Hind 'The internal colonial concept', *Comparative Studies in Society and History*, 1984, vol. 26, no. 3.

7 A. Orridge 'Uneven development and nationalism: 2', *Political Studies*, 1981, vol. 29, no. 2, p. 190; see also Chaloult 'Internal colonialism'.

8 See for example Orridge 'Uneven development and nationalism: 1/2', *Political Studies*, 1981, vol. 29, nos. 1/2.

9 Love 'Modeling internal colonialism'; Michael Hechter, 'Internal colonialism revisited', in E. A. Tirykian and R. Rogowski (eds) *New Nationalisms of the Developed West*, Boston, Allen and Unwin, 1985; Harold Wolpe 'The theory of internal colonialism: the South African case', in Ivan Oxaal, T. Barnett, and D. Booth (eds) *Beyond*

the *Sociology of Development: Economy and Society in Latin America and Africa*, London, Routledge, 1975.

10 Hechter specifically attempts to take account of the latter situation by his concept of the segmental cultural division of labour. See M. Mechter and M. Levi 'The comparative analysis of ethno-regional movements', *Ethnic and Racial Studies*, 1979, vol. 2, no. 3.

11 Most of the recent work on internal colonialism, including that by Hechter, has focused on the developed states of the West. This partly reflects simply increased interest in ethnicity in developed states, but it is in part a product of the long-standing assumption that whereas ethnicity in the 'Third World' is simply traditional primordialism, ethnicity in the West needs a situational explanation. Once such an assumption is rejected it becomes feasible to consider the applicability of theoretical arguments developed with reference to the industrialized West to the 'new states'.

12 The ambiguities are evident in perhaps the first extended discussion of the concept, in Pablo Gonzalez Casanova 'Internal colonial and national development', *Studies in Comparative International Development*, 1965, vol. 1, no. 4.

13 Wolpe 'The theory of internal colonialism', p. 244.

14 M. Hechter *Internal Colonialism: The Celtic Fringe in British National Development. 1536–1966*, Berkeley, University of California Press, 1975, p. 5.

15 M. Hechter 'Ethnicity and industrialization: On the proliferation of the cultural division of labor', *Ethnicity*, 1976, vol. 3, no. 3, p. 217.

16 Hechter *Internal Colonialism*, p. 9.

17 See Wolpe 'The theory of internal colonialism'; also Donald Rothchild 'State and ethnicity in Africa', in Neil Nevitte and Charles H. Kennedy (eds) *Ethnic Preference and Public Policy in Developing States*, Boulder, Colo., Lynne Rienner, 1986, pp. 20–2.

18 Hechter *Internal Colonialism*, p. 10.

19 Hechter and Levi 'The comparative analysis', p. 263.

20 Hechter and Levi 'The comparative analysis', p. 263.

21 Hechter *Internal Colonialism*, p. 37.

22 Hechter and Levi 'The comparative analysis'.

23 Walker Connor 'Prospects for stability in Southeast Asia: the ethnic barrier' in Kusuma Snitwongse and Sukhumbhand Paribatra (eds) *Durable Stability in Southeast Asia*, Singapore, Institute of Southeast Asian Studies, 1987.

24 Yoshihara Kunio *The Rise of Ersatz Capitalism in South-East Asia*, Singapore, Oxford University Press, 1988.

25 Kevin Hewison *Power and Politics in Thailand*, Manila, Journal of Contemporary Asia Publishers, 1989.

26 Taken from Keyes *Thailand*, p. 159.

27 Bruce London *Metropolis and Nation in Thailand: The Political Economy of Uneven Development*, Boulder, Colo., Westview, 1980; Nobuko Ichikawa 'Geographic implications of foreign investment in Thailand's industrialization', *Southeast Asian Journal of Social*

Science, 1991, vol. 19, nos. 1/2.

28 In 1960 per capita incomes were 26.5 per cent of those in Bangkok and 71 per cent of the national average. In 1983 they were 24 per cent of those in Bangkok and 66 per cent of the national average. From the figures quoted in Keyes *Thailand*, p. 159.

29 Peter Richards *Basic Needs and Government Policies in Thailand*, Singapore, ILO Study, Maruzen Asia, 1982, pp. 6–8; Paul T. Cohen 'Opium and the Karen: a study of indebtedness in Northern Thailand', *Journal of Southeast Asian Studies*, 1984, vol. 15, no. 1, p. 160.

30 Government policies since the early 1950s towards the hill tribe communities are surveyed in Anthony R. Walker 'In mountain and *ulu*: a comparative history of development strategies for ethnic minority peoples in Thailand and Malaysia', *Contemporary Southeast Asia*, 1983, vol. 4, no. 4. See also Kachadpai Burusapatana and Porntipa Atipas 'Thai government policies on minorities', *Southeast Asian Journal of Social Science*, 1988, vol. 16, no. 2.

31 London *Metropolis and Nation*, pp. 95–103.

32 Keyes *Thailand*, p. 127. See also Edward Van Roy *Economic Systems of Northern Thailand*, Ithaca/London, Cornell University Press, 1971, pp. 23–5. *Khon Muang* culture is different from Central Thai culture in various respects, most notably its dialect, its matrilinearity and the traditional importance of *miang* (fermented tea leaves) in the diet. Anchalee Singhanetra-Renard *Northern Thai Mobility 1870–1977: A View From Within*, PhD thesis, University of Hawaii, 1983, pp. 73–8.

33 Nicholas Tapp *Sovereignty and Rebellion: The White Hmong of Northern Thailand*, Singapore, Oxford University Press, 1989, p. 69. The main tribal groups in the North are the Karen, Meo (Hmong), Lahu, Yao, Akha, H'tin, Lisu, Lua and Kha Mu. The total hill tribe population was estimated at over half a million in 1988, with the two largest groups being the Karen (271,000) and the Hmong (82,000). Tribal Research Institute *The Hill Tribes of Thailand*, Chiang Mai, 1989, p. 4.

34 Chavivun Prachuabmoh and Chaiwat Satha-Anand 'Thailand: a mosaic of ethnic tensions under control', *Ethnic Studies Report*, 1985, vol. 3, no. 1, p. 26.

35 Tapp *Sovereignty and Rebellion*, pp. 73–4. The Hmong (Miao) constitute about 10 per cent of the hill communities of Thailand, and are divided into two main dialect-cultural subgroups, the White and the Green.

36 Tapp *Sovereignty and Rebellion*, p. 64.

37 Tapp *Sovereignty and Rebellion*, p. 37; and Robert G. Cooper 'The tribal minorities of Northern Thailand', *Southeast Asian Affairs 1979*, Singapore, Institute of Southeast Asian Studies, 1979, pp. 325–6.

38 Tapp *Sovereignty and Rebellion*, p. 65. The increasing incidence of landlessness and the type of government policies which contribute to this are discussed in Andrew Turton 'The current situation in

the Thai countryside', in A. Turton, J. Fast and M. Caldwell (eds) *Thailand: Roots of Conflict*, Nottingham, Spokesman, 1978.

39 Charles F. Keyes (ed.) *Ethnic Adaptation and Identity: The Karen on the Thai Frontier with Burma*, Philadelphia, Institute for the Study of Human Issues, 1979; 'Introduction', pp. 1–23. Tapp argues that for the Hmong, messianic Christianity offers 'a way of remaining Hmong without being assimilated by the state'. Tapp *Sovereignty and Rebellion*, p. 103.

40 Tapp *Sovereignty and Rebellion*, p. 39.

41 Tapp *Sovereignty and Rebellion*, p. 77.

42 Somjai Rakjiwit *The Jungle Leads the Village* (edited by Robert Zimmerman), Bangkok, USOM, 1974, p. 281 and Section 3 on the North.

43 W. Donner *The Five Faces of Thailand: An Economic Geography*, London, Hurst, 1978, p. 589.

44 This outline of the ethnic structure of the Northeast is from Donner *Five Faces of Thailand*, p. 593.

45 C. F. Keyes *Isan: Regionalism in Northeast Thailand*, Ithaca, Data paper 65, Southeast Asia Program, Cornell University, 1967, p. 12.

46 Rattporn Sangtada *Isan (Northeast Thailand): A Select Bibliography*, Sydney, BISA Special Project, University of Sydney, 1986, p. xvii.

47 This began on an *ad hoc* basis during the 1890s, but was institutionalized in the resident commissioner system for the towns in the 1890s, and thereafter in the 'Thesaphiban' system of provincial administration which progressively eroded the powers of local élites. Kennon Breazeale *The Integration of the Lao States into the Thai Kingdom*, PhD thesis, Oxford University, 1975. Also Keyes *Isan*, p. 17.

48 In the 1950s 65 per cent to 75 per cent of paddy areas was used for glutinous rice, but this proportion has been falling.

49 Glutinous rice is used for eating in the North and Northeast, elsewhere it is used for brewing and sweets. There is only very limited export to Laos, Burma and Korea.

50 L. Maprasert *The Domestic Product of Thailand and its Regional Distribution*, PhD thesis, University of London, 1965, p. 76.

51 Grit Permtanjit *Political Economy of Dependent Capitalist Development: Study of the Limits of the Capacity of the State to Rationalize in Thailand*, PhD thesis, University of Pennsylvania, 1981. Also published by Social Research Institute, Chulalongkon University, 1982, n.b. pp. 94–100.

52 Breazeale *The Integration of the Lao States*.

53 London *Metropolis*, p. 95.

54 Grit *Political Economy*, pp. 97–9.

55 There are clearly problems as to the reliability and comparability of the data bases, but it is interesting to compare Zimmerman's calculation for 1930/31, that Northeast incomes were 29.78 per cent of Central Region incomes, with the figures given by Chantagul for 1976, which show Northeast incomes (adjusted for price differences) as 24.2 per cent of Central Regional incomes.

The survey data on regional incomes for the 1930s is presented in Constance M. Wilson *Thailand: A Handbook of Historical Statistics*, Boston, Hall, 1969, Tables vii, 2, 3, 4, 5, 6. For the 1976 data see Preeda Chantagul, Kumphol Puapanich, Rajanikorn Setthoe, Chiraphan Guladilok and Supriya Suthamnuwat 'Regional development in Thailand', in Regional Development Research Unit *Regional Development in Southeast Asian Countries*, Tokyo, Institute of Developing Economies, 1979, p. 395, Table 1.16.

56 Keyes *Thailand*, p. 159. Between 1960 and 1979, while Bangkok's per capita income rose by 440 per cent from 5,630 to 30,161 baht; that for the Northeast increased by only 360 per cent, from 1,082 to 4,991 baht. This means that the Northeast's average income declined from 19.2 per cent to 16.5 per cent of Bangkok's during this period. Sidney Goldstein and Alice Goldstein *Migration in Thailand: A Twenty-Five Year Review*, Hawaii, Papers of the East–West Population Institute, No. 100, 1986, p. 47. See also the data on regional disparities in per capita income presented in the Government of Thailand *Third National Economic and Social Development Plan (1972–1976)*, Bangkok, Office of Prime Minister, 1972, pp. 87–98 and Table 6.2.

57 *Statistical Summary of Thailand*, National Statistical Office, Bangkok, 1985.

58 From Phaichitr Uathavikul 'Regional planning and development: the case of Thailand', in Vichitvong Na Pombhejara (ed.) *Readings in Thailand's Political Economy*, Bangkok, Bangkok Printing, 1978, Table 8 (p. 47), and Table 10 (p. 51). Note that 81.7 per cent of all special programme expenditure went to the Northeast. Foreign development loans to the Northeast also increased from a negligible level prior to 1963, to 17.54 per cent of the national total in 1965 and 10.13 per cent in 1966. The Northeast also received about 70 per cent of 'anti-communism' aid from the USA. Turton 'The current situation', p. 117.

59 C. J. Dixon 'Development, regional disparity and planning: the experience of Northeast Thailand', *Journal of Southeast Asian Studies*, 1977, vol. 8, no. 2, p. 223.

60 Theodore D. Fuller, Peerasit Kamnuansilpa, Paul Lightfoot, and Sawaeng Rathanamongkolmas *Migration and Development in Modern Thailand*, Bangkok, National Institute of Development Administration, 1982, p. 36.

61 Investment incentives were offered under the Industrial Development Acts of 1962 and 1972. By 1972 the Northeast contained 28.5 per cent of manufacturing firms in Thailand, and the number of manufacturing industries established there averaged 2,200 per year between 1977 and 1984. National Statistical Office *Statistical Reports of Region: Northeastern Region*, Bangkok, 1988, Table 89; United Nations *Thailand*, pp. 28–9.

62 United Nations *Thailand*, pp. 28–9. The government investment policies were partially counteracted by the lending policies of the banking sector whereby, between 1970 and 1982, there was a net

outflow of funds from the Northeast for investment in Bangkok businesses. Nalinee Homasawin *A Regional Analysis of Financial Structures in Thailand: Growth and Distribution 1970–1982* M.Econ dissertation, Thamasat University, Bangkok, 1984, p. 99.

63 Goldstein *Migration*, p. 3.

64 Chou Meng Tarr 'The nature of structural contradictions in peasant communities of Northeastern Thailand', *Southeast Asian Journal of Social Science*, 1988, vol. 16, no. 1; World Bank Country Study *Thailand: Income Growth and Poverty Alleviation*, June 1980. Note also that while the World Bank reported 48 per cent of the Northeast below the poverty line in 1975/6, the 1978–80 socio-economic survey of the National Statistical Office reported a figure of 67 per cent. The figures are reproduced in Medhi Krongkaew and Aphichat Chamratrithirong *Poverty in the Northeast: A Study of Low Income Households in the Northeastern Region of Thailand*, Quezon City, Philippines, Council For Asian Manpower Studies, University of the Philippines, Discussion Paper, 84–10, 1984.

65 (a) Hans Luther 'Peasants and state in contemporary Thailand', *International Journal of Politics*, vol. 7, no. 4, 1978/9, p. 63; and Turton 'The current situation', p. 108. The rural poverty line was here defined as under 6,000 baht per household.

   (b) Goldstein *Migration*, Table 1 (p. 6).

   (c) Richards *Basic Needs*, p. 7. The poverty line here was 165 baht per person at 1975/6 prices.

   (d) National Statistics Office *Statistical Report: Northeast*, 1988. The poverty line was 10,000 baht per household.

   (e) Quoted in Krongkaew and Chamritriwithirong *Poverty in the Northeast*, p. 12.

   (f) Official village survey of Buriram Changwat in 1979, quoted in Chou 'The nature of structural contradictions', pp. 39–40. The poverty line here was 10,000 baht household income. Note that the 1984 (d) statistics for the Northeast give the equivalent figure for Buri Ram as 62.3 per cent, which is only slightly higher than the 1984 (d) figure of 59.6 per cent for the Region as a whole, so that the 1979 figure might be similarly representative.

   (g) These are the most 'optimistic' statistics, from the National Statistics Office, Household Surveys, see World Bank Country Study *Thailand: Towards a Development Strategy of Full Participation*, 1980, Table 3.16 (p. 62). Note that the poverty line of 10,000 baht, used for the 1979 and 1984 figures, is well below the World Bank standards of 15,600 for an average peasant household of 6.7 persons. If the World Bank criterion were used, then the 1984 (d) figure would rise to about 65 per cent.

66 Turton 'The current situation', p. 108–9.

67 Note, however, that the World Bank Report of 1980 concluded that income disparities in the Northeast remained low and were

only increasing in higher income villages. World Bank *Thailand: Income Growth*, pp. 25–7.

68 Dixon gives the figures for the Northeast for average paddy holdings, as 1929, 0.8 hectares; 1936, 1.1 hectares; 1963, 3.97 hectares. See Dixon 'Development', p. 218. Richards gives a figure of 5.1 hectares for 1973/4 and Goldstein gives a 1974 figure of 5.07 hectares. See Richards *Basic Needs*, p. 5; and Goldstein *Migration*, p. 6.

69 Chou 'The nature of structural contradictions', pp. 30–4. Chou found these problems to be less intense in the Northeast than in the North, but that they were increasing. Thus he found 12.9 per cent of landholdings fully rented, and another 10 per cent part-rented; these proportions being much higher than those given in the regional statistics for 1968/9. The regional figures are given in Turton 'The current situation', p. 112. In 1968/9, in the Northeast, owner-operators counted for 97.33 per cent, tenants for 0.62 per cent and part-owner/tenants for 2.05 per cent.

70 Chou 'The nature of structural contradictions', p. 45. This vulnerability of the poor indebted peasantry contrasts with the advantages enjoyed by the richer peasants, who have been able to get subsidized low interest credit, for example from the government Bank for Agriculture and Agricultural Credit (BAAC). Indeed, Paul Lightfoot and Jacqueline Fox found that: 'Subsidized credit actually worsens the position of the poor by enabling middle- and large-scale farmers to accumulate increasing shares of agricultural resources.' Paul Lightfoot and Jacqueline Fox *Institutional Credit and Small-Scale Farmers in Northeastern Thailand*, Centre for South-East Asian Studies Occasional paper No. 5, University of Hull, 1983, p. 43.

71 Turton 'The current situation', pp. 114–19, and Luther 'Peasants and the state', pp. 70–1. See also the comments on various government officials in Mai Chueang *Some Pertinent Village Attitudes in Northeast Thailand*, Bangkok, USOM, 1967.

72 Economist Intelligence Unit *Thailand: Prospects and Policies*, Special Report No. 161, 1984, p. 35.

73 Luther 'Peasants and state', p. 96.

74 Luther 'Peasants and state', p. 98.

75 The weakness and ineffectiveness of the land reform legislation of the mid-1970s is outlined in Turton 'The current situation', pp. 119–21.

76 Luther 'Peasants and state', p. 98.

77 Chou 'The nature of structural contradictions', p. 29.

78 Chou 'The nature of structural contradictions', p. 56.

79 Turton 'The current situation', p. 127.

80 Turtòn 'The current situation', p. 127.

81 Keyes *Isan*, p. 37.

82 The sample surveys of the National Statistical Office indicated in 1985 that 1.4 per cent of the Bangkok population had in-migrated in the previous two years. Of these 43.4 per cent were from the Northeast. The corresponding figures for the previous years were

1982, 38.7 per cent; 1983, 47.4 per cent and 1984, 48.8 per cent. The large majority of these Northeastern migrants were village farmers. See *Survey of Migration into the Bangkok Metropolis, 1985*, National Statistical Office, Table 1 (p. 5) and Table 13 (p. 24).

83 Mai Chepaeng *Some Pertinent Village Attitudes*, p. 11.

84 Keyes *Isan*, p. 38.

85 Keyes *Isan*, p. 39. This attitude is clear in Pira Sudham's portrayal of a Northeastern girl in Bangkok, who 'tried not to let a word of "Lao" escape from your mouth for fear of it being known that you come from the poorest part of the country.' Pira Sudham *People of Esarn*, Bangkok, Siam Media International Books, 1987, p. 60.

86 In 1969 95 per cent of 4th grade students in Bangkok advanced to 5th grade, but only 14 per cent of Northeastern Region students did so. R. Gurevich 'Language, minority education, and social mobility: The case of rural Northeast Thailand', *Journal of Research and Development in Education*, 1976, vol. 9, no. 4, p. 139. Gurevich did his research in Northeastern villages in 1969 and 1970.

87 W. J. Gedney 'Thailand and Laos', in T. A. Sebeok *et al.* (eds) *Linguistics in East Asia and Southeast Asia*, The Hague, Mouton, 1967. Quoted in Gurevich 'Langage', p. 139.

88 Gurevich 'Language', p. 141.

89 Gurevich 'Language', p. 140.

90 Keyes *Isan*, p. 20.

91 For a description of the role of village headmen in Northern Thailand, which is probably applicable also to the Northeast, see Kenneth Robert Ayer *Changing Patterns of Patronage in Northern Thailand*, PhD thesis, Stanford University, 1980, pp. 216–7.

92 Luther 'Peasants and state', p. 90.

93 Luther 'Peasants and state', p. 94.

94 Luther 'Peasants and state', p. 43. An example of the oppressive activities of government officials is provided in the following newspaper item; 'Police Lieutenant-General Boonthin Wongrakmit . . . said that in his previous position as commissioner for the north-eastern region of the country, suspects were always killed during their arrest if "we were sure that they were underworld figures . . . . I worked in the north-eastern region for 37 years and always used the drastic measure. And it worked."' *Straits Times*, 6 December, 1991.

95 S. I. Alpern 'Insurgency in Northeast Thailand: a new cause for alarm', *Asian Survey*, 1975, vol. 15, no. 8, p. 686.

96 Keyes *Isan*, p. 3.

97 C. F. Keyes 'Ethnic identity and loyalty of villages in Northeastern Thailand', in I. McAlister (ed.) *Southeast Asia: The Politics of National Integration*, New York, Random House, 1973, p. 359.

98 Luther 'Peasants and state', p. 54.

99 Keyes 'Ethnic identity', p. 360.

100 Mai Chuepaeng *Some Pertinent Village Attitudes*, pp. 11, 14. The order of two sentences from p. 14 has been reversed so as to make the implied argument explicit.

101 Keyes *Isan*, p. 3.
102 Hechter *Internal Colonialism*, p. 34.
103 Kanok Wongtrangan *Communist Revolutionary Process: A Study of the Communist Party of Thailand*, PhD thesis, Johns Hopkins University, 1981, pp. 259–60; Luther 'Peasants and state', p. 55; Keyes *Thailand*, pp. 55–6.
104 Chai-Anan Samudavanija 'Thailand: A stable semi-democracy', in L. Diamond, J. L. Linz and S. M. Lipset (eds) *Democracy in Developing Countries. Vol. 3: Asia*, Boulder, Colo., Lynne Reinner, 1989, p. 324.
105 Keyes *Isan*, pp. 26–7.
106 Pridi held effective power only briefly from 1944 to 1947, while Phibun was PM or in effective charge from 1938 to 1944 and again from 1947 to 1957.
107 Keyes *Isan*, pp. 28–9. Between 1944 and 1947, when Pridi was in power, the Northeastern Saakachip (Co-operative) Party MPs supported Pridi, and some became Cabinet members; however some supported the anti-Pridi Democratic Party.
108 Keyes *Isan*, pp. 39–40.
109 Keyes *Isan*, p. 41.
110 Keyes *Isan*, p. 42.
111 Zimmerman 'Insurgency', p. 25; Turton 'The current situation', p. 131.
112 David A. Wilson 'Thailand and Marxism' in Frank N. Trager (ed.) *Marxism in Southeast Asia*, Stanford, Stanford University Press, 1959, p. 81.
113 See the essays in W. J. Klausner *Reflections on Thai Culture*, Bangkok, Siam Society, 1987; especially that on 'Power and hooliganism'.
114 Keyes *Isan*, p. 47. Keyes notes that several of the pro-government MPs from the Northeast also campaigned actively for regional development. In April 1958 they threatened to break away and form a Northeastern party if development projects were not begun, and in May twenty-one MPs of various parties met to demand regional development initiatives.
115 J. Coast *Some Aspects of Siamese Politics*, New York, Institute of Pacific Relations, 1953, p. 50.
116 Quoted in Keyes *Isan*, pp. 53–4, from the *Bangkok Post*, 15 December, 1961.
117 Keyes *Isan*, pp. 33–4.
118 Keyes *Isan*, pp. 34–5.
119 Keyes *Isan*, p. 53.
120 Luther 'Peasants and state', p. 84.
121 Keyes *Isan*, p. 55.
122 R. Prizzia *Thailand in Transition: The Role of Oppositional Forces*, Hawaii, Asian Studies at Hawaii No. 32, University of Hawaii Press, 1985, p. 8.
123 Prizzia *Thailand in Transition*, p. 12.
124 Zimmerman 'Insurgency', p. 22.

125 M. Ladd Thomas 'Communist insurgency in Thailand: factors contributing to its decline', *Asian Affairs: An American Review*, 1986, vol. 13, no. 1, pp. 17–18.
126 Luther 'Peasants and state', p. 80.
127 Luther 'Peasants and state', p. 79.
128 Zimmerman 'Insurgency', p. 27.
129 Somchai Rakjiwit *The Jungle Leads the Village*, pp. 196, 120. According to some reports the communists also sought to mobilize support in the Northeast by portraying themselves in messianic terms as the bringers of a new 'Phi Bun' deliverance. See Louis E. Lomax *Thailand: The War That Will Be*, New York, Vintage, 1967, pp. 71–2.
130 Zimmerman 'Insurgency', p. 25.
131 Somchai Rakjiwit *The Jungle Leads*.
132 Zimmerman 'Insurrection', p. 22.
133 Alpern 'Insurgency', p. 685.
134 Justus M. van der Kroef 'Thailand: a new phase in the insurgency?', *Pacific Community*, 1977, vol. 8, no. 4, p. 600.
135 M. Stuart-Fox 'Factors influencing relations between the Communist Parties of Thailand and Laos', *Asian Survey*, 1979, vol. 19, no. 4, p. 348.
136 Stuart-Fox 'Factors influencing relations', p. 350.
137 This would accord with other cases where village-level support for ethno-regional rebellion involves an 'unrealistic' combination of goals, in which the aim of the removal of all frontiers and barriers to pan-ethnic unification coexists with the goal of maintaining access to the benefits of membership of the present state, rather than seceding and becoming a member of the less developed neighbouring state. See David Brown, 'Borderline politics in Ghana: The National Liberation Movement of Western Togoland', *Journal of Modern African Studies*, 1981, vol. 18, no. 4.
138 Stuart-Fox 'Factors influencing relations', p. 351.
139 Stuart-Fox 'Factors influencing relations'; Ladd Thomas 'Insurgency'.
140 T. A. Marks 'Thailand: The threatened kingdom', *Conflict Studies*, 1980, no. 115, p. 13. Compare this estimate with the 1977 estimate by a Thai Security Command officer, that 'in the northeast of the country the insurgents now could count on 3,500 "hard core" members, plus an additional 60,000 sympathizers'. Van der Kroef 'Thailand', p. 608.
141 R. Sean Randolph and W. Scott Thompson *Thai Insurgency: Contemporary Developments*, Beverley Hills/London, Washington Papers Vol. ix, Center for Strategic and International Studies, Georgetown University, Sage, 1981, p. 33.
142 Maurice M. Tanter 'Welcome to the domino that didn't fall', *Reason*, 18 July, 1986, pp. 24–32.
143 Zimmerman 'Insurgency', p. 33.
144 Randolph and Thompson *Thai Insurgency*, p. 34.
145 J. L. S. Girling 'Northeast Thailand: Tomorrow's Viet Nam?',

Foreign Affairs, 1968, vol. 46, no. 2, p. 391.
146 James Haffner 'View from the village: participatory rural development in North East Thailand', *Community Development Journal*,
1987, vol. 22, no. 2; Andrew Turton *Production, Power and
Participation in Rural Thailand: Experiences of Poor Farmers' Groups*,
Geneva, United Nations Research Institute for Social Development, 1987.
147 For a portrayal of the Northeast in these terms see Paul Handley
'How the other half live', *Far Eastern Economic Review*, 18 July,
1991, pp. 47–8.
148 Charles F. Keyes 'Economic action and Buddhist morality in a Thai
village', *Journal of Asian Studies*, 1983, vol. 42, no. 4.
149 Andrew Turton 'Patrolling the middle ground: methodological
perspectives on "everyday peasant resistance"', *The Journal of
Peasant Studies*, 1986, vol. 13, no. 2; 'Thailand: North-east Passage',
Economist, 23 February, 1991, p. 30; Paul Handley, 'Thailand:
the Land Wars', *Far Eastern Economic Review*, 31 October, 1991,
pp. 15–16.
150 Paul Handley 'Where money talks', *Far Eastern Economic Review*, 2
April, 1992, p. 12, and 'Traveller's tales', *Far Eastern Economic
Review*, 30 April, 1992, p. 30.
151 Andre Gunder Frank 'The development of underdevelopment', in
R. I. Rhodes (ed.) *Imperialism and Underdevelopment*, New York/
London, Monthly Review Press, 1970.
152 Hechter 'Ethnicity and industrialization', p. 217.
153 Hechter and Levi 'Comparative analysis', p. 270.
154 Joseph R. Rudolph and Robert J. Thompson (eds) *Ethnoterritorial
Politics, Policy, and the Western World*, Boulder, Colo., Lynne
Rienner, 1989, pp. 7.
155 One implication, which might well apply to the present resurgence
of ethnic unrest amongst the Pattani Malays, is that, should the
state respond to peripheral unrest by concessions which increase
political autonomy, facilitate the emergence of indigenous élites,
and promote the legitimacy of ethnic nationalist ideologies, then
this would serve to increase the likelihood of an ethnic nationalist
upsurge, rather than to reduce it.

6 Class, state and ethnic politics in Peninsular Malaysia

1 This approach is adopted by most of the chapters in S. Husin Ali
(ed.) *Ethnicity, Class and Development: Malaysia*, Kuala Lumpur,
Persatuan Sains Sosial Malaysia, 1984. See also R. S. Milne 'Politics,
ethnicity and class in Guyana and Malaysia', *Social and Economic
Studies*, 1977, vol. 26, no. 1. The most systematic and careful
example of this approach is that by Judith Nagata 'The status of
ethnicity and the ethnicity of status: ethnic and class identity in
Malaysia and Latin America', *International Journal of Comparative
Sociology*, 1976, vol. 17, nos. 3/4.
2 Karl Marx *Manifesto of the Communist Party*, in Lewis S. Feuer (ed.)

Marx and Engels: Basic Writings on Politics and Philosophy, London, Fontana, 1969, p. 51.

3 Ralph Miliband *Marxism and Politics*, Oxford, Oxford University Press, 1977, Chapter 5. For a rather different view of 'relative autonomy', see Nicos Poulantzas *Classes in Contemporary Capitalism*, London, NLB, 1975, Pt. 2.3.

4 Theda Skocpol *States and Social Revolution*, Cambridge, Cambridge University Press, 1979, p. 32.

5 Poulantzas *Classes in Contemporary Capitalism*, p. 164.

6 Hamza Alavi 'The state in post-colonial societies: Pakistan and Bangladesh', in Harry Goldbourne (ed.) *Politics and State in the Third World*, London, Macmillan, 1979, p. 42. See also, in the same volume, J. S. Saul 'The state in post-colonial societies: Tanzania'. Also Issa G. Shivji *The Class Struggles in Tanzania*, London, Heinemann, 1976. Whereas Alavi talks of the 'bureaucratic-military oligarchy', Shivji employs the term 'bureaucratic bourgeoisie'.

7 Poulantzas *Classes in Contemporary Capitalism*, pp. 186–9.

8 The distinction between the two approaches is established, and applied to the Malaysian case, in Redha Ahmad 'Capital accumulation and the state in Malaysia', *Ilmu Masyarakat*, 1985, No. 8.

9 W. Ziemann and M. Lanzendorfer 'The state in peripheral societies', *Socialist Register: 1977 a Survey of Movements and Ideas*, 1977, London, Merlin.

10 For broadly compatible views of the relationship between state and classes in Malaysia, see T. Salem 'Capitalist development and the formation of the bureaucratic bourgeoisie in Peninsular Malaya', *Kajian Malaysia*, 1983, vol. 1, no. 2; and Jomo Kwame Sundaram 'Malaysia's New Economic Policy: A class perspective', *Pacific Viewpoint*, 1984, vol. 25, no. 2.

11 There is no consensus amongst class analysts as to the characterization of the Malaysian state, but this three-phase model is certainly the most widespread, with the major disagreement concerning the extent to which the post-1969 state ought to be characterized simply as the agency of the bureaucratic bourgeoisie, rather than as mediating between competing class interests. The model is employed explicitly, for example, in Toh Kin Woon and Jomo Kwame Sundaram 'The nature of the Malaysian State and it's implications for development planning', in K. S. Jomo and K. G. Wells (eds) *Fourth Malaysian Plan*, Kuala Lumpur, Persatuan Ekonomi Malaysia, 1983. The 'mediating' characterization of the third phase is argued, for example, in Redha Ahmad 'Capital accumulation and the state'.

12 This is indicated in Marx's argument that the peasantry, in that they do not form an interactive community, 'do not form a class'. Karl Marx *The Eighteenth Brumaire*, in Marx and Engels *Selected Works*, London, Lawrence and Wishart, 1968, p. 172.

13 Laclau's examination of the relationship between class and ideology is related to ethnic consciousness in Malaysia in Zawawi

Ibrahim 'Malay peasants and proletarian consciousness', *Bulletin of Concerned Asian Scholars*, 1983, vol. 15, no. 4.

14 This link between class and ethnicity, though not the term 'ethno-class', is discussed in John Rex *Race and Ethnicity*, Milton Keynes, Open University Press, 1986, pp. 79–83. For some recent reflections on the relationship between Malay identity, class, and Malaysian efforts to interpret their changing social environments, see Joel S. Kahn, 'Class ethnicity and diversity: some remarks on Malay culture in Malaysia', in Joel S. Kahn and Francis Loh Kok Wah (eds) *Fragmented Vision: Culture and Politics in Contemporary Malaysia*, Sydney, Allen and Unwin, 1992.

15 Toh Kin Woon 'The role of the Malaysian State in the restructuring of employment', *Jurnal Ekonomi Malaysia*, 1982, no. 6. See pp. 57–61.

16 Richard Sklar 'Political science and national integration: a radical approach', *Journal of Modern African Studies*, 1967, vol. 5, no. 1.

17 Note that this was not the initial decolonization strategy, embodied in the plan for an ethnically neutral Malay Union. Rather it was an *ad hoc* strategy which emerged in response to the anti-colonialism of the Malayan Communist Party. This is discussed below.

18 Frank Furedi 'Britain's colonial wars: playing the ethnic card', *Journal of Commonwealth and Comparative Politics*, 1990, vol. 28, no. 1.

19 To some extent this process of transition was already under way prior to colonial rule, see P. L. Burns 'Capitalism and the Malay states', in Hamza Alavi (ed.) *Capitalism and Colonial Production*, London, Croom Helm, 1982.

20 Ozay Mehmet 'Colonialism, dualistic growth and the distribution of economic benefits in Malaysia', *Southeast Asian Journal of Social Science*, 1977, vol. 5, nos 11/12.

21 Jomo Kwame Sundaram *A Question of Class: Capital, The State and Uneven Development in Malaya*, New York, Monthly Review Press, and Manila, Journal of Contemporary Asia Publishers, 1988, pp. 190–1.

22 Collin E. R. Abraham 'Racial and ethnic manipulation in colonial Malaya', *Ethnic and Racial Studies*, 1983, vol. 6, no. 1; and Helen Hill 'Class relations within neo-colonialism in Southeast Asia', in K. Mcleod and E. Utrecht *The ASEAN Papers*, Queensland, Transnational Corp, 1978.

23 By 1900 Malaya was producing only one-third of its rice requirements. Hill 'Class relations', p. 74.

24 For this debate, see Paul H. Kratoska 'Rice cultivation and the ethnic division of labor in British Malaya', *Comparative Studies of Society and History*, vol. 24, no. 2, 1982; and Lim Teck Ghee 'British colonial administration and the ethnic division of labour in Malaya', *Kajian Malaysia*, 1984, vol. 2, no. 2.

25 John Funston *Malay Politics in Malaysia: A Study of UMNO and PAS*, Kuala Lumpur, Heinemann, 1980, p. 31.

26 Viswanathan Selvaratnam 'Ethnicity, inequality, and higher edu-

cation in Malaysia', *Comparative Education Review*, 1988, vol. 32, no. 2, p. 175.

27 At the time of the Second World War there were less than 32 Malays in the senior arm of the administration, the Malayan Civil Service. Even after the rapid Malayanization of the public service in the 1950s, Malays only held 29.3 per cent of the senior posts as of 1962. Mavis Puthucheary 'The administrative élite', in Zakaria Haji Ahmad (ed.) *Government and Politics of Malaysia*, Singapore, Oxford University Press, 1987, Table 6.1 (p. 96).

28 The percentage of Indians in estate labour is the figure for 1972; otherwise the data is from the 1957 statistics on occupation and ethnic group, reproduced in James V. Jesudason *Ethnicity and the Economy: The State, Chinese Business, and Multinationals in Malaysia*, Singapore, Oxford University Press, 1990, p. 37.

29 Jomo *Question of Class*, Table 11.5 (pp. 300–1).

30 Jomo *Question of Class*, Table 11.2 (pp. 292–3). The distinction between employer and own-account worker is not made in the 1957 and 1970 statistics.

31 The figures are those for 1970. Toh 'The role of the Malaysian State', Table 3 (p. 39).

32 The figures quoted by Zainudin are $144 per month for Malays and $217 for Chinese, a proportion of 1:1.5. Osman-Rani quoting the Household Income Survey, gives a ratio of 1:2.158. See M. Zainudin Salleh and Zulkifly Osman 'The economic structure' in E. K. Fisk and H. Osman-Rani (eds) *The Political Economy of Malaysia*, Kuala Lumpur, Oxford University Press, 1982, p. 143; H. Osman-Rani 'Economic development and ethnic integration: the Malaysian experience', *Sojourn*, 1990, vol. 5, no. 1, Table 3 (p. 9).

33 Tai Yoke Lin 'Inter-ethnic restructuring in Malaysia, 1970–80: The employment perspective', in Robert B. Goldman and A. Jeyaratnam Wilson (eds) *From Independence to Statehood*, London, Frances Pinter, 1984.

34 For the urban areas see Dipak Mazumdar *The Urban Labor Market and Income Distribution: A Study of Malaysia*, New York, Oxford University Press, 1981, pp. 184–90. Note that such racial segregation is probably weakest in the larger multi-national enterprises.

35 This discussion is derived from Martin Brennan 'Class, politics and race in modern Malaysia', in Richard Higott and Richard Robison (eds) *Southeast Asia: Essays in the Political Economy of Structural Change*, London, Routledge, 1985.

36 To designate one of the bourgeois class fractions as the Malay 'aristocracy' is apparently not respectful of the Marxist terminology. The justification is that the Malay aristocrats have functioned as land and timber owners, capital investors, and administrators, so as to maintain their dominant position in society. Their non-bourgeois origins and status coexist, therefore, with their bourgeois roles.

37 Albert Lau *The Malayan Union Controversy*, Singapore, Oxford

University Press, 1991.

38 The AMCJA-PUTERA was an *ad hoc* coalition of those excluded from the Malayan Federation constitutional negotiations. It contained Malay and non-Malay organizations but was dominated by socialist and proletarian movements. After allying with the Chinese Chamber of Commerce to organize mass demonstrations, this united front divided on class lines. Many of the worker-based movements were banned at the onset of the communist rebellion. The IMP grew out of the Communities Liaison Committee and was an attempt by both the British administration and the Chinese and Malay bourgeoisies to wean mass support away from the MCP. It was a non-communal party founded by Dato Onn, the leader of UMNO, and Tan Cheng Lock, the MCA leader. It was distrusted both by the subordinate classes and by the bourgeoisie because of its attempt to combine populist economic and 'anti-feudal' policies with a pro-colonial political stance; for both class groups, therefore, it was 'highly suspect'. See Khong Kim Hoong 'The early political movements before Independence', in Zakaria *Government and Politics*.

39 Khong 'The early political movements', p. 12.

40 Khong 'The early political movements', pp. 15–6.

41 Many Indians held aloof from the PMFTU, in part because the conditions and wages for Indian labour were markedly inferior to those of the Chinese. Thus when the British dismembered the PMFTU it was predominantly Indian anti-communist unions, many of whom eventually amalgamated into the National Union of Plantation Workers, who formed the Malayan Trade Union Congress. Sinnappah Arasaratnam *Indians in Malaysia and Singapore*, Kuala Lumpur, Oxford University Press, 1979, p. 139; Jesudasan *Ethnicity and the Economy*, pp. 41–2.

42 The role of the MCP in promoting Chinese interests is stressed in Anthony Short 'Communism, race and politics in Malaysia', *Asian Survey*, 1970, vol. 10, no. 12.

43 Such Malay support became evident in the early stages of the emergency, when over 1,000 Malays were detained, and army intelligence reported that 'more Malays appear to be joining the bandits'. Furedi 'Britain's colonial wars', pp. 72–3; and Hua Wu Yin *Class and Communalism in Malaysia: Politics in a Dependent Capitalist State*, London, Zed, 1983, Chapters 3 and 4, n.b. pp. 97–8.

44 Furedi 'Britain's colonial wars', p. 82.

45 Funston *Malay Politics*, pp. 40–1.

46 Funston *Malay Politics*, p. 88.

47 Funston *Malay Politics*, p. 292.

48 Funston *Malay Politics*, pp. 75–87.

49 Funston *Malay Politics*, p. 77.

50 Funston *Malay Politics*, Chapter 5.

51 The term is that employed by Jomo Kwame Sundaram in 'The ascendance of Bureaucrat capitalists in Malaysia', *Alternatives*,

1981, no. 8.

52 Mavis Puthucheary *The Politics of Administration: The Malaysian Experience*, Kuala Lumpur, Oxford University Press, 1978, pp. 24–38.

53 Toh Kin Woon and Jomo Kwame Sundaram 'The nature of the Malaysian State and its implications for development planning', in Jomo Kwame Sundaram and K. J. Wells (eds) *The Fourth Malaysian Plan*, Kuala Lumpur, Persatuan Ekonomi Malaysia, 1983, pp. 23–43.

54 Keng Pek Koon *Chinese Politics in Malaysia: A History of the Malaysian Chinese Association*, Singapore, Oxford University Press, 1988, p. 56.

55 Heng *Chinese Politics*, p. 57.

56 Heng *Chinese Politics*, pp. 59–61.

57 Heng *Chinese Politics*, p. 76.

58 Sinnappah Arasaratnam *Indians in Malaysia*, p. 124.

59 Rajeswary Ampalavanar *The Indian Minority and Political Change in Malaya, 1945–1957*, Kuala Lumpur, Oxford University Press, 1981, pp. 213–20.

60 Sinnappah Arasaratnam *Indians in Malaysia*, p. 131.

61 Hill 'Class relations', p. 77.

62 Arendt Lijphart 'Consociational democracy', *World Politics*, 1969, vol. 21, no. 2, p. 213.

63 Toh and Jomo 'The nature of the Malaysian State', p. 37.

64 On the tolerance of status disparities in each racial group see Judith A. Nagata 'Perceptions of social inequality in Malaysia' in Judith A. Nagata (ed.) *Pluralism in Malaysia: Myth and Reality*, Leiden, Canadian Association for South Asian Studies, Brill, 1975.

65 Funston *Malay Politics*, p. 187.

66 Heng *Chinese Politics*, pp. 215–6.

67 Leon Comber *13 May 1969: A Historical Survey of Sino-Malay Relations*, Kuala Lumpur, Heinemann, 1983, pp. 70–1.

68 Gordon Means *Malaysian Politics: The Second Generation*, Singapore, Oxford University Press, 1991, p. 7.

69 The exact figures for this ratio quoted by Osman-Rani are 2.158 for 1957/8 and 2.541 for 1970. The income figures quoted by Zainudin generate corresponding ratio figures of 1.88 and 2.46. Osman-Rani 'Economic development', Table 3 (p. 9); Zainudin 'The economic structure', Table 7.9 (p. 143).

70 The figure is for 1947, and compares to 4 per cent in 1980. From Jomo *A Question of Class*, Appendix 2, pp. 322–3.

71 Hing Ai Yun 'Capitalist development, class and race', in Husin Ali *Ethnicity Class and Development*, p. 303.

72 The remaining 114 were British, there being no non-Malay Malayans. Puthucheary *The Politics of Administration*, Table 5.2 (p. 54).

73 This occurred partly because of enhanced investment opportunities for indigenous businessmen arising from state incentives, to fill the gap left by declining foreign investment. Hing 'Capitalist devel-

opment', p. 304.

74 Indicated by the rapid increase in Malay employment in manufacturing between 1957 and 1970, from 266,000 (2.6 per cent of Malays) to 731,000 (5.1 per cent of Malays). See Jomo *A Question of Class*, Table 11.3 (pp. 294–5). Note that Malay-owned businesses expanded less quickly, though by 1970 they constituted 14.2 per cent of all those registered. Jesudason *Ethnicity and the Economy*, p. 102.

75 The latter two figures are for 1970. Puthucheary *The Politics of Administration*, Tables 5.2, 5.3, 5.7 (pp. 54–7).

76 Osman-Rani 'Economic development', p. 2.

77 In terms of the alternative measures of income disparity, the mean/median ratio rose from 1.241 to 1.599, an increase of 29 per cent; and the Gini coefficient rose from 0.342 to 0.466, an increase of 36%. Osman-Rani 'Economic development', pp. 7–8. See also H. J. Ragayah, Mat Zinn and Ishak Shari, 'Some aspects of income inequality in Peninsular Malaysia, 1957–1970', in N. T. Oshima and T. Mizoguchi (eds) *Income Distribution by Sectors and over time in East and Southeast Asian Countries*, Manila, CAMS, 1978, pp. 228–58.

78 Osman-Rani 'Economic development', p. 10. Ikemoto's calculations show that 'the period 1957–70 is a period of inequalization both within race and between rural and urban areas accompanying an absolute decrease in income of the "poor", leaving the inequality between races unchanged.' Yukio Ikemoto 'Income distribution in Malaysia: 1957–80', *The Developing Economies*, 1985, vol. 23, no. 4, p. 357.

79 Hing 'Capitalist development', p. 305.

80 Karl Von Vorys *Democracy Without Consensus: Communalism and Political Stability in Malaysia*, Princeton, Princeton University Press, 1975, p. 236.

81 Calculated from Osman-Rani 'Economic development', Table 2 (p. 8).

82 Sudhir Anand *Inequality and Poverty in Malaysia: Measurement and Decomposition*, New York, Oxford University Press, 1983, p. 96.

83 Osman-Rani 'Economic development', p. 7.

84 Heng *Chinese Politics*, p. 257.

85 Von Vorys *Democracy Without Consensus*, p. 305.

86 Loh Kok Wah 'The socio-economic basis of ethnic consciousness: The Chinese in the 1970s', in Hussin Ali *Ethnicity, Class and Development*, pp. 93–112.

87 Chandra Muzaffar 'Has the communal situation worsened over the last decade? Some preliminary thoughts', in Hussin Ali *Ethnicity, Class and Development*, p. 360. It is relevant that Penang has a predominantly Chinese population.

88 Funston *Malay Politics*, pp. 197–8.

89 This is argued, for example, by Michael Stenson: 'The Malay-instigated race riots of May 1969 arose from a form of transferred frustration having its roots in intra-Malay class conflict. Directed at

the most immediate and visible object of Malay frustration, urban non-Malays who were demanding political power to go with their manifest material affluence, the youthful rioters were unconsciously warning the too complaisant, too accommodatory UMNO élite which had for so long collaborated with the urban non-Malays while failing to uplift its own racial group.' Michael Stenson 'Class and race in West Malaysia', *Bulletin of Concerned Asian Scholars*, 1976, vol. 8, no. 2, p. 48.

90 J. S. Furnivall *Colonial Policy and Practice*, New York, New York University Press, 1956, p. 304.

91 Choo Keng Kum *The Changing Urban Structure in Penisular Malaysia (1957–1970)*, University of Utah, PhD thesis, 1978, p. 226.

92 Choo *The Changing Urban Structure*, p. 256.

93 Choo *The Changing Urban Structure*, p. 110.

94 Calculated from Choo *Changing Urban Structure*, Table (p. 315).

95 Mazumdar *The Urban Labor Market*, p. 202.

96 Hans-Dieter Evers 'Ethnic and class conflict in urban South-East Asia' in Hans-Deiter Evers (ed.) *Sociology of South-East Asia: Readings on Social Change and Development*, Kuala Lumpur, Oxford University Press, 1980, pp. 121–4.

97 Mazumdar *The Urban Labor Market*, pp. 183–90.

98 Anand *Inequality and Poverty*, p. 203. He concluded that race itself accounted for less than 5 per cent of overall income inequalities.

99 Anand *Inequality and Poverty*, p. 168.

100 Mazumdar *The Urban Labor Market*, pp. 268–70.

101 For all racial groups in urban areas, the share of income accruing to the poorest 40 per cent of the population fell rapidly from 1957 to 1970. Osman-Rani 'Economic development', Table 1 (p. 7).

102 Anand *Inequality and Poverty*, p. 173. For a full discussion see Muzamdar *The Urban Labor Market*, Pt. III.

103 Mazumdar *The Urban Labor Market*, pp. 323–7.

104 Alvin Rabushka 'Racial stereotyping in Malaya', *Asian Survey*, 1971, vol. 9, no. 7.

105 Comber *13 May 1969*, p. 64.

106 Puthucheary *The Politics of Administration*, pp. 53–5.

107 Mavis Puthucheary 'The administrative élite', in Zakaria *Government and Politics*, p. 99.

108 Jesudason *Ethnicity and the Economy*, p. 51.

109 Tham Seong Chee 'Ideology, politics and economic modernization: The case of the Malays in Malaysia', *Southeast Asian Journal of Social Science*, 1973, vol. 1, no. 1, pp. 46–9.

110 Jesudason *Ethnicity and the Economy*, pp. 51–2.

111 Hua *Class and Communism*, pp. 145–6.

112 Funston *Malay Politics*, pp. 178–83.

113 Speech by Tungku Abdul Rahman to UMNO leaders, 6 May, 1966, *Straits Times*.

114 The political dominance of the Malays was thrown into doubt by the incorporation into Malaysia of the predominantly Chinese Singapore, and by Lee Kuan Yew's demand for a 'Malaysian

Malaysia'. Malay dominance, which had hitherto been taken some-what for granted, would now have to be actively asserted.

115 *Straits Times* report of UMNO General Assembly, 2 August, 1966.
116 Quoted in Von Vorys *Democracy Without Consensus*, p. 284.
117 Jomo 'The ascendance of bureaucrat capitalists'.
118 For a discussion of the role of the state in balancing the interests of international capitalism, the comprador bourgeoisie, and the state bureaucrats; and attempting at the same time to control the peasantry, see F. Ha-Lim 'The state in West Malaysia', *Race and Class*, 1982, vol. 14, no. 1, pp. 33–45.
119 Diane K. Mauzy *Barisan Nasional: Coalition Government in Malaysia*, Kuala Lumpur, Marican, 1983, p. 140.
120 For overviews which stress the negative impact of the pro-*Bumiputra* policies in benefiting only Malay élites but alienating the Chinese, see Mah Hui Lim 'Affirmative action, ethnicity and integration: the case of Malaysia', *Ethnic and Racial Studies*, 1985, vol. 8, no. 2; Thomas Sowell *Preferential Policies*, New York, Morrow, 1990, pp. 41–51.
121 Just Faaland, J. R. Parkinson, Rais Saniman *Growth and Ethnic Inequality: Malaysia's New Economic Policy*, Kuala Lumpur, Dewan Bahasa dan Pustaka, 1990, p. 57.
122 R. S. Milne 'The politics of Malaysia's New Economic Policy', *Pacific Affairs*, 1976, vol. 49, no. 2. The phrase 'bureaucratic entre-preneurs' is here credited to Dr. Mohd. Nor Abdullah. See p. 249, note 67.
123 Tai Yoke Lin 'Inter-ethnic restructuring', Tables 4.1, 4.2, 4.3 (pp. 46–8). Note that these figures do not tally with those noted by Gordon Means, who suggests that between 1969 and 1973 98 per cent of all public service recruits for government service, and 99 per cent of those recruited into the armed forces, were Malays. Means *Malaysian Politics*, p. 26.
124 Salem 'Capitalist development'.
125 Toh 'The role of the Malaysian State'.
126 There is a particularly strong correlation, for Malays, between higher education and higher earnings. See Mazumdar *The Urban Labor Market*, p. 201. The employment of Malay as the language of education was crucial in facilitating Malay economic advancement. The relationship is examined in D. John Grove 'Restructuring the cultural division of labor in Malaysia and Sri Lanka', *Comparative Political Studies*, 1986, vol. 19, no. 2, pp. 179–99.
127 Jomo 'Malaysia's New Economic Policy', pp. 160–8.
128 E. T. Gomez *Politics in Business: UMNO's Corporate Investments*, Kuala Lumpur, Forum, 1990, p. vii and p. viii.
129 Osman-Rani 'Economic development', pp. 8–9. The mean/median ratio increased from 1.451 in 1970 to 1.481 in 1976, then down to 1.466 in 1984. The reduction in the gap between mean Malay and mean Chinese incomes was from a ratio of 2.541 in 1970 to 2.281 in 1976, to 1.763 in 1984. In Gini ratio terms, this was a reduction from 0.466 in 1970 to 0.494 in 1976, to 0.469 in 1984. During the

period of the Fifth Plan, between 1946 and 1990, mean *Bumiputra* incomes improved, as a percentage of Chinese incomes, from 56.7 per cent to 58.8 per cent. *Sixth Malaysia Plan*, Kuala Lumpur, 1991.

130 Ikemoto 'Income distribution', p. 366.

131 Mazumdar *The Urban Labor Market*, p. 201. Note also that the NEP, in viewing the country's economic problems in ethnic terms, detracted attention away from the problem of Chinese and Indian poverty. See Mavis Puthucheary 'Public policies relating to business and land, and their impact on ethnic relations in Peninsular Malaysia', in Goldman and Jeyaratnam Wilson *From Independence to Statehood*, pp. 147–72.

132 Stenson 'Class and race', p. 49.

133 Hing 'Capitalist development', p. 311.

134 Chandra Muzaffar 'Has the communal situation worsened?', p. 378.

135 Jesudason *Ethnicity and the Economy*, p. 159.

136 Lim Mah Hui 'The ownership and control of large corporations in Malaysia: the role of Chinese businessmen', in Linda Y. C. Lim and L. A. Peter Gosling (eds) *The Chinese in Southeast Asia. Vol 1.*, Singapore, Maruzen Asia, 1983, p. 311.

137 The appointment of Malays to nominal management and ownership positions with companies effectively run by Chinese.

138 Bruce Gale *Politics and Business A Study of Multi-Purpose Holdings Berhad*, Singapore, Eastern Universities Press, 1985, Chapter 5.

139 Ahmad 'Capital accumulation', pp. 19–23; Milne 'The politics of Malaysia's New Economic Policy', pp. 251–3; E. T. Gomez *Money Politics in the Barisan Nasional*, Kuala Lumpur, Forum, 1991, pp. 47–55.

140 Between 1970 and 1976 the wealthiest 20 per cent of Chinese in Malaysia managed to increase their share of incomes from 52.6 per cent to 56.1 per cent, though by 1984 their share dropped back to 51 per cent. Osman-Rani 'Economic development', p. 7.

141 Stenson 'Class and race', p. 51.

142 Chandra Muzaffar *Islamic Resurgence in Malaysia*, Selangor, Penerbit Fajar Bakti, 1987, pp. 15–16.

143 Tai Yoke Lin, 'Inter-ethnic restructuring', pp. 49–50. See also Toh Kin Woon, 'Education as a vehicle for reducing economic inequality', in Husin Ali *Ethnicity, Class and Development*.

144 Zainah Anwar *Islamic Revivalism in Malaysia: Dakwah among the Students*, Selangor, Pelanduk Publications, 1987, pp. 21–2.

145 Muzaffar *Islamic Resurgence*, p. 31.

146 Muzaffar *Islamic Resurgence*, p. 31.

147 Zainah Anwar *Islamic Revivalism*, p. 30.

148 Zainah Anwar *Islamic Revivalism*, p. 35.

149 Chandra Muzaffar *Islamic Resurgence*, Chapter 4.

150 Faaland *Growth and Ethnic Inequality*, p. 311.

151 James C. Scott *Weapons of the Weak: Everyday Forms of Peasant Resistance*, New Haven, Yale University Press, 1985, p. 53.

152 Scott estimates that rice production increased by 2.5 times its

previous level as a result of the 'green revolution'. Scott *Weapons of the Weak*, p. 55.

153 K. S. Jomo *Growth and Structural Change in the Malaysian Economy*, London, Macmillan, 1990, pp. 148 and 152.

154 Jomo *Growth and Structural Change*, p. 153.

155 For a summary account of some of these studies see K. S. Jomo and Ishak Shari *Development Policies and Income Inequality in Peninsular Malaysia*, Kuala Lumpur, Institute of Advanced Studies, 1986, pp. 49–58. For the counter-argument, that state investments did not promote income inequalities, at least amongst Kelantan rice farmers in the Kemubu Project, see R. T. Shand 'Income distribution in a dynamic rural sector: some evidence from Malaysia', *Economic Development and Cultural Change*, 1987, vol. 36, no. 1, pp. 35–50.

156 Jomo *Growth and Structural Change*, p. 153.

157 Scott *Weapons of the Weak*, p. 56.

158 Scott *Weapons of the Weak*, p. xvii.

159 Scott *Weapons of the Weak*, p. 56.

160 Between 10,000 and 15,000 rice farmers were involved in the Muda protests. Other protests included the Baling demonstration of November 1974, relating to falling rubber prices, and the unrest on the FELDA land resettlement schemes in 1978 and 1979. See Ha-Lim 'The state in West Malaysia', pp. 33–45. The interweaving of class consciousness with ethnic consciousness, to produce manifestations of political discontent is examined, in the case of the Malay rural proletariat, in Zawawi Ibrahim 'Malay peasants and proletarian consciousness'.

161 Shamsul Amri Baharuddin 'The patron–client relations as an aspect of peasant ideology: a note with reference to Malay peasant society', *Akademika*, 1982, vol. 20/21.

162 Zawawi Ibrahim 'Perspectives on capitalist penetration and the reconstitution of the Malay peasantry', *Jurnal Ekonomi Malaysia*, 1982, vol. 5. The perception of peasant class interests in culturally-defined terms is discussed in Scott *Weapons of the Weak*, p. 135, and in Clive S. Kessler *Islam and Politics in a Malay State: Kelantan 1938–1969*, Ithaca, Cornell University Press, 1978, pp. 164–70 and Chapter 11.

163 David Brown 'Crisis and ethnicity: legitimacy in plural societies', *Third World Quarterly*, 1985, vol. 7, no. 4.

164 Sharon Siddique and Leo Suryadinata 'Bumiputra and Pribumi: Economic nationalism (indigenism) in Malaysia and Indonesia', *Pacific Affairs*, 1981–2, vol. 54, no. 4.

165 Muzaffar *Islamic Resurgence*, p. 24.

166 Muzaffar *Islamic Resurgence*, p. 56.

167 Muzaffar *Islamic Resurgence*, p. 24.

168 The NEP ended in 1990 and is replaced by the New Development Policy (NDP), formulated in the Second Outline Perspective Plan (OPP2), and launched in the Sixth Malaysian Plan of 1991–5. The plan gives greater priority to the private sector and to the goal of

growth, but there is no sign of any intention to dismantle the various pro-*Bumiputra* institutions and provisions of the NEP.

7 Ethnicity, nationalism and democracy

1 Meinecke's *Kulturnation* was the cultural community which did not necessarily possess, but had the potential for, national consciousness; whereas the *Staatsnation* was the active consciousness of political community. Kohn's distinction was between a western version of nationalism as a subjective, rational, civic association; and an eastern European form of nationalism which was derived from the objective organic unity of the community. Friedrich Meinecke *Cosmopolitanism and the National State*, New Jersey, Princeton University Press, 1970; Hans Kohn *The Idea of Nationalism: A Study in its Origins and Background*, New York, Collier-Macmillan, 1967.

Bibliography

Abraham C. E. R. 'Racial and ethnic manipulation in colonial Malaya', *Ethnic and Racial Studies*, 1983, vol. 6, no. 1.

Action Committee for Indian Education *Report of the Action Committee on Indian Education: At the Crossroads*, Singapore, 1991.

Adorno T. W., Frenkel-Brunswick E., Levinson D. J. and Sanford R. N. *The Authoritarian Personality*, New York, Harper and Row, 1950.

Ahmad Z. H. (ed.) *Government and Politics of Malaysia*, Singapore, Oxford University Press, 1987.

Akhmadi H. *Breaking the Chains of Oppression of the Indonesian People: Defense Statement at his Trial on Charges of Insulting the Head of State*, Bandung, June 1979, Ithaca, Cornell Modern Indonesia Project, Translation Series, Cornell University, 1981.

Alavi H. 'The State in post-colonial societies: Pakistan and Bangladesh', in H. Goulbourne (ed.) *Politics and State in the Third World*, London, Macmillan, 1979.

Alavi H. (ed.) *Capitalism and Colonial Production*, London, Croom Helm, 1982.

Allport G. *The Nature of Prejudice*, Boston, Beacon, 1954.

Alpern S. I. 'Insurgency in Northeast Thailand: a new cause for alarm', *Asian Survey*, 1975, vol. 15, no. 8.

Anantaraman V. *Singapore Industrial Relations System*, Singapore, Singapore Institute of Management/McGraw-Hill, 1990.

Anderson B. R. O'G 'Current data on the Indonesian military élite', *Indonesia*, Ithaca, Cornell Southeast Asia Program (various issues).

Anderson B. R. O'G. 'The idea of power in Javanese culture' in Claire Holt (ed.) *Culture and Politics in Indonesia*, Ithaca, Cornell University Press, 1972.

Anderson B. R. O'G and Kahin A. (eds) *Interpreting Indonesian Politics: Thirteen Contributions to the Debate*, Ithaca, Cornell Modern Indonesia Project, Cornell University, 1982.

Ayer K. R. *Changing Patterns of Patronage in Northern Thailand*, PhD thesis, Stanford University, 1980.

Aziz I. J. 'Key issues in Indonesian regional development', in H. Hill (ed.) *Unity and Diversity: Regional Economic Development in Indonesia since 1970*, Singapore, Oxford University Press, 1989.

Backtiar H. W. *The Indonesian Nation: Some Problems of Integration and Disintegration*, Singapore, Institute of Southeast Asian Studies, 1973.

Banton M. *Racial and Ethnic Competition*, Cambridge, Cambridge University Press, 1983.

Benjamin G. 'The cultural logic of Singapore's multiracialism', in Riaz Hassan (ed.) *Singapore: Society in Transition*, Singapore, Oxford University Press, 1976.

Betts R. *Multiracialism, Meritocracy and the Malays of Singapore*, PhD thesis, Massachusetts Institute of Technology, 1975.

Black A. *State, Community and Human Desire*, Hemel Hempstead, Harvester-Wheatsheaf, 1988.

Boileau J. M. *Golkar: Functional Group Politics in Indonesia*, Jakarta, Centre for Strategic and International Studies, 1983.

Boland B. J. *The Struggle of Islam in Modern Indonesia*, The Hague, Martinus Nijhoff, 1971.

Brass P. (ed.) *Ethnic Groups and the State*, Beckenham, Croom Helm, 1985.

Breazeale K. *The Integration of the Lao States into the Thai Kingdom*, PhD thesis, Oxford University, 1975.

Brennan M. 'Class, politics and race in modern Malaysia', in Richard Higott and Richard Robison, (eds) *Southeast Asia: Essays in the Political Economy of Structural Change*, London, Routledge, 1985.

Brown D. 'Borderline politics in Ghana: the national liberation movement of western Togoland', *Journal of Modern African Studies*, 1981, vol. 18, no. 4.

Brown D. 'Crisis and ethnicity: Legitimacy in plural societies', *Third World Quarterly*, 1985, vol. 7, no. 4.

Brown D. 'From peripheral communities to ethnic nations: separatism in Southeast Asia', *Pacific Affairs*, 1988, vol. 61, no. 1.

Brown D. 'The corporatist management of ethnicity in contemporary Singapore' in Garry Rodan (ed.) *Singapore Changes Guard: Social, Political and Economic Directions in the 1990s*, Melbourne, Longman Cheshire, 1993.

Burns P. L. 'Capitalism and the Malay states', in Hamza Alavi (ed.) *Capitalism and Colonial Production*, London, Croom Helm, 1982.

Buzan B. *People, States and Fear: The National Security Problem in International Relations*, Brighton, Wheatsheaf, 1983.

Cady J. *A History of Modern Burma*, Ithaca, Cornell University Press, 1958.

Campbell J. (ed.) *The Portable Jung*, Harmondsworth, Penguin, 1976.

Casanova P. G. 'Internal colonialism and national development', *Studies in Comparative International Development*, 1965, vol. 1, no. 4.

Chai-Anan Samudavanija 'Thailand: a stable semi-democracy', in L. Diamond, J. L. Linz and S. M. Lipset (eds) *Democracy in Developing Countries, Vol. 3: Asia*, Boulder, Colo., Lynne Reinner, 1989.

Chaloult N. B. and Chaloult Y. 'The internal colonialism concept: methodological considerations', *Social and Economic Studies*, 1979, vol. 28, no. 4.

Chan Heng Chee *The Politics of Survival 1965–1967*, Singapore/Kuala Lumpur, Oxford University Press, 1971.

Chan Heng Chee 'Politics in an administrative state: where has all the politics gone?', in Seah Chee Meow (ed.) *Trends in Singapore*, Singapore, Singapore University Press, 1975.

Chan Heng Chee 'Language and culture in a multi-ethnic society: a Singapore strategy', paper presented for the MSSA International Conference on Modernization and National Cultural Identity, Kuala Lumpur, 10–12 January, 1983.

Chan Heng Chee 'The PAP and the structuring of the political system', in K. S. Sandhu and P. Wheatley (eds) *Management of Success: The Moulding of Modern Singapore*, Singapore, Institute of Southeast Asian Studies, 1989.

Chan Heng Chee and Evers H-D. 'Nation-building and national identity in Southeast Asia' in S. N. Eisenstadt and Stein Rokkan (eds) *Building States and Nations, Vol 2*, Beverly Hills/London, Sage, 1973.

Chandra Muzaffar 'Has the communal situation worsened over the last decade? Some preliminary thoughts', in S. Husin Ali (ed.) *Ethnicity, Class and Development: Malaysia*, Kuala Lumpur, Persatuan Sains Sosial Malaysia, 1984.

Chandra Muzaffar *Islamic Resurgence in Malaysia*, Selangor, Penerbit Fajar Bakti, 1987.

Chao Tzang Yawnghwe 'The Burman military: holding the country together?', in Joseph Silverstein (ed.) *Independent Burma at Forty Years: Six Assessments*, Ithaca, Cornell Southeast Asia Program, Cornell University, 1989.

Chavivun Prachuabmoh and Chaiwat Satha-Anand 'Thailand: A mosaic of ethnic tensions under control', *Ethnic Studies Report*, 1985, vol. 3, no. 1.

Chen P. (ed.) *Singapore Development Policy and Trends*, Singapore, Oxford University Press, 1983.

Chew Sock Foon *Ethnicity and Nationality in Singapore*, Ohio, Center for International Studies, Ohio University, 1987.

Chiew Seen-Kong 'The socio-cultural framework of politics', in Jon S. T. Quah, Chan Heng Chee and Seah Chee Meow (eds) *Government and Politics of Singapore*, Singapore, Oxford University Press, 1987.

Choo Keng Kun *The Changing Urban Structure in Penisular Malaysia (1957–1970)*, University of Utah, PhD thesis, 1978.

Chou Meng Tarr 'The nature of structural contradictions in peasant communities of northeastern Thailand', *Southeast Asian Journal of Social Science*, 1988, vol. 16, no. 1.

Christie R. and Jahda M. (eds) *Studies in the Scope and Method of the 'Authoritarian Personality'*, Glencoe, Free Press, 1954.

Clammer J. *Singapore: Ideology, Society, Culture*, Singapore, Chopmen, 1985.

Clapham C. 'Clientelism and the State', in Christopher Clapham (ed.) *Private Patronage and Public Power: Political Clientelism in the Modern State*, London, Pinter, 1982.

Clapham C. (ed.) *Private Patronage and Public Power: Political Clientelism in the Modern State*, London, Pinter, 1982.

Clapham C. *Third World Politics: An Introduction*, London, Croom Helm 1985.

Coast J. *Some Aspects of Siamese Politics*, New York, Institute of Pacific Relations, 1953.

Cohen P.T. 'Opium and the Karen: a study of indebtedness in Northern Thailand:, *Journal of Southeast Asian Studies*, 1984, vol. 15, no. 1.

Comber L. *13 May 1969: A Historical Survey of Sino-Malay Relations*, Kuala Lumpur, Heinemann, 1983.

Connor W. 'Nation-building or nation-destroying', *World Politics*, 1972, vol. 24, no. 3.

Connor W. 'A nation is a nation, is a state, is an ethnic group, is a . . . ', *Ethnic and Racial Studies*, 1978, vol. 1, no. 4.

Connor W. 'Eco- or ethno-nationalism?', *Ethnic and Racial Studies*, 1981, vol. 7, no. 3.

Connor W. 'Ethnonationalism', in M. Weiner and S. P. Huntington (eds) *Understanding Political Development*, Boston, Little Brown, 1987.

Connor W. 'Prospects for stability in Southeast Asia: the ethnic barrier', in Kusuma Snitwongse and Sukhumbhand Paribatra (eds) *Durable Stability in Southeast Asia*, Singapore, Institute of Southeast Asian Studies, 1987.

Cooper R.G. 'The tribal minorities of Northern Thailand', *Southeast Asian Affairs 1979*, Singapore, Institute of Southeast Asian Studies, 1979.

Crawford C., Smith M. and Krebs D. (eds), *Sociobiology and Psychology: Ideas, Issues and Applications*, Hillsdale, Lawrence Erlbaum, 1987.

Crone D. K. 'State, social elites, and government capacity in Southeast Asia', *World Politics*, 1988, vol. 40, no. 2.

Crouch H. *The Army and Politics in Indonesia*, Ithaca, Cornell University Press, 1978.

Crouch H. 'Patrimonialism and military rule in Indonesia', *World Politics*, 1979, vol. 31, no. 4.

Crouch H. *Domestic Political Structures and Regional Economic Cooperation*, Singapore, Institute of Southeast Asian Studies, 1984.

Darling F. C. *Thailand: New Challenges and the Struggle for a Political and Economic Take-Off*, Bangkok, American–Asian Educational Exchange, 1969.

Dawood D. and Sjafrizal 'Aceh: the LNG boom and enclave development', in H. Hill (ed.) *Unity and Diversity: Regional Economic Development in Indonesia since 1970*, Singapore, Oxford University Press, 1989.

De Silva K. M., Duke P., Goldberg E. S. and Katz N. (eds) *Ethnic Conflict in Buddhist Societies: Sri Lanka, Thailand and Burma*, London, Pinter, 1988.

De Silva K. M. and May R. J. (eds) *Internationalization of Ethnic Conflict*, London, Pinter, 1991.

Deleuze G. and Guattari F. *Anti-Oedipus: Capitalism and Schizophrenia*, London, Athlone, 1984.

Deyo F. C. *Dependent Development and Industrial Order: An Asian Case Study*, New York, Praeger, 1981.

Diamond L., Linz J. L. and Lipset S.M. (eds) *Democracy in Developing Countries, Vol. 3: Asia*, Boulder, Colo., Lynne Reinner, 1989.

Dipak Mazumdar *The Urban Labor Market and Income Distribution: A Study of Malaysia*, New York, Oxford University Press, 1981.

Dixon C. J. 'Development, regional disparity and planning: the experience of Northeast Thailand', *Journal of Southeast Asian Studies*, 1977, vol. 8, no. 2.

Djiwandono Soedjati and Yong Mun Cheong (eds) *Soldiers and Stability in Southeast Asia*, Singapore, Institute of Southeast Asian Studies, 1988.

Donner W. *The Five Faces of Thailand: An Economic Geography*, London, Hurst, 1978.

Doob L. W. *Patriotism and Nationalism: Their Psychological Foundations*, New Haven, Yale University Press, 1964.

Dorodjatun K. J. and Simatupang T. A. M. 'The Indonesian experience in facing non-armed and armed movements: lessons from the past and glimpses of the future', in Kusuma Snitwongse and Sukhumbhand Paribatra (eds) *Durable Stability in Southeast Asia*, Singapore, Institute of Southeast Asian Studies, 1987.

Drake C. *National Integration in Indonesia: Patterns and Policies*, Honolulu, University of Hawaii Press, 1989.

Eisestadt S. N. *Traditional Patrimonialism and Modern Neo-Patrimonialism*, Beverly Hills/London, Sage, 1973.

Eisenstadt S. N. and Rokkan S. (eds) *Building States and Nations, Vol 2*, Beverly Hills/London, Sage, 1973.

Ellinwood D. C. and Enloe C. H. *Ethnicity and the Military in Asia*, New Brunswick, Transaction, 1981.

Emmerson D. K. 'The military and development in Indonesia', in Soedjati Djiwandono and Yong Mun Cheong (eds) *Soldiers and Stability in Southeast Asia*, Singapore, Institute of Southeast Asian Studies, 1988.

Enloe C. H. 'Ethnic diversity: the potential for conflict', in Guy L. Pauker, Frank H. Golay and Cynthia H. Enloe *Diversity and Development in Southeast Asia*, New York, McGraw-Hill, 1977.

Enloe C. H. *Ethnic Soldiers: State Security in Divided Societies*, Athens, University of Georgia Press, 1980.

Erikson E. H. *Identity: Youth and Crisis*, London, Faber and Faber, 1968.

Erikson E. H. *Dimensions of a New Identity*, New York, Norton, 1974.

Esman M. J. 'Communal conflict in Southeast Asia', in Nathan Glazer and Daniel P. Moynihan *Ethnicity: Theory and Experience*, Cambridge, Harvard University Press, 1975.

Esman M. J. 'Two dimensions of ethnic politics', *Ethnic and Racial Studies*, 1985, vol. 8, no. 3.

Evers H-D 'Ethnic and class conflict in urban South-East Asia' in Hans-Deiter Evers (ed.) *Sociology of South-East Asia: Readings on Social Change and Development*, Kuala Lumpur, Oxford University Press, 1980.

Evers H-D (ed.) *Sociology of South-East Asia: Readings on Social Change and*

Development, Kuala Lumpur, Oxford University Press, 1980.

Faaland J., Parkinson J. R., Rais Saniman *Growth and Ethnic Inequality: Malaysia's New Economic Policy*, Kuala Lumpur, Dewan Bahasa dan Pustaka, 1990.

Fanon F. *Black Skin, White Masks*, London, MacGibbon and Kee, 1968.

Feith H. *The Wilopo Cabinet, 1952–1953: A Turning Point in Post-Revolutionary Indonesia*, Ithaca, Cornell University, Modern Indonesia Project, 1958.

Feith H. *The Decline of Constitutional Democracy in Indonesia*, Ithaca, Cornell University Press, 1968.

Feuer L. S. (ed.) *Marx and Engels: Basic Writings on Politics and Philosophy*, London, Fontana, 1969.

Fisk E. K. and Osman-Rani H. (eds) *The Political Economy of Malaysia*, Kuala Lumpur, Oxford University Press, 1982.

Fox J. J, Garnaut R., McCawley P. and Mackie J. A. C. (eds) *Indonesia: Australian Perspectives (Volume 2)*, Canberra, Australian National University, 1980.

Frank A. G. 'The development of underdevelopment', in R. I. Rhodes (ed.) *Imperialism and Underdevelopment*, New York/London, Monthly Review Press, 1970.

Freund J. *The Sociology of Max Weber*, Middlesex, Penguin, 1966.

Fromm E. *The Sane Society*, New York, Fawcett, 1955.

Frosh S. *The Politics of Psychoanalysis: An Introduction to Freudian and Post-Freudian Theory*, London, Macmillan, 1987.

Frosh S. 'Psychoanalysis and racism', in Barry Richards (ed.) *Crises of the Self: Further Essays on Psychoanalysis and Politics*, London, Free Association Books, 1989.

Fukuyama F. *The End of History and the Last Man*, New York, Free Press, 1992.

Fuller T. D., Peerasit Kamnuansilpa, Lightfoot P. and Sawaeng Rathanamongkolmas *Migration and Development in Modern Thailand*, Bangkok, National Institute of Development Administration, 1982.

Funston J. *Malay Politics in Malaysia: A Study of UMNO and PAS*, Kuala Lumpur, Heinemann, 1980.

Furedi F. 'Britain's colonial wars: playing the ethnic card', *Journal of Commonwealth and Comparative Politics*, 1990, vol. 28, no. 1.

Furnivall J. S. *Colonial Policy and Practice*, Cambridge, Cambridge University Press, 1948, and New York, New York University Press, 1956.

Furnivall J. S. *The Governance of Modern Burma*, New York, Institute of Pacific Relations, 1958.

Gale B. *Politics and Business: A Study of Multi-Purpose Holdings Berhad*, Singapore, Eastern Universities Press, 1985.

Geertz C. *The Religion of Java*, Chicago, University of Chicago Press, 1960.

Geertz C. (ed.) *Old Societies and New States: The Quest for Modernity in Asia and Africa*, New York, Free Press of Glencoe, 1963.

Geertz C. 'The integrative revolution', in Clifford Geertz (ed.) *Old Societies and New States: The Quest for Modernity in Asia and Africa*, New

York, Free Press of Glencoe, 1963.

Geertz C. *The Interpretation of Cultures: Selected Essays*, New York, Basic, 1973.

Gehan Wijeyewardene (ed.) *Ethnic Groups Across National Boundaries in Mainland Southeast Asia*, Singapore, Institute of Southeast Asian Studies, 1990.

Gibbons D. 'The spectator culture: a refinement of the Almond and Verba model', *Journal of Commonwealth Political Studies*, 1971, vol. 9, no. 1.

Girling J. 'Northeast Thailand: tomorrow's Viet Nam?' *Foreign Affairs*, 1968, vol. 46, no. 2.

Glazer N. and Moynihan D. P. *Ethnicity: Theory and Experience*, Cambridge, Harvard University Press, 1975.

Goldman R. B. and Jeyaratnam Wilson A. (eds) *From Independence to Statehood*, London, Frances Pinter, 1984.

Goldstein S. and Goldstein A. *Migration in Thailand: A Twenty-Five Year Review*, Hawaii, Papers of the East–West Population Institute, No. 100, 1986.

Gomez E. T. *Politics in Business: UMNO's Corporate Investments*, Kuala Lumpur, Forum, 1990.

Gomez E. T. *Money Politics in the Barisan Nasional*, Kuala Lumpur, Forum, 1991.

Gopinathan S. 'Education' in Jon S. T. Quah, Chan Heng Chee and Seah Chee Meow (eds) *Government and Politics of Singapore*, Singapore, Oxford University Press, 1987.

Goulbourne H. (ed.) *Politics and State in the Third World*, London, Macmillan, 1979.

Government of Singapore, *Singapore: The Next Lap*, Singapore, Times, 1991.

Government of Thailand, *Third National Economic and Social Development Plan (1972–1976)*, Bangkok, Office of Prime Minister, 1972.

Gregory A. *Recruitment and Factional Patterns of the Indonesian Political Elite: Guided Democracy and the New Order*, PhD thesis, Columbia University, 1976.

Gregory A. 'The influence of ethnicity in the evolution of the Indonesian military elite' in D. C. Ellinwood and C. H. Enloe (eds) *Ethnicity and the Military in Asia*, New Brunswick/London, Transaction Books, 1981.

Grit Permtanjit *Political Economy of Dependent Capitalist Development: Study of the Limits of the Capacity of the State to Rationalize in Thailand*, PhD thesis, University of Pennsylvania, 1981. Also published by Social Research Institute, Chulalongkon University, 1982.

Group for the Advancement of Psychiatry *Us and Them: The Psychology of Ethnonationalism*, Report No. 123, New York, Brunner/Mazel, 1987.

Grove J.D. 'Restructuring the cultural division of labor in Malaysia and Sri lanka', *Comparative Political Studies*, 1986, vol. 19, no. 2.

Gurevich R. 'Language, minority education, and social mobility: the case of rural Northeast Thailand', *Journal of Research and Development in Education*, 1976, vol. 9, no. 4.

Ha-Lim F. 'The State in West Malaysia', *Race and Class*, 1982, vol. 14, no. 1.

Haffner J. 'View from the village: participatory rural development in north east Thailand', *Community Development Journal*, 1987, vol. 22, no. 2.

Hall C. S., Lindzey G., Loehlin J. and Manosevitz M. *Introduction to Theories of Personality*, New York, Wiley, 1985.

Hasan M. di Tiro *The Price of Freedom*, National Liberation Front of Acheh, Sumatra, Norsborg, Sweden, 1981.

Hassan R. (ed.) *Singapore: Society in Transition*, Kuala Lumpur, Oxford University Press, 1976.

Hassan R. *Families in Flats: A Study of Low Income Families in Public Housing*, Singapore, Singapore University Press, 1977.

Hechter M. *Internal Colonialism: The Celtic Fringe in British National Development, 1536–1966*, Berkeley, University of California Press, 1975.

Hechter M. 'Ethnicity and industrialization: on the proliferation of the cultural division of labor' *Ethnicity*, 1976, vol. 3, no. 3.

Hechter M. 'Internal colonialism revisited', in E. A. Tirykian and R. Rogowski (eds) *New Nationalisms of the Developed West*, Boston, Allen and Unwin, 1985.

Hechter M. 'Rational choice theory and the study of race and ethnic relations', in John Rex and David Mason (eds) *Theories of Race and Ethnic Relations*, Cambridge, Cambridge University Press, 1986.

Hechter M. and Levi M. 'The comparative analysis of ethno-regional movements', *Ethnic and Racial Studies*, 1979, vol. 2, no. 3.

Heeger G. A. *The Politics of Underdevelopment*, London, Macmillan, 1974.

Heng Pek Koon *Chinese Politics in Malaysia: A History of the Malaysian Chinese Association*, Singapore, Oxford University Press, 1988.

Hewison K. *Power and Politics in Thailand*, Manila, Journal of Contemporary Asia Publishers, 1989.

Higott R. and Robison R. (eds) *Southeast Asia: Essays in the Political Economy of Structural Change*, London, Routledge, 1985.

Hill H. 'Class relations within neo-colonialism in Southeast Asia', in K. McLeod and E. Utrecht *The ASEAN Papers*, Queensland, Transnational Corp, 1978.

Hill H. (ed.) *Unity and Diversity: Regional Economic Development in Indonesia since 1970*, Singapore, Oxford University Press, 1989.

Hind R. J. 'The internal colonial concept', *Comparative Studies in Society and History*, 1984, vol. 26, no. 3.

Hing Ai Yun 'Capitalist development, class and race', in S. Husin Ali (ed.) *Ethnicity, Class and Development: Malaysia*, Kuala Lumpur, Persatuan Sains Sosial Malaysia, 1984.

Ho Wing Meng 'Value premises underlying the transformation of Singapore', in K. S. Sandhu and P. Wheatley (eds) *Management of Success: The Moulding of Modern Singapore*, Singapore, Institute of Southeast Asian Studies, 1989.

Holbrook D. *Human Hope and the Death Instinct*, Oxford, Pergamon,

1971.

Holt C. (ed.) *Culture and Politics in Indonesia*, Ithaca, Cornell University Press, 1972.

Horowitz D. L. *Ethnic Groups in Conflict*, Los Angeles/London, University of California Press, 1985.

Hua Wu Yin *Class and Communalism in Malaysia: Politics in a Dependent Capitalist State*, London, Zed, 1983.

Husin Ali S. (ed.) *Ethnicity, Class and Development: Malaysia*, Kuala Lumpur, Persatuan Sains Sosial Malaysia, 1984.

Inland Revenue Department *Report on the Survey of Employment of Graduates*, Singapore, 1980.

Institute of Policy Studies *The Singaporean: Ethnicity, National Identity and Citizenship*, Press Release, Singapore, 1990.

Jackson K. D. 'A bureaucratic polity: a theoretical framework for the analysis of power and communications in Indonesia', in K. D. Jackson and L. W. Pye *Political Power and Communications in Indonesia*, Berkeley, University of California Press, 1978.

Jackson K. D. 'The political implications of structure and culture in Indonesia', in K. D. Jackson and L. W. Pye (eds) *Political Power and Communications in Indonesia*, Berkeley, University of California Press, 1978.

Jackson K. D. and Pye L. W. (eds) *Political Power and Communications in Indonesia*, Berkeley, University of California Press, 1978.

Jackson K. D. and Moeliono J. 'Participation in rebellion: the Dar'ul Islam in West Java', in R. W. Liddle (ed.) *Political Participation in Modern Indonesia*, New Haven, Yale University Press, 1973.

Jenkins A. *The Social Theory of Claude Levi-Strauss*, London, Macmillan, 1979.

Jesudason J. *Ethnicity and the Economy: The State, Chinese Business, and Multinationals in Malaysia*, Singapore, Oxford University Press, 1990.

Jomo K. S. 'The ascendance of bureaucrat capitalists in Malaysia', *Alternatives*, 1981, no. 8.

Jomo K. S. 'Malaysia's new economic policy: a class perspective', *Pacific Viewpoint*, 1984, vol. 25, no. 2.

Jomo K. S. *A Question of Class: Capital, The State and Uneven Development in Malaya*, New York, Monthly Review Press, and Manila, Journal of Contemporary Asia Publishers, 1988.

Jomo, K. S. *Growth and Structural Change in the Malaysian Economy*, London, Macmillan, 1990.

Jomo K. S. and Ishak Shari *Development Policies and Income Inequality in Peninsular Malaysia*, Kuala Lumpur, Institute of Advanced Studies, 1986.

Jomo K. S. and Wells K. G. (eds) *Fourth Malaysian Plan*, Kuala Lumpur, Persatuan Ekonomi Malaysia, 1983.

Kachadpai Burusapatana and Porntipa Atipas 'Thai government policies on minorities', *Southeast Asian Journal of Social Science*, 1988, vol. 16, no. 2.

Kahin A. R. (ed.) *Regional Dynamics of the Indonesian Revolution: Unity from Diversity*, Honolulu, University of Hawaii Press, 1985.

Kahn J. S. 'Ideology and social structure in Indonesia', in B. R. O'G. Anderson and A. Kahin (eds) *Interpreting Indonesian Politics: Thirteen Contributions to the Debate*, Ithaca, Cornell Modern Indonesia Project, Cornell University, 1982.

Kahn J. S. 'Class, ethnicity and diversity: some remarks on Malay culture in Malaysia', in Joel S. Kahn and Francis Loh Kok Wah (eds) *Fragmented Vision: Culture and Politics in Contemporary Malaysia*, Sydney, Allen and Unwin, 1992.

Kahn J. S. and Loh Kok Wah F. (eds) *Fragmented Vision: Culture and Politics in Contemporary Malaysia*, Sydney, Allen and Unwin, 1992.

Kanok Wongtrangan *Communist Revolutionary Process: A Study of the Communist Party of Thailand*, PhD thesis, Johns Hopkins University, 1981.

Kasfir N. *The Shrinking Political Arena: Participation and Ethnicity in African Politics*, Los Angeles, University of California Press, 1976.

Kassim I. *Problems of Elite Cohesion: A Perspective from a Minority Community*, Singapore, Singapore University Press, 1974.

Kedourie E. *Nationalism*, London, Hutchinson, 1960, revised 1986.

Kellas J. G. *The Politics of Nationalism and Ethnicity*, London, Macmillan, 1991.

Kessler C. S. *Islam and Politics in a Malay State: Kelantan 1938–1969*, Ithaca, Cornell University Press, 1978.

Keyes C. F. *Isan: Regionalism in Northeast Thailand*, Ithaca, Data Paper 65, Southeast Asia Program, Cornell University, 1967.

Keyes C. F. 'Ethnic identity and loyalty of villagers in Northeastern Thailand', in I. McAlister (ed.) *Southeast Asia: The Politics of National Integration*, New York, Random House, 1973.

Keyes C. F. (ed.) *Ethnic Adaptation and Identity: The Karen on the Thai Frontier with Burma*, Philadelphia, Institute for the Study of Human Issues, 1979.

Keyes C. F. 'Economic action and Buddhist morality in a Thai village', *Journal of Asian Studies*, 1983, vol. 42, no. 4.

Keyes C. F. *Thailand: Buddhist Kingdom as Modern Nation-State*, Boulder, Colo./London, Westview, 1987.

Khong Kim Hoong 'The early political movements before independence', in Zakaria Haji Ahmad (ed.) *Government and Politics of Malaysia*, Singapore, Oxford University Press, 1987.

King D. Y. 'Indonesia's new order as a bureaucratic polity, a neo-patrimonial Régime or a bureaucratic authoritarian régime: what difference does it make?' in B. Anderson and A. Kahin (eds) *Interpreting Indonesian Politics: Thirteen Contributions to the Debate*, Ithaca, Cornell Modern Indonesia Project, Cornell University, 1982.

King D. Y. and Ryass Rasjid M. 'The Golkar landslide in the 1987 elections: the case of Aceh', *Asian Survey*, 1988, vol. 28, no. 9.

Klaren, P. F. and Bossert T. J. (eds) *Promise of Development: Theories of Change in Latin America*, Boulder, Colo., Westview, 1986.

Klausner W. J. *Reflections on Thai Culture*, Bangkok, Siam Society, 1987.

Kohn H. *The Idea of Nationalism: A Study in its Origins and Background*, New York, Collier-Macmillan, 1967.

Kratoska P. H. 'Rice cultivation and the ethnic division of labor in British Malaya', *Comparative Studies of Society and History*, 1982, vol. 24, no. 2.

Kusuma Snitwongse and Sukhumbhand Paribatra (eds) *Durable Stability in Southeast Asia*, Singapore, Institute of Southeast Asian Studies, 1987.

Ladd Thomas M. 'Communist insurgency in Thailand: factors contributing to its decline', *Asian Affairs: An American Review*, 1986, vol. 13, no. 1.

Lanternari V. 'Ethnocentrism and ideology', *Ethnic and Racial Studies*, 1980, vol. 3, no. 1.

Lasch C. *Haven in a Heartless World: The Family Besieged*, New York, Basic, 1977.

Lasswell H. 'The selective effect of personality', in Richard Christie and Marie Jahda (eds) *Studies in the Scope and Method of the 'Authoritarian Personality'*, Glencoe, Free Press, 1954.

Lau A. *The Malayan Union Controversy*, Singapore, Oxford University Press, 1991.

Leach E. R. *Political Systems in Highland Burma*, Boston, Beacon, 1954.

Lehman F. R. 'Who are the Karen, and if so, why', in C. F. Keyes, (ed.) *Ethnic Adaptation and Identity: The Karen on the Thai Frontier with Burma*, Philadelphia, Institute for the Study of Human Issues, 1979.

Leifer M. 'Communal violence in Singapore', *Asian Survey*, 1964, vol. 4, no. 10.

Lemarchand R. 'Political clientelism and ethnicity in tropical Africa: competing solidarities in nation-building', *American Political Science Review*, 1972, vol. 66, no. 1.

Lev D. S. *Islamic Courts in Indonesia: A Study in the Political Bases of Legal Institutions*, Berkeley, University of California Press, 1972.

Levi M and Hechter M. 'A rational choice approach to the rise and decline of ethnoregional political parties', in E. A. Tiryakian and R. Rogowski (eds) *New Nationalisms in the Developed West*, Boston, Allen and Unwin, 1985.

Levi-Strauss C. *The View From Afar*, Harmondsworth, Penguin, 1985.

Levine R. A. and Campbell D. T. *Ethnocentrism: Theories of Conflict, Ethnic Attitudes and Group Behaviour*, New York, Wiley, 1972.

Li T. *Malays in Singapore: Culture, Economy and Ideology*, Singapore, Oxford University Press, 1988.

Lichbach M. I. 'An evaluation of "Does economic inequality breed political conflict?" Studies', *World Politics*, 1989, vol. 41, no. 4.

Liddle R. W. *Ethnicity, Party, and National Integration: An Indonesian Case Study*, New Haven/London, Yale University Press, 1970.

Liddle R. W. 'Ethnicity and political organization: three East Sumatran cases', in C. Holt (ed.) *Culture and Politics in Indonesia*, Ithaca, Cornell University Press, 1972.

Liddle R. W. (ed.) *Political Participation in Modern Indonesia*, New Haven, Yale University Press, 1978.

Lieberman V. B. 'Ethnic politics in eighteenth century Burma' *Modern Asian Studies*, 1978, vol. 12, no. 3.

Lightfoot P. and Fox J. *Institutional Credit and Small-Scale Farmers in Northeastern Thailand*, Centre for South-East Asian Studies Occasional Paper No. 5, University of Hull, 1983.

Lijphart A. 'Consociational democracy', *World Politics*, 1969, vol. 21, no. 2.

Lim J-J and Vani S. (eds) *Armed Separatism in Southeast Asia*, Singapore, Institute of Southeast Asian Studies, 1984.

Lim L. Y. C. and Gosling L. A. P. (eds) *The Chinese in Southeast Asia, Vol.1*, Singapore, Maruzen Asia, 1983.

Lim Mah Hui 'The ownership and control of large corporations in Malaysia: the role of Chinese businessmen', in Linda Y. C. Lim and L. A. Peter Gosling (eds) *The Chinese in Southeast Asia, Vol.1*, Singapore, Maruzen Asia, 1983.

Lim P. *Ethnic Strategies in Singapore Politics*, B.Soc.Sci. Academic Exercise, Political Science, National University of Singapore, 1990.

Lim Teck Ghee 'British colonial administration and the ethnic division of labour in Malaya', *Kajian Malaysia*, 1984, vol. 2, no. 2.

Lintner B. 'The internationalization of Burma's ethnic conflict', in K. M. De Silva and R. J. May (eds) *Internationalization of Ethnic Conflict*, London, Pinter, 1991.

Lintner B. 'The Shans and the Shan State of Burma' in *Contemporary Southeast Asia*, 1984, vol. 5, no. 4.

Lipset S. M. *Political Man*, New York, Doubleday, 1960.

Lodge G. and Vogel E. (eds) *Ideology and National Competitiveness*, Cambridge, Harvard Business School Press, 1987.

Loh Kok Wah 'The socio-economic basis of ethnic consciousness: the Chinese in the 1970s', in S. Husin Ali (ed.) *Ethnicity, Class and Development: Malaysia*, Kuala Lumpur, Persatuan Sains Sosial Malaysia, 1984.

Lomax L. E. *Thailand: The War That Will Be*, New York, Vintage, 1967.

London B. *Metropolis and Nation in Thailand: The Political Economy of Uneven Development*, Boulder, Colo., Westview, 1980.

Love J. L. 'Modeling internal colonialism: history and prospect', *World Development*, 1989, vol. 17, no. 6.

Luther H. 'Peasants and State in contemporary Thailand', *International Journal of Politics*, 1978/9, vol. 7, no. 4.

McAlister I. (ed.) *Southeast Asia: The Politics of National Integration*, New York, Random House, 1973.

MacIntyre A. *Business and Politics in Indonesia*, Sydney, Allen and Unwin, 1990.

McKay J. 'An exploratory synthesis of primordial and mobilizationist approaches to ethnic phenomena', *Ethnic and Racial Studies*, 1982, vol. 5, no. 4.

Mackie J. A. C 'Integrating and centrifugal factors in Indonesian politics since 1954' in J. J. Fox, R. Garnaut, P. McCawley and J. A. C. Mackie (eds) *Indonesia: Australian Perspectives* (Volume 2), Canberra, Australian National University, 1980.

Mackie J. A. C., Feith H., Nazaruddin Sjamsuddin, MacDonald H. *Contemporary Indonesia: Political Dimensions*, Melbourne, Centre of

Southeast Asian Studies, Monash University, 1978.

McLeod K. and Utrecht E. (eds) *The ASEAN Papers*, Queensland, Transnational Corp, 1978.

McVey R. 'Nationalism, Islam and Marxism: the management of ideological conflict in Indonesia', Introduction to Soekarno, *Nationalism, Islam and Marxism*, Ithaca, Cornell University Press, 1970.

McVey R. 'Faith as the outsider: Islam in Indonesian politics' in J. Piscatori (ed.) *Islam in the Political Process*, Cambridge, Cambridge University Press, 1983.

McVey R. 'Separatism and the paradoxes of the nation-state in perspective' in Lim Joo-Jock and S. Vani (eds) *Armed Separatism in Southeast Asia*, Singapore, Institute of Southeast Asian Studies, 1984.

Mah Hui Lim 'Affirmative action, ethnicity and integration: the case of Malaysia', *Ethnic and Racial Studies*, 1985, vol. 8, no. 2.

Mai Chueang *Some Pertinent Village Attitudes in Northeast Thailand*, Bangkok, USOM, 1967.

Mallow J. M. (ed.) *Authoritarianism and Corporatism in Latin America*, Pittsburgh, University of Pittsburgh Press, 1977.

Maprasert L. *The Domestic Product of Thailand and its Regional Distribution*, PhD thesis, University of London, 1965.

Marcuse H. *Eros and Civilization*, Boston, Beacon, 1955.

Marks T. A. 'Thailand: The threatened kingdom', *Conflict Studies*, 1980, no. 115.

Marx K. *The Eighteenth Brumaire*, in K. Marx and F. Engels *Selected Works*, London, Lawrence and Wishart, 1968.

Mauzy D. K. *Barisan Nasional: Coalition Government in Malaysia*, Kuala Lumpur, Marican, 1983.

May R. J. 'Ethnic separatism in Southeast Asia', *Pacific Viewpoint*, 1990, vol. 31, no. 2.

Means G. *Malaysian Politics: The Second Generation*, Singapore, Oxford University Press, 1991.

Medard J. F. 'The underdeveloped State in tropical Africa: political clientelism or neo-patrimonialism', in C. Clapham (ed.) *Private Patronage and Public Power: Political Clientelism in the Modern State*, London, Pinter, 1982.

Meinecke F. *Cosmopolitanism and the National State*, New Jersey, Princeton University Press, 1970.

Migdal J. S. *Strong Societies and Weak States: State–Society Relations and State Capabilities in the Third World*, New Jersey, Princeton University Press, 1988.

Miliband R. *Marxism and Politics*, Oxford, Oxford University Press, 1977.

Milne R. S. 'The politics of Malaysia's New Economic Policy', *Pacific Affairs*, 1976, vol. 49, no. 2.

Milne R. S. 'Politics, ethnicity and class in Guyana and Malaysia', *Social and Economic Studies*, 1977, vol. 26, no. 1.

Milne R. S. 'Corporatism in the ASEAN countries', *Contemporary Southeast Asia*, 1983, vol. 5, no. 2.

Minogue K. R. *Nationalism*, London, Batsford, 1967.

Morris E. E. *Islam and Politics in Aceh: A Study of Center–Periphery Relations in Indonesia*, PhD thesis, Cornell University, 1983.

Morris E. E. 'Aceh: Social revolution and the Islamic vision', in Audrey R. Kahin (ed.) *Regional Dynamics of the Indonesian Revolution: Unity from Diversity*, Honolulu, University of Hawaii Press, 1985.

Nagata J. A. 'What is a Malay?: Situational selection of ethnic identity in a plural society', *American Ethnologist*, 1974, vol. 1, no. 2.

Nagata J. A. 'Perceptions of social inequality in Malaysia' in Judith A. Nagata (ed.) *Pluralism in Malaysia: Myth and Reality*, Leiden, Canadian Association for South Asian Studies, Brill, 1975.

Nagata J. A. (ed.) *Pluralism in Malaysia: Myth and Reality*, Leiden, Canadian Association for South Asian Studies, Brill, 1975.

Nagata J. A. 'The status of ethnicity and the ethnicity of status: ethnic and class identity in Malaysia and Latin America', *International Journal of Comparative Sociology*, 1976, vol. 17, nos. 3/4.

Nalinee Homasawin *A Regional Analysis of Financial Structures in Thailand: Growth and Distribution, 1970–1982*, M.Econ dissertation, Thamasat University, Bangkok, 1984.

Nazaruddin Sjamsuddin 'Regionalism and national integration in Indonesia: the Acehnese experience' in Jamie Mackie, Herb Feith, Nazaruddin Sjamsuddin and Hamish MacDonald, *Contemporary Indonesia: Political Dimensions*, Melbourne, Centre of Southeast Asian Studies, Monash University, 1978.

Nazaruddin Sjamsuddin 'Issues and politics of regionalism in Indonesia: evaluating the Acehnese experience', in Lim Joo-Jock and S. Vani *Armed Separatism in Southeast Asia*, Singapore, Institute of Southeast Asian Studies, 1984.

Nazaruddin Sjamsuddin *The Republican Revolt: A Study of the Acehnese Rebellion*, Singapore, Institute of Southeast Asian Studies, 1985.

Nevitte N. and Kennedy C. H. (eds) *Ethnic Preference and Public Policy in Developing States*, Boulder, Colo., Lynne Rienner, 1986.

Newman S. 'Does modernization breed ethnic political conflict', *World Politics*, 1991, vol. 43, no. 3.

Nobuko Ichikawa 'Geographic implications of foreign investment in Thailand's industrialization', *Southeast Asian Journal of Social Science*, 1991, vol. 19, nos. 1/2.

Noonan K. M. 'Evolution: A primer for psychologists' in Charles Crawford, Martin Smith and Dennis Krebs (eds) *Sociobiology and Psychology: Ideas, Issues and Applications*, Hillsdale, Lawrence Erlbaum, 1987.

O'Donnell G. *Modernization and Bureaucratic-Authoritarianism*, Berkeley, University of California, 1973.

O'Donnell G. 'Corporatism and the question of the State' in J. M. Mallow (ed.) *Authoritarianism and Corporatism in Latin America*, Pittsburgh, University of Pittsburgh Press, 1977.

O'Donnell G. 'Towards an alternative conceptualization of South American politics' in Peter F. Klaren and Thomas J. Bossert *Promise of Development: Theories of Change in Latin America*, Boulder, Colo., Westview, 1986.

Okamura J. Y. 'Situational ethnicity', *Ethnic and Racial Studies*, 1981, vol. 4, no. 4.

Orridge A. 'Uneven development and nationalism: 1/2', *Political Studies*, 1981, vol. 29, nos 1/2.

Oshima N. T. and Mizoguchi T. (eds) *Income Distribution by Sectors and over Time in East and Southeast Asian Countries*, Manila, CAMS, 1978.

Osman-Rani H. 'Economic development and ethnic integration: the Malaysian experience, *Sojourn*, 1990, vol. 5, no. 1.

Oxaal I., Barnett T. and Booth D. (eds) *Beyond the Sociology of Development: Economy and Society in Latin America and Africa*, London, Routledge, 1975.

Ozay Mehmet 'Colonialism, dualistic growth and the distribution of economic benefits in Malaysia', *Southeast Asian Journal of Social Science*, 1977, vol. 5, nos 11/12.

Pauker G., Golay F. H. and Enloe C. H. *Diversity and Development in Southeast Asia*, New York, McGraw-Hill, 1977.

Pettigrew G. M., Fredrickson G. M., Knobel D. T., Glazer N. and Ueda R. *Prejudice*, Cambridge, Belknap/Harvard University Press, 1982.

Phaichitr Uathavikul 'Regional planning and development: the case of Thailand', in Vichitvong Na Pombhejara (ed.) *Readings in Thailand's Political Economy*, Bangkok, Bangkok Printing, 1978.

Pira Sudham *People of Esarn*, Bangkok, Siam Media International Books, 1987.

Piscatori J. (ed.) *Islam in the Political Process*, Cambridge, Cambridge University Press, 1983.

Poulantzas N. *Classes in Contemporary Capitalism*, London, NLB, 1975.

Powell J. D. 'Peasant society and clientelist politics', *American Political Science Review*, 1970, vol. 64, no. 2.

Preeda Chantagul, Kumphol Puapanich, Rajanikorn Setthoe, Chiraphan Guladilok and Supriya Suthamnuwat 'Regional development in Thailand', in Regional Development Research Unit, *Regional Development in Southeast Asian Countries*, Tokyo, Institute of Developing Economies, 1979.

Prizzia R. *Thailand in Transition: The Role of Oppositional Forces*, Hawaii, Asian Studies at Hawaii no. 32, University of Hawaii Press, 1985.

Puthucheary M. *The Politics of Administration: The Malaysian Experience*, Kuala Lumpur, Oxford University Press, 1978.

Puthucheary M. 'Public policies relating to business and land, and their impact on ethnic relations in Peninsular Malaysia', in Robert B. Goldman and A. Jeyaratnam Wilson (eds) *From Independence to Statehood*, London, Francis Pinter, 1984.

Puthucheary M. 'The administrative élite', in Zakaria Haji Ahmad (ed.) *Government and Politics of Malaysia*, Singapore, Oxford University Press, 1987.

Pye L. W. *Politics, Personality, and Nation Building: Burma's Search for Identity*, New Haven/London, Yale University Press, 1962.

Quah J. S. T., Chan Heng Chee and Seah Chee Meow (eds) *Government and Politics of Singapore*, Singapore, Oxford University Press, 1987.

Rabushka A. 'Racial stereotyping in Malaya', *Asian Survey*, 1971, vol. 9, no. 7.

Rabushka A. and Shepsle K.A. *Politics in Plural Societies*, Columbus, Merrill, 1972.

Ragayah H. J., Mat Zin and Ishak Shari 'Some aspects of income inequality in Peninsular Malaysia, 1957–1970', in N. T. Oshima and T. Mizoguchi (eds) *Income Distribution by Sectors and over Time in East and Southeast Asian Countries*, Manila, CAMS, 1978.

Rajah, A. 'Ethnicity, nationalism and the nation-state: the Karen in Burma and Thailand', in Gehan Wijeyewardene (ed.) *Ethnic Groups Across National Boundaries in Mainland Southeast Asia*, Singapore, Institute of Southeast Asian Studies, 1990.

Rajeshwari Gose (ed.) *Protest Movements in South and South-East Asia: Traditional and Modern Idioms of Expression*, Hong Kong, Centre of Asian Studies, University of Hong Kong, 1987.

Rajeswary Ampalavanar *The Indian Minority and Political Change in Malaya, 1945–1957*, Kuala Lumpur, Oxford University Press, 1981.

Randolph R. S. and Scott Thompson W. *Thai Insurgency: Contemporary Developments*, Beverly Hills/ London, Washington Papers Vol ix, Center for Strategic and International Studies, Georgetown University, Sage, 1981.

Rattporn Sangtada *Isan (Northeast Thailand): A Select Bibliography*, Sydney, BISA Special Project, University of Sydney, 1986.

Redha Ahmad 'Capital accumulation and the State in Malaysia', *Ilmu Masyarakat*, 1985, no. 8.

Regional Development Research Unit *Regional Development in Southeast Asian Countries*, Tokyo, Institute of Developing Economies, 1979.

Reid A. *The Blood of the People: Revolution and the End of Traditional Rule in Northern Sumatra*, Kuala Lumpur, Oxford University Press, 1979.

Renard R. 'Minorities in Burmese History', in K. M. De Silva, Pensri Duke, Ellen S. Goldberg and Nathan Katz (eds) *Ethnic Conflict in Buddhist Societies: Sri Lanka, Thailand and Burma*, London, Pinter, 1988.

Rex J. *Race and Ethnicity*, Milton Keynes, Open University Press, 1986.

Rex J. and Mason D. (eds) *Theories of Race and Ethnic Relations*, Cambridge, Cambridge Univerisy Press, 1986.

Reynolds V., Falger V. and Vine I. (eds) *The Sociobiology of Ethnocentrism*, London, Croom Helm, 1987.

Rhodes R. I. (ed.) *Imerialism and Underdevelopment*, New York/London, Monthly Review Press, 1970.

Richards B. (ed.) *Crises of the Self: Further Essays on Psychoanalysis and Politics*, London, Free Association Books, 1989.

Richards P. *Basic Needs and Government Policies in Thailand*, Singapore, ILO Study, Maruzen Asia, 1982.

Rieff P. *Freud: The Mind of the Moralist*, Chicago, University of Chicago Press, 1979.

Robison R. *Power and Economy in Suharto's Indonesia*, Manila, Journal of Contemporary Asia Publishers, 1990.

Robison R. and Girling J. 'Southeast Asian area studies political science methodology: four essays', in *Asian Studies Association of Australia Review*, 1985, vol. 9, no. 1.

Rodan G. *The Political Economy of Singapore's Industrialization: National*

State and International Capital, London, Macmillan, 1989.

Rodan G. (ed.) *Singapore Changes Guard: Social, Political and Economic Directions in the 1990s*, Melbourne, Longman Cheshire, 1993.

Ronen D. *The Quest for Self-Determination*, New Haven/London, Yale University Press, 1979.

Roth G. 'Personal rulership, patrimonialism and empire-building in the new states', *World Politics*, 1968, vol. 20, no. 1.

Rothchild D. 'State and ethnicity in Africa', in Neil Nevitte and Charles H. Kennedy (eds) *Ethnic Preference and Public Policy in Developing States*, Boulder, Colo., Lynne Rienner, 1986.

Rothchild D. and Olorunsola V. A. (eds) *State Versus Ethnic Claims: African Policy Dilemmas*, Boulder, Westview Press, 1983.

Rothschild J. *Ethnopolitics: A Conceptual Framework*, New York, Columbia University Press, 1981.

Roy M. 'The Oedipus complex and the Bengali family in India (a study of father-daughter relations in Bengal)', in Thomas R. Williams (ed.) *Psychological Anthropology*, The Hague, Mouton, 1975.

Rudolph J. R. and Thompson R. J. (eds) *Ethnoterritorial Politics, Policy, and the Western World*, Boulder, Colo., Lynne Rienner, 1989.

Salem T. 'Capitalist development and the formation of the bureaucratic bourgeoisie in Peninsular Malaya', *Kajian Malaysia*, 1983, vol. 1, no. 2.

Sandhu K. S. 'Historical role of the Sikhs in the development of Singapore', in *Seminar Report on Sikh Youth and Nation-Building*, Singapore, Sikh Advisory Board, 1989.

Sandhu K. S. and Wheatley P. (eds) *Management of Success: The Moulding of Modern Singapore*, Singapore, Institute of Southeast Asian Studies, 1989.

Saul J. 'The State in post-colonial societies: Tanzania' in Harry Goulbourne (ed.) *Politics and State in the Third World*, London, Macmillan, 1979.

Schmitter P. C. 'Still the century of corporatism?' in Schmitter and G. Lembrucht (eds) *Trends Towards Corporatist Intermediation*, London, Sage, 1979.

Schmitter P. C. and Lembrucht G. (eds) *Trends Towards Corporatist Mediation*, London, Sage, 1979.

Schrieke B. *Indonesian Sociological Studies 1*, The Hague/Bandung, Van Hoeve, 1955.

Schwartzman S. 'Corporatism and patrimonialism in the seventies' in James M. Mallow (ed.) *Authoritarianism and Corporatism in Latin America*, Pittsburgh, University of Pittsburgh Press, 1977.

Scott G. M. 'A resynthesis of primordial and circumstantial approaches to ethnic group solidarity: towards an explanatory model', *Ethnic and Racial Studies*, 1990, vol. 13, no. 2.

Scott J. C. 'Patron–client politics and political change in Southeast Asia', *American Political Science Review*, 1972, vol. 66, no. 1.

Scott J. C. *Weapons of the Weak: Everyday Forms of Peasant Resistance*, New Haven, Yale University Press, 1985.

Seah Chee Meow (ed.) *Trends in Singapore*, Singapore, Singapore

University Press, 1975.
Seah Chee Meow and Seah L. 'Education reform and national integration', in Peter S. J. Chen (ed.) *Singapore Development Policy and Trends*, Singapore, Oxford University Press, 1983.
Selth A. *The Anti-Fascist Resistance in Burma, 1942–1945: The Racial Dimension*, Occasional Paper 14 (undated), Centre for Southeast Asian Studies, James Cook University of North Queensland.
Shamsul Amri Baharuddin 'The patron–client relations as an aspect of peasant ideology: a note with reference to Malay peasant society', *Akademika*, 1982, nos 20 and 21.
Shand R. T. 'Income distribution in a dynamic rural sector: some evidence from Malaysia', *Economic Development and Cultural Change*, 1987, vol. 36, no. 1.
Shee Poon Kim *The PAP in Singapore, 1954–1970: A Study in Survivalism of a Single-Dominant Party*, PhD thesis, Indiana University, 1971.
Shee Poon Kim 'The evolution of the political system', in Jon S. T. Quah, Chan Heng Chee and Seah Chee Meow (eds) *Government and Politics of Singapore*, Singapore, Oxford University Press, 1987.
Shivji I. G. *The Class Struggles in Tanzania*, London, Heinemann, 1976.
Short A. 'Communism, race and politics in Malaysia', *Asian Survey*, 1970, vol. 10, no. 12.
Shotam N. P. 'Language and linguistic policies', in K. S. Sandhu and P. Wheatley (eds) *Management of Success: The Moulding of Modern Singapore*, Singapore, Institute of Southeast Asian Studies, 1989.
Siddique S. and Suryadinata L. 'Bumiputra and Pribumi: economic nationalism (indigenism) in Malaysia and Indonesia', *Pacific Affairs*, 1981–2, vol, 54, no. 4.
Siegal J. T. *The Rope of God*, Berkeley/Los Angeles, University of California Press, 1969.
Siegal J. T. *Shadow and Sound: The Historical Thought of a Sumatran People*, Chicago/London, University of Chicago Press, 1979.
Silalahi H. T. 'The 1977 General Elections: the results and the role of traditional authority relations in modern Indonesian society', *Indonesian Quarterly*, 1977, vol. 5, no. 3.
Silalahi H. T. 'The 1987 Election in Indonesia', *Southeast Asian Affairs 1988*, Singapore, Institute of Southeast Asian Studies, 1988.
Silverman I. 'Race, race differences, and race relations' in C. Crawford, M. Smith and D. Krebs *Sociobiology and Psychology: Ideas, Issues and Applications*, Hilsdale, Lawrence Erlbaum, 1987.
Silverstein J. *Burmese Politics: The Dilemma of National Unity*, New Brunswick, Rutgers University Press, 1980.
Silverstein J. 'Ethnic protest in Burma: its causes and solutions', in Rajeshwari Gose (ed.) *Protest Movements in South and South-East Asia: Traditional and Modern Idioms of Expression*, Hong Kong, Centre of Asian Studies, University of Hong Kong, 1987.
Silverstein J. (ed.) *Independent Burma at Forty Years: Six Assessments*, Ithaca, Cornell Southeast Asia Program, Cornell University, 1989.
Singhanetra-Renard A. *Northern Thai Mobility 1870–1977: A View From Within*, PhD thesis, University of Hawaii, 1983.

Sinnappah Arasaratnam *Indians in Malaysia and Singapore*, Kuala Lumpur, Oxford University Press, 1979.
Sklar R. 'Political science and national integration: a radical approach', *Journal of Modern African Studies*, 1967, vol. 5, no. 1.
Skocpol T. *States and Social Revolution*, Cambridge, Cambridge University Press, 1979.
Sloan W. M. 'Ethnicity or imperialism', *Comparative Studies in Society and History*, 1979, vol. 21, no. 1.
Smith A. D. *The Ethnic Revival*, Cambridge, Cambridge University Press, 1981.
Smith A. D. 'State and homelands: the social and geopolitical implications of national territory', *Millenium: Journal of International Studies*, 1981, vol 10, no. 3.
Smith A. D. *The Ethnic Origins of Nations*, Oxford, Blackwell, 1986.
Smith A. D. *National Identity*, London, Penguin, 1991.
Smith M. *Burma: Insurgency and the Politics of Ethnicity*, London/New Jersey, Zed, 1991.
Smith M. G. *The Plural Society in the British West Indies*, Berkeley, University of California Press, 1965.
Snitwongse K. and Sukhumbhand Paribatra (eds) *Durable Stability in Southeast Asia*, Singapore, Institute of Southeast Asian Studies, 1987.
Somjai Rakjiwit *The Jungle Leads the Village* (edited by Robert Zimmerman), Bangkok, USOM, 1974.
Sowell T. *Preferential Policies*, New York, Morrow, 1990.
Stack J. F. 'Ethnic mobilization in world politics: the primordial perspective', in J. F. Stack *The Primordial Challenge: Ethnicity in the Contemporary World*, New York, Greenwood, 1986.
Stack J. F. *The Primordial Challenge: Ethnicity in the Contemporary World*, New York, Greenwood, 1986.
Steinberg D. J. *Burma: A Socialist Nation of Southeast Asia*, Boulder Col., Westview, 1982.
Steinberg D. J. 'Constitutional and political bases of minority insurrections in Burma', in Lim Joo-Jock and S. Vani (eds) *Armed Separatism in Southeast Asia*, Singapore, Institute of Southeast Asian Studies, 1984.
Steinberg D. J. (ed.) *In Search of Southeast Asia: A Modern History*, Sydney, Allen and Unwin, 1987.
Steinberg D. J. *The Future of Burma: Crisis and Choice in Myanmar*, Lanham, University Press of America, 1990.
Stenson M. 'Class and race in West Malaysia', *Bulletin of Concerned Asian Scholars*, 1976, vol. 8, no. 2.
Stone J. 'Ethnicity versus the State' in Donald Rothchild and Victor A. Olorunsola (eds) *State Versus Ethnic Claims: African Policy Dilemmas*, Boulder, Colo., Westview Press, 1983.
Stuart-Fox M. 'Factors influencing relations between the Communist Parties of Thailand and Laos', *Asian Survey*, 1979. vol. 19, no. 4.
Sudhir Anand *Inequality and Poverty in Malaysia: Measurement and Decomposition*, New York, Oxford University Press, 1983.
Suryadinata L. 'Government policy and national integration in

Indonesia', *Southeast Asian Journal of Social Science*, 1988, vol. 16, no. 2.

Suryadinata L. *Pribumi Indonesians, The Chinese Minority and China*, Singapore, Heinemann, 1992.

Tai Yoke Lin 'Inter-ethnic restructuring in Malaysia, 1970–80: the employment perspective', in Robert B. Goldman and A. Jeyaratnam Wilson (eds) *From Independence to Statehood*, London, Frances Pinter, 1984.

Tan Peng Chuan *Advisory Committees and Policymaking in Singapore*, B.Soc.Sci Academic Exercise, Political Science, National University of Singapore, 1990.

Tan Teng Lang *The Evolving PAP Ideology: Beyond Democratic Socialism*, B.Soc.Sci. Academic Exercise, Political Science, National University of Singapore, 1983.

Tapp N. *Sovereignty and Rebellion: The White Hmong of Northern Thailand*, Singapore, Oxford University Press, 1989.

Taylor R.H. 'Burma's national unity problem and the 1974 Constitution', *Contemporary Southeast Asia*, 1979, vol. 1, no. 3.

Taylor R. H. 'Perceptions of ethnicity in the politics of Burma', *Southeast Asian Journal of Social Science*, 1982, vol. 10, no. 1.

Taylor R. H. *An Undeveloped State: The Study of Modern Burma's Politics*, Centre of Southeast Asian Studies, Working Paper No. 28, Monash University, Clayton, Australia 1983.

Taylor R. H. *The State of Burma*, London, Hurst, 1987.

Tham Kok Wing *National Campaigns in Singapore Politics*, B.Soc.Sci Academic Exercise, Political Science, National University of Singapore, 1983.

Tham Seong Chee 'Ideology, politics and economic modernization: the case of the Malays in Malaysia', *Southeast Asian Journal of Social Science*, 1973, vol. 1, no. 1.

Theobald R. 'Patrimonialism', *World Politics*, 1982, vol. 34, no. 4.

Tinker H. *The Union of Burma*, London, Oxford University Press, 1967.

Tiryakian E.A. and Rogowski R. (eds) *New Nationalisms in the Developed West*, Boston, Allen and Unwin, 1985.

Toh Kin Woon 'The role of the Malaysian State in the restructuring of employment', *Jurnal Ekonomi Malaysia*, 1982, no. 6.

Toh Kin Woon 'Education as a vehicle for reducing economic inequality' in S. Husin Ali (ed.) *Ethnicity, Class and Development: Malaysia*, Kuala Lumpur, Persatuan Sains Sosial Malaysia, 1984.

Toh Kin Woon and Jomo Kwame Sundaram 'The nature of the Malaysian State and it's implications for development planning', in K. S. Jomo and K. J. Wells (eds) *The Fourth Malaysian Plan*, Kuala Lumpur, Persatuan Ekonomi Malaysia, 1983.

Trager F. N. (ed.) *Marxism in Southeast Asia*, Stanford, Stanford University Press, 1959.

Trager F. N. *Burma: From Kingdom to Republic*, New York, Praeger, 1966.

Tribal Research Institute *The Hill Tribes of Thailand*, Chiang Mai, 1989.

Tudor H. *Political Myth*, New York, Praeger, 1972.

Turton A., Fast J. and Caldwell M. (eds) *Thailand: Roots of Conflict*, Nottingham, Spokesman, 1978.

Turton A. 'The current situation in the Thai countryside', in A. Turton, J. Fast and M. Caldwell (eds) *Thailand: Roots of Conflict*, Nottingham, Spokesman, 1978.

Turton A. 'Patrolling the middle ground: methodological perspectives on "everyday peasant resistance"', *The Journal of Peasant Studies*, 1986, vol. 13, no. 2.

Turton A. *Production, Power and Participation in Rural Thailand: Experiences of Poor Farmers' Groups*, Geneva, United Nations Research Institute for Social Development, 1987.

Van der Kroef J. M. 'Thailand: A new phase in the insurgency?', *Pacific Community*, 1977, vol. 8, no. 4.

Van Roy E. *Economic Systems of Northern Thailand*, Ithaca/London, Cornell University Press, 1971.

Vasil R. *Governing Singapore*, Singapore, Eastern Universities Press, 1984.

Vichitvong Na Pombhejara (ed.) *Readings in Thailand's Political Economy*, Bangkok, Bangkok Printing, 1978.

Viswanathan Selvaratnam 'Ethnicity, inequality, and higher education in Malaysia', *Comparative Education Review*, 1988, vol. 32, no. 2.

Von Vorys K. *Democracy Without Consensus: Communalism and Political Stability in Malaysia*, Princeton, Princeton University Press, 1975.

Walker A. R. 'In mountain and *Ulu*: a comparative history of development strategies for ethnic minority peoples in Thailand and Malaysia', *Contemporary Southeast Asia*, 1983, vol. 4, no. 4.

Walzer M. 'Pluralism in political perspective' in M. Walzer, E. T. Kantowicz, J. Higham and M. Harrington *The Politics of Ethnicity*, Cambridge/London, Belknap, Harvard University Press, 1982.

Walzer M., Kantowicz E. T., Higham J. and Harrington M. *The Politics of Ethnicity*, Cambridge/London, Belknap, Harvard University Press, 1982.

Weber Max *The Theory of Social and Economic Organization*, New York, Free Press, 1957.

Weiner M. 'Political change: Asia, Africa and the Middle East', in M. Weiner and S. P. Huntington (eds) *Understanding Political Development*, Boston, Little Brown, 1987.

Weiner M. and Huntington S. P. (eds) *Understanding Political Development*, Boston, Little Brown, 1987.

Wertheim W. F. 'From aliran to class struggle in the countryside of Java', *Pacific Viewpoint*, 1969, vol. 10, no. 1.

Williams T. R. (ed.) *Psychological Anthropology*, The Hague, Mouton, 1975.

Williamson P. J. *Varieties of Corporatism: A Conceptual Discussion*, Cambridge, Cambridge University Press, 1985.

Willmott W. E. 'The emergence of nationalism' in K. S. Sandhu and P. Wheatley (eds) *Management of Success: The Moulding of Modern Singapore*, Singapore, Institute of Southeast Asian Studies, 1989.

Wilson C. M. 'Burmese-Karen Warfare, 1810–1850: a Thai view', in De

Witt C. Ellinwood and Cynthia H. Enloe *Ethnicity and the Military in Asia*, New Brunswick, Transaction, 1981.

Wilson C. M. *Thailand: A Handbook of Historical Statistics*, Boston, Hall, 1969.

Wilson D. A. 'Thailand and Marxism' in Frank N. Trager (ed.) *Marxism in Southeast Asia*, Stanford, Stanford University Press, 1959.

Wolpe H. 'The theory of internal colonialism: the South African case', in Ivan Oxaal, T. Barnett and D. Booth (eds) *Beyond the Sociology of Development: Economy and Society in Latin America and Africa*, London, Routledge, 1975.

Yasunaka A. 'Basic data on Indonesian political leaders', in *Indonesia*, 10, Oct. 1970.

Yoshihara Kunio *The Rise of Ersatz Capitalism in South-East Asia*, Singapore, Oxford University Press, 1988.

Young, C. *The Politics of Cultural Pluralism*, Madison/London, Wisconsin University Press, 1976.

Yukio Ikemoto 'Income distribution in Malaysia: 1957–80', *The Developing Economies*, 1985, vol. 23, no. 4.

Zainah Anwar *Islamic Revivalism in Malaysia: Dakwah among the Students*, Selangor, Pelanduk Publications, 1987.

Zainudin Salleh and Zulkifly Osman 'The economic structure' in E. K. Fisk and H. Osman-Rani (eds) *The Political Economy of Malaysia*, Kuala Lumpur, Oxford University Press, 1982.

Zawawi Ibrahim 'Malay peasants and proletarian consciousness', *Bulletin of Concerned Asian Scholars*, 1983, vol. 15, no. 4.

Zawawi Ibrahim 'Perspectives on capitalist penetration and the reconstitution of the Malay peasantry', *Jurnal Ekonomi Malaysia*, 1982, no. 5.

Ziemann W. and Lanzendorfer M. 'The State in peripheral societies', *Socialist Register 1977: A Survey of Movements and Ideas*, London, Merlin, 1977.

Zimmerman R. F. 'Insurgency in Thailand', *Problems of Communism*, 1976, vol. 25, no. 3.

Zolberg A. R. *Creating Political Order: The One-Party States of West Africa*, Chicago, Rand McNally, 1966.

Index